INFORMATION TECHNOLOGY

DESIGN AND APPLICATIONS

INFORMATION TECHNOLOGY

DESIGN AND APPLICATIONS

EDITED BY NANCY D. LANE & MARGARET E. CHISHOLM

G.K. Hall & Co.

Boston

First published 1991
by G.K. Hall & Co.
70 Lincoln Street
Boston, Massachusetts 02111

10 9 8 7 6 5 4 3 2 1

Library of Congress Cataloging-in-Publication Data

Information Technology: Design and Applications /
   edited by Nancy D. Lane and Margaret E. Chisholm
      p. cm.
    Includes index.
    ISBN 0-8161-1908-2. – ISBN 0-8161-1909-0 (pbk.)
    1. Library science – Technological innovations.
    2. Information technology. 3. Libraries – Automation.
   I. Lane, Nancy D. II. Chisholm, Margaret E.
   Z678.9.I59   1990
   020'.285 – dc20   90-43577
                                    CIP

Contents

Foreword

We are in the midst of John Naisbitt's proclaimed change from an industrial society to an information society, popularized by his 1982 book, *Megatrends*. Each day we face a multitude of information options and decisions, and we have made tremendous advances over the last few decades in how we manage the increasing amounts of information available. By gaining a better understanding of information management, we have been able to effect global change. For the first time, local health officials in many Third World countries have access to relatively up-to-date medical information. Satellite transmission allows for the rapid, global "sharing" of research and the commmunication of news. Within hours of the earthquakes in Iran in June 1990, for instance, virtually every country in the world was aware of the catastrophe and began delivering humanitarian aid. We are living proof of Marshall McLuhan's "global village" theory.

In spite of the advances in information management, we are experiencing many of the symptoms of "information overload." For instance:

- Between 6,000 and 7,000 scientific articles are written each day.

- The quantity of scientific and technical information now increases by more that 13 percent annually.

- The *Wall Street Journal* reported in 1988 that less than 50 percent of all information received from satellites in the last 10 years has been processed.

Our challenge is to develop and incorporate faster and more efficient means to filter, process, store, and retrieve information. Today's information professionals are hard-pressed to acquire and maintain all the print materials they need for their collections to meet the needs of their users. At the same time, administrative budgets aren't increasing at nearly the rate that new publications and other sources of information are being developed.

While advancements in technology have allowed us to manage information better, this technology has also placed tremendous pressure on our financial resources. Some may ask why we need to continue pushing forward. When is it enough? If our methods of information storage, retrieval, and access cannot keep pace with the information explosion, we run the risk of closing the door on a cure for cancer or AIDS, more efficient management of our environmental resources, or a clue that allows us to put an astronaut on Mars. To progress, we must understand and have access to the information of the past.

From the course I taught at the University of Michigan School of Information and Library Studies in spring 1990, the need was evident for an introduction to a broad range of information technologies and the ways they are being applied in the real world today and may be applied in the future. Enormous resources from many different industry sources are being brought to bear on the issues of information access, preservation, and distribution. Significant breakthroughs in technology are expected in the 1990s, and these may have a sizable impact on productivity and literacy.

The stakes are much too high for us to rest on the laurels of our past technological achievements, and that is why the timing of this book is so critical. There are some tremendous advancements taking place right now, in the areas of CD-ROM technology, micrographics, and advanced networking applications. Only by understanding the applications being instituted today can we push for and manage the changes tomorrow. This book is a wonderful starting point.

Joseph Fitzsimmons
President
UMI (University Microfilms International)
Ann Arbor, Michigan

Preface

Recently I taught an introductory course in the University of Washington's Continuing Education Certificate Program in Library Automation. At that time, I could find no text that covered a wide range of information technologies, giving brief background information while concentrating on applications in librarianship and related fields such as education, communication, journalism, and publishing.

Judith Frey, then continuing education coordinator for the Graduate School of Library and Information Science at the university, encouraged me to edit such a text. This book, which I have compiled jointly with the director of the graduate school, Dr. Margaret Chisholm, is the result.

I would like to thank Judith, as well as the students in the introductory course who put up with pages and pages of photocopies, for the inspiration to carry through with this project. I would also like to thank the University of Canberra, which supported my sabbatical at the University of Washington, and Sue Wright, who did the word processing of the glossary and index.

Nancy D. Lane

Introduction

Nancy D. Lane and Margaret E. Chisholm

Information technology is pervasive. It has changed the way we bank, shop, communicate, travel, and entertain ourselves. It changes our lives incrementally, so that we are often unaware of the effect that a new product or process will ultimately have.

For example, writers who compose on word processors find it frustrating to go back to a typewriter with correcting tape, let alone a manual one. Yet, initially, learning to use word-proccssing software may have proved an even more frustrating experience. Or perhaps a better example: Many of you never experienced life before the photocopier. Can you imagine the hours and hours that were spent taking notes from books and journals by hand? There was also a time when you could bank only during bankers' hours – 10 A.M. to 3 P.M. on weekdays. Too bad if you needed money for the weekend, and you missed closing by five minutes. Now the cash machine is a standard fixture of every shopping center.

These changes have all occurred in the past 20 years. The changes that emerge during the next 20 years may be even more dramatic and far-reaching. It is the purpose of this book to describe the developments in information technology that are now becoming commonplace in business and industry, education and the arts. Although the mechanics of these technologies are explained briefly, the focus is primarily on their present and future applications to the field of library and information science. Such a background will give students and practitioners sufficient understanding of these technologies to read more widely in the current journal literature. The references and suggested readings in each chapter provide a starting point for further reading.

There are some purposeful omissions from this overview. As most students will be taking courses in introductory computing, this topic is not discussed. Basic computing concepts and terms, such as input, CPU, and RAM, are not defined when used in the text, but are explained in the glossary.

▪ 1 ▪

Data Communications

Joseph Ford

Data communications is the transmission and reception of digital information between or among components of a computerized information system. The components may be two or more computers, in a machine-to-machine configuration; they may be a computer terminal and a host computer, operating in real time on an information query; or they may be a terminal and its associated printer, recording or printing the results of an information search. Data communications is a subject of the wider field of telecommunications.

In most, if not all, information technology applications, the delivery channel or conveyance between users and the information machinery itself involves data communications. It is difficult to overemphasize the importance of data communications, whether historically, as a key development of information technology; economically, as the means of making information technology possible by allowing the dissemination of information to remote users; or functionally, as the adjunct or spur to added development in other sectors of information technology.

HISTORY OF DATA COMMUNICATIONS

Historically, modern data communications is an outgrowth of five related, nineteenth-century discoveries and technologies, which grew to maturity before the mid-twentieth century. First is the telegraph, developed by Samuel F. B. Morse in the 1840s and subsequently introduced virtually worldwide as a system of transmitting messages using a discrete encoding scheme, Morse code. Morse code uses a two-state method of transmission (long and short pulses of electricity, or dot and dash). Each character in the alphabet, as well as some special and numeric characters, is represented by a series of long and short pulses. The number of pulses required for each character varies from two to as many as four. In its earliest form, the pulses were turned on and off, or modulated, by a hand-controlled key.

The second, and more important technology, is the telephone. Invented by Alexander Graham Bell in 1876, the telephone used some of the characteristics of the telegraph: copper wire, low direct-current voltage, and a technique for transmitting and controlling that voltage in transmission. Bell substituted for the telegraph key a combination of electrically operated sending and receiving diaphragms for the mouthpiece and earpiece. The sending diaphragm responded to the pressure of soundwaves and transmitted voltage that varied by the amount of pressure. On receipt, the variable voltage controlled another diaphragm through an electromagnetic device that reproduced the sound originally sensed at the transmission diaphragm.

The wavelike nature of electrical current is the major physical principle underlying modern data communications. The discoverer of this principle, the third of the five on which data communications depends, was Heinrich Hertz, a nineteenth-century German physicist, whose work on electromagnetism established that electrical currents oscillated or vibrated in a wavelike form. He further developed the capability for controlling the propagation and measurement of such waves. He is memorialized by the use of his name as the symbol for the frequency of oscillation and its measurement (hertz, contracted to Hz, equal to one cycle per second).

The fourth development, and second principle of electrical currents, is that they can be discharged from an antenna into the atmosphere, or into a vacuum, and be received and recreated. The discoverer of this principle was Guglielmo Marconi, the Italian physicist who in 1894-95 demonstrated that Heinrich Hertz's electrical oscillations could be freed from the wires and transmitted as radio-wave signals for reception by a companion receiving device. This discovery ultimately led to the vast number of electronic communications applications called wireless or radio, including radar, microwave, and satellite transmission.

With an understanding of electrical currents and the means to control them in order to send a signal, the remaining requirement was how to code the signal for computers. While one could argue that the French telegrapher J. M. E. Baudot developed the first digital code, used for Telex transmission, the more applicable contributor was an American engineer named Herman Hollerith. In 1890, Hollerith developed for the United States Bureau of the Census a method of encoding information on a punched paper card, which could be scanned by an electromechanical device. The card could be perforated in several discrete locations for each piece of data, with the presence or absence of perforations signaling either an "on" or "off" state. This binary representation, called a bit, forms much of the encoding characteristic of computing machinery and the data communications that link the machinery to users and to other machines.

What is important in this discussion of physical properties, their discoverers, and the technical applications that resulted? The answer is multifold. First, much of what we use and rely on comes out of technologies first developed for other purposes. This fact is an important element of modern data communications because it clearly points out the evolutionary nature of data communications, as communications engineers adapted voice technology and radio technology for data communications purposes.

Second, perhaps less important, is that modern data communications operates on a continuum of historical research and development, which stretches backward 100 or more years and forward to a future whose shape is coming into increasingly sharp focus. Any student, user, or developer of information technology is in the debt of a number of scientists and technologists.

Finally, the economics of information technology and the communications that tie users and systems together is crucial to the evolutionary development just described. If information technology developers or communications engineers were required to invent, from scratch, a data communications system without the foundation of telegraph, voice, radio, and computing technologies that went before, they would face an insurmountable task.

PRINCIPLES AND TERMINOLOGY

To begin the discussion of data communications, one assumes a transmission path, or medium, between components, with transmission and reception equipment to send, receive, and manage a communications signal. The signal is generated or propagated by one or more electronic components, and is encoded in one of the many computer communications code sets, or binary representations of alphabetic, numeric, and special characters.

The management or control of the signal relies on a protocol, or set of conventions for signal management shared by all components in the exchange. If the transmission path, or circuit, is metallic (that is, consisting of copper wires), the signal will consist of electrons in an electrical current measured in volts. If the transmission path is a fiber-optic channel, or light guide, the signal will consist of light pulses. Other data communications paths may include radio-frequency channels for satellite, microwave, or data radio.

The communications path will link devices, such as a host computer and a terminal or printer, using a channel or circuit in a network. In short-distance metallic communications circuits, a signal may operate on a *parallel* path, that is, one involving several wires sending a signal pulse simultaneously. Such paths may link a terminal to a printer. For example, the common Centronics parallel cable (named for the firm that devised the standard for such short-distance communications) consists of 35 wires, each one carrying a separate control or signal function. In contrast, a signal may be transmitted on a *serial* path. A single wire among as many as 25 carries actual signal information, and the others provide grounding and control functions.

Digital and Analog Signals

Morse code, as well as the subsequent five-bit Baudot telegraphic code developed for teletype in the 1890s by Baudot, was in a sense binary because it employed only two states of being. Data communications also presumes only two forms of signal, either 1 or 0, thus providing digital transmission. This is in sharp contrast to an analog transmission such as the human voice, which may modulate a signal in many different frequencies while the speaker talks.

This distinction is of critical importance in data communications: communications signals between machines operate in very strictly defined patterns. They consist of pulses of voltage in metallic or radio-frequency circuits, or of light in fiber-optic circuits. These pulses have specific durations and shapes, measured by the frequency and intensity of their propagation. Essentially the bandwidth, or carrying capacity of a transmission medium such as a copper-wire circuit, describes its maximum data transmission carrying rate.

It is important to remember that the first data communications systems were built on top of the voice systems that preceded them. The requirements for data communications were superimposed on top of the voice communications systems. This critical fact has controlled much of the research and development work involved in data communications equipment (DCE) and data terminal equipment (DTE), as well as in the transmission media themselves. DCE and DTE are discussed in more detail later in this chapter. The communications system developed for voice assumed an analog requirement, with the voice signal changing frequency and intensity.

TRANSMISSION METHODS AND MEDIA

As previously noted, the entire data communications environment depends on transmitting and receiving a signal that has been altered, or modulated, to encode digital information. That is, data communications depends on a flow of electrical current, or light pulses in fiber-optic transmission. The signal oscillates, or behaves as a sine wave, as discovered by Hertz; and the communications equipment modulates the rate of oscillation, or alters the shape of the sine wave. The information, or intelligent content of the signal, is carried in these wave-form changes, or modulations.

Signals are generated by sending a pulse of electricity of a specific voltage, shape, and duration. The bit rate, or the frequency of the pulses measured in bits per second (bps), is the standard for measuring digital data transmission speed. (The information content of the bits is explained later in this chapter.) Sometimes mistakenly referred to as baud or baud rate, bits per second is roughly equivalent to the bandwidth of a transmission path. For example, a standard voice-grade telephone line is expected to transmit signals ranging from a low of 300 Hz up to 3000 Hz. The bandwidth is therefore 2700 Hz, which is roughly equivalent to the 2400 bits per second that the channel can convey without use of complex modulation techniques.

These modulation techniques fall into three basic types, which are related to the form of the sine wave and the ways in which the wave may be modulated. The first type is amplitude modulation (AM), which modifies the strength of the signal and is represented by an increase in the height of the sine wave above its mid-line. The second type is frequency modulation (FM), which changes how often the signal wave oscillates, or how many complete cycles of the signal wave would be generated in a fixed amount of time, such as one second. The third type is called phase shift, sometimes referred to as PSK, for phase shift key. Phase shift modulation changes the shape of the signal, so that the regular form of the sine wave is suddenly modified to reverse the direction, and then abruptly reversed again. The outer ends of the wave are chopped off and replaced by small but discrete and highly recognizable V-shaped troughs.

By mixing these modulation techniques together, and with the use of ever-more sensitive electronic components, DCE designers have been able to raise transmission speeds sharply, while improving reliability and reducing component size and cost.

Metallic Circuits and Radio-Frequency Transmission

A variety of media exists in which data communications signals pass from transmitting end to receiving end. Most frequently, data is transmitted on metallic circuits, consisting of copper or aluminum wires or cables. The construction of the wiring and cables may vary greatly depending on the volume of data to be carried and the environment in which the transmission is to take place.

The simplest wire in practical use is probably the telephone wire, with its two, three, or four separate strands of small-gauge copper. Called *twisted pair*, these unshielded wires are used frequently in low-speed and local data transmission—for example, in carrying the signal from a computer terminal and its associated DTE, such as a modem, to or through the public switched telephone network. Since the length of such a data cable is generally short, from a few feet to a few miles, and its intended data transmission requirement is for low-speed and intermittent data, there is little problem with any of the three major impediments to error-free transmission described below.

Errors, or noise, may occur in metallic circuit data transmission when any of the following conditions exist. First, the quality of the signal may degrade, or attenuate, due to the resistance of the wire carrying the signal. At low speeds, between 300 bps and 19,200 bps (also noted as 19.2 kilobits per second or Kbps), this attenuation generally falls within the error detection and correction (EDC) capability of the DTE. EDC involves examining the contents of the bit stream, identifying errors (usually through some mathematical computation), and then correcting the errors. Frequently the correction involves having the incorrect portion of the bit stream retransmitted.

Errors also occur when, for example, magnetic fields created in electrical wiring, lighting, or around electric motors distort or modify a communications signal as it passes along the wire. This is called electromagnetic interference (EMI). Finally, radio-frequency interference (RFI) results from the intrusion of high-frequency signals into a communications channel, such as from a transmission facility, or from the electrical signals being conveyed along the circuits of a computer.

The effects of EMI or RFI are best dealt with by shielding cables, or routing them through noninterfering environments. Metallic circuits designed to carry high volumes of data, or to carry data over long distances and in environments where externally based electrical interference exists, use wire or cable that is shielded against such interference. Such shielding may consist of several protective layers: an outer layer of plastic, then copper or aluminum foil, then a plastic jacket that contains the actual conductive wire. Cable television (also called Community Antenna Television or CATV) is transmitted via coaxial cable and employs such a shielded wire, whose properties of high bandwidth and low susceptibility to interference make it very useful in data communications applications.

Other transmission media include those in the high-frequency range associated with radio wavelengths. In the technological aftermath of World War II, radar and its highly focused, very shortwave radio waves, called microwaves, were adapted to communications. Operating in a "line of sight" manner, microwave communications employs point-to-point radio transmission operating above 1 billion Hz and up to 30 billion Hz, termed gigahertz (GHz). Much of the long-distance telephone network in North America has been based on microwave transmission since the early 1960s. With an increasing reliance on fiber optics for high-volume, long-distance traffic, microwave will likely be used in special circumstances, such as local, high-volume private networks.

Fiber Optics

Strands of very pure glass as fine as .0005 inches, developed by Corning Glass in the early 1970s, introduced the new and exciting technology of fiber optics to the communications industry. Fiber optics and its companion transmission and reception technologies of lasers and light-emitting diodes are rapidly replacing or supplementing metallic and radio-frequency communications.

Fiber-optic lines employ a strand or bundles of strands of very fine and very pure glass. The strands may be as thin as a human hair or thinner. Supplied in lengths of about 3/4 of a mile, and spliced together to make longer lengths, fiber-optic cables have recently gone into service for trans-Atlantic and trans-Pacific communications. They are also in use in North America for short, medium, and long distance communications, generally between major switching centers. With the base of installed miles growing by some estimates as much as 80 percent per year, and with anticipated growth rates to stay nearly as high through the mid-1990s, fiber optics is on the way to becoming the dominant transmission medium for long- and mid-distance communications.

A number of installations of fiber-optic cables are taking place as well in the local telephone subscriber loop, that portion of the public switched network (PSN) that connects telephones in individual residences or buildings with the central office. Optical fiber's very high bandwidth and ability to carry a variety of signals simultaneously make it an excellent medium for installations such as campus networks. Its physical properties lend themselves to high-volume communications.

The properties of fiber-optics that make it so attractive for communications are its very high bandwidth of up to 100 million Hz (or megahertz, abbreviated MHz) or more, its immunity to EMI and RFI, its per-mile cost equivalency to copper, its low susceptibility to terrestrial or weather interference (which can plague the new higher-frequency microwave), its low signal attenuation characteristics, and its security. These characteristics are all highly desirable in data communications, and all combine to push fiber optics as the preferred medium for data communications, particularly in medium- and long-distance applications.

Fiber strands conduct communications as pulses of light, with the light pulses generated either by laser or light-emitting diode. A laser produces a high-intensity beam of radiation of a frequency within or near the range of visible light; a light-emitting diode is a semiconductor that produces light when it receives an electric current. The pulses, ideally suited for digital communications, are modulated at very high rates, approaching 50 billion times per second in laboratory settings. The light pulse, once launched down the strand, follows the strand even if it is bent, provided the bend is not too tight. It is reflected off the highly reflective cladding that surrounds the strand

and, in an environment where resistance to flow is virtually nil, suffers very low attenuation. At the receiving end, diodes sense the arrival of a pulse and emit an electronic pulse or avalanche of electrons in response, which is amplified and directed to the communications or computer control devices prepared to receive a digital signal. Communications engineers sometimes refer to the optical portion of such communications as the optical regime, and the portion that operates on electrical and electronic principles as the electrical regime.

COMMUNICATIONS CONTROLS, CODES, AND NETWORKS

Regardless of the physical characteristics of the channel, it will have a variety of flow control and management characteristics. Controlling the flow of a digital signal originally constituted the greatest challenge to system designers and operators. Communications control is defined as synchronizing and managing the rate of transmission and reception of a communications signal, recognizing and acknowledging the start and finish of characters and messages, maintaining the quality of the signal as it moves through the transmission media, and identifying and correcting transmission errors.

These control functions may also describe whether the signals move in one direction or both directions and, if in both directions, whether in one direction at a time or both directions simultaneously. The directional nature of the data flow is called *simplex* if it is in one direction only, as in home cable TV. If bidirectional, in only one direction at a time it is called *half duplex,* and in both directions at a time, *full duplex.* Typically, low-speed data flow on a two-wire metallic circuit is simplex or half duplex. A full duplex circuit requires a four-wire circuit (two twisted pairs).

Protocols

Other control functions, brought together under the term protocol, describe the error detection and correction methods, the rate of flow in bits per second, the form of timing or synchronization of the flow, and the methods by which two or more components in the circuit exchange acknowledgment of the flow control. A great variety of protocols exists. Some are referred to as character-level because they control transmission and attempt to detect and correct errors at the individual character level. Others are referred to as bit-level, particularly those associated with much higher transmission bit rates. They employ sophisticated mathematical algorithms to scan bit patterns and reject those blocks of data that cannot be valid because of transmission errors.

Some bit-level protocols include High-level Data Link Control (HDLC) and Synchronous Data Link Control (SDLC), both of which manage blocks of data placed in frames. These frames, incorporating both information bits and control bits, are transmitted and received in groups, with the sequence of each individual frame described within the frame, so that as a group of frames arrives each frame will contain its sequence number. This framing process allows receiving equipment, operating under computer control, to scan, approve, and acknowledge large volumes of data very quickly. When a transmission error occurs and the receiving equipment detects it, it calls for a retransmission of the frame containing an error.

This scanning and acknowledgment process also operates on the character level and provides the basis for most error correction. When data that contains errors arrives, the receiving DTE is generally designed to call for a retransmission of the corrupted data, rather than to attempt to reconstruct the data.

Computer Codes

The basic data communications code for digital information is the American Standard Code for Information Interchange (ASCII). ASCII is a seven- or eight-bit code – that is, each character may be represented by either seven or eight bits per character. Seven bits suffices to transmit 128 characters (2 to the 7th power), where each of seven bit locations may have the two states 1 (on) or 0 (off). In its eight-bit version, ASCII can accommodate 256 characters (2 to the 8th power). Developed in 1963, ASCII is the most commonly used code for low-speed data communications, typically under 19.2 Kbps.

Another code set common to the International Business Machines (IBM) hardware environment is called the Extended Binary-Coded Decimal Interchange Code (EBCDIC). EBCDIC is exclusively eight-bit.

These code sets match each numeric, alphabetic, and special character to a sequence of eight bits, called a byte, in a pattern that is unique to that character. The alphabetic character *B*, for example, is represented in ASCII with the unique bit pattern 1000010. The lowercase ASCII *b* is represented by a different bit pattern, 1100010. In turn, each character has its own pattern or code.

The transmission and reception of these strings of 1s and 0s must be tightly managed if they are not to become unintelligible garbage at the receiving end. Among the critical issues in managing a bit stream is timing the flow, so that the pattern of 1s and 0s is properly synchronized at both ends. Timing can be accomplished in two ways: by managing at the byte, or character, level, called asynchronous communications; or at the block of characters level, called synchronous communications.

Essentially, an asynchronous communications channel lacks a commonly agreed upon timing mechanism or internal clock. Without that clock, which is present in synchronous systems, the DCE or DTE must supply the synchronization for each character. They accomplish the task by inserting one start bit before and one or two stop bits after each byte. In the process, they add as many as three bits to the seven bits required to represent a character, an overhead of more than 40 percent. The sending equipment adds the framing bits to each character or byte, and the receiving equipment senses their presence and removes them as it converts the analog pulses to a digital form.

In a synchronous system, DCE and DTE transmit characters in blocks, either as a whole computer terminal screen or as a field of data from the screen. The modems and control units are synchronized by a timing pulse that automatically signals between components that a certain state of affairs exists, for example, that the first modem is beginning to transmit a block of characters, which will not be framed on an individual character basis as with asynchronous communications. The second modem is then prepared to receive the data block in its entirety. Modems are discussed in more detail later in this chapter.

Other control functions relate to detecting and correcting errors. A garbled signal quickly loses its usefulness and must be either corrected or retransmitted. At the character level, one method of error detection involves a technique called *parity checking*. In ASCII, the DCE or DTE counts the number of 1 bits in the seven bits composing the character and then may force the eighth data bit into parity. For example, if both pieces of equipment in a DCE pair are set to operate on even parity, and the number of 1 bits in the character is odd (say three or five), then the eighth bit would be set to 1. The addition of the 1 bit brings the character into even parity. If the bit count of 1s is already even (say two or four), the eighth bit would be set to 0. In odd parity, an even number of 1 bits would be set odd by adding a 1 in the eighth bit position.

In receiving a character or block of characters, the modem or control unit verifies the number of 1 bits. If they are not in parity–that is, if the parity is set to even and there is an odd number of 1 bits–an error has occurred in generating or transmitting that character. The receiving DCE or DTE, which operates in tandem with the sending unit in regard to the error detection scheme, then refuses to acknowledge the receipt by returning a NAK or No Acknowledge signal, which forces the sending DCE to retransmit the character or block again.

A frame containing errors may be detected by the receiving component, and if those errors cannot be corrected, the individual frame will be retransmitted by the sending component. The framing process employs techniques that are applied in most synchronous communications such as SDLC, HDLC, and another called the X.25 packet protocol.

The X.25 protocol, developed as a standard by the Consultative Committee on International Telephony and Telegraphy (an international standards organization known best by its initials, CCITT), has become popular in a variety of settings. It is in use in networks such as Tymnet and Telenet, which are discussed later in this chapter.

Transmission Networks

Whatever the type and capacity of the communications medium, it eventually must be configured into a communications network. At its simplest, the network will be a point-to-point network, consisting of a single line, or circuit, perhaps connecting a computer terminal to a host computer. Typical configurations for such a network would have a low speed of 1200 to 2400 bps, in asynchronous mode, using voice-grade telephone lines with two modems, one at each end of the network. Such point-to-point circuits are typical of the applications in many library settings, such as a branch's circulation terminal connected to the library's central computer system.

As network requirements grow in complexity, a variety of technical and economic factors begin to affect the engineering and topology, or architecture, of the network. For example, with several remote sites requiring access to a central host computer, the costs of leasing a separate private line for each circuit may become prohibitive, particularly if an alternative exists for sharing the use of a single line. By developing control capabilities, it is possible to have many terminals on a circuit, in different locations in a point-to-multipoint network. These multipoint circuits can significantly lower leased-line charges without degrading service.

Such networks employ either *contention* or *polling* techniques to allow all of the terminals to gain access to the host. Contention techniques include assigning priority levels to different devices, or to specific messages, and then having the device or terminal request permission to control the circuit to transmit the message. In a typical example of polling, the host computer or its DCE signals each terminal on a multipoint network in a predetermined sequence. If a terminal has a message for the host, that message is then transmitted to the host. While the host is processing the transaction from the first terminal, the second terminal is polled, or asked if it has a message, and if so, to send the message. The entire polling sequence proceeds in this manner. When the first terminal's turn comes again, its transaction at the host computer may be completed, so the host's response to the original message is returned to the first terminal.

In such a polled environment, each terminal has equal access to the circuit; if there are 10 terminals, each has one-tenth of the total circuit time. To improve efficiency, engineers apply dynamic polling techniques to a multipoint network. For example, a terminal that does not respond to three straight polls may not be in use and, therefore, can be passed over in some way, such as in one out of three subsequent polling sequences. Instead, its polling sequence may be assigned to a terminal that has consistent and heavy traffic at each poll.

These two basic network topologies, point-to-point and point-to-multipoint, while describing many data communications networks, leave one common type remaining: the value-added networks (VANs). Such networks are also referred to as enhanced service providers by the Federal Communications Commission (FCC). VANs are operated by communications carriers such as Tymnet and Telenet, which have added protocol, packet switching, and other performance enhancements to their carrying capacity.

Packet Switching

These multipoint, multipath networks employ packet switching to enhance the efficiency of their leased data lines. Packet switching, using an X.25 or similar protocol, allows a message to move in segments or packets between host and terminal, or between host and host, following whichever path will most efficiently handle individual packets. Since the packet assembly process assigns sequence and control information to each packet, the packets may move on different circuit segments toward their destination, where they will be disassembled into the proper sequence. The process of packet assembly and disassembly takes place in a piece of DCE called a packet assembler-disassembler (PAD).

As commercial data communications providers, the VANs maintain nodes in most metropolitan areas in North America and in many remote locations where sufficient traffic warrants their installation. Nodes consist of incoming phone lines, modems, PADs, and computerized channel control equipment. Users wanting to access a remote host computer, for example to search the Dialog information service, would place a data call to their local VAN node, where the initial call setup would take place. This setup includes logging on to the VAN for the session for billing purposes and initializing access to the node located at the host site.

With the session initiated, each search request or command sent between the user's terminal and the host would be assembled by the PAD and sent toward the host or terminal. Since all nodes in the VAN are interconnected, a variety of potential paths exists between the user's node and the host node. The control equipment at each node monitors the traffic level on segments of circuit associated with that node. When it receives a packet headed toward the host computer, the control equipment selects the most efficient path available at that time. Packets arriving subsequently may be routed on different paths, to be properly disassembled and sequenced when they arrive at the destination node.

These packet-switched networks are also in use for private data communications networks. Several of the VANs will install and maintain data communications nodes for the use of single corporations or users, linking sites either through the multipath networks in general use or through private leased lines.

Finally, the growth of microcomputers and the need to access and share files, printers, and other microcomputer components, as well as the need to access large-scale computers, has given rise to a new form of data communications network, the local area network (LAN). By definition, a LAN is closed; it does not communicate outside the immediate area or building in which it is located and links together microcomputer or mainframe computer resources within its area. Chapter 2 covers LANs in detail.

DATA COMMUNICATIONS EQUIPMENT

By its nature, data communications presumes that, at the minimum, each end of the communications channel has equipment to perform the functions described thus far. The transmission and reception functions, the flow control functions, the error detection and correction functions, and the conversion functions from one transmission form to another all require some machine manipulation and management of the communications process.

Most electronic equipment employed in data communications falls into one of two areas: data terminal equipment or data communications equipment. The distinction between these two may be understood simply by answering two questions. First, does the equipment transmit, receive, display, or print information from a computer system? If so, it is probably DTE. Second, does the equipment manage the transmission of, propagate, convert, or control signals? If so, it is probably DCE.

While the distinction between DTE and DCE may sometimes be blurred, as in a modem card installed in a microcomputer that uses a software package to control data transmission, the functions of control versus display separate the two types when the equipment itself falls into both areas. In control functions, the modem is the common denominator at low data transmission speeds.

Modems

Typically, transmission over the public switched network or leased lines requires conversion from a purely digital signal to an analog form. The transmission/reception equipment for the conversion is called a modem, for

MOdulator-DEModulator. The modem takes the digital signal and transmits it through a system that ultimately alters the signal through impedance (the resistance to the flow of electrons that exists in a metallic circuit), or another of the processes described earlier in this chapter.

Because the frequencies and techniques being used to represent a digital signal in an analog system require methods common to both partners in the modem pair, the standards involved in designing and manufacturing modems have become matters of international importance. The standards set by Bell Telephone/American Telephone and Telegraph (AT&T) in designing their 300- to 1200-bps modems have been adopted by virtually all other North American manufacturers of DCE. Lumped together as type 103 for 300-bps modems and type 212A for 1200-bps, these Bell standards have dominated their respective markets. Modems that adhere to these standards are described as *Bell-compatible*.

At transmission rates of 2400 bps and above, there is considerably more diversity and confusion. The CCITT has developed a variety of standards in use in Europe, and increasingly in North America as well.

Labeled with V. followed by a numeric or alphabetic designation, such as V.22 or V.33 bis, the CCITT standards seem to be emerging as the predominant design guidelines for modem manufacturers. With their more recent research support and ability to take advantage of new computer and communications technology, the CCITT standards and hardware manufactured to these standards promise higher speeds, better error detection and correction, and more flexibility in using the capacity of the communications channels. More information on data communications standards is provided later in this chapter.

Multiplexers

Because the bandwidth of a transmission channel may potentially carry more information than a single modem pair can transmit and control over that channel, and because one high-speed channel is typically less expensive than the number of lower-speed channels required for an equivalent amount of bandwidth, the multiplexer has become an essential part of high-volume data communications.

The multiplexer, sometimes called *mux*, was developed by the telephone and telegraph industries in the 1930s and 1940s as a means of optimizing channel use in long-distance communications. Essentially, muxes divide a channel in one of two ways: longitudinally, by splitting one communications path into several discrete channels; and laterally, by dividing the channel into slices of time, each slice being applied to one of two or more channels.

The first method, involving the frequency division multiplexer (FDM), was the original technique for getting more use out of telephone lines. FDMs transmit and receive on different frequencies for different channels, with the channels bundled together in one wire or cable. While FDMs are not used as much now, they still represent useful technology.

The second type of mux, the time division multiplexer (TDM), and its derivative, the statistical time division multiplexer (STDM, or stat mux), treat a communications path as a single channel, but give portions of the channel to different devices on a rotating time basis. This process, called *interleaving,* makes efficient use of communications channels.

Imagine three data terminals attached via three separate access ports to one computer, but sharing a common communications line for a part of the distance between the computer's and the terminals' locations. Since none of the three will require full-time use of the path, a pair of TDMs will allocate the entire channel for the brief duration of each message or signal between each terminal and the computer. After each device has concluded its transmission/reception, the TDM will sense that conclusion and turn the channel over to one of the other devices.

The STDM operates with more control than simply handing off channel access from one device to another. In effect, it controls the channel allocation based on message traffic between terminal and computer. If one terminal or device has no message requirement, its time slot is allocated to another terminal, or the duration of the time slot may be lengthened or reduced.

Modems and multiplexers are frequently incorporated into the same device, providing both signal conversion and channel optimizing in one component.

Protocol Converters

In data communications networks involving many manufacturers' equipment, converting signals from differing standards to a commonly transmitted standard and then converting back to a form recognized by the other devices involved in the transaction may require protocol conversion. Somewhere in the communications path between devices of differing protocols must be a control capability which either converts from one protocol to another or emulates a dominant protocol.

For example, a terminal manufactured by Digital Equipment Corporation that operates on the VT-220 protocol will require some intervention in a communications network attached to an IBM-manufactured computer. Such intervention and conversion may take place in a single-function device, called a *protocol converter,* which changes a VT-220 formatted signal to an IBM EBCDIC format signal, and back. The changes in the signal might involve both information, such as bit patterns for individual characters, and control functions, such as end of message marks.

Communications Controllers

Increasingly, data communications functions such as packet assembly-disassembly, multiplexing, analog-digital conversion, protocol conversion, error detection and correction, and routing selection are being incorporated into communications controllers. These specialized data communications devices may involve only a few functions or many, including dynamic management of a communications network, management and statistical reporting of communications activity, and establishment of alternative paths in the event of device or circuit failure.

DATA COMMUNICATIONS STANDARDS

By its nature, data communications presupposes a very high level of machine control of the communications process. That machine control then demands that the machines interact in ways that are predictable. The need for predictable interaction necessitates standards, or commonly understood and agreed upon techniques, codes, operating speeds, error detection and correction, and a host of other requirements.

Much standards work has grown out of products and services supplied by large corporations. As noted earlier, AT&T's modems created de facto standards for low-speed data communications, and these standards at one time dominated the North American market. IBM's Systems Network Architecture (SNA), which generally conformed to international standards under development at the time of its introduction in 1974, has become a de facto standard for hardware environments using IBM equipment or software.

Despite the very large role played by commercial firms, standards by and large must be reviewed, adopted, and published by one of the national or international standards-setting organizations to achieve formal status. As noted earlier, the CCITT, an international organization specifically devoted to standards and a part of the International Telecommunications Union, exists to develop and recommend standards without having direct commercial interest in specific products. Another influential international organization is the International Organisation for Standardisation (ISO).

A variety of such organizations exists in North America as well. These include among others the American National Standards Institute (ANSI), the Electronic Industries Association (EIA), the Institute of Electrical and Electronics Engineers (IEEE), and the Computer and Business Equipment Manufacturers Association (CBEMA).

The standards development and implementation process is often long and arduous. Since many participants in standards setting depend on income from sales of products that will operate according to the standards being discussed, there is much give and take involved in identifying common ground in highly technical areas. Frequently, new developments in technology or the need to exploit marketing opportunities mean that formalizing standards is just bowing to reality: a manufacturer has a new product that is being well received, and that employs novel or innovative technical characteristics. Wishing to gain greater acceptance for this innovation and having the advantage of being first to develop a product, the manufacturer proposes that a standards organization adopt the manufacturer's characteristics, with appropriate review and modification, as a recognized standard. In an environment where reliable interaction between components is critical, other manufacturers or suppliers will eventually want to conform to the new standard and will appreciate having it formally approved.

Some of the most important data communications standards are shown in Table 1.1. The terms used in the ISO and IEEE standards are explained in chapter 2.

Table 1.1. Major Data Communications Standards

Promulgating Organization	Standard Designation	Standard Description
EIA	RS-232C	Circuit connections between DTE and DCE, and circuit electrical characteristics, all using serial binary data.
	RS-449	Circuit connections between DTE and DCE using 37-pin and 9-pin connections, all using serial binary data.
ISO	7498	Basic reference model of Open Systems Interconnection (OSI).
CC:TT	X.25 X.28 X.29	Interconnection between DTE and DCE for terminals; interconnection to a PAD; interconnection between PADs for exchange of information and control; all use packet-switched networks.
	V.21 thru V.29	Standards for modems operating at data rates between 300 and 9600 bps, both on dial-up and leased lines.
IEEE	488	Interconnection between devices using parallel data interface.
	802.3	Broadband and baseband bus using CSMA/CD.
	802.4 802.5	Broadband and baseband bus for token passing; token passing access method.

DATA COMMUNICATIONS IN LIBRARIES

Library applications of data communications have largely been at the lower end of the information technology potential. The transmission rates are typically low (probably not over 19.2 Kbps) with metallic media for transmission, and the applications primarily involve remote site access to information systems for text transmission, retrieval, and display. Examples include public library branches with circulation control terminals or public access catalog terminals.

Given the circumstances of most libraries, as branches or agencies of state or local government, or as parts of private, nonprofit institutions, they are not often required to invest in leading-edge research or to implement new or costly technology. For these reasons, and because library needs have been served well by existing technologies, libraries have generally used mature, dependable, and affordable data communications. These technologies include a great deal of data transmitted over the local telephone subscriber loop.

Public Libraries

A typical public library wishing to automate its circulation function would probably opt for a minicomputer or small mainframe computer at a central site, with computer terminals and modems at branch locations for remote access. The terminals may employ multiplexers to reduce line charges and improve communications channel efficiency. Likely they would operate between 2400 and 9600 bps, over copper wires leased from the local telephone company. The channel would probably be full or half duplex. If it is full duplex, the circuit would be four-wire. Depending on the terminal and computer equipment manufacturer, the circuit would operate either synchronously, using a bit-level protocol like SDLC, or asynchronously, using a simple protocol like ASCII/TTY. (TTY is the contraction of Teletype, an early data communications application, which remains in use.)

When a library has very high data communications traffic and its branches or constituents are very remote from the central site, or when it is part of a large regional system, it may use the higher-speed facilities of the long-distance network. In that case, the telecommunications carrier, or company, would connect the library traffic onto a backbone circuit, which may operate at 56 Kbps. The backbone circuit is that part of a multipoint circuit that is in use by all the devices communicating on it. In the integrated services digital network (ISDN) discussed later in this chapter, the backbone circuit, called a T-1 circuit, may operate at 1.544 megabits per second (a million bits per second, abbreviated Mbps).

Some innovative data communications applications have come to light in public library settings, including the use of data radio and cable television facilities. In the case of data radio, at least two public library agencies with branches widely scattered across thinly populated territory have implemented data communications using packet data and radio modems. While the initial cost is substantially higher than either leased-line or dial-up metallic circuits due to the complexity of the equipment and comparative scarcity of suppliers, the operating costs are substantially less. The technology involves the use of highly linear radio transmission, or radio transmitters and receivers that are aimed with some precision toward each other. The use of a radio-frequency signal, operating in the FM range of approximately 475 MHz, allows data communications that is truly wireless, and yet in many ways still operates much like a leased-line synchronous system.

Cable television can lend itself to data transmission. The bandwidth of the transmission medium, coaxial cable, is quite high; at the lower end of the transmission spectrum, there is little demand on the bandwidth for television transmission because of potential interference from other electronic devices. In addition, coaxial cable can support a substantial capacity for voice and data channels in addition to television. Several public libraries have arranged to use cable television facilities for linking branches to a central site, being required only to retrofit the necessary equipment to the systems to enable data transmission.

Academic Libraries

Because of campus data communications facilities, academic libraries have been in a position to operate in more technically advanced environments. While it is difficult to develop a model academic library, there are certain campus network environments common enough to be useful as models.

Frequently the library is simply one of a number of automated information resources on campus. The physical environment, often clustered around a group of buildings, is conducive to sharing resources and facilities. The variety of communications applications on campus often includes voice, data, and video or image transmission. Because of the number of applications, the variety of requirements, and the high number of users concentrated in a small area, there is frequently a high degree of expertise either on site or readily available from contracting agencies such as the telephone company and switch manufacturers.

In such an environment, it makes sense that the campus communications system would have broadband capability—that is, the ability to handle several channels of communications simultaneously on the same facility. In order to do so, the campus network might be coaxial, shielded twisted-pair, or fiber-optic. If fiber optics have not yet arrived on campus, they might be expected by the early 1990s. The communications system should be able to handle the data requirements of a variety of hardware manufacturers, so either it would be hardware-independent using the widely accepted Transmission Control Protocol/Internet Protocol (TCP/IP) or it would include a great variety of protocol conversion equipment and software. It would have a number of nodes, or locations where communications may enter and exit the campus network. At these nodes would be switches, protocol converters, and access to subnetworks or local area networks. In this type of environment, access to library information would be readily available from faculty offices and student housing.

IMPLICATIONS FOR FUTURE DIRECTIONS

The implications of recently emerged standards and technologies point toward a communications future very different from the current environment. It seems quite clear that by the middle or late 1990s, most communications will be digital, whether involving voice, data, or images. The impetus for digitization will be the very high bandwidth available on fiber optics and revitalized metallic circuits, and the economics of handling multiple communications requirements with a single set of transmission media and equipment.

Four major factors drive the development of all-digital communications. First is the proposed standard developed by the ISO and the CCITT in the mid-1970s for ISDN. Second is the development of the preferred transmission medium, fiber optics; and third is the continuing enhancement of microprocessor technology for managing and controlling digital communications.

The fourth major factor, and the controlling one, is economic. The international nature of business and its associated communications means that no corporation or communications carrier can afford to develop a separate large-scale, stand-alone communications system for voice, another for data, and a third for video. All evidence for future directions suggests that agreed-upon standards and the ability to transmit voice, data, and image on a common set of channels with common controls and equipment will dictate a fully digital system.

These four parallel developments have already caused changes in the data communications industry. First, the standards-setting process has become significantly more international in scope in the last 10 years, as the ISO and the CCITT have become extremely important forces in the North American standards process. Second, communications carriers have been making enormous investments in fiber optics, with estimates of up to 80 percent annual growth in fiber-optic circuit miles per year in the late 1980s, and the expectation for growth to continue at that rate into the mid-1990s. Third, the penetration of fiber optics into the local subscriber loop has begun. Admittedly, the first such installations were either in very high-volume applications or represented pilot projects. Because of the trend toward the digitization of all traffic, including voice, even standard telephone service has begun to convert analog voice signals to digital form, beginning with automated private branch exchanges (PBXes).

Emerging standards and the services they will help shape point to the increased digitization of all communications traffic. Two separate sets of standards in particular presuppose all-digital environments and are aimed at some of the most pressing problems in a highly mechanized and highly complex communications world. The first such set of standards, proposed by the ISO, is called Open Systems Interconnection (OSI). OSI is discussed in detail in chapter 2.

In addition to OSI, the emerging ISDN standards are intended to provide for bandwidth and common switching. Given the need to transmit enormous amounts of data, communications carriers and corporations with significant interest in communications will make investments in a variety of information technology applications. Many of these are not difficult to imagine: on-demand publishing for the scientific and technical community, for whom timeliness is critical and for whom the print version of an article might frequently appear weeks later than a machine-readable version from a publisher; custom video showings from any of a variety of vendors who can be accessed through the local subscriber loop; custom news magazines, with voice, text, and image capability, organized as a type of selective dissemination of information; and image and voice combined for telephone service.

As noted earlier, ISDN is the outgrowth of a set of standards first proposed by the CCITT in the 1970s and now being embraced in both Europe and North America. ISDN services are all digital, including voice, from the point of entry of the signal into the network to its destination. In the late 1980s, ISDN "rollouts" or introductions of services in North American corporations or major metropolitan areas seemed to be largely focused on voice and data applications using common switching, or communications control, and common transport, or cabling. The promise of video being incorporated may require additional bandwidth beyond the ISDN standards of 1.544 Mbps in North America, and 2.048 Mbps in Europe.

T-1 is a standard for the 1.544-Mbps digital facility. It will form the so-called primary rate for ISDN in North America. Among the interesting departures between European and North American ISDN plans is the European standard being defined at 2.048 Mbps. Interfacing between the two facilities will require conversion software and hardware to maintain a connection for communication that originates at one standard and terminates at another.

These data rates may be divided into separate channels of 16, 32, and 64 Kbps. The minimum preferred ISDN transmission capability in North

America includes two 64-Kbps channels (termed B channels) and a single 16 Kbps-channel (a D channel) for managing the signals that flow on the B channels. While this capacity seems high, it is too little for full motion video.

In fact, one criticism of ISDN is that it may already offer too little capacity. The recent improvements in very high speed local data transmission, where 16 Mbps is now becoming a common application on metallic circuits for LANs, may make ISDN services too restricted as the primary transmission format for all digital information.

Clearly, the role of information technology planners is made both more complex by these developments and more rewarding. Despite a potential need for more capacity, if each library in North America, for example, had the minimum standard described in ISDN, it would have at its disposal 144 Kb of bandwidth. This amount of capacity would be adequate for high-speed digital facsimile, slow-scan video, voice, and data transmission, all on the same channels and controlled by the same equipment. This capacity would make possible a number of services, including full-text information retrieval and capture and on-demand electronic publishing, that are now available only at prices far beyond the average public or academic library budget.

The implications of ISDN in combination with OSI for information services are many and varied. The potential exists for a full and complete automated information network that would permit authorized users to access whatever information they needed to perform their jobs, enhance their recreational interests, or communicate with anyone who was also connected to the network.

There are obviously a number of potential effects that might disrupt current service patterns or that could change the sociology of information delivery. It is not difficult to see that with on-demand publishing the role of some current information providers could be seriously degraded: Who would need the library if the patrons' current information requests could be delivered at their desks on an information appliance attached to a high-capacity communications channel?

There are also technical and economic factors that will affect the implementation of this emergent communications environment. Given the many billions of dollars required to upgrade the North American communications plant, there must be someone to pay for the upgrade. Much of the existing plant can be converted or used, but much of it, including customer premises equipment (CPE), may not provide sufficient functionality in an OSI/ISDN environment.

To summarize, the changes in communications will have substantial effects on publishing, information delivery, and libraries. One can only conjecture; what is certain is that all these information technology applications may be very different in 10 years.

SUGGESTED READING

Monographs

Boss, Richard W. *Telecommunications for Library Management.* White Plains, N.Y.: Knowledge Industries, 1985.

Jacob, M. E. L. *Telecommunications Networks: Issues and Trends.* White Plains, N.Y.: Knowledge Industries, 1986.

Journals

Datapro Reports on Data Communications.

Telephony.

Network World.

Information Technology and Libraries.

Library Hi Tech.

Communications Week.

▪ 2 ▪

Networks

Kerry Webb

Computer networks provide the facilities of individual systems to users beyond the immediate area. A computer may have a number of terminals attached to it in the same building, but there are certain limitations on the type of terminal that may be connected and, more important, on the distance between the computer and the terminal. Computer networks are used so that a wider range of equipment can be connected over a wider area.

A network consists of at least one computer (also known as a processor), transmission media (which may include further computer equipment), and terminal equipment (including terminal controllers). Of course, that is only the hardware; a network also requires specific software, mostly in the host computer(s) and associated communications controllers, but often in the terminal equipment. A typical network configuration is shown in Figure 2.1.

Networks may extend over a vast area or be limited to one room. They may contain one processor or one hundred. The processors may range from microcomputers to supercomputers. An examination of all types of networks is beyond the scope of this book, but there are two types of networks of particular interest to libraries: local area networks (LANs), which link terminals or computers within a small geographic area such as a building or a college campus; and bibliographic networks, which may spread across a town, state, country, or several countries around the world. LANs and bibliographic networks operate using similar basic physical concepts, but there are many differences in how they are managed.

LOCAL AREA NETWORKS

LANs have developed since the 1970s as a way of providing computing resources to a number of users within an organization in an economical manner. The significance of "local" is that the users are all associated with one organization and have similar and predictable requirements.

Furthermore, the organization has a great deal of control over the facilities that are offered to the users and the way in which these facilities are used.

Figure 2.1. A Typical Network Consisting of a Central Host Computer, Terminal Controllers, and Terminals

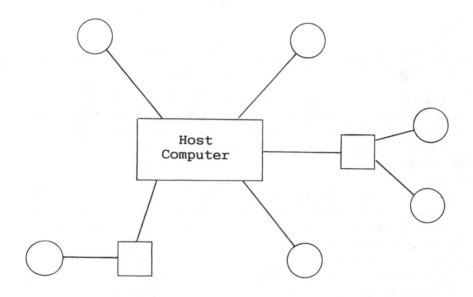

Terminal controller

Terminal

Characteristics

A LAN consists of processing components (processors, servers, terminals, disk drives, printers, and so on) and cabling that carries messages between the components. Its characteristics include:

1. The topology, or the way in which the components are linked together. The basis of the link (as with all computer networks) is a transmission medium that can carry a signal. Whatever the medium, the topology of the network is characterized by its geometric shape and depends on the type and amount of the traffic on the network.

   The topology may be a star, in which there is a central computer with all other elements linked to it; a ring, in which cables link adjacent elements, including the processor(s), forming a closed loop; or a bus, which is like the ring but with open ends, in which equipment at the ends passes messages back along the bus as required. These three topologies are illustrated in Figure 2.2. With a ring or a bus, the message contains data plus indicators of the source and destination of the message. With a star, where the source and destination are implicit in the link, the addresses do not appear in the message in the same way.

2. The cabling medium, which consists of twisted-pair wiring, coaxial cable, or fiber-optic cable. (Larger networks may use microwave transmission, but because LANs are limited in geographic area, this is not appropriate for them.) While twisted-pair wiring is inexpensive and easy to lay, the transmission rates it can support are low, and therefore the efficiency of the LAN is limited. The other types of cable can provide faster transmission. Fiber-optic cable has the added benefits of more security and freedom from electrical interference that may affect cabling carrying electrical current.

3. The number of channels, described as baseband or broadband. A baseband network can handle only one channel, which is all that may be needed for most LANs. A broadband network can handle many channels, providing a facility for several types of communication on the network, including voice, video, and data.

4. The protocol, which is the set of rules governing communication on the LAN. The protocol controls the way in which messages are passed from one component to another, the way in which "collisions" between messages are prevented when more than one component wishes to transmit, and the way in which messages are

removed from the network when they have been received. Examples of protocols are Carrier Sense Multiple Access–Collision Detection (CSMA/CD) and Token Passing.

CSMA/CD uses the technique (called *carrier sense*) of checking before transmission to see if another node in the network is sending a message and, if so, waiting until the line is clear. The message is transmitted to all nodes, which must check to see if it is intended for them. Should two nodes begin transmission simultaneously, the resulting signals on the line become corrupted. To overcome this possibility, the transmitting node can check its own transmitted message; if there is a difference, it stops the transmission (called *collision detection*). After a random interval, the message can be retransmitted.

In token passing, a "token" is passed from one node to another in a ring or a bus, with the node being able to transmit a message only when it holds the token. In this way, only one message can be sent at a time.

Figure 2.2. LAN Topologies

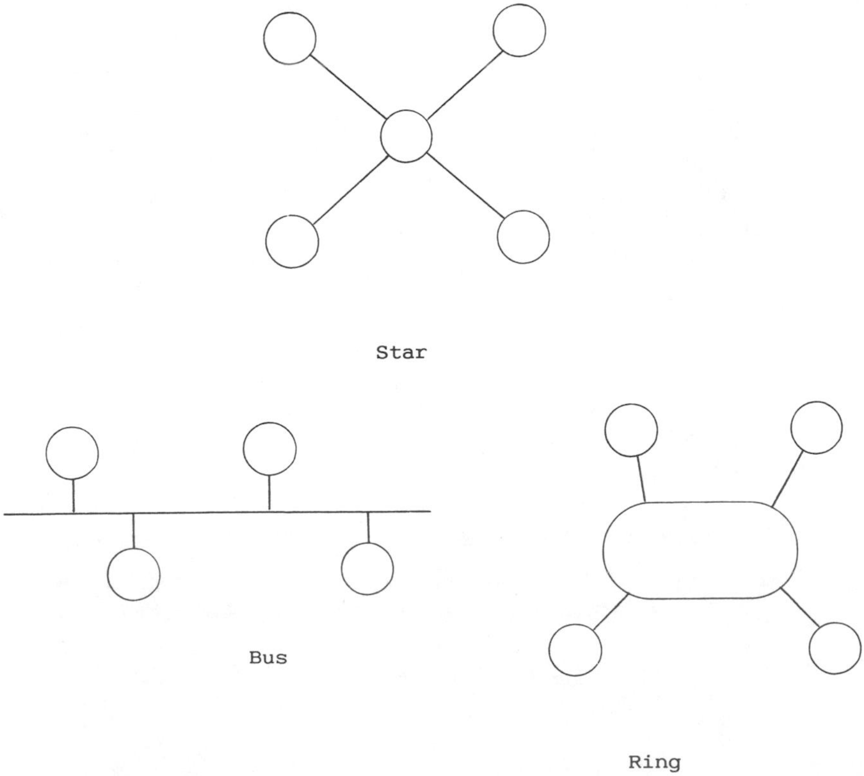

Star

Bus

Ring

Benefits

The basic principle of a LAN is that computing resources (such as processors, disk storage, printers, and communication gateways or switched access to other networks) are shared among users. Clearly, users could each have these resources attached to their workstations (and many users do), but for a large part of the time, most of these resources would not be in use. A LAN offers more cost-efficient use of this equipment.

Consider the case of an office where there are eight potential users of a computer system that provides word processing, spreadsheets, and database access. (These software applications are explained in detail in chapters 8 and 9.) To equip each user with a personal computer, disk drive, laser printer, modem, and software could cost around $40,000. However, if they can share a large capacity disk drive, laser printer, and communications facility to other networks, it would be possible to provide each user with a terminal on a LAN for less than half of that amount.

The benefits of LANs extend beyond mere financial savings. Files stored on a central facility may be made available to any user on the LAN with the authority to read or update them. This avoids the inefficiency of different users inputting the same data. Furthermore, only one backup operation is needed, rather than having to rely on all users performing their own.

It is not only data that can be shared. Systems and software can also be made available to a wider range of users more economically. A LAN may contain a number of processors, each operating a range of software, such as an integrated library management system, database systems, and spreadsheets. The cost of common software for word processing or spreadsheets, for example, is less for a network version supporting a number of users than for the same number of copies for individual personal computers.

Other benefits are possible only because of the existence of the LAN. The most significant of these is the use of electronic mail. By sending a message to another user on the LAN, you avoid the frustration of "telephone tag"; you ensure that the message says exactly what you want it to say; and you have a record of when it was sent and whether or not it was received. Electronic mail also enables a user to deal with the messages at the most convenient time.

The shared resources on a LAN are controlled by processors known as *peripheral servers,* most commonly *file servers* (controlling high-capacity disk drives) and *printer servers.* A file server makes it possible for users' private files to be stored economically on a central device and for common files to be accessed by a number of users. This is typically achieved by the use of file directories (pointing to groups of files), which, together with tables of passwords, control which users may access which groups of files on the disks.

The file server queues requests from multiple users of the same disk and prevents multiple access to common files if such a file is being amended at that time.

Printer servers provide control of access to the printer or printers on the LAN. Because of the shared nature of the LAN, several users may frequently wish to print documents at the same time. The printer server may write these documents to temporary disk storage until the printer is free (a technique known as *spooling*), or may record the details of the document to be printed (file name, format, number of copies, etc.) so that it can be retrieved and printed later.

Disadvantages

Despite the benefits in terms of functionality and cost associated with the use of LANs, there are some significant drawbacks. Indeed, these drawbacks in various forms are the reason why we have not yet seen the predicted explosion of LANs.

The greatest disadvantage is the loss of independence for individual users. If personal computer users want another software package or a better laser printer, they can buy it, install it, and use it any way they want. On a network, it is not that easy. Decisions on what equipment to purchase and how it is to be used are made on behalf of the network, not each user. Furthermore, the user must accept that the performance of a terminal on the network in terms of speed may well be less than that of a personal computer.

Network resources such as printers are not as easy to use as on a personal computer. The printer is usually located some distance away from most users, and a user may have to negotiate with others to ensure that the appropriate stationery (plain, letterhead, or adhesive labels) is loaded at the appropriate time.

With the benefits of multiple access to data comes the necessity of ensuring that two or more users do not update the same record at the same time. Some LANs prevent even read-only access to files that are being printed at the time.

Finally, there is the requirement for a network administrator. Such administrators perform much of the work that personal computer support staff do, but on a larger scale. They buy and install new software and hardware and ensure that system backups are performed. They are also responsible for continual monitoring of the system and performing whatever tuning is required. This tuning may involve acquiring more hardware or adjusting the software to provide better network performance. It also involves telling users to remove unwanted files from the central disk storage. Finally, the duties of an administrator include planning for future network growth.

BIBLIOGRAPHIC NETWORKS

A bibliographic network is a network consisting of a central computer system with a large database of catalog records linked by telecommunications facilities to libraries. A bibliographic network has the same general attraction for users as any other network. Users remote from the base location of the host computer require access to the data and processing functions of the host. This is particularly attractive to libraries because of the size of the database required for library applications and the complexity of processing associated with this data.

Functions

The most common service offered by bibliographic networks is shared cataloging–the reason for the success of such networks as the Online Computer Library Center (OCLC), the Research Libraries Information Network (RLIN), the University of Toronto Library Automation System (UTLAS), and the Western Library Network (WLN). A cataloger wishing to catalog a particular item can access a host computer containing millions of records contributed by national cataloging agencies (for example, the Library of Congress [LC] or the British Library) or by other users of the network.

If there is a record on the system for the item, the cataloger can choose to accept it and have the system produce appropriate products: microfiche records, spine labels, records on magnetic tape, and so on. At the same time, holdings information for the cataloger's library can be added to the record on the database, thereby enhancing the union catalog, or combined list of holdings, for the community. If the record is not present or (in some systems) if the cataloger chooses not to accept the standard of cataloging recorded on the database, a new record for the item can be added to the system, together with holdings data.

In either case, the user has access to an enormous amount of data and sophisticated functions on the host computer. These functions, in addition to the sophisticated search facilities used to find the record in the first place, may include:

1. Input of cataloging data, with verification of certain fields to ensure that they conform to standard formats.

2. Access to authority files to ensure that authorized forms of names and subjects are used.

3. Addition of holdings to the database for the compilation of a union catalog.

4. Aggregation of cataloging records to user files so that bulk cataloging products such as microfiche or magnetic tape files can be produced.

5. Acquisitions, which may include electronic ordering of material and accessioning of the material when it is delivered.

6. Routing of messages requesting interlibrary loans (ILLs), monitoring the status of these requests, and providing statistics on ILL traffic.

Bibliographic networks, however, face an uncertain future. Most grew out of shared cataloging functions, which then spawned resource-sharing activities, particularly the maintenance of union catalogs, which permitted searching as part of general information retrieval or interlibrary loan. The base, though, remained shared cataloging, and without it, particularly the contribution of cataloging data from member libraries, the other functions cannot be supported economically.

Trends toward Local Processing

The change in circumstances has been brought about by the introduction in many member libraries of local processing systems and the use of large files of bibliographic data on compact disc-read only memory (CD-ROM). (CD-ROM is discussed in greater detail in chapter 7). By doing original or copy cataloging on a network, a library can easily add information concerning its holdings to the union catalog, thereby increasing the resource for all network users. But if, for good economic reasons, the library decides that it is preferable to perform original cataloging on its local system, there is no guarantee that any original cataloging or holdings data will ever be added to the network's database.

The problem is compounded by the ready availability of data on CD-ROM, for example, the LC MARC (Library of Congress MAchine Readable Cataloging) files offered by a number of vendors and the planned provision of other MARC files from various national sources. Many libraries, particularly public libraries, can find an acceptable percentage of their cataloging data on such products.

This trend toward local cataloging has been observed for some time, along with other changes in usage that provide a degree of doubt concerning the future viability of some networks. For instance, the amount of searching on the online union catalogs in RLIN and OCLC has increased at a time when the demand for cataloging and acquisitions services has leveled off. Clearly, the requirement for comprehensive union catalogs as aids to resource sharing for collection development and ILL is greater than ever, but the growth in the underlying database of holdings is in danger of decreasing.

In some networks, there is the possibility of purchasing holdings data in the same way that cataloging data is acquired from sources such as LC. The Australian Bibliographic Network (ABN), for instance, offers incentives to major libraries that have not been members of the network to add their retrospective holdings to the system. This enables the ABN database to be a more comprehensive resource-sharing tool, for the benefit of all its members.

New Products and Services

What has become clearer in recent times is that all networks have realized that they have become businesses and must act in a businesslike way, even if they continue in some cases as not-for-profit organizations. This realization has been marked in various ways. OCLC, WLN, and CLASS (Cooperative Library Agency for Systems and Services) have changed their names (while retaining their acronyms) to reflect a wider market than their initial geographic areas. WLN and OCLC have changed their corporate status to become private bodies separate from their founding parent bodies.

These changes have of necessity had an impact on the way the networks are governed. In their early days, with just a few committed users, there was typically a board of user representatives who would meet regularly to plan the overall development of the network. As the size of the network grew, however, changes were made in the way these representatives were elected and in their level of responsibility as the organization developed from a publicly funded cooperative to a multimillion dollar corporation. WLN, for instance, with several licensees of its software around the world, has had to consider how its licensees' interests could be represented on its governing body, which is largely directed towards its network users in the Pacific Northwest of the United States.

These matters have demanded a great deal of attention from the networks, but as organizations with a need to survive as business enterprises, their most significant challenge has been the identification of new products and services. Many of these products have been based upon the existing resource of the network. WLN's LaserCat is a CD-ROM-based union catalog of the network's holdings, which has gained wide acceptance in smaller libraries as an alternative to online searching and in larger member libraries as a complement to online activity. OCLC also provides CD-ROM products as well as local processing systems for smaller libraries.

Other products and services offered have originated from an examination of how the network may meet specific needs of current and potential members. Many such services are not based on utilization of investment in hardware and software, but on people-based cooperative activities. One example is the brokerage of online products from commercial vendors such as Dialog, where members receive discounts arranged by the network. Another is the provision of consultancy services for activities such as retrospective conversion of card catalogs into machine-readable form or disaster planning.

In many cases, the charging mechanisms for networks are also changing. When they started, with a smaller range of services, it was common to levy basic subscription charges, possibly based upon the size of the member library or its annual acquisitions budget. This has given way to charges for products aligned to their production costs – a more businesslike approach, but one which can be at odds with consideration of the public good. For instance, networks must consider whether the amount that they charge for providing an online cataloging service should take into account the economic and other benefits arising from a comprehensive online catalog for resource sharing.

Systems Interconnection

For various reasons, and not only as a reaction to uncertain economic futures, there has been considerable interest from networks in interconnection of their computer systems. Although this is important for networks in all countries, it is particularly critical in the United States, where the lack of a central controlling network has created a number of separate entities, each contributing to the resource. There is little likelihood that a single system will ever encompass the whole of the country's online catalog (or even the majority of it), so other solutions have been pursued.

The most significant development so far has been the Linked System Project (LSP), which has at various times involved LC, RLIN, WLN, and OCLC. LSP is based broadly on the Open Systems Interconnection (OSI) protocols, discussed later in this chapter. The initial LSP activity has resulted in the transfer among LC, RLIN, and OCLC of name authority records on a daily basis for the maintenance of the Name Authority File residing at LC.

There is no doubt that in the future there will be more applications of intersystem communications based on OSI. In Canada, there has been much development of protocols for both interlibrary loan and directory services. However, the area likely to have the biggest impact is intersystem searching, which will permit users to conduct searches in the language of their own system on any other system or network to which they are connected.

OPEN SYSTEMS INTERCONNECTION

Systems developers and users have been concerned for many years about the problem of communication between systems of different vendors (and in some cases, different systems from the same vendor). This is because each vendor has designed its own communications facilities for its own computers.

In this way, the dominant computer vendors have virtually imposed their standards upon those less prominent. The best example of this is IBM, whose Systems Network Architecture (SNA) is the most widely used proprietary "standard" in the world of computer communications. Other computer vendors whose users wanted to communicate with IBM systems have had to make SNA-compatible facilities available on their systems.

Non-IBM systems also need to communicate with other different non-IBM systems, so vendors needed to provide facilities to enable connection to computers from Digital, Unisys, Fujitsu, ICL, and so on. Clearly, this was a heavy burden to most suppliers and their users, so there began an exploration of a general communications philosophy that would provide a standardized means for any system to interact with any other, regardless of the system vendor. This resulted in the concept of Open Systems Interconnection, the framework within which standards for communication between computer systems can be developed. The International Organisation for Standardisation (ISO) has been developing this framework, officially known as the Reference Model of Open Systems Interconnection, based on a number of principles.

The first and best-known principle is that the model is based upon seven layers—that is, the communication process between one user program and another on a different system comprises seven groups of activities. In determining the layers, these are the main rules used:

1. A layer should be created where a different level of abstraction is needed.

2. Each layer should perform a well-defined function.

3. The function of each layer should be chosen with an eye toward defining internationally standardized protocols.

4. The layer boundaries should be chosen to minimize the information flow across those boundaries.

5. The number of layers should be large enough so that distinct functions need not be thrown together in the same layer out of necessity and small enough so that the architecture does not become unwieldy.

Seven Layers of OSI

The individual layers are described below. Each uses the layers at the lower levels to provide services for those at the higher levels. However, it must be stressed that for nearly all users of computer networks it is not necessary to have a full understanding of the functions of the layers. It is more important to understand the benefits and costs of OSI, which are dealt with later in this chapter.

1. The *physical layer* has the function of transmitting bits of data over a physical medium, whether it is a copper cable, an optical fiber or a microwave link. The standards at this layer specify matters such as voltage levels, how to establish a physical connection, duration of individual signals, and the number and functions of pins in the plug connecting the system to the network.

2. The *data link layer* has the responsibility of converting the facility provided by the physical layer into an error-free environment for the network layer. It composes the input data from the network layer into data frames, transmits them in order, and processes frames sent from the receiving system, which acknowledges receipt of the data. In this way, lost or distorted frames can be retransmitted as required.

3. The *network layer* is concerned with the operation of the communications network, which provides the communication between computer systems. This network is usually a packet-switched network provided by a network vendor, such as Telenet or Tymnet. Whereas the unit of data for the physical layer was a bit, and for the data link layer a frame, for the network layer it is a larger component – the packet. (For a discussion of bits, frames, and packets, see chapter 1.) This layer accepts data from the higher-level layers, converts them to packets, and ensures that the packets arrive at the required destination. The destination is important because this layer is also concerned with routing, and it must keep track of the paths of the packets as they pass through intermediate network nodes on their way to the receiving system.

4. The *transport layer* acts as an interface between the session layer and the communications network. In this layer, decisions are made about how the data are transmitted throughout the network, and the degree of error checking required for the transmission of data. Whereas communication between systems may involve intermediate nodes in the network, each of which implements the three lower layers, the transport layer occurs only in the sending and receiving computers.

5. The *session layer* is used to establish and manage a connection between the two systems. The establishment includes verification that there is permission for the systems to communicate and

agreement on modes of communication (full or half duplex). This layer may also manage some error recovery functions, especially if the lower layers are at all unreliable.

6. The *presentation layer* performs a variety of transformations on the data presented to it. This may include data compression, encryption, or conversion between character sets such as American Standard Code for Information Interchange (ASCII) and Extended Binary-Coded Decimal Interchange Code (EBCDIC). There may also be conversions between control characters used by different types of terminals.

7. The *applications layer* contains one or more general-purpose functions that can be used by user programs. Note that this layer is part of the OSI structure and not part of the user program itself. The functions contained in this layer may include file transfer, message handling, terminal emulation, or interlibrary loan messaging.

Benefits and Costs of OSI

The benefits of OSI are most apparent for smaller vendors and their users. When OSI-based communications products are widely available in the systems of major vendors, these smaller vendors will need to supply only an OSI interface with their systems, rather than a specific interface for IBM, Digital, Fujitsu, and so on. This should result in less expensive systems for their users.

The problem is that there is less benefit for the major vendors, and they will be less eager to develop OSI facilities, although they will do so in order to remain competitive. Furthermore, many vendors will also continue to offer products based on their own communications standards for the interconnection of their own systems. For instance, IBM has indicated that SNA will remain the standard for communication between IBM systems, despite their OSI developments.

Thus, smaller vendors will have the option of offering either SNA- or OSI-based products for communication with IBM systems and will probably offer both for some time. Depending on the demand from users, products based on Digital or Unisys standards, for example, may be replaced by those communicating via OSI.

There are short-term costs for all vendors in developing new products, and these, of course, are passed on to the users. Those most affected will be users of major vendors, especially IBM users. These major vendors have rarely had to be concerned with other proprietary standards, but they will now be required by market forces to offer OSI-based products. Despite these costs, as standards are finalized, OSI will be introduced by all vendors as the accepted means of communicating between different computer systems.

SUGGESTED READING

Crawford, Walt. *Current Technologies in the Library: An Informal Overview.* Boston: G.K. Hall, 1988.

Jesty, P. H. *Networking with Microcomputers.* Oxford: Blackwell Scientific, 1985.

Kibirige, Harry M. *Local Area Networks in Information Management.* New York: Greenwood, 1989.

Sugnet, Chris, ed. "Networking in Transition: Current and Future Issues." *Library Hi Tech* 24 (1988): 101-19.

Tanenbaum, A. S. *Computer Networks,* 2d ed. Englewood Cliffs, N.J.: Prentice-Hall, 1988.

▪ 3 ▪

Telecommunications Applications

Joel M. Lee

Telecommunications technologies, like many others, tend to develop and change at a rate far faster than applications for them appear in the field. Even in the last decade of this century, when the rate of technological change is, at least according to conventional wisdom, so much faster than it was 50 or 60 years before, it is not difficult to perceive the time lag between the introduction of a technological advance and the ability of the marketplace to assimilate it.

The factors that contribute to this delay are particularly evident in the realm of telecommunications technologies, which are certainly much older than many other information technologies described in this book. Adoption of these technologies in a given field is often delayed or restricted for such reasons as the cost of equipment purchase and operation, difficulty or complexity of its use, limitations inherent in the technology, or lack of readily available applications.

These barriers are more often matters of perception than reality. Although use of any new technology will unquestionably involve some investment of both human and financial resources, the least tractable obstacle to a technology's integration into daily lives is human resistance to change. That there were still libraries without telephone service in the 1980s was only partly due to those libraries' limited funding; there were still a few public library boards who actually chose not to install telephones lest the staff be disturbed in their work by reference questions.

As we examine applications of several major telecommunications technologies and describe their benefits and disadvantages, it is important to keep in mind that their most daunting barrier is inertia. Their greatest challenge is to prove themselves so superior to existing methods that even the most dubious are compelled to adopt them.

This chapter describes electronic mail, electronic bulletin boards and teleconferencing, telefacsimile (FAX), and online information retrieval systems. This list is not comprehensive, nor are the technologies themselves independent of one another; indeed, they are often closely related and have a comparable base of key applications. However, these five are the most important used in the library, information, and communication professions. The focus of these technologies is primarily on interactions between peers – individuals and groups – and secondarily on information delivery. Such a focus is reflective foremost of the nature of the technology itself, as well as of the question inevitably asked of a new technology: "What will *I* use it for?"

Attempting to be definitive in the realm of telecommunications is a risky endeavor. The field is too much subject to the impact of technical development, the cycles of legal, regulatory, and economic forces, and the whims of personal opinion and the marketplace, for one to be completely conclusive and unambiguous. Therefore, the statements made in this chapter are, like most prices, subject to change without notice.

ELECTRONIC MAIL

Electronic mail, or *email*, the transmission of messages between correspondents using telecommunications connections through a computer system, is the most appropriate medium with which to begin. Communication by mail represents one of the most basic requirements of individuals, groups, organizations, and societies. By understanding mail and how it works, we can understand the objectives of any communications technology, especially those that are text- or graphics-oriented.

Thus, electronic mail is covered to a depth greater than are other communications technologies in this chapter. The strategy in this approach is to view electronic mail as a model that embodies a number of functions and issues common to most, if not all, other communications applications of information technologies. Electronic mail, like the other technologies we will discuss, breaks down an act of communication – mail in this case – into fundamental components and functions that, with the logic and power of the computer, can be assembled into any configuration appropriate to the particular communication objective at hand. The essence of email is to be found in that objective.

Characteristics of Mail and Other Messages

Although speech is the most fundamental method of communication, it has one critical limitation – the requirement that it be conducted in real time, with the speaker and listener both in contact with one another. Another limitation is that there is no record of the communication, unless someone specifically documents it by writing or by some other method. Correspondence is an ancient form of communication that overcomes this limitation, permitting the transmission of messages between persons without the requirement of real-time contact. It is helpful to view mail, as well as other kinds of messages, as having certain characteristics or properties. These characteristics are evident in both hardcopy and electronic messages.

Direction and Objects

Mail may be said to go in different directions and have different objects – that is, it goes *out* from the sender *to* the recipient(s), and comes *in* to one *from* someone. Mail received by one person may be forwarded to a third party for action. While mail always has a primary recipient, it may also have one or more secondary recipients, such as a person who is sent a courtesy copy of a letter. A message may be sent from one person to another, or it may be sent from one person to many persons. Messages from one group may be directed to another group, or from a group to an individual.

Status

Messages have varying degrees of priority. They may be ordinary communications of no special importance; or they may be urgent, in which case they are sent in hardcopy by express mail or courier, or by electronic mail or telefacsimile. The priority assigned a message by a sender may well conflict with that accorded to it by its recipient, and vice versa. A message that is highly confidential might require special protection from unauthorized readers.

When mail is received it is categorized as inbound mail and may be placed in an "in tray"; outbound mail is similarly classified. Some types of messages are repetitive in nature and regularly follow the same, often standardized, format; these messages can be structured as forms, and filling out forms is a feature often automated in email systems.

Disposition

Once received, messages are (at least ideally) acted upon; there may be a reply or a cycle of replies (in and out) until the transaction is concluded and the item of mail is disposed of. The message might be destroyed immediately, filed or retained for a certain period, or preserved indefinitely. Messages and the transactions they represent thus have a position in time; they may be currently pending, or concluded and past.

Writing by hand is notably a single-copy technology; even typewriters, carbon paper, and photocopy machines have mitigated this limitation only to a degree. Only messages that have been created and retained in electronic form can be readily reused for output in another medium.

Development and Acceptance of Electronic Mail

The notable precursors of today's electronic mail systems are the teletypewriter and Telex/TWX machines. Extensions of telegraphy, they represent one of the earliest and most durable efforts to merge telecommunications with a mechanism for generating text in order to automate its transmission. The teletypewriter is a form of telegraph machine equipped with a keyboard on which messages are typed, creating electrical impulses that are transmitted through telegraph wires. Telex (TELetypewriter EXchange) uses a teletypewriter connected to the telephone exchange to transmit messages. Developed in Europe in the late 1930s, the international Telex network achieved wide acceptance in government and industry, surpassing the speed and efficiency of postal and courier services. Although rapidly being supplanted by electronic mail and FAX, and despite its slow speed of approximately 50 bits per second (bps), this technology has served many fields effectively, including newswire services transmitting reports around the world and libraries exchanging interlibrary loan (ILL) requests.

Communication by Telex requires a dedicated machine, set to receive any incoming messages, just as a telephone sits idle waiting for inbound calls. Sending an outbound message is comparable to placing a telephone call; typing on the machine, the operator connects to the Telex network, enters the Telex address of the recipient, and types the outbound message. Access to the network is by subscription, with charges for messages based on time and characters transmitted, plus the cost of equipment. An open communications network, any Telex user may send messages to any other whose address is known, and directories of Telex numbers have been widely published. Telex users worldwide number in the millions.

Electronic mail's flowering as a technology resulted from the increases achieved in the early to mid-1970s in the storage capabilities of computers, but its greatest growth as an industry came from the establishment of time-sharing systems. With time-sharing, the cost of maintaining large computing facilities can be spread among a large number of users. Users gain access to host systems from remote sites through telecommunications networks dedicated to the transmission of digital data over voice or higher grade telephone lines.

While individual companies or organizations might maintain their own private telecommunications networks, commercial data networks like Telenet and Tymnet have had the greatest impact in making electronic mail, online information retrieval services, and many other time-sharing computer applications widely available in many market sectors. Such commercial services are referred to as public data networks because they are available to the public, with billing generally handled through arrangements with time-sharing services or directly with the networks. Individual users may dial into a public line available to many users, or into a privately leased line supplied by the network. Telenet and Tymnet offer their services in and provide access to host computers in many countries. Datapac is a primary Canadian network.

While some corporations have installed electronic mail software on their own mainframe computers, bypassing time-sharing providers altogether, others have migrated gradually away from time-sharing systems to in-house based email. Email software used on in-house systems may be acquired from the computer's manufacturer or a third party software producer, or even leased from a time-sharing vendor.

Electronic mail is an industry of major proportions, with millions of mailboxes worldwide. The Electronic Mail Association conservatively estimates that there are 7,000,000 email users in North America alone, residing on vendor time-sharing systems or on in-house corporate systems (but excluding those on local bulletin board systems). Message-based revenues resulting from these users were $500 million at the end of the 1980s, with implications for an additional $300-$400 million in ancillary areas such as communications software and related services.

Today, commercial email services are provided by an array of vendors, including Telenet, British Telecom's (BT) Tymnet (formerly Dialcom), CompuServe, and iNET2000[tm]. U.S. resellers of these services include the Regional Bell Operating Companies (RBOCs) and such value-added resellers of commercial products as the American Library Association's ALANET[r] (BT Tymnet) and the American Bar Association's ABA/net[tm] (iNET, formerly with Dialcom). Telecom Gold is BT's U.K. offering and Envoi 100[tm] is the predominant system in Canada. Throughout the world a profusion of BT licensees, national postal and telecommunications agencies (PTTs for post, telephone, and telegram), and in-house systems support a growing user base. Outside the United States, where the distribution of responsibility for email services between public and private sectors is different, with email, telephone, and other services being offered by PTTs, email has grown more slowly, but growth is still evident.

Operation

In computer-based electronic mail, a host computer system performs the role of postal service. An individual holds an electronic mailbox or address stored in a central computer, and all other users of the email system have their own addresses. Messages are addressed from sender to recipient, but those messages actually reside in the host computer. In these "store and forward" systems, the senders create the messages at their sites and transmit them to the computer; the recipients must connect to the host computer in order to retrieve the message.

This process identifies a key difference in methodology between electronic and hardcopy mail: delivery. Whereas postal and courier services ordinarily deliver mail to the recipients' sites (except when they choose to have a box at the post office), electronic mail messages must actively be retrieved by the recipients, in addition to being actively entered into the system by the senders.

An electronic mail message generally follows the ordinary memorandum format, including the elements *Date, To, From,* and *Subject.* Email systems offer, in varying degrees, the ability to incorporate within a single message an array of options to accomplish particular objectives for that communication. For example, if the sender of a message to a primary recipient also sends a copy to a secondary recipient with the primary recipient's knowledge (by a note on the message), the copy is referred to as a courtesy copy. A copy sent to a secondary recipient without the primary recipient's knowledge is called a blind copy because it is "blind" to the primary recipient. Courtesy copies, blind copies, automatic acknowledgments (return receipts), or even password security for confidential messages may be offered by the provider. Distribution lists may support group mailings of the same message.

Forms for purchase orders, claims, questionnaires, reports, and so on can be set up in many systems so that users are automatically prompted to fill in each element of the form, which is then transmitted as an email message. Interfaces to the Telex network or other email systems may be offered as a separate function or invoked for a single message sent as intrasystem mail. The ability to transmit a message to a receiving FAX machine was added to some vendor offerings in the mid-1980s.

Although email systems can be reached with a dumb computer terminal, they are most effectively used with microcomputers (also known as personal computers or PCs) or mainframe computers that permit text to be saved and edited offline. Messages may of course be keyed online, and even a fairly primitive bulletin board's email component will have some kind of online text editor. However, offline message preparation is advantageous inasmuch as there are no connect or telecommunications charges being incurred while the text is composed and a familiar word processor may be used to create it.

As microcomputer access to email vendors has grown, providers have increasingly offered file transfer and batch mail facilities to maximize the use of their systems in the growing PC environment. File transfer refers to the electronic transmission of text documents, database files, encoded computer programs, spreadsheets, etc., in contrast to messages. Batch mail refers to groups of mail messages, transferred to and processed by an electronic mail service as a batch. Such a facility offers users time savings by eliminating the need to repeat command sequences for each message.

Privacy and security of messages are generally guaranteed by password access to the user's identification (ID) code (i.e., electronic mailbox), plus in some cases a password for access to an individual message. Email systems have different levels of security for users and system managers; their sophistication may vary, but their objective of preserving the confidentiality of correspondence is common to all systems. Individual users usually can and should change their passwords periodically to prevent abuse; some corporate and governmental systems require regular or even automatic password changes. Furthermore, system providers regularly back up and preserve copies of software, messages, and other electronically stored content, so that in case of equipment or telecommunications failures lost data can be restored.

Applications

Applications of email are as diverse as the uses of hardcopy mail. Those information-oriented professions that have been either less well endowed financially or less inclined to shift from established tradition or habit have been slower to adopt electronic mail than private enterprise, a pattern seen among these same professions with regard to other technologies. Noteworthy applications of email are found in a number of fields, and a few of them are described below.

Business

Electronic mail had its first applications in large business environments, especially where regular communications between home and field offices are complicated by busy meeting schedules and time zone differences. Daily news bulletins, memoranda, policy notices, and other communications may be sent through the electronic mail system along with general messages to individuals. Forms are often mounted on corporate systems to facilitate field staff's entering orders, claims, sales reports, or other communications that are repetitive in structure and regular in frequency. Transfers of financial and other data files are regularly conducted in corporate email environments.

Libraries

The most frequently mentioned email application in libraries is interlibrary loan, a service whereby a library obtains for its patrons materials that it does not own or have available. As a library operation, ILL is particularly time sensitive in its objective of reader service. However, it has traditionally been very cumbersome to administer and slow in responding to users' requests for information or materials.

ILL is characterized by standardized forms of some complexity, elaborate codes or protocols between borrowing and lending libraries, and a strong resistance on the part of some librarians to placing requests for materials by telephone. Extended periods of time may pass between the various mailings of requests, responses, and desired materials due to the slow pace of hardcopy mail services; even where library consortia have established their own delivery services in addition to or in lieu of the postal service, handling hardcopy requests inevitably adds delays to the process.

Electronic mail applications of interlibrary loan began to appear in the late 1970s and early 1980s among medical libraries, which often need journal articles and other materials quickly for direct patient care. By transmitting the ILL request instantly using electronic mail, medical and other libraries have been able to achieve reductions in turnaround time between a request's initiation and the delivery of materials.

Publishing

The publishing industry, especially the periodical press, has made effective use of electronic mail for transferring manuscripts prepared in the field to the publisher's production facilities. News reporters with portable computers can write their texts and transmit them to their editors, who then revise them and forward them to production – all without the need for rekeying. This method provides substantial time savings, not only through higher transmission speeds (e.g., 1200 or 2400 bps versus Telex's 50 bps), but also through eliminating the need to rekey the author's manuscript upon receipt.

The same pattern is followed by journal article authors and their editors and publishers. For example, Meckler Corporation, which publishes several journals and newsletters in the library, information, and telecommunications fields, uses a number of geographically dispersed editors and authors, many of whose manuscripts and editorial communications are transmitted by electronic mail, stored at the production offices, and processed through composition systems into the resulting typeset products.

The time and cost savings achieved by reducing or eliminating duplicative keyboarding had become a major objective of publishers by the early 1980s, with ever increasing numbers of manuscripts being submitted by authors on magnetic media for conversion directly into publishers' editorial and production systems. Electronic mail transmission of time-sensitive text set an early precedent for this production method.

Equipment and Networks

Electronic mail requires at minimum a dumb computer terminal with a modem operating at 300 bps or faster, and a telephone line. As dumb terminals have no significant memory or computing capabilities, their utility for some of the more powerful features of electronic mail is limited. A modem-equipped personal computer with a printer is now considered basic equipment, and a modem operating at 2400 bps is preferable to 300 or 1200 bps. Connections at 4800 and 9600 bps are now being introduced in time-sharing systems.

A PC must have telecommunications software to drive the modem and to perform the functions of sending and receiving files or batched messages prepared offline. Ordinarily, the PC will be used for more functions than just telecommunications, such as word processing, database management, or spreadsheet applications. (These are discussed in chapters 8 and 9.) Indeed, if the workstation is additionally equipped with a telefacsimile board (a microcomputer peripheral device containing a circuit board, telephone connection, and special printer that enables the computer to be used as a FAX machine), the user can send a FAX to a receiving machine.

Costs

A subscription of some kind is usually required by the commercial electronic mail services, ordinarily with an associated registration, billing, or other such fee. These charges may be one-time, ongoing, or a combination of both. Usage charges are based on a mix of elements: connect time to the host computer (at prime or nonprime times); telecommunications charges (at prime or nonprime times); message-related fees, such as kilocharacter traffic (i.e., units of 1,000 characters transmitted or received) or per-message charges; and surcharges for special utilities like file transfers, database access, international message transfers, text stored online, etc.

The Byzantine charging structures of the time-sharing electronic mail systems make cost projections difficult in the extreme. One rule of thumb in the library field suggests that with regular use of basic mail services, a library can expect to spend $500 to $750 per year on email. Another states that the average user will spend three-quarters to one hour online sending and receiving email each month. This author's recent experience in a small business environment with moderate email activity plus occasional database searches and file transfers, on the part of four individuals, results in billings of about $150 per month. Thus, a network of 100 libraries might incur charges of $4,000 per month – or a fraction of that amount, depending on the applications selected, baud rates, user expertise, text stored in the host system, and the priority the network's sponsor gives to email.

In the case of BITNET, an academic and research-oriented email system, the individual user ordinarily pays little or no direct charge. BITNET software is made available to academic institutions and consortia, who mount it on their own mainframe computers. They share the cost of dedicated telephone lines and provide the service to foster scholarly communication and the exchange of research activities and data.

Training

Some electronic mail systems are easier to learn to use than others, but all require an expenditure of time and effort to develop sufficient proficiency in using the equipment and the system to make optimal use of its functions. Online tutorials and documentation, regardless of their quality, are helpful – indeed essential – tools, and training classes are the most desirable way of learning a system; however, they only modify, and never eliminate, the learning curve.

Interconnections

Electronic mail systems have traditionally been closed networks; only those who use the same email system have been able to communicate directly with one another. An exception is Western Union's EasyLink^{tm}, which in addition to its own computer-based email offers connections with the Telex/TWX network, which it owns and operates. Electronic mail, which in the United States has been largely provided by private, nongovernmental firms, is a highly competitive business, made even more so by the divestiture of telephone monopolies and the opening of the email business to RBOCs. Directories of groups of email users within a single provider's system are usually proprietary, further limiting interorganizational access except where organizations work together to establish directory exchanges.

More important, there were few technical standards for electronic mail systems, so that until the 1980s, when the Consultative Committee for International Telephone and Telegraph (CCITT) X.400 standard for interfaces between electronic mail systems became fully developed, it was impracticable to transmit messages between incompatible systems. Even after adoption of X.400, competing vendors of email services resisted the interchange of email across systems. They were naturally reluctant to risk loss of market share by implementing the standard even though they had ostensibly adopted it. However, led by BT Tymnet, increasing numbers of X.400 interfaces were announced by the end of the 1980s in the electronic mail marketplace. Impetus was added by the U.S. government's requirement that X.400 interfaces be provided by their email suppliers.

Currently, without broad implementation of X.400, email users often must subscribe to two or more electronic mail systems. This requirement has both financial and operational implications and is a deterrent to adoption of the technology. A potential email user wishing to correspond with users distributed among several email networks may simply reject electronic mail altogether and choose other more convenient technologies, or accept the vagaries of traditional hardcopy mail and telephones.

In-House versus Public Systems

Within the electronic mail industry an issue of concern is the balance between in-house systems and publicly available time-sharing systems. A number of organizations whose level of email use requires extremely large computing resources have opted to mount electronic mail software on their own systems instead of purchasing the service from a time-sharing vendor. Others, especially those with limited geographic dispersal and communications needs, find use of an in-house email service adequate for their lesser, more circumscribed requirements. Local area networks (LANs) have become enormously popular within small organizations or departments, and email is often included with the LAN software, as discussed in Chapter 2.

Time-sharing email services, and the telecommunications networks whose revenues in part depend on them, have had to grapple with the challenge presented by migration to in-house systems. One technique these services have adopted is shifting the balance of email time between online and offline activities. By providing facilities supportive of local microcomputers and by altering their rate structures, the email vendors have reduced the amount of time a user must spend connected to the remote host. Some vendors have also chosen to make their software available for lease on in-house systems.

Benefits, Challenges, and Trends

Interlibrary loan applications alone demonstrate the substantial time savings that can be achieved with electronic mail. Because messages are transmitted instantly, they are immediately available to the recipient. Email users, especially those who must communicate with individuals in other geographic regions and time zones, hail the reduction in "telephone tag" achieved by electronic mail. It has been estimated that as many as two-thirds of all business phone calls fail to reach the desired party on the first attempt, and that up to half the second attempts are unsuccessful. Electronic mail reduces the need for phone calls, and with it, the number of missed calls.

Potential Drawbacks

These time-saving benefits can easily be negated by the failure of one correspondent to check for and respond to incoming email. Both senders and recipients must connect regularly with the email system to check for inbound messages. This factor is critical to the success of electronic mail and most clearly demonstrates the challenge email embodies with respect to altering procedures and daily routines. Checking the mail is perhaps the most difficult change for new email users to make as they integrate the technique into the workday. It is extremely easy to forget, ignore, or be distracted from this new routine until it becomes a habit.

Furthermore, while it is customary for mail to appear on one's desk through long-established office procedures for mail handling, obtaining electronic mail may involve leaving the primary workstation and walking to a computer station. It has been observed that use of email decreases as distance to a terminal increases. Convenience of access to equipment used for electronic mail is essential.

Such issues, although potential drawbacks, can be overcome if management establishes regular email use as a priority and encourages it through convenient placement of sufficient numbers of terminals. Some managers assume they must themselves access the email system, whereas they have delegated hardcopy mail to administrative staff. This assumption is a misconception; it is appropriate that administrative staff be trained to manage electronic mail just as they do other kinds of correspondence and communications.

Other drawbacks to electronic mail include such technical problems as local terminal or software failure, user error, or host system failures, which, despite vendor backup procedures, can cause loss of data. Telecommunications links are susceptible to interference or interruption from faulty transmission lines, electrical storms, or even sunspots. Transmissions should be routed from the modem to a phone line; intermediate lines like in-house switchboards can degrade transmission quality. Data network "line noise" (static leading to "garbage characters" being inserted in the transmission) can interrupt transmissions. Such problems are frustrating at the least, but can also deter electronic mail users entirely.

Cost Issues

Another rule of thumb heard in forums on electronic mail states that an ordinary business letter costs $12.00 to $15.00 to compose, type, copy, and post, including indirect costs; the postage stamp is only $.25. In contrast, an email message might involve a higher direct cost of $.35 or $.50. However, because electronic mail provides instantaneous transmission, a multiplicity of functions that can be combined in a single message (e.g., copies, acknowledgments, group mailings), and the possibility of reusing text without rekeying, it offers the potential for considerable savings in indirect costs, most notably in high volume situations.

At the same time, although administrators are accustomed to telephone, postage, and photocopying bills, they have been known to blanch at billings in the hundreds of dollars from an email service provider. The unquantifiable benefits of email are easily forgotten in such circumstances, as are the additional ancillary information services that might have been included in the invoice.

Multiple Functions

Electronic mail systems seldom operate in isolation from other functions performed on the host systems. Even in single-user bulletin boards email is only one of several offerings. Corporate email may be one component of a larger management information and communications system, which might include access to financial records, data-processing programs, text-editing systems, or other computer-based activities.

Public email systems generally offer a variety of commercially distributed databases, providing access to such timely information as newswires, airline schedules, market data, and financial news. Special communications facilities, such as text-to-FAX transmission and links to the Telex network, often enhance the product line of the commercial email vendor. Users of these systems, including individual corporations and professional associations, may distribute their own electronic newsletters or other information to their constituents using facilities offered by the vendor. These ancillary services add value to the electronic mail network and facilitate integration of information dispersed with communications to achieve more informed and effective performance on the part of the user.

Electronic Junk Mail

Like hardcopy mail, electronic mail can be used to send unsolicited correspondence, especially of a promotional nature. People are accustomed to dealing with hardcopy junk mail; a quick glance and a flick of the wrist constitute the usual disposition of unsolicited mail. Electronic junk mail is particularly irksome and unwelcome because, being computer-based, it must be reviewed piece by piece in sequence and disposed of. More important, most email users pay to read their inbound messages, and electronic junk mail is a potential financial burden as well as an annoyance.

Most email system managers actively discourage their users from using the system for promotional purposes except in ways that may be provided expressly for advertising, such as bulletin boards. Delinquent users might even be barred for abusing the system with junk mail. As discussed later in this chapter, the issue of electronic junk mail has achieved national attention in connection with FAX machines.

Alternatives to Electronic Mail

The burgeoning of FAX use and the introduction of voice mail have been viewed by some as harbingers of doom for electronic mail. Experience has not yet borne out this view, but FAX and voice mail probably do present the most serious challenges to electronic mail's position among the alternative communications technologies.

Facsimile overcomes the limitations of closed email networks and the complexities of computer equipment. However, text transmitted by FAX cannot be readily utilized as can digitized text messages sent by electronic mail. FAX transmits graphic data, and while it is possible to convert text to FAX, the reverse technology has not been developed. Also, the image that comes out of the FAX machine may not be of adequate quality for scanning into digital form.

Voice mail (also included with and/or referred to as audiotext) is a technology for the recording and digital storage of messages. The familiar answering machine records messages as analog signals on magnetic tape. Voice mail digitizes the recording, and voice mail systems additionally may provide for forwarding, reply, and other options. Call-routing systems often found in business are audiotext applications and usually include message components of varying levels of sophistication.

Voice mail may prove to be more challenging to electronic mail than FAX, as voice mail and other audiotext applications increase in number and develop in sophistication. Most consumers are now familiar with corporate telephone systems answered by a recording that directs the caller to dial certain numbers for certain services, with human operator intervention as a last, rather than first, resort.

Voice mail is entirely comparable to electronic mail, except that the object of transmission is a recorded voice message that is digitized as audio and stored in the host computer. As voice mail evolves from being slightly more than a centralized answering machine to include reply, forward, copy, and other options, it will no doubt erode some of the usage base of electronic mail for certain categories of message. Some of the same issues that apply to electronic mail also apply to voice mail, however, including the need to dial to a central host to send and retrieve messages, and the fact that the recording cannot be converted to a nonaudio medium.

ELECTRONIC BULLETIN BOARD AND CONFERENCING SYSTEMS

Picture for a moment a large cork bulletin board in a student union, library, or other building centrally located on a university campus. The bulletin board will no doubt be divided into sections according to various categories: housing sought or available for rent, jobs wanted or offered, student-run campus activities of various kinds, official rule notices, or calendars of events. There may be a section for individual personal messages, or even a separate message board. Typed, printed, or handwritten on sheets of paper or cards, the notices are tacked or taped to the board according to their category. Some of the notices, such as an advertisement for typing services, or a notice of a yard sale, might have been printed or typed and cut in such a way that tabs can be torn from the bottom of the page for taking away the phone number or address of the sponsor.

This kind of bulletin board is the exact model upon which electronic bulletin board systems (BBSes), in their most fundamental aspects, are based. The bulletin board is primarily a mechanism for one-to-many or many-to-many communications, like the typing service's ad or the music department's announcement of an upcoming recital. Even in this hardcopy example, however, there is a mechanism to link the bulletin board message to some kind of one-to-one communication. The phone number tab is a device for encouraging a contact to arise from information posted on the board.

In the electronic bulletin board system, electronic mail options provide the linking mechanism between the one-to-many message and ensuing one-to-one messages. Unlike a hardcopy bulletin board, the electronic version facilitates additional communications by fostering chains of one-to-many messages on a particular topic, as well as chains of commentary (i.e., many-to-many messages) for all users to review. Thus, the electronic BBS functions as something that a wall-bound board cannot: a means for conducting dynamic ongoing discussion or a conference, with many users communicating with many others on a single subject. (I will hereafter regretfully use the gerund *conferencing* for systems that support conferences. The noun has been used as a verb so frequently that it is now common usage, as is the case with *access.*)

Conferencing may take place in two modes using electronic systems. Group meetings may be conducted in real time, that is, when the participants are online at the same time, interacting through their keyboards and screens instead of by voice or face to face. More frequently, electronic conferences are carried out in "non-real time," according to schedules more or less at the discretion of the participants, without the requirement that all be connected to the host at the same time. Conferencing facilitates two particular types of communication less significant in electronic mail systems: passive and group communications.

Passive communications are characterized by the unstructured and voluntary nature of perusing a bulletin board and choosing to act on a posted notice. Use of the adjective *passive* to characterize bulletin board communications reflects the fact that using a BBS is usually a voluntary, often recreational activity. Access frequently takes place from the user's home, or at odd hours during the workday.

Because BBS content is usually addressed to or from many users, it lacks the individual focus and direction of one-to-one communications. Furthermore, private correspondence is structurally separate from group BBS communications, so that additional steps are required for the user to make use of both functions.

Group communications are discussions and resulting actions involving more than two participants, activities to which ordinary means of written communication are inhospitable. As electronic mail can substitute for one-to-one voice communication between individuals, so BBSes and conferencing systems can supplement and even substitute for group conference calls and face-to-face meetings. It is an interesting phenomenon that electronic BBSes and conferences, through their very presence and availability, often stimulate communications among individuals who do not know one another personally, but who share certain interests addressed in the BBS.

Operation and Applications

Structurally, the BBS is simply an electronic rendering of the wall board described earlier. At log-on, the user is presented with a menu of available sections, usually including one where private email messages between individuals can be posted. Additional message sections of the board are set up according to topic or area of group interest, so that the user selects the desired section within the BBS. Unlike wall boards, the electronic BBS may offer one or more *libraries* to their users. In these libraries may reside public domain software contributed by users or the system operator (SYSOP) – the individual, group, or organization that operates and manages the electronic bulletin board system, including provision and maintenance of host computer equipment, in-bound telephone lines, and BBS content. The users may download (i.e., transfer from the host computer) files for their own use. Text files provided by users may also be stored in BBS libraries, with their content depending on the nature of the BBS.

Access to the board is controlled by the SYSOP or sponsoring agency. First-time users of free bulletin boards may be prompted to complete an online questionnaire about themselves; name and address verification may follow before the SYSOP will grant full levels of access to sections. Admission to individual sections may be restricted by the SYSOP to individual categories of user. Some BBS sections are in the nature of "clubs" that users "join" and participate in; others may be limited according to such criteria as age, gender, or sexual preference in addition to topical interest, as is usually the case with "adults only" boards.

Access and Use

Upon selecting a particular message section, users may scan and read existing messages. In some cases a user's access is indexed so that only new messages are read, bypassing items already reviewed. After reading, the user may have the option of replying privately to the sender of the message, or of commenting publicly for other users. In the latter case, a primary message may be followed by a long string of responses, limited in length only by the limitations of the BBS software and the host equipment's storage capacity.

Users may post their own notices to the board for others to review and comment on; if the software allows it, the notices may be posted anonymously. Recreational users frequently adopt *handles* or codenames by which they are known to other users, reflecting the style adopted in citizen's band radio. These handles, which may also function as IDs or passwords, provide the user with an alter ego, a measure of privacy, and even an air of mystery. Like electronic mail, notices may be prepared offline and transmitted to the system.

Public or consumer boards generally revolve around interests common to their users. These may range from the juvenile (there being numerous BBSes for kids) to the adult (including X-rated dating boards for those of every proclivity). Especially popular, as one might expect, are special interest groups, or SIGs, for the technology-minded. These may be sponsored by an information utility, like those on CompuServe. *Byte* magazine's BIX bulletin board and the board offered by Apple Computer are good examples of BBSes where users may exchange questions, experiences, tips, and software. A user may voluntarily perform the SYSOP role, or a member of the sponsor's staff may manage the BBS.

Many libraries became interested in bulletin boards in the mid-1980s as an inexpensive means for providing access to information about the library and the community for computer-minded patrons. The databases mounted on these BBSes might contain calendars of library programs, book and movie reviews, or other content of interest to the community. Book reserves and interlibrary loans are among the operational functions BBSes support. Patrons may be able to contribute to the BBS in addition to library staff.

Most library bulletin boards have appeared in public library settings or in library systems and networks. The number of academic library-oriented BBSes is increasing, however, especially as part of campuswide email and communication networks of which the library is a member or host.

Real-Time Chats

Some electronic communications services offer a facility for two-way (i.e., one-to-one) private online conversations between users, referred to as a chat. To new BBS users this way of communicating may seem bizarre and inefficient, but it can in fact be captivating and enjoyable. (It is, perhaps unfortunately, out of the scope of this chapter to describe in detail the psychodynamics of online chats and the personal interactions that take place among BBS users.)

Additionally, the system may offer one or more group chat modes, whereby more than two users may engage in conversation. As with two-way chats, the messages transmitted are in first-in-first-out (FIFO) order, and the pace at which these group conversations proceed may seem agonizingly slow, depending on the speed of the host system and the typing and modem speeds of the participants. Open conferences may be available to all users online at the same time, while closed conferences may be available only to designated members who access them by password or conference name.

Messages keyed in open conferences are visible to all participants. The commands for access to these conversations may match the name of the facility, such as BT Tymnet's NET-TALK, or American People Link's Partyline; the latter includes chat, private conferences called *codes* (for the codenames users establish to enter them), and open lines numbered 0 to 99. Real-time conferencing systems may also allow for the exchange of private messages not visible to all participants, the electronic analogue to passing notes during a meeting.

Group chats and partylines can be extremely lively and entertaining, especially with participants who are congenial, compose well, and type quickly. The informality and sociability of these group conversations can foster positive discussion, whereas the formality of business-oriented sessions seems to dampen enthusiasm. Thus, group chats may technically be conferences, but it stretches the point to consider them so.

Real-Time Conferences

Face-to-face meetings are usually convened with a set agenda of discussion issues and the specific objective of reaching conclusions and taking action on agenda items through the processes of group deliberation and voting. In many organizations, rules of parliamentary procedure govern the conduct of group proceedings, at least official ones.

In electronic versions of real-time conferences, facilities to reach conclusions through votes, to edit documents, or to formulate action plans are the logical extension of the chains of text and comments featured in topical bulletin boards. Toward this decision-making end, and to make access to conferences, notices, and commentary as fast and effective as possible, a number of conferencing software programs have been developed and installed in mainframe systems. These conferencing programs may include balloting or polling functions, and online editors can be used for group editorial work on documents.

As in telephone conference calls, all participants in a real-time online teleconference must be online at the same time. This requirement means that each user must have a modem-equipped PC or terminal and dedicated telephone line. Common baud rates and reasonable typing skills are also desirable. The cost for an online teleconference would generally consist of the total connection-related charges of all participants, primarily hourly usage and telecommunication network charges. Of course the host system must have adequate hardware and software resources to support this kind of application without degradation of response time.

The online teleconference is probably not the best way to conduct a formal meeting, however. I experienced an interactive online conference with the executive board of the Association for Library and Information Science Education (ALISE) in spring 1986 using BT Tymnet's NET-TALK facility. There were seven participants from California to Nova Scotia in this Saturday morning session, and during the 45 minutes the meeting lasted (interrupted just short of the agenda's completion by a system crash), the participants were able to cover most of the scheduled items.

Unfortunately, the waiting between messages was protracted by users' uncertainty as to who should be "speaking" next, a problem less frequent in face-to-face meetings. Disconnects experienced by the Canadian participant caused several interruptions, and the use of the private message feature added yet more delay. Still, the board completed most of its agenda and, more important, learned which issues truly required group deliberation and which could be dispensed with quickly. Having saved several thousand dollars in travel expenses on this one meeting, ALISE has continued to conduct one meeting annually online, but using a bulletin board instead.

In my experience, the face-to-face group meeting is still the preferred means for conducting real-time conferences, despite the challenges of logistics, scheduling, and travel expenses. Interpersonal and social factors additionally carry considerable weight in the preference on the part of most organization members for in-person contact, and there are compelling psychological, political, and professional reasons for an organization to assign major priority to such meetings. Alternative methods for conducting meetings, such as conference calls, real-time online teleconferences, BBS and non-real-time teleconferences, and video teleconferences, all suffer from significant weaknesses; these include timing, ease of use, and lack of personal interaction.

Non-Real-Time Conferences

An example of a non-real-time teleconference is the Online Librarian's Microcomputer User Group (OLMUG). Organized by PC-minded librarians, this BBS and conferencing service offers information exchange, problem-solving help, and cooperative software evaluation. It uses the Confer II software, and while the SYSOPs are based in California, the program operates on a mainframe computer at Wayne State University in Detroit, Michigan.

The Well is a West Coast-based BBS and conferencing service whose users access it through the Tymnet public data network, thereby incurring only telecommunications charges. It contains an extensive set of conferences covering many different political, religious, social, and professional interests. A conference for librarians on The Well was of some interest within the field.

The greatest use of conferencing systems other than in public bulletin board and information systems seems to take place in academic and research-oriented environments, where scholars and researchers have a number of electronic mechanisms in place for the exchange and discussion of ideas and projects. A number of research-oriented groups reside on BITNET, some of which use the system to transfer quantitative data from field sites to project coordinators, while others produce regular electronic newsletters. An example is the PACS-L conference on patron access issues with some 600 BITNET users, which has initiated a refereed electronic journal, *PACS Review*. While these may not be results-oriented conferences like board meetings, they do provide an inexpensive forum for deliberation whether or not action results. In the longer term, the growth of electronic journals versus printed ones will have significant implications for scholarly communication and publishing.

Equipment and Costs

Microcomputer BBSes are relatively inexpensive to operate, which is one reason for their popularity among individual libraries and other organizations, and among PC hobbyists. The BBS requires a microcomputer dedicated to its support; in this PC reside the software for operating the BBS and the content provided by the SYSOP and users. The system's capacity for storing messages and files is limited only by the storage capacity of the supporting equipment. The number of users who may access the board at one time is limited by the number of telephone lines and modem ports the software, PC, and SYSOP are able to support.

The telecommunications component of BBSes can be the most costly, both for users and SYSOPs, especially when phone lines and related equipment expand the BBS operator's hardware configuration. Recreational BBS SYSOPs may simply contribute these costs as the price of their hobby; others, however, have turned their BBSes into money-making activities, with monitored use time charged to users by credit card in the way public systems might do. Organizations may similarly offer their BBS as a service, or seek cost recovery or profit through memberships or use-based fees.

Local users ordinarily incur only the price of a telephone call to dial into a BBS. However, those interested in BBSes in other geographic areas can incur substantial toll charges for long-distance access. Public data networks, particularly Telenet's PC Pursuit service, have facilitated interstate access to BBSes by offering an inexpensive, credit card-based service for higher volume nonprime-time users wanting access to BBSes outside their regions.

For a moderate monthly fee the user gains dial access to any bulletin board desired, at connect rates lower than long-distance calls, which also may be lower than information utilities' marked up telecommunications rates.

Individuals and groups interested in starting a BBS must be prepared for considerable ongoing work: file maintenance, password control for new subscribers, program debugging, etc. Many BBSes purge their files of old messages after a set time, and users who do not access the system for 30 days or other predetermined period may be dropped from the list of active users.

The profusion of BBS software available varies in sophistication. Programs are available for various operating systems (MS-DOS, CP/M, etc.), hardware models (Commodore, IBM, Radio Shack, Apple), and levels of sophistication (messages, file transfers, library storage). Among the most popular have been the following: Fido, TBBS (The Bread Board System), ABBS from Software Sorcery, PMS (People's Message System), and Oracomm; others appear in journals and directories for popular computing like *The Computer Phone Book* and *Public Computing*.

For teleconferences, the software that supports the BBS or conferencing service must offer the desired features. In the case of mainframe-based systems, multifunction teleconference software includes the following: Delphi, Participate, Caucus, and Confer II. Facilities among them tend to be similar, but with varying levels of sophistication and speed; more significant, the vocabularies they apply to the diverse elements and functions within the conference may vary greatly.

Benefits, Challenges, and Trends

BBS and teleconferencing enthusiasts are excellent at proselytizing on their behalf. The audiences most inclined toward BBSes have been fellow PC users and other recruits who become aficionados of PC technology or of the dynamics of BBSes themselves. The novelty, spontaneity, and personal interactions afforded by these systems easily engage the new user, and the information exchanges are potentially quite profitable, so that for many using online chatting the BBS becomes almost addictive. However, the novelty can wear off quickly, and when other demands reduce the time available for exploring the varied offerings of BBSes, usage drops off. The passive, voluntary nature of BBS communications makes them vulnerable to periodic changes in their lists of users, and even eventual failure for lack of interest or momentum.

In the working environment, success is much harder to achieve and sustain for the voluntary BBS or conference. All the issues identified earlier for electronic mail (training, access to equipment, cost) are further impediments to the use of BBSes. In the work setting, BBSes and teleconferences seem to be most successful where there are strong motivations for participation and where work schedules allow for their use. Membership association committee processes, focused projects of researchers or other academics, or regular priority transactions like interlibrary loan are more likely to succeed because of the priority assigned them by their sponsors.

While inertia, diminished interest, or loss of funding can lead to the demise of a BBS, theft of equipment rather frequently causes a system to cease operation. While individuals who operate BBSes are the usual victims, libraries and other institutions have also suffered such losses.

Abuse of the system by unethical users is one of the risks of operating a BBS or conferencing system. The legislative and regulatory environment for electronic communications is different from and less well developed than that for hardcopy communications and published materials, placing some burden of risk on system managers. As BBSes grew during the mid-1980s, there was increased awareness of special interest boards for such radical groups as neo-Nazis, and communications that some might consider obscene could be found in the many sexually oriented boards. False advertising could be posted in the "for sale" sections of public boards, and a copy of one library's BBS disks was confiscated by the Secret Service because of a public message construed as a death threat against the president of the United States. There have been some attempts to hold BBS operators liable for the content posted in and usage made of their systems.

Email providers and bulletin board SYSOPs generally use administrative mechanisms to protect themselves and other users from any liability arising from illegal or inappropriate use of the system and associated files and records. Disclaimers and statements of prohibited uses are ordinarily included in the subscription terms of commercial systems or in the sign-up questionnaires of free access BBSes. Operators of sexually oriented boards explicitly state the adult nature of the BBS at log-on and require that all users state that they are 18 years or older. Operators are required to guard assiduously not only their own privacy, but also that of their users, about whom they might hold address, telephone, and other personal information on file.

BBS software also offers various technical facilities for dealing with these matters. Some include filters, whereby the texts of posted messages are compared against a list of forbidden words. System operators can control level of access approved for individual users in varying degrees ranging from bulletin board sections to even individual messages.

As legislation affecting the content of telecommunications technology develops, and as societies grapple with questions of censorship, free speech, and privacy, these issues will continue to receive focus and concern.

Alternatives to BBSes

PC- and mainframe-based bulletin board and conferencing systems have competed with each other since such systems were developed. The speed, storage capacity, and remote access capability characteristic of mainframe systems have become features of increasingly powerful microcomputer systems and data networks' consumer-oriented services like PC Pursuit. PC Pursuit is a consumer-oriented service of the Telenet data network that offers individuals low-cost access to a variety of hosts using Telenet telecommunication lines. The usage charge is a flat monthly fee usually billed to the user's credit card. Costs of setup, maintenance, and use and the politics of sponsorship may become to an even greater extent the determining factors in the success of special interest and organizational BBSes, and even recreational boards.

The video conference, discussed in more detail in chapter 4, may be a more effective electronic vehicle for real-time teleconferencing. Participants can see and hear one another as they speak, materials for display can be repaired in advance, and participants do not require keyboard skills. The most critical issues in videoconferencing are program planning and cost.

Producing educational conferences, such as the CD-ROM Video Teleconferences produced by the College of DuPage (Illinois) in 1987 and 1989, is very much like producing an educational television program, with the associated scripts, sets, production facilities, and professional presenters. Collateral print materials are important supplements to the conference, and careful coordination is required with participants at multiple receiving sites. Transmission facilities and downlinks at local sites are required. Production and air time alone can approach an investment of $50,000. In corporate teleconferencing, there may be less formality and fewer programmatic elements, especially if the objective is conducting a meeting that would otherwise have involved travel to a central site, but the costs of an effective meeting are still high; there are anecdotal reports of corporate videoconferences costing $1,000,000.

Real success and widespread adoption of conferencing through telecommunications will eventually come to pass, but only when the economics of available meeting methods change further. Although group meeting expenses are substantial, the convention and collateral industries such as travel and hotel are sufficiently competitive to permit organizations to continue conducting more conferences in person than electronically. More important, only when a method for electronic conferencing offers most of the benefits of in-person meetings at a price competitive with in-person meeting costs will electronic conferencing achieve its broadest success. This shift in the economics of conferencing had not occurred by the beginning of the 1990s.

TELEFACSIMILE

Telefacsimile (also known as FAX, facsimile, and telefax) is the transmission of an image from a sending machine to a receiving machine in a remote location using telecommunications. That image might be a printed text, handwritten document, photograph, or graphic.

How did we function without FAX? Before FAX machines achieved the status of standard office equipment during the mid-1980s, how many deadlines were missed, transactions delayed, documents lost in the mails, and bills paid for overnight courier service? The editors of this book, located on two separate continents an ocean apart, have jointly edited the manuscripts of these chapters using FAX. I have saved weeks in getting news releases published by sending them by FAX. Even some of my recently filed mortgage papers were transmitted by facsimile. The almost indispensable FAX machine is the most recent addition to the menu of communications technologies at the disposal of information professionals.

Although the earliest facsimile experiments date to the mid-19th century, and the first commercial FAX networking was developed in Europe in the first decade of this century, substantial growth in the technology and the telefax business took place in North America during the 1930s and 1940s. The several incompatible systems available during that period had been developed for transmitting graphics and were most frequently used for news photographs and for weather data directed to seafaring naval and merchant marine vessels. Law enforcement had also used telefacsimile effectively to dispatch photos, drawings, and fingerprints. The technology at that time converted the image to analog signals.

Using telephone lines for digital FAX was developed in the 1960s. It was not until the early 1980s, however, that digital FAX machines sufficiently improved their copy quality and transmission speed to make the technique attractive in a wide variety of settings.

Operation and Equipment

The operator uses the telephone dial built into the sending FAX machine to enter the telephone number of the receiving machine. The page to be sent is fed into the machine, which optically scans the image on the page, converts it to digital signals, and transmits them through the voice-grade telephone line. The receiving FAX machine, upon "answering the phone," receives the transmission, converts it from digital form back into a graphic image, and prints it out, commonly onto a specially coated paper supplied in rolls.

FAX etiquette requires that the first page sent be a cover sheet that notes the names, addresses, and telephone numbers (voice and FAX) of sender and recipient, along with the number of pages being sent (including the cover sheet itself) and the name and number of a FAX operator to contact in case of transmission trouble. This cover sheet alerts recipients to the number of pages they can expect to receive, not only for timing purposes, but also to determine that the transmission was successfully completed. Idle FAX machines, except those at telephones used also for voice calls, are usually left turned on and in the receive mode, so that FAXes may be received unattended at any time.

Telefacsimile machines are categorized according to the standards for the communications protocols between FAX machines formulated by the CCITT. FAX machine standards are classified in groups according to the speed with which they transmit and receive data: Group I (four to six minutes per page), Group II (two to three minutes), and Group III (one minute or less). Group IV, introduced in the mid-1980s, provides clearer images and offers faster speeds by transmitting signals through the packet-switching techniques used by online services. FAX machines are ordinarily able to identify and adjust to the group category of the receiving FAX machines, a process known as *automatic stepdown.*

Telefacsimile requires only a modest financial investment on the user's part. FAX machines under $1,000 were common in the early 1990s, as increased competition in the burgeoning FAX industry greatly increased the supply of available machines. A voice-grade telephone line is required; although a dedicated line may not be necessary if the user's FAX traffic is relatively low, it is certainly desirable. If the user's phone line doubles for voice and FAX, a correspondent may have to call the user with notification that a FAX will be sent. Because FAX machines include a setting to receive FAXes automatically, it is highly preferable to allocate a phone line to sending and receiving FAX messages without their competing with other kinds of telecommunications.

The capabilities of the machine required will depend on the usage volume, finances, and technological interests of the purchaser. FAX units may include such features as a telephone instrument, automatic stepdown, automatic redial after a busy signal, automatic document feeding, transaction reports, and automatic dialing from a programmed directory of phone numbers. Plain paper FAX machines were introduced in the late 1980s, as a response to dissatisfaction with the rolls of slick, curling FAX paper.

While Group IV machines may be costly at first, their price should drop as demand increases, as was the case with earlier models. The use of packet-switching networks and non-voice-grade telephone lines to carry FAX data may be a more daunting economic hurdle for higher level FAX machines. The differing economics of data networks and voice networks may lead to variable selection of FAX machine group on a per-application basis; the volatility of the voice telephone and data communications industries makes the economics even harder to predict.

Applications

News publishers and wire services were early users of telefacsimile when the industry developed in the 1930s and 1940s. In those years of rapidly unfolding historical events the wirephoto was certainly an invaluable tool. FAX is still used by those who work in public relations and the press to transmit all kinds of timely information.

The substantially greater speed and image quality of Group II and Group III machines have enhanced FAX's application in publishing, where it frequently supports the most time-sensitive aspects of editorial and production processes, such as late editing and correction of manuscripts by authors and editors, or corrections between publisher and typesetters.

Libraries

Again, medical libraries provide early examples of FAX applications. Sending interlibrary loan requests and photocopied journal articles or chapters was a library FAX application as early as the mid-1960s, and the timeliness of telefax makes it especially attractive in the medical library setting. Other kinds of library materials are sent by FAX as well; the library literature reports experiments with communications between library branches and with reference information requests.

Commercial services and information brokers that provide document retrieval services to their clients offer FAX as a premium option for sending urgently needed documents. UMI Article Clearinghouse, a service introduced in 1983 by University Microfilms for supplying hardcopy articles from its microform journal collections, began offering a telefacsimile option for articles ordered by its customers soon after the service began operating.

Other Industries

Certain signals mark the point at which a technology's adoption may be considered universal. These signals include its appearance as a topic in general interest mass market news and current events publications; display advertisements in airline passengers' magazines directed at the business traveler and in Sunday newspaper business sections; and mail order sales ads in technically oriented popular magazines, like those for PC users.

If these points on the mass media barometer can be considered accurate measures, then telefacsimile, which is readily evident in all these media, is now a universally adopted technology for information transfer in a broad array of settings, including business, finance, medicine, government, and education. FAX numbers increasingly appear on business cards and corporate letterheads, and, significantly, news coverage of the telecommuting that became increasingly common in the traffic-snarled 1980s almost invariably included the FAX machine as a basic tool of the home office, along with the PC and plain paper photocopier. Automobiles equipped with cellular mobile telephones are known to carry FAX machines as well.

Benefits, Challenges, and Trends

Telefacsimile has proved itself to be an easy, manageable, and affordable technology. Programmable dialing, automatic redial, and other functions allow a FAX machine to be used with little operator attention and only minimal training. Faster and potentially cheaper than courier and messenger services, FAX has quickly become integrated into day-to-day operations in many organizations. Except for the initial purchase or lease of the FAX equipment and the periodic restocking of comparatively expensive FAX paper, the only direct cost associated with telefacsimile is the cost of telephone calls. While long-distance traffic, especially international calls, can incur substantial charges, some FAX units can be programmed to dial at nonprime times when long-distance rates are lower.

Little has appeared in the literature to suggest the point at which the advantage of telefacsimile's timeliness is counteracted by the expense of sending extremely long or numerous FAX messages. It may be that this issue can be resolved only by judgment on the part of the FAX user or administrator responsible for selecting which technology to apply to a particular communication.

Reusability of Transmissions

A significant weakness in telefax is the single-copy nature of a FAX transmission. As noted earlier, FAX sends digitized graphic images; FAX has much in common with copying, and images sent by facsimile are actually digitized photocopies. Technology is available and widely used to convert digitized text (ASCII code) directly into FAX format; telefacsimile boards are increasingly popular peripheral add-ons to microcomputers, and their cost is gradually declining from about $1,500. Several electronic mail services offer facilities for sending email messages to FAX machines. These techniques can bypass the step of printing a document before feeding it into the FAX machine, except when typographic elements are needed.

The reverse technology, conversion of FAX signals into digital text or graphics for reuse in other systems, has not been developed. Without such a capability, FAX recipients of text or images to be used in other electronic systems must recreate the FAX's content. Because the image produced by a FAX machine is fuzzy, especially if the source document was unclear, optical character recognition (OCR) technology may not work well with FAX documents so that text must be rekeyed. The extent to which Group IV machines will solve this problem is unknown. Electronic mail therefore remains a more effective telecommunications technology for content that must be reused in other electronic systems.

Junk FAX

The Connecticut state legislature passed a law in 1989 establishing penalties for sending unsolicited telefacsimile transmissions. The statute resulted not only from the complaints of citizens, but also from the legislators themselves. Abetted by the automatic sending and group distribution features of more sophisticated FAX machines, and using FAX numbers found in widely published directories, some marketers had used telefacsimile as a new way to send their promotional messages to a broad audience, capitalizing on the urgency associated with FAXes. However, users received so many unsolicited FAXes that their machines were tied up for extended periods with no means for blocking the transmissions, and many rolls of costly paper were consumed. These marketers' abuse of the technology led to the adoption of this and similar statutes elsewhere.

Clearly, promotional junk FAX, like junk email, is an inappropriate application of the technology. Junk hardcopy mail, as observed with regard to email, involves no direct cost and little effort on the part of the recipient to dispose of it; this is obviously not the case with FAX.

Alternatives to FAX

The differences between electronic mail and telefacsimile, and their relative merits and weaknesses, have already been described. The addition of certain FAX capabilities by commercial email systems has also been noted. Competition in the email industry will only become more intense as FAX usage continues to expand. The difficulty and complexity of using electronic mail systems, especially compared with an almost effortless technology like telefacsimile, will become even greater marketing and training challenges for email providers. Furthermore, there will be continuing pressure to make email systems easier to use and to improve PC interfaces to online email systems.

While simplicity of use is an important criterion, users of telecommunications technologies should be concerned lest one method's use be so mindlessly easy that it obscures both its own weaknesses and the potential benefits of alternative technologies.

ONLINE INFORMATION RETRIEVAL SYSTEMS

Online information retrieval systems are one of the most important telecommunications applications in the information industry. The design and use of information retrieval systems are the subjects of a very substantial body of published literature. The objective here is to describe briefly how these systems came about and have developed, and to identify the trends and issues that have implications for their telecommunications components.

History and Background

Online information systems represent the merging of two separate paths of technological development: the computerization of typesetting for print abstracting and indexing (A&I) services and other major serial publications, and the creation of computer-based systems for the storage and retrieval of large numbers of bibliographic citations. Development of both began in the mid-1950s.

Experiments at batch mode searching of machine-readable bibliographic data began in 1954, culminating in the public availability of the National Library of Medicine's MEDLARS system in 1964. Online interactive searching of machine-readable bibliographic files was first attempted in 1960 at the Systems Development Corporation (SDC), and by late 1964 SDC demonstrated a full-fledged retrieval system, which was made available to other organizations the following year. Government contracts that led to the Lockheed Dialog bibliographic retrieval system began in 1966, with the commercially available service offered in 1972. Mead Data Central, noted for its role in online retrieval from full-text databases, introduced its LEXIS legal information service in 1972. Other systems for bibliographic, full-text, and numeric databases developed during the 1960s and 1970s.

Online interaction with the information retrieval system implies a telecommunications link from the remote terminal to the host computer, and the ready availability of telecommunications networks to connect distant users to retrieval systems has been absolutely essential to the success of online information systems. Public data networks like Telenet and Tymnet have served the needs of users accessing online database systems since their earliest availability, and some database providers like Dialog have reached sufficient levels of use to warrant establishing their own proprietary networks.

Types of Databases

Databases may be categorized in two major groups: reference and source databases. Reference databases contain bibliographic, directory, or other citations referring the user to primary information sources. Source databases contain the primary information itself – textual, numeric, or other raw data, or even encoded computer software.

Reference databases are further subdivided into bibliographic and referral databases. Bibliographic databases contain index references to primary sources; they may additionally include abstracts of or extracts from the cited text. Referral databases contain descriptive, directory, or other information on individuals, organizations, employment opportunities, or other nonbibliographic references.

Source databases include full-text databases, offering the complete texts of newspapers, journals, encyclopedias, and other published information sources; and numeric databases, containing statistical, economic, or other data made available for analysis by the user. Some categories of source data may be considered in either category depending on their use in relation to a particular search; such data would include chemical formulas and patents. As digitized graphics technologies have developed, diagrams and other images have been incorporated into databases.

Production and Distribution

With over 3000 databases on the market, the online industry is clearly a substantial one. Data are produced by an organization that gathers and disseminates information, such as a publicly or privately funded research center, commercial or nonprofit A&I service, or traditional publisher of newspapers, reference books, or other materials. While database producers may publish print products for which the electronic form might originally have been a by-product, others produce databases that appear only electronically with no associated print counterpart.

There are several patterns of distribution of machine-readable databases. Database vendors like Dialog Information Services are time-sharing services that offer large numbers of databases accessed using a search command language specific to the system. Other organizations, like the H.W. Wilson Company, not only produce bibliographic data but also are the sole or primary distributors of the data. Some providers include databases as value-added services complementary to their primary offering; electronic mail providers offering database access in addition to their electronic mail and other telecommunications functions are included in this category of distributor.

Applications

Because bibliographic references to scientific and technical documents maintained in libraries were the first applications of computerized information retrieval systems, libraries and information centers quickly and naturally became key centers for access. However, they were soon surpassed by the growing number of business and financial users. The falling prices and broad distribution of microcomputers have led also to a substantial consumer market.

Libraries

For the library profession, managing, financing, and, most of all, using online retrieval systems had become major topics of conference programming and publishing by the mid-1970s. Since that time, a number of journals have been established, and several competing online-oriented conferences are held at various times of the year.

Combined with the growth through the 1970s and 1980s of union (i.e., multilibrary) catalogs and serials lists, the establishment of cooperative collection development plans and specialized document repositories, the improvements in interlibrary loan protocols and procedures, and the appearance in the 1980s of fee-based document delivery services and information brokers outside the institutional library environment, the online information system became essential to retrieving the universe of information, regardless of its location. If a library identified a needed item it did not hold, the item could probably be obtained relatively quickly and easily from another library or commercial service. Telecommunications could support both identification and retrieval of the desired item.

By the end of the 1980s the online industry had reached a level of maturity. Online searches are offered as a service in substantial numbers of libraries of all kinds in North America, especially in academic and special or corporate libraries, as well as in Europe, Australia, and other regions of the world. Searching techniques for information retrieval systems are now considered basic skills for the entry-level information professional, and online searching is included in library and information science curricula.

Business, Industry, and the Professions

Business and industry are primary users of online source databases of many kinds. Whether access to the online service is obtained through the corporate library, information center, research department, or other organizational unit, electronic data from online sources are integral to many kinds of businesses and professions.

The legal and medical professions not only use bibliographic databases, but also increasingly rely on full-text sources, especially in the law where machine-readable versions of laws, codes, court opinions, and other texts are widely available. Indeed, value-added information services, such as ABA/net and ALANET mentioned with reference to electronic mail, have been developed for a number of professionally oriented groups, and electronic information networks exist in the fields of nursing, realty, medicine, pharmacy, and others.

Financial and statistical data are gathered by a large and growing number of international, governmental, and both privately and publicly funded research organizations. This information is often made available to outside agencies, including corporations, where it is used in economic planning, market research, forecasting, and other research activities essential to ongoing successful business. While some of the data are distributed on magnetic tapes or other media for use on local computer systems, numeric and other source data are also included in many online systems. Records of patents, trademarks, chemical formulas, and other primary data are critical to the successful development, manufacturing, marketing, and distribution of innumerable products of business and industry.

Consumers

That end-user searching has been such a frequent topic in online conferences and journals is indicative of the interest of individual consumers in their own information retrieval, be they located in academic institutions, government agencies, corporate headquarters, home offices, or the household recreation room. Database vendors have developed end-user-oriented search interfaces and subscription options, such as BRS Menus and Dialog After Dark.

Value-added consumer utilities like CompuServe (discussed in chapter 4) offer databases on their own computers or through telecommunications gateway links to outside hosts. The end user is the primary focus of EasyNet,^{tm} a gateway service accessed by telecommunications, that assists the user in formulating a search and choosing a database, connects with the database host and conducts the search, and presents the results to the user.

Equipment and Costs

In the home, the only requirements for access to online databases are a modem-equipped terminal or microcomputer, a telephone line, and the money to pay subscription, usage, or other charges. Use of online retrieval systems in an organizational setting, however, involves a number of significant administrative and financial issues, but online services can provide immeasurable benefit to the library and its users.

Equipment and Software

While a dumb 300 bps terminal might have been the only affordable option in the early days of online information services, requirements now considered basic are a microcomputer with a high-speed (1200 if not 2400 bps) modem and telecommunications software, and a printer. Because printouts of records retrieved during an online session are usually hard to use and unattractive, especially when large numbers of citations are retrieved, librarians and other users quickly sought better means for presenting search results. Downloading the results (i.e., saving them to the user's computer disk) has become a standard practice, with word-processing software used to reformat the results so that they are suitable for presentation.

Pre- and postprocessing search software began to appear in the mid-1980s. These programs sought to conserve costly online time, facilitate offline construction of searches in complex systems and files, and support reformatting of search results into bibliographies or reports. Among the popular packages are *Pro-Search* and *Pro-Cite*. *Pro-Search*, introduced by the Menlo Corporation in 1984 as In-Search and renamed in 1985, focused on search formulation, log-on, and online searching. *Pro-Cite* (originally Personal Bibliographic System) was developed for creating bibliographies in standard citation form. The two programs work as complementary packages, with *Pro-Search* addressing presearch processing needs, and *Pro-Cite* converting downloaded search results to presentation format. Utility programs called "Biblio Links" convert records from the formats used by various database vendors to the standardized format required by the software, the U.S. MARC (machine-readable cataloging) format. Other examples of pre- and postprocessing search software packages are *Sci-Mate* (Institute for Scientific Information) and *Search Helper* (Information Access Corporation).

Pricing and Contracts

Online searching involves various levels of charges, in addition to connect time or kilocharacter traffic charges for telecommunications links. Database producers and vendors set usage rates according to a variety of factors, including connect time; records displayed online (e.g., for downloading or immediate printout); records printed offline and shipped by hardcopy mail (e.g., for large bibliographies); or records sent by the vendor's electronic mail system. Contracts or subscriptions to database services may be required. Costs may be reduced by nonprime time use, with volume discounting, or through group purchase plans offered by a number of cooperatives that broker database subscriptions and training services.

Connect time charges for files on major vendor systems may range from $35 per hour for a government-produced database, to well over $150, and even more for highly specialized files. Charges for online record displays and offline prints may range from 10 cents to 25 cents, or up to $1 or more. Telecommunications connect charges are usually in the range of $6 to $10 per connect hour, with surcharges for access to and from overseas hosts – a real concern as databases all over the world are made available worldwide.

Training

Training has always been an important aspect of online searching and continues to be a point of resistance on the part of many librarians and others who delay or reject implementation of online search services for reasons other than funding and hardware. Even someone with a general education in online systems will require additional training in connection with individual specialized databases or systems, new techniques and system enhancements, and continuing education for purposes of current awareness and maintaining skills.

Classes, online tutorials, videos, and interactive software are all methods used for training database users in system access and searching, and each method involves costs. Training may be included as part of a subscription fee, or involve an additional charge. Documentation, including database descriptions, instructional materials, and such secondary literature as journals and monographs, must also be considered in financing the online search service.

Training classes are usually offered by vendors, often in close coordination with database producers. Vendors usually offer a selection of courses for beginning, intermediate, and advanced users, and classes may focus on databases within specific industries or subject areas. Classes may be presented in many cities in addition to the vendor's headquarters location, and training or update sessions may be held concurrently with major professional meetings. Regional cooperatives or local organizations may become authorized training agents for the vendor, broadening the availability of educational offerings and building on the expertise of individual users in many geographic areas, types of library, and subject specialties.

Administration and Funding

Online searching as an organizational service involves a number of funding, administrative, and staffing issues. The funding sources that must be developed to support the online searching unit have been the most controversial aspect of the service, not only because of its direct and indirect costs, but also because the extraordinary nature and costs of online information suggested early on that library users be charged for the service. Corporate libraries might have an easier time accommodating usage charges, with search fees often billed to other departments or outside clients. Public, academic, and other libraries and information centers that are publicly funded or that have traditionally offered all services without additional charge faced a more difficult issue in the 1980s.

Although the "fee versus free" issue sparked much debate in library meetings and publications, the majority of libraries offering online services chose to deal pragmatically with the issue by constructing fee schedules for their users. While some libraries do subsidize all fees for user searching, at least within some basic parameters, more are charging users for some or all direct costs associated with searching, with overheads covered by the library.

The need for equipment and training for online services implies an administrative structure and staffing pattern. Maintaining records to track billing from vendors and charges to users is an additional paperwork requirement. Staff scheduling must accommodate, in addition to direct client service and administrative functions, time to prepare search queries and to process and reformat search results. Where searching is built into orientation or instructional programs for library patrons, search specialists assume responsibility for informing and educating users, in addition to meeting their own training requirements.

Benefits, Challenges, and Trends

Clearly, there are numerous and often complicated factors to consider in managing an online search service, but at the same time, the benefits of online services have secured their position within the majority of libraries and information centers. Most significantly, online retrieval systems offer access to information with a power, ease, and comprehensiveness that was utterly unattainable with print-based information sources. Today, it can be asserted that any information not documented in a database accessible through an online information retrieval system can be considered inaccessible.

The post-World War II expansion in scientific and technical research and the resulting explosion in information resources added urgency to issues of bibliographic and physical control of information that had been sought for centuries. Only after introduction of the computer could the kinds of services described here be created, much less exploited. Furthermore, research that led to these systems fostered the discipline of information science, which in turn has led to a rethinking of librarianship and other information-oriented professions. Advanced research in such areas as indexing theory, systems design, patterns of information-seeking behavior, and scholarly communications has resulted in improvements to existing systems and affected the functionality of new systems. It has also had a beneficial effect on the development of microcomputer database management systems and information management software, which is discussed in chapter 9.

The benefit of online information retrieval systems can be summarized using terminology codified as part of the mission of the International Federation of Library Associations and Institutions: universal bibliographic control for the achievement of universal availability of publications. The relevance of online information services to this review of telecommunications applications is their fundamental reliance on telecommunications links to carry information to the user.

Local Database Distribution

As large academic and research institutions grew in both their on-site computing capabilities and their use of machine-readable information sources, it became clear from the economics of online retrieval systems with their pay-as-you-go pricing structures that total reliance on online vendors could no longer be sustained. Large institutional users began, first with data files in the public domain and then with commercially produced sources, to obtain licenses to mount databases on their local systems. Although local retrieval software was first applied to these files, institutions were later able to negotiate licenses to the retrieval software of some commercial database vendors.

Such a move was certainly advantageous to the institutions, which could then make the data available to large numbers of users in their institutionwide networks, all linked to centralized computing facilities. Database producers and vendors recognized the advantages of direct relationships with high-volume institutional licensees, which might otherwise be forced to limit searching for users who held potential for ongoing use after they left the institution. Furthermore, by licensing their software they could protect themselves from the competition of other software providers.

The number of institutions and vendors engaging in such relationships was still small at the end of the 1980s, so that their longer term impact on the online information vendors was not clear. However, this new shift in balance in the information distribution equation, combined with other changes described below, is certain to lead to major changes in the field.

Gateway Services and Expert Systems

Two problems confronting the online user are the need to subscribe to multiple database services to gain access to all desired databases, and the differences in command languages among systems. Local database distribution is helpful to bridge these gaps for some databases and in some institutional settings; however, this option is currently unavailable to the majority of users. An alternative approach is a gateway service, which provides links from one system to others, together with a standardized command language that facilitates searching on different hosts.

EasyNet, mentioned earlier, is one online version of such a gateway service. Designed for end users and inexperienced searchers, its menu and prompting structure aids users formulating their queries, and conducts the search for them, obviating the need for multiple subscriptions to multiple vendors. Another feature of EasyNet is its implementation of the Common Command Language (CCL), a new standard for search commands in information retrieval systems, being considered for adoption by the International Organisation for Standardisation (ISO) but not yet widely implemented in the online industry.

EasyNet cannot perhaps be characterized as an expert system, that is, with an interface that matches the user's own mode of expression, and with precise and unfailingly accurate search results. Such systems, discussed in more detail in chapter 10, are within the province of the field of artificial intelligence (AI). AI has developed some specialized systems, but none with the breadth of scope of current online systems.

EasyNet has been extremely successful in many settings, including libraries, because its objective is easy access to a wealth of information sources without the impediments of administrative and training requirements that online systems entail. While comprehensive literature searches and highly technical, specialized subjects or genres (like patents or formulas) require complex search strategies and command structures, a substantial number of information needs can be met by a system like EasyNet.

Microcomputer Software

The pre- and postsearch software discussed above reflects an interest on the part of information users in minimizing their direct online use charges by shifting as much of the burden as possible away from online time; this shift is similar to the online-offline shift seen among electronic mail users. One reaction of vendors to such changing use patterns has been to preserve their revenue bases by altering charging structures. For example, online retrieval systems began charging for records displayed online only when it became clear that searchers were downloading those records and paying only connect time, in order to reformat and print them on-site instead of buying offline prints. Communications, searching, and database management software development, along with the continually improving speed and storage capacity of modems and PCs, will lead to further comparable cycles of action and reaction among vendors and users of online systems.

Alternatives to Online Information Retrieval Systems

The most significant alternative technology to the online system has been compact disc-read only memory (CD-ROM), which combines the massive storage capacity (550 megabytes) of 5¼-inch optical discs with PC-based retrieval systems. CD-ROM and other optical information systems began to appear in the mid-1980s. The number of commercially available CD-ROM products grew quickly from a handful to some 300 by 1989. Optical disc and CD-ROM technologies are discussed in detail in chapters 6 and 7.

CD-ROM use is entirely offline, so that no connect time or telecommunications charges are incurred. Like a print A&I service, CD-ROMs can be searched an unlimited number of times for the single price of the product's subscription. Though early CD-ROMs were rather extravagantly priced, competitive market forces and growing numbers of purchasers quickly modified CD-ROM pricing.

Because CD-ROM publishers have packaged both databases and retrieval software together, CD-ROM was positioned to compete with online systems. Although the files available online might be more up to date than those on CD-ROM, libraries and other CD-ROM users chose to sacrifice information currency for unlimited searching for a fixed price. Migration to CD-ROM began soon after the technology was introduced. Online vendors quickly modified their search software to operate in the PC/CD-ROM environment and issued CD-ROMs, positioning themselves as key players in the marketplace. The H. W. Wilson Company even packaged its CD-ROM products so that a subscription included both unlimited CD-ROM searching and access to their WILSONLINE online service, with online searching free of all charges except telecommunications.

When online retrieval services were introduced, publishers of print A&I services were concerned, as reflected in the literature of the time, with migration from print to online. These publishers did in fact lose some print subscribers, but the greater audience afforded them by online services actually expanded their revenue base. Although it is too soon to predict the economic outcome of migration from online to CD-ROM, it is certain that the trend will continue.

TELECOMMUNICATIONS CHALLENGES

The product line of a single vendor of telecommunications or database services may contain a diverse set of offerings, including electronic mail, bulletin boards, teleconferencing, telefacsimile interfaces, and information retrieval services – in short, all the technologies described in this chapter. The emphasis a vendor gives a particular service depends on that vendor's primary corporate objectives. Dialog's electronic mail and bulletin board offerings are designed to complement its primary line of database products; in contrast, the databases available to BT Tymnet users seek to enhance the communications services that are its principal focus.

There have been some reports and studies in the literature of applications that combine two or more of these technologies, such as electronic mail plus FAX (e.g., email for interlibrary loan requests, FAX for document delivery) and online searching plus electronic mail (e.g., search result transmission by electronic mail). Software packages for communications, search formulation, and postsearch processing have integrated several functions associated with telecommunications applications.

The integration within a single vendor's product line of a multiplicity of services and the development of ancillary software packages reflect two important forces. First, vendors expand and modify their offerings in reaction to technologies and services that might threaten their market share. Second and more important, these multiple offerings are responses to users' ever greater demands for easy, single-source access to all of the communications and information services they need. Unrealistic as this demand may now seem given the complexity of each service and the competitive marketplace in which providers must function, users continue to demand it, and system developers increasingly will respond. The trend toward integration will profoundly affect the telecommunications and information industries described here.

Telecommunications technologies face substantial challenges in the marketplace and present significant challenges to users. A newly introduced technology must compete with others that are firmly established or even habitual, and whose use, economics, and benefits are well understood.

As this chapter has sought to demonstrate, the user must address numerous issues before deciding whether to adopt a particular technology for a particular application. These issues include financial, operational, training, and psychological factors. Once the new technique has been adopted, individuals and organizations alike must adapt to it, learn to use it, and change their comfortable work habits to accommodate it.

Proponents and providers of telecommunications must remember that the contemporary user applying them must select from an array of potentially useful technologies. Face-to-face meetings, two-way and conference calls, electronic mail, teleconferences, bulletin boards, and telefacsimile are all available methods; each has its advantages and limitations, and each is appropriate to particular situations.

The principal challenge presented by telecommunications is selection, making the appropriate match between the application and the technology best suited to it. This selection process is continual, involves a number of often subtle factors, and is conducted in a dynamic working environment. The cycle of analysis, evaluation, selection, and adoption that must be applied to communications technologies will continue to be an important responsibility of information professionals as new telecommunications applications are devised and as new methods are introduced.

SUGGESTED READING

This bibliography was compiled with the invaluable assistance of Carolyn V. Pearson, Graduate School of Library and Information Science, University of Washington, whose work on this project is greatly appreciated.

Electronic Mail

Birks, Grant, Scott Inrigg, and Maureen Towaij. "EDIS (Electronically Distributed Information Service)." In *ASIS 85: Proceedings of the 48th ASIS Annual Meeting 1985,* vol. 22, edited by Carol A. Parkhurst, 15-18. White Plains, N.Y.: Knowledge Industry Publications for the American Society for Information Science, 1985.

Green, Alan. *Communicating in the '80s: New Options for the Nonprofit Community.* Washington, D.C.: Benton Foundation, 1983. ED247919.

Mayer, Ira. *The Electronic Mailbox.* Hasbrouck Heights, N.J.: Hayden Book Co., 1985.

Vervest, Peter. *Innovation in Electronic Mail.* Amsterdam: Elsevier Science Publishers, 1986.

Bulletin Boards and Teleconferencing

Dewey, Patrick R. "Electronic Bulletin Boards: Applications in Libraries." *Library Journal* 111, no. 18 (1 November 1986): Library Computing Supplement, LC10-LC19.

_____. *Essential Guide to Bulletin Board Systems.* Westport, Conn.: Meckler, 1986.

National Directory of Bulletin Board Systems. Westport, Conn.: Meckler, annual.

Telefacsimile

Boss, Richard W., and Hal Espo. "The Use of Telefacsimile in Libraries." *Library Hi Tech* 5, no. 1 (Spring 1987): 33-42.

Buchan, James H., and Linda L. Alter. "The Authoritative Guide on the Use of Telefacsimile in Libraries: An Occasional Paper." State Library of Ohio. *Occasional Papers* 2, no. 3 (November 1988).

Buyer's Laboratory. "Test Reports on 19 Facsimile Machines." *Library Technology Reports* 24, no. 5 (November/December 1988): 613-716.

Online Information Retrieval Systems

Buckland, Michael. "Combining Electronic Mail with Online Retrieval in a Library Context." *Information Technology and Libraries* 6, no. 4 (December 1987): 266-71.

Harter, Stephen P. *Online Information Retrieval: Concepts, Principles and Techniques.* Orlando, Fla: Academic Press, 1986.

Hawkins, Donald T., and Louise R. Levy. "Front End Software for Online Database Searching." Part I. *Online* 9 (November 1985): 30-36; Part II. *Online* 10 (January 1986): 33-40; Part III. *Online* 10 (May 1986): 49-58.

Lee, Joel M., William P. Whitely, and Arthur W. Hafner. "Electronic Publishing in Library and Information Science." In Patricia F. Stenstrom and Dale S. Montanelli, eds., "Library Literature in the 1980s." *Library Trends* 36, no. 1 (Spring 1988): 673-93.

Maloney, James. "Online Information Services." In *ALA World Encyclopedia of Library and Information Services.* 2d ed., 611-21. Chicago: American Library Association, 1986.

Palmer, Roger C. *Online Reference and Information Retrieval.* 2d ed. Littleton, Colo.: Libraries Unlimited, 1987.

Saffady, William. "The Availability and Cost of Online Search Services." *Library Technology Reports* 24, no. 3 (May/June 1988): 291-497.

Sieburth, Janice F. *Online Search Services in the Academic Library: Planning, Management, and Operation.* Chicago: American Library Association, 1988.

▪ 4 ▪

Television and Video

Margaret E. Chisholm and K. Michael Malone

In any evaluation of television as an information technology, one inevitably encounters the central conflict inherent in the medium's two principal properties: television as conduit (the transmission of images) and television as content (the images thus transmitted). While the hardware/software dichotomy characterizes all information technologies to one extent or another, television's potential as an information dissemination technology has been uniquely and unfortunately circumscribed by the widespread public equation of television's technological possibilities with the nature and quality of traditional commercial television content.

Yet, in many respects, the technology of television can readily be seen as the apex of all efforts to express, record, and swiftly – even instantaneously – disseminate the vast array of images, actions, observations, perceptions, thoughts, ideas, and feelings that constitute the foundation of what our society regards as information.

THE HISTORY OF TELEVISION

The lineage of television is a complex one indeed; its roots include such nineteenth-century inventions as the photograph, telegraph, telephone, phonograph, and motion picture, as well as such scientific phenomena as electromagnetic waves and the theory of the electron. Television's prime progenitor, however, was the radio – both as a technology and as a social, political, and economic force. It is no small coincidence that the three major television networks in the United States (NBC, CBS, and ABC) began in the mid-1920s as radio networks.

Although the wireless transmitter, capable of transmitting coded radio signals from ship to ship and ship to shore, was patented in 1896 by Guglielmo Marconi, it was not until a decade later that the broadcasting potential of radio was conceived. Through the efforts of two American pioneers, Lee de Forest and Reginald Fessenden, the two primary obstacles impeding the development of radio broadcasting–voice transmission and sufficient sound wave amplification–were overcome.

The major obstacle facing television, however, was the development of a means by which images could be dissected and conveyed through the air via electromagnetic waves. The first efforts to devise such a system, begun as early as 1884, employed mechanical means such as revolving drums or discs, as in the Nipkow disc. These discs functioned by allowing light waves to pass between the light source and the scene to be televised. As the disc was rapidly spun, the light waves passed through holes placed on the disc in a spiral design and were then converted into electric impulses, which were carried via electromagnetic waves to a receiver. The receiver, which also employed a disc, converted the electric impulses back into light waves, thus reconstituting and revealing the transmitted image.

The first successful trans-Atlantic television transmission was accomplished in 1928 by a Scottish inventor, John Logie Baird, using just such a system. The mechanical scanning technique was also the means by which German broadcasters began regular television service in 1935 and by which British broadcasters inaugurated their transmissions in 1936.

Ultimately, a system based upon electronic scanning proved superior in the delivery of a sufficiently well defined image. This electronic system had in fact evolved from the invention of the cathode-ray tube in 1897 by Karl Braun in Germany. In 1907 and 1908, respectively, Russian scientist Boris Rosing and British scientist A. A. Campbell Swinton, completely independently of one another, conceived of a transmitter that would employ a beam of electrons to scan the scene to be televised, thereby yielding electrical signals identical to the scene itself. These electrical signals would travel by means of electromagnetic waves and then be converted back into electrical signals in the receiver, releasing the electron beam that would in turn recreate the scene on the receiver's photosensitive screen. In the 1920s and 1930s, the independent research team at Marconi-EMI under the huge and imposing auspices of the Radio Corporation of America (RCA), began building upon this basic concept to form the scientific basis for modern television.

Although a variety of nascent American television stations had undertaken fitful efforts throughout the 1930s to provide television service to American audiences, NBC's April 30, 1939, broadcast of the opening of the World's Fair in New York City, which featured a speech by President Franklin D. Roosevelt, is considered to be the birth of television service in the United States.

Technical Standards

A swift proliferation of competing technical standards for television transmission–put forth largely by receiver manufacturers like RCA who were eager to have their system adopted as the national standard – moved the Federal Communications Commission (FCC), which had responsibility for allocating the electromagnetic spectrum frequencies on which radio and television operated, to establish the National Television Standards Commmittee (NTSC). In early 1941, after comparing the competing systems, the NTSC recommended that the picture should comprise 525 horizontal, interlaced scanning lines.

Interlaced scanning refers to the practice of transmitting in two separate frames the horizontal scan lines that compose the complete television picture. The first frame consists of the odd-numbered lines, and the second frame consists of the even-numbered lines. This method of scanning eliminates the picture flicker that would otherwise occur if lines 1 through 525 were scanned in direct order. The NTSC also recommended a frame frequency rate of 30 frames per second and an *aspect ratio* (the ratio of horizontal units to vertical units) of 4:3.

With its adoption of the NTSC recommendations, the FCC granted permission to television stations to begin commercial television service on 1 July 1941. On that date, WNBT (NBC), WCBW (CBS), and W2XWV (DuMont, a short-lived third network) aired a wide range of programming, including news, quiz shows, baseball, dance lessons, and an art exhibit borrowed from the Metropolitan Museum of Art. However, the bombing of Pearl Harbor by the Japanese on 7 December 1941 and the ensuing U.S. entry into World War II heralded a rapid decline in television service, as the minds and materials that had been so arduously directed toward the development of television were now to be dedicated to the war effort.

Although broadcasting was resumed in the immediate postwar period, complications involving the equitable allocation of the electromagnetic spectrum prompted the FCC to put a "temporary" freeze on the assigning of transmitting licenses while it studied the situation. This temporary freeze was in effect from September 1948 until June 1952, when the FCC returned to the task of licensing transmitters. With that, television service expanded prodigiously and proceeded to capture the American imagination. According to Erik Barnouw, a preeminent television historian, the inauguration of television as a truly mass medium occurred on 19 January 1953 when 68.8 percent of the American television audience watched as Lucy Ricardo (Lucille Ball) gave birth to Little Ricky on *I Love Lucy*.[1]

Color Television and UHF

Two further technical complexities soon vexed the young industry, however. The first concerned color television, whose development and introduction were impeded by the inability of existing black and white sets to receive the signals generated by the majority of the competing color television systems.

Indeed, the FCC required that the signals produced by the system that would win their approval – and thus become the industry standard – must be capable of reception (though not in color, of course) by current black and white sets. Although the FCC eventually selected in 1953 a system developed by RCA in which red, green and blue picture-tube phosphors are combined variously to produce a range of colors, the high cost of producing color programming, combined with the expense of color television sets, kept color broadcasting to a minimum until the mid-1960s.

The second complexity involved the difficulties experienced by television stations whose frequency allocation was in the UHF (ultrahigh frequency) range (channels 14-83). In comparison to VHF (very high frequency) signals (channels 2-13), UHF signals are less hearty when making the journey from transmitter to receiver and often are weakened or blocked altogether by terrestrial obstructions such as buildings or trees. In addition, television sets that were not equipped with costly UHF converters could not receive UHF programming.

In response, the FCC interceded in 1963 and, authorized by the passage of the All-Channel Television Receiver Act of 1962, was able to require that all new television sets be equipped to receive all channels.

TELEVISION TODAY

As a technology, television currently enjoys extraordinary penetration into American society. According to 1988 statistics, 98 percent of all U.S. homes have at least one television, and those households watch television for an average of seven hours and six minutes per day, although the mental energy each individual devotes to the act of television viewing naturally varies widely.[2] In addition, the development and expansion of such alternative forms of signal delivery as coaxial cable and satellites have combined with inexpensive videotape technology to afford viewers far more options in program selection and considerably more control over when and under what conditions those selections are viewed.

For broadcasters and cablecasters, program production, signal transmission, cable installation, operation and maintenance, and the services of highly trained professional and technical staffs cost millions of dollars, even for relatively small operations. However, because of the funding structures of commercial broadcast television, public television, and cable television, combined with the enormous economies of scale afforded by the vast market penetration of television and videotape, TV viewers actually pay very little – directly, anyway – for the costly programming they receive. When compared to the home delivery of newspapers or magazines or the purchase of hardbound books, even cable television with all the frills remains an information bargain.

In spite of television's widespread popularity, its capacity to perform as a legitimate provider of information, education, and even entertainment is frequently attacked by sociologists, artists, politicians, religious leaders, writers, educators, print journalists, and others. Some of their criticisms, like those lodged by Marie Winn,[3] target television's properties as a conduit. Most, however, are directed toward television's content, which is considered variously as a tranquilizer responsible for the erosion of productivity and the deterioration of human interaction, and as a pernicious catalyst to action that incites viewers, particularly children, to mimic behaviors – usually violent or otherwise antisocial in nature – which they have seen on television. That television's content reflects and reinforces – and occasionally exploits – our society's values, hopes, and fears is perhaps closer to the truth.

Today's television is available through broadcast, cable, and satellite. Videotape provides still another alternative.

Broadcast Television

Broadcast television is the oldest and perhaps most familiar form of television. On the conduit side, the television signal is generated when a television or video camera electronically scans an object or a scene and converts its light and sound values into matching electrical signals. The light or video signal is then superimposed onto a carrier wave forming an amplitude modulation (AM) signal, while the sound or audio signal is modulated onto a carrier wave forming a frequency modulation (FM) signal. These signals can then be either broadcast "live" or recorded on videotape for later transmission.

Broadcasting – literally, scattering widely – occurs when the AM and FM signals are transmitted on the television station's FCC-assigned spectrum frequency, which has been allocated in either the VHF or UHF range. Because of the relatively large amount of video and audio information required to construct an adequate television signal, a correspondingly large portion of the electromagnetic frequency range – 6 megahertz (MHz) per TV channel – must be reserved for transmission. The signal is then ready for amplification, the purpose of which is to boost the power of the signal without changing its structure, thereby enabling it to be carried over a distance with sufficient fidelity to be intelligibly received by the TV set.

In the television receiver, the signal is captured through the antennae and again amplified, prior to its extraction, or demodulation, from the electromagnetic carrier wave, to give it added strength. Following amplification, the video and audio signals are demodulated, synchronized, and converted from electrical signals back into the same specific light and sound values as those which composed the original object or scene.

Interestingly, the apparent motion of the televised image is in fact the result of the speed with which each frame of video values is replaced. Each frame, which consists of hundreds of thousands of tiny dots of varying light intensity and color distribution laid out in 525 horizontal lines (the NTSC standard), is replaced at the rate of 30 per second, thus taking advantage of the human physiological phenomenon of persistence of vision and giving the illusion of motion.

Subscription and Low-Power Television

Two variations on the broadcasting theme are subscription television (STV) and low-power television (LPTV). Although STV is transmitted via electromagnetic waves like conventional television, its signal is "scrambled" by the station that originates it. However, for a monthly fee paid to the station – the subscription – viewers can obtain a decoding device, which, when attached to the receiver, unscrambles the signal so that the station's programming (usually similar to that provided by a premium cable channel, described later in this chapter) can be intelligibly displayed.

Low-power television stations, which are limited to 10 watts VHF and 1000 watts UHF to avoid interference with full-power TV stations, provide signals that can be received within a 10- to 33-mile radius. LPTV typically serves isolated, sparsely populated areas that are geographically inhospitable to broadcast signals and financially unattractive to cable companies for wiring purposes. While they do provide some locally produced programming, LPTV stations usually serve as area translators, that is, they capture transmissions of video and audio information emanating from regular-power TV stations and convert or "translate" them from their original electromagnetic frequency to another, usually lower, frequency. LPTV stations serve as translators for both network-originated broadcast signals and subscription or cable television signals, whose unscrambled reception requires a decoder.

Commercial Television

In terms of content, American broadcast television falls into two quite distinct categories – commercial and public – whose programming characteristics are profoundly influenced by the manner in which they derive their financial support. Commercial television, as the name implies, finances the enormous costs of program production and transmission through fees paid by companies that buy air time from networks (ABC, CBS, Fox, and NBC), their affiliates, or independent stations for the purpose of advertising their products or services to the viewing audience. This arrangement offers significant rewards to the network whose programming enables its affiliates to deliver consistently the largest number of viewers – the *real* product in the transaction between station and sponsor – to the advertiser. However, the networks are thus tied to the yoke of the ratings game, which in turn impels those responsible for content to seek programming that has the capacity to attract the largest possible audience, often by appealing to the more basic interests – the so-called lowest common denominator – of its members.

Typically, programming on commercial television consists of a network-supplied mix of situation comedies; police, medical, and law dramas; action-oriented crime or intrigue programs; sports events; talk, quiz, and game shows; children's cartoons; daily newscasts and weekly investigative reports; and feature-length made-for-TV or previously theatrically released films. In addition to programming supplied by the networks, network affiliates also produce their own local newscasts, talk shows, and public affairs programming; air runs of syndicated shows; and screen a variety of films, specials, and local interest material. Reruns and older films usually constitute the majority of programming offered by independent stations.

Public Television

Although American public television stations, loosely organized under the Public Broadcasting Service (PBS) banner, are not unaffected by ratings, their philosophy, combined with the nature of their funding structure – government support, nonprofit foundation grants, corporate sponsorships, and donations solicited from viewers – enables them to air content whose audience size would be small by commercial TV standards. Unlike some public broadcasting systems, like Japan's NHK network, which assure their comparative affluence by assessing fees from TV owners in the form of licenses, U.S. public broadcasting stations are chronically underfunded in their efforts to purchase and produce programming that meets the legendary high standards of PBS.

American public television had its genesis in the educational radio movement of the 1920s and 1930s; this heritage has exerted considerable influence on the development of public television throughout its evolution. In the early 1950s, a public television – then called noncommercial educational television (ETV) – commonly found its home in universities, state and local agencies, and community development organizations, with limited programming options. However, with the establishment of the Educational Television and Radio Center, which later became National Educational Television (NET), ETV programming became more systematic and sophisticated, with programs on the humanities, political and economic issues, and international affairs.

ETV ultimately gave way to public television proper when the Public Broadcasting Act of 1967 created the Corporation for Public Broadcasting (CPB), which in turn established the Public Broadcasting Service. An agency designed to select – but not produce – programming suitable for all American public television stations, PBS soon became a central point of program distribution. Under the guidance of the CPB and PBS, public television in the United States has sought to entertain as well as educate and inform, airing such unabashedly entertaining fare as *Monty Python* in addition to more standard educational programming.

Currently, PBS programming features news and its analysis; documentaries; musical performances; classic films; American Playhouse productions; how-to shows in food preparation, carpentry, and household repair; a variety of dramas and comedies produced by the British Broadcasting Corporation; science-oriented programs; and an array of specials. In particular, high-quality prosocial children's programming could well be considered one of PBS's most significant contributions to American television – and to American society – to date; *Mister Roger's Neighborhood* and *Sesame Street* remain model efforts in the development of educational programming that genuinely appeals to children and provides them with a stable social context within which to explore the vicissitudes of childhood. In addition to programming intended for either general education or entertainment, many public television stations cooperate with local community colleges or other educational institutions to provide instructional television transmissions for use in conjunction with specific courses.

Cable Television

Unlike broadcast television, which utilizes a very limited resource – the electromagnetic spectrum – for its transmission, cable television delivers its programming through the use of coaxial cable capable of carrying up to 100 channels.

Originally called Community Access Television (CATV), cable television was conceived in 1950 as a solution to the problem of poor broadcast signal reception in communities whose access to standard line-of-sight TV signals was impeded by the presence of tall buildings or large mountains. Typically, an antenna would be placed atop the offending obstruction to collect the incoming clear broadcast signals; the captured full-strength signals would then be relayed via coaxial cable (usually strung along phone lines or buried in trenches) down to the homes below. A small monthly fee would be assessed to subscribers to support the service, which could be either publicly or privately owned.

At first, broadcasters applauded cable television's capacity as a conduit through which otherwise unserved communities could receive television service. After all, the technology of cable enabled network, network-affiliated, and independent television stations alike to expand significantly their audience size – and therefore their advertising revenues. In the mid-1960s, however, as cable technology improved and signals from stations well beyond the local television range could be received by the growing number of cable subscribers, broadcasters began to fear that the increased viewing options thus available would serve to fractionalize their audience and decimate their advertising revenues.

Programming Content

Broadcasters' anxieties intensified in the 1970s. Their initial concern was the development of non-network-affiliated superstations – notably WTBS (Atlanta), WGN (Chicago), and WOR (New York). These superstations provided 24-hour-a-day programming (a mix of old movies, reruns, and sports), which was relayed coast-to-coast first by microwave and later by satellite. Their next concern was the introduction of premium cable channels, such as Home Box Office (HBO), which cablecast unedited, recently released feature films and other high-demand entertainment programming, often produced exclusively for cable, for a small fee in addition to the basic monthly charge.

In the 1980s, cable television blossomed with a diversity of programming across its many channels that squarely challenged the long-standing dominance of the commercial television networks. By 1980, 19.8 percent of U.S. households had been wired with cable; by 1988, the number had exceeded 50 percent.[4] Further, cable television's capacity to utilize its coaxial cable connection to provide teletext, videotex, and other interactive services has revealed cable's potential as a two-way, increasingly personalized, and responsive tool of electronic communication. Teletext and videotex services are discussed in chapter 5.

While commercial televison, funded solely through advertising revenue, must provide content that consistently attracts the largest possible audience in order to remain profitable, cable television can afford to draw significantly smaller audiences to its plethora of diverse, specialized programming and still turn a handsome profit because it is supported by revenue generated through both advertising and subscribers' fees. The basic monthly cable subscription charge ranges from about $12 to $20, with premium channels each adding $4 to $7 to the bill. In addition, cable television has the attractive capacity to *narrowcast*, to aim programming at specialized or minority audiences, thus allowing its subscribers to select television program content in much the same way as they might choose a book from a library or bookstore – based on their individual needs, wants, and interests.

The content of cable television tends to vary according to the character of the channel – often called a network – on which it is carried. Superstations, such as WTBS, usually offer broadcast television reruns, sports, and older films, while channels like the Arts and Entertainment Network, the Learning

Channel, the Cable News Network, and the Entertainment and Sports Programming Network devote their programming to specific content areas.

Additionally, most cable companies, in their negotiations with local communities for area cable franchises, agree to reserve at least one channel for the purpose of providing members of the community with an opportunity to develop their own noncommercial programming. Commonly, such an arrangement includes free use of production facilities and equipment provided by the cable company. Also, like many PBS stations, cable companies frequently offer channel space over which local community colleges or universities can cablecast instructional television programming to students enrolled in selected telecourses.

Specialized Cable Systems

Essentially a miniature cable system with a satellite feed, satellite master antenna television (SMATV) provides a variety of standard and premium cable programming options to residents of apartment or condominium complexes, either as a perquisite to attract renters or buyers, or as a fee-based service. Like conventional cable television, SMATV can offer a selection of individualized services, such as electronic banking or shopping and home security alarms, that are based upon cable's interactive properties.

Pay per view (PPV), another relatively recent addition to the system of cable programming distribution, allows cable companies to cablecast extremely high-demand programming, such as championship boxing matches, only to those subscribers who are willing to pay a special fee for reception. Made possible by the increasingly sophisticated cable reception and decoding devices that cable companies install in subscribers' homes, the PPV strategy enables cable companies to supplement their available sources of income, or revenue streams, when cablecasting highly expensive programming. Currently, it is speculated that the PPV format may eventually supplant the commercial home video business by allowing subscribers to use cable's interactive capacity to order and receive films or other programming of their own choosing for a small additional charge to their monthly bill.

Closed-circuit television (CCTV), often found in schools or businesses, is a form of buildingwide cable television consisting of a video camera, a videocassette recorder, and one or more television monitors or receivers. CCTV is commonly used for surveillance purposes in hospitals, stores, banks, and correctional facilities. More recently, many department stores and other commercial concerns have adopted the closed-circuit television format to augment window and floor displays for advertising purposes.

Many educational and research institutions utilize CCTV in conjunction with cable links, microwave relays, and telephone lines for slow-scan TV. With slow-scan television, the video images are conveyed by video cameras via modem links and standard telephone lines to a receiving location where they are reassembled and displayed on a video monitor. Because of the slow pace at which telephone lines can transmit the complex video information, slow-scan video images customarily require several minutes to receive and reconstitute full pictures. Slow-scan video images are commonly used to supplement telephone conferences and can consist of one- or two-way still pictures of participants as well as any diagrams or illustrations. With the development of large and increasingly affordable videoconferencing facilities (described later in this chapter), interest in slow-scan television has diminished considerably.

Satellite Television

As a relatively inexpensive alternative to standard terrestrial signal transmission, the communications satellite has, since the late 1970s, enabled cable and broadcast television to reach far larger audiences and to achieve far greater flexibility in programming. In addition to its capacity to aid in the transmission of television in its conventional sense, satellite technology has also spawned a growing satellite videoconferencing industry, which employs the video camera, the satellite, and the receiver/monitor to link people via video in much the same way telephones link people via audio.

Satellite broadcasting technology combines the notion of conventional broadcasting – the transmission of video and audio signals via VHF, UHF, and microwave – with the concept of radar, which detects the presence of objects by "broadcasting" radio waves toward them and then charting the dimensions of the reflected waves to determine the objects' locations and other characteristics.

In 1948, the U.S. Army Signal Corps successfully demonstrated that the moon – a satellite of the natural variety – could be used as a backdrop against which microwave signals, sent from earth at relatively low power, could be bounced and then recovered with minimal signal degradation. In 1957, the USSR launched the first human-made satellite, Sputnik – meaning, literally, fellow wayfarer. The United States followed soon after with its 1 January 1958 launching of Explorer I.

The satellite age thus inaugurated, the 1960s witnessed enormous advancements in satellite sophistication. Soon satellites were no longer passive signal-bouncing mirrors doomed to float in elliptical orbits that restricted their utility to the times during which they appeared overhead. Instead, they were launched into geosynchronous orbits located in an arc approximately 22,300 miles above the earth, which enabled them to circle the earth at the same speed as the planet itself was rotating, thereby ensuring constant access to the satellites' services. In addition, satellites became active;

through transponders, they could receive and amplify signals before transmitting them back to earth, which served to increase signal strength.

Transmission

Television transmission via satellite occurs when a modulated TV signal, conveyed either over-the-air or by cable, is received by a satellite earth station – the *uplink* – which converts the signal's frequency from the VHF or UHF range to a vastly higher and more potent microwave frequency. Its frequency thus boosted, the signal is then powerfully amplified and beamed out at the appropriate satellite. The targeted satellite receives the signal within seconds, lowers its frequency slightly to avoid interference with the continuing flow of uplink messages, amplifies it, and then transmits it back to earth again from its downlink antennae.

The resulting satellite-transmitted signal spreads earthward in a roughly conical pattern, striking up to 40 percent of the earth's surface in what is called the satellite's *footprint*. The signal can now be received by any appropriately tuned earth station. The earth station captures the signal through a parabolic antenna – the *dish* – and focuses it through a feedhorn into an amplifier, in order to give it additional strength. Following amplification, the signal is converted from the extremely high carrier wave frequency to one that is comprehensible to conventional TV receivers, essentially reversing the uplink process. Once converted, the signal passes through the air or via cable to the receiver, where it is demodulated and transformed back into intelligible television images.

Earth Station Ownership

Initially, earth stations were used largely by cable companies like HBO wishing to cablecast premium channels or superstations like WTBS; the number of cable company-owned earth stations grew from 500 in 1977 to almost 5000 in 1982.[5] More recently, the broadcast networks have adopted satellite technology as the means by which they deliver their programming to affiliated stations, often sharing earth station construction costs with their affiliates. Earth stations can also be found in apartment and condominium complexes, hotels, and even bars through the development of SMATV.

In addition, an increasing number of individuals have built or purchased for their private use small home earth stations, which, depending on their size, power, and sophistication, are capable of capturing for viewing some or all of the unscrambled television signals transmitted by any satellite in the footprint where the home earth station happens to be located. Home satellite earth stations can be built or purchased for $1000 to $4000 and up, depending on the model.

The practice of home earth station reception of television signals has been vigorously opposed by the broadcast networks and the cable industry alike, however. The networks are vexed because the programming that they beam to affiliates is often unedited and not intended for reception in its raw form. For cable companies, these interceptions represent a significant threat to their financial solvency because those with home satellite dishes are able to pirate their signals, obtaining them without paying the monthly service charge assessed to cable subscribers for the same programming.

For their part, many home earth station owners – particularly those living in rural areas without access to either quality broadcast signals or cable – argue that the earth station merely enables them to obtain the same programming as that available to viewers who receive adequate signals or are served by cable companies. Indeed, they argue, many home earth station owners have attempted to pay cable programmers such as HBO for the programs they receive, only to be informed that the programmers can make such contracts only with cable companies.

However, despite aggressive opposition from the broadcasting and cable industries, home earth station reception of unscrambled signals was legalized in 1984 through an amendment to the Communications Act of 1934, the major piece of legislation that governs communications in the United States. In response, many premium programmers such as HBO moved quickly to scramble their signals with sophisticated and expensive encryption or encoding systems; such computer-based technology enables the programmers to change the code daily, if necessary, to prevent signal piracy. Thus, they can offer owners of home earth stations the opportunity to subscribe by paying a monthly fee of $12 to $14 per channel and by purchasing a decoder that deciphers the scrambled satellite signal for $300 to $400.

These decoders have also played a role in the development of the increasingly popular satellite PPV service. Like its counterpart in cable television, satellite PPV permits programmers to offer special, high-demand programs to home earth station subscribers who own the decoders. Subscribers simply notify the programmers that they wish to view the special program; the programmers then temporarily allow the appropriate decoders to decipher the special signal, after which the subscribers are automatically billed.

Specialized Satellite Services

A variation on home satellite reception, multipoint distribution service (MDS) has emerged to provide satellite programming to subscribers without home earth stations. MDS providers negotiate with premium cable programmers to receive their satellite transmissions and then rebroadcast them over the air through line-of-sight microwave relays to their subscribers, whose receivers have been modified to accept the microwave signals.

Signal transmission via direct broadcasting satellite (DBS) constitutes another variation. DBS seeks to provide multiple-channel satellite programming to households equipped with special, comparatively small rooftop dish antennae ranging from 18 to 36 inches in diameter. Because the satellite transponders used by DBS transmit at much higher power than do conventional satellites (70 watts or higher for DBS, as compared with only 4 or 5 watts for standard transponders), their signals can be detected by much smaller and less expensive dishes.

While DBS has attained considerable use in Europe and Japan, its development in the United States has been minimal, largely because of the high cable penetration rate and DBS's inability either to undercut the price of cable or to offer a greater selection of viewing options. Even though DBS could be an ideal way to reach homes in rural areas that have not been wired for cable (and are not likely to be), the fact is that many such homes already own home earth stations whose size and power are sufficient to access the same programming from standard-power satellite transponders.

Videoconferencing

A new industry born of the dynamic convergence of television technology and satellite signal transmission, videoconferencing enables large corporations and other organizations to communicate with branches or field offices via two-way audio and one- or two-way video links. Some corporations have made the significant financial investment of $120,000 and up required to install organizationwide videoconferencing facilities (which include video cameras, uplinks, earth stations, and monitors, as well as leased satellite transponder time and trained staff), with monthly operating costs averaging $12,000. Most companies, however, currently opt to rent the fully equipped videoconferencing facilities located at many major hotels, universities, and television stations if their videoconferencing needs are too infrequent to justify the installation of an in-house system.

Initially, the impetus for videoconferencing was largely to reduce travel costs associated with the many out-of-town meetings in which large, multistate, or multinational corporations are involved. Since its introduction and expansion, however, videoconferencing has been extended to the realm of teaching and training with the establishment of the National Technological University (NTU). Under the auspices of the Association for Media-Based Continuing Education for Engineering (AMCEE), NTU coordinates group instruction packages that enable working engineers to pursue graduate coursework through instructional television courses beamed directly via satellite to the videoconferencing facilities located in their workplace. Thus the students can have real-time interactive audio and video links with their instructors.

VIDEOTAPE

Although often considered synonymous with the development of television, videotape technology was not introduced until 1956, when the Ampex Corporation unveiled its videotape recorder (VTR), a black and white reel-to-reel system that used two-inch videotape. Despite its heft, bulk, and high cost, the VTR was swiftly and gratefully adopted by the television industry, which could at long last be liberated not only from the ephemeral, gaffe-prone transmissions that characterized early live television, but also from the costliness and time delays that were associated with the labor-intensive practice of recording television programs, especially news broadcasts, on film stock.

The next major advancement in videotape recording occurred in 1965 when Sony–the first of several Japanese electronics firms that would ultimately dominate video technology–announced its Portapak system, a black and white reel-to-reel VTR that combined a new scanning design with transistorized recording to achieve genuine portability. Throughout the 1960s and 1970s, videotape technology gained extensive acceptance in U.S. business and industry. In addition, refinements in video cameras, recording and editing equipment, and monitors, along with the development of color videotape, joined with rapidly declining prices to establish videotape as an attractive alternative to film for many applications.

Videocassette Recording

Introduced in 1972 by the Philips company and intended solely for home use, the videocassette recorder (VCR) allowed viewers to time shift television programming aired at inconvenient times by recording the desired TV shows off the air and replaying them at their leisure. The Philips VCR was followed in 1975 by the Sony Betamax and in 1976 by the JVC Video Home System (VHS). Although the three competing systems all used one-half-inch videotape, they were nonetheless incompatible due to differing cassette sizes and recording speeds. Eventually, the issue of incompatibility led to a long-fought, costly, and bitter rivalry among the systems; only in the 1980s did JVC's VHS model emerge the clear victor.

Currently, VCR penetration in the United States continues to grow, with 58.1 percent of all American households with televisions now owning VCRs.[6] One significant result of the rapid proliferation of VCRs was the swift development and expansion of the commercial home video industry, which produces prerecorded videocassettes–whose content ranges from high-demand feature films to foreign language instruction – and offers them to viewers for sale or rent.

The home-use camcorder, a combination video camera/VCR weighing as little as 3 1/2 lbs and priced under $1000, constitutes a relatively new variation on the VCR theme. By allowing viewers to make their own video recordings of family activities or special events, the camcorder increases the VCR's programming options, which are otherwise limited to taped broadcast, cable or satellite programming, and prerecorded videocassettes obtained through rental or purchase. In a sense, the camcorder adds a new dimension to the video experience by empowering viewers to create their own television programming.

Videotape Technology

Videotape, the central figure in video technology, consists of a long, thin strip of narrow, stretch-resistant plastic, one side of which is coated with minute, easily magnetized oxide particles and treated with an adhesive designed to cause the particles to cling to the plastic strip. Videotape width can vary from one-quarter inch to two inches, depending on its intended use (for example, television program production, surveillance, or home videos), and the tape itself can be wound on an open reel or encased in a hard plastic cassette.

The process of videotape recording begins when electrical signals generated by a video camera are received by a VTR or VCR by means of direct input jack, antenna, satellite dish, or coaxial cable connection. Once received, these signals are demodulated and reduced to their component parts: video and audio, plus a control signal designed to regulate the picture's stability and the tape's speed. They are then dispatched to the recorder's video and audio control heads, where they are transformed from electrical impulses into matching magnetic impulses. As the videotape slowly winds past the video and audio control heads, its coating of minute oxide particles suddenly becomes frozen into a pattern that is identical to the magnetic charge emitted from the newly transformed signals. During playback, as the tape's magnetically charged patterns wind past the video and audio control heads, they are detected by the heads and converted back into electrical signals. The resulting electrical signals are processed by the receiver or monitor, which then displays the videotaped images.

In terms of content, in theory at least, videotape technology's possibilities are infinite; its capacity to record the wealth of broadcast, cable, and satellite television programming and to play commercially prerecorded videocassettes as well as personally taped home videos enables viewers to attain a kind of self-determination in the face of the Information Age – or, more accurately, the Entertainment Age. In some respects, videotape has also served to demystify television by allowing viewers to capture and manipulate its transmissions, freeing them from the tyranny of the television time schedule and offering them the opportunity to replay programming at will, either for study or for the sheer pleasure of reviewing it in much the same way as one might reread a favorite book.

APPLICATIONS

With the introduction of videotape technology and the proliferation of signal delivery options, television's ability to serve as a credible information technology – a means by which information can be recorded, processed, disseminated, and stored – has achieved growing acknowledgment among those in the library and information profession, as well as those in the fields of journalism, communications, advertising, and public relations.

This acknowledgment has not been without reservations, however. Because of their traditional reliance upon print as the predominant form of information transmission, some library and information professionals have harbored a distrust of information packaged and conveyed via such nonprint media as film, television, and videotape.

Indeed, for decades, this same print bias served to fuel a bitter rivalry between the newspaper, magazine, and book publishing industries and the film, television, and videotape industries. The visual media were frequently assailed as intellectually inferior purveyors of popular culture, while the print media were characterized as humorless and snobbish guardians of the status quo who viewed TV and films with great disdain.

Journalism and Publishing

The field of journalism was perhaps the most obvious early adapter of television's capacity to package and communicate information. Literally from the first day of FCC-approved commercial TV broadcasts in 1941, television journalists have recognized and utilized – and occasionally exploited – the medium's ability to record and transmit the sounds and images of life in their efforts to report the news. Today, through the use of highly portable video cameras, VTRs, and editing decks, as well as mobile satellite uplink facilities, TV journalists on a local, national, and international level can collect, compile, and communicate their news stories with a flexibilty and timeliness that render earthly distance almost negligible.

Because of its massive penetration into the American household – and therefore into the American mind – television has become an integral part of the advertising and public relations industry. Through the efforts of market research firms to develop detailed audience profiles, advertisers and public relations specialists are increasingly able to channel their advertising energies toward those segments of the viewing audience that are most likely to be responsive to the product, service, or message in question. Indeed, until the introduction of the home-use VCR, television's linear nature–a function of the fact that its signals are delivered in a specific sequence that is unalterable save through the use of a VCR–ensured that advertisers obtained a more or less captive audience for their commercials.

More recently, however, viewers using videocassette recorders to time-shift TV programming have employed the VCR's fast-forward function to speed through–or "zap"–the commercials that interrupt (but also ultimately pay for) television programming. Although this trend has generated considerable dismay and frustration among television stations, advertisers, and advertising agencies, some media observers have noted that the level of viewer attention required to accurately zap through a series of commercials ensures that at least a portion of the advertisement's visual information, particularly graphics indicating products or services, is perceived by viewers as they speed through the commercial interruptions.[7]

Interestingly, the viewer zapping phenomenon has served to send a clear message to advertisers and their agencies that commercials in their present form are tedious at best and noisome at worse; as a result, a number of perceptive advertising agencies have responded with more creative and entertaining commercials. One example of advertisers' efforts to adapt to changing viewer tastes (or, more accurately, to viewers' increasing power to control what is viewed) is the infomercial, which strives to offer an entertaining and informative backdrop against which to make a commercial pitch. Infomercials, which generally run between 5 and 30 minutes, were pioneered by independent broadcast stations and cable channels, largely due to their much cheaper advertising fees.

A number of innovative publishers have also endeavored to look beyond the obvious differences between print and video in their effort to see the information content underlying both media. The video magazine, a videocassette "published" at regular intervals in a format that closely resembles its print counterpart, represents certain publishers' recognition of videotape's attractive content-packaging possibilities. Containing special features, regular departments, and other standard magazine fare, the video magazine format enables publishers to continue to provide their subscribers with informative, entertaining, and appealing content–publishing's established forte–while allowing that content to be delivered through a technology capable of liberating publishers and readers from the traditional limitations of print.

In addition to the video magazine, a wide variety of prerecorded videocassettes are being marketed by several new companies in much the same style as publishers market books. Although these companies do sell some feature-length films on video, their primary focus is nonfiction, with videos available in such categories as health and fitness, music, comedy, sports, nature and outdoor activities, how-to, and hobbies. In many cases, these videos are priced in the $10-$40 range, approximating the current cost of many hardbound books.

Libraries

Many library and information professionals have also proven to be enthusiastic adapters of videotape technology. In the early 1980s, the swift growth of the commercial home video industry prompted many public libraries in the United States to begin collecting and lending a wide array of entertainment, hobby, and educational videocassettes. Although controversial at first, library video collections quickly became commonplace. By 1986, nearly 70 percent of U.S. public libraries serving populations of 25,000 or more were lending videocassettes whose content ranged from full-length feature films to how-to and travel videos.[8] Although, in general, the content of library video collections tends to be somewhat more eclectic than that available at most commercial video rental stores, it is entertainment, and not education in the strictest sense, that continues to be the primary focus.

The widespread library implementation of video lending services underscores the emergence of a larger movement within the library and information profession to recognize, collect, access, and utilize information in all its forms, including print, film, audio- and videotape, computer files, compact and optical disc, online databases, and broadcast, cable and satellite television. In particular, this broader vision of information collection, access, and use has sparked a new spirit of cooperation between libraries and the television and video industries.

In one recent collaboration, the American Library Association joined with the Annenberg/CPB Project to develop a guide to *Voices and Visions,* a 13-hour PBS series designed to showcase American poets from Walt Whitman to Sylvia Plath. Together, the guide and the series strive to act as an incentive to interest readers and viewers alike in further exploring the richness of American poetry.

In another ongoing collaboration, the Library of Congress and the CBS television network have joined forces to integrate books and television programming through their *Read More About It* effort. In the project, the CBS network airs a 60- to 90-second spot announcement after the conclusion of a major network prime-time broadcast that has dealt with a dramatic topic such as AIDS, alcoholism, or mental illness. In the spot, a celebrity–usually one of the preceding program's featured performers–introduces several books recommended by the Library of Congress for further exploration of the topic and encourages viewers to visit their local library to "read more about it." The program also distributes the topical booklists to libraries shortly before the production is televised.

In addition to collecting and lending prerecorded videocassettes, a number of U.S. public libraries have experimented with operating their own cable television public access channels, offering library-produced programming, serving as an information center for upcoming community activities, and even providing on-air reference services in response to viewer telephone calls. Indeed, with the many options afforded by broadcast, cable, and satellite signal delivery, as well as those offered by videotape technology, libraries in the 1990s are uniquely poised to play the same key leadership role in the world of TV and videotape that they have played so well in the world of print and computer-based information. As more and more information is packaged in video form, viewers – or, more accurately, users – will increasingly require intellectual and physical access to that information, and library and information professionals, trained to analyze, evaluate, and organize information in all its forms, can ensure that access.

Education

In the broader context of communication, television and videotape are being utilized in a growing array of applications. Some applications are quite informal, as in the case of a Washington, D.C., law firm that subscribes to the Cable Satellite Public Affairs Networks (C-SPAN) television channel in order to acquaint its new attorneys with the legislative proceedings of the U.S. House of Representatives. Others, like the National Technological University program of satellite-delivered telecourses, involve a very formal structure. Still other applications fall somewhere in between, as when videotape is used to develop a battery of employee orientation and training materials.

In particular, schools from kindergarten to university level have proliferated uses for television and videotape. The medium's great appeal to the young has enabled teachers to lure reluctant readers into the world of the written word by integrating scripts from students' favorite TV shows into standard reading assignments, subtly reminding youngsters that much of human life – even the interesting parts – is based upon the written word. For those schools with videotape-recording equipment, off-air broadcasts can be taped and used to supplement teaching materials for the sciences, the humanities, and other subjects. Many schools have also acquired video cameras and have begun to train students in video production. In addition, an increasing number of schools, colleges, and universities are taking advantage of the cable television public access channel by transmitting their own locally produced programming.

The growing educational videocassette market has also served to provide additional options to teachers for the presentation of their subjects, while the swiftly decreasing cost of home-use camcorders has enabled some students to produce "video term papers." Satellite signal delivery of programs from distant places, combined with videotape technology, has also been employed as an aid to instruction – either by content (for example, propagandized news broadcasts to illustrate the implications of state-controlled media) or by the language in which the transmissions are presented (for example, in Spanish for students studying that language).

Continuing education in law, medicine, engineering, library science, computer science, and an array of other disciplines has also proven to be an area in which television and videotape technology can play an important role. Whether transmitted via satellite to videoconferencing facilities or packaged in prerecorded videocassettes, continuing education programs can be delivered to participants – individually or in groups – quickly, conveniently, and cheaply. The American Hospital Video Network, which beams medical news and continuing education programming for medical professionals to over 7,000 U.S. hospitals, represents a particularly innovative and successful use of TV and videotape technology to communicate information and educational material.

The potential applications of television and videotape technology throughout society are growing exponentially as new technologies are developed and integrated with older ones to form useful hybrids in a rapidly evolving information chain. The enormous utility afforded by television's visual and aural properties and its instantaneous transmissibility serves to extend and enhance the reach of human eyes and ears. In addition, videotape technology's capacity to record, process, display, and store vast amounts of video information will enable researchers years hence to gain a comprehensive and realistic view of our day-to-day life.

ADVANTAGES

In any attempt to assess the relative advantages of television and videotape in the broad context of modern information technology, one is immediately struck by the enormous, enduring, and fundamental appeal of the fully integrated visual and sound signals that compose the television and videotape image. Whether conveying fantasy-escape content, information-education content, or a combination of both, the video image engages our senses and captures our attention in a way that printed matter seldom can.

The capacity of television and videotape to simulate the action of the two most prominent of the human senses – seeing and hearing – in a manner that (often erroneously) implies immediacy and authenticity affords the two technologies an appeal largely denied to print-borne information. In addition, television, as a means of signal transmission, and videotape, as a recording medium, can deftly incorporate printed, photographed, and filmed materials as part of their visual transmissions, thus appropriating both the content and the character of other media into their own information repertoire.

Further, television constitutes a truly mass medium, whose airwave, cable, and satellite transmissions can reach an incredible 98 percent of American households, a penetration unrivaled by any other information technology. Indeed, because of its unique visual base, television can bypass even literacy as a basic prerequisite; thus, television can serve as a crucial information link to the illiterate.

Perhaps the most significant – and conspicuous – advantage of television and videotape, however, can be found in their capacity to collect, transmit, and preserve the wealth of information, raw and processed, that abounds in the ephemeral world of day-to-day (indeed minute-to-minute) human existence. In the short term, television and videotape serve as vital tools of instantaneous communication across small distances or vast ones; in the long term, they stand to create a kind of videotape quilt, composed both of fiction and fact, that will help future societies to understand and learn from our society's experiences through its legacy of videotaped "life" and other images.

In addition to performing independently as information technologies, television and videotape offer great promise as components of other information technologies. In particular, the integration of computer technology with information stored on videotape will yield, at long last, a unified incarnation of print and video images. Even on the low-technology side, videotape and television can be used in conjunction with printed materials in a tangible recognition of the useful symbiosis of the two formats.

DISADVANTAGES

The disadvantages to which commercial broadcast television has traditionally been heir stem largely from the influence of its funding structure upon the development of programming content. Because its level of advertising revenue is contingent upon high audience ratings, commercial broadcast television often seeks to draw those requisite large audiences by broadcasting programming high in such provocative content as sexual innuendo or violence. As an unfortunate result of this practice, many well-crafted programs that dramatize more sophisticated and complex plots and feature performers whose talents include qualities other than youth and physical beauty are dropped by network programmers seeking to deliver ever larger audiences to advertisers.

Curiously, although public television does occasionally air programming high in violent content – *I, Claudius, Medea* and *King Lear* being obvious examples – it has traditionally done so with a sense of propriety and social responsibility that has characteristically been absent in most commercial broadcast television. In many ways, public television has evolved into a kind of television public library, striving to provide content of genuine interest to a diversity of people while also attempting to place the act of information- and entertainment-seeking in the broader context of human social experience and fulfillment. Both PBS and the public library offer their respective publics what they say they want, and both hold as a kind of article of faith the idea – the hope – that most viewers, given the opportunity, will naturally want better programming, which both public television and public libraries also seek to provide.

Indeed, in some respects, through the rapid growth of cable, satellite, and videotape, viewers are discovering and clearly enjoying an array of diverse programming, which includes, in large part, information, entertainment, and educational material that is free of violence altogether. Increasingly, viewers are demonstrating that their interests defy easy prediction and that commercial television, in its ambitious and costly efforts to decipher audience viewing tastes, has spent too much time trying to learn what people are watching, and too little time trying to discern what people would like to watch, if it were available. The networks have simply overlooked the fact that, as television comes to be used more and more as an information technology, viewers will increasingly expect it to behave like one; they expect it to serve them, giving them the information, education, and entertainment they need and want when they need and want it – services that cable, satellite, and videotape technology can easily provide.

Cable Television

For cable television, the primary disadvantage comes not from its programming but from its means of transmission. The same interactive capacity that affords cable such attractiveness as a signal carrier also has the potential of compromising viewer privacy, since the information that cable companies regularly collect in their routine of service – premium channel selections, pay-per-view choices, home-shopping purchases, home security and fire alarm information, and home-banking transactions – could easily be misused if obtained by unauthorized parties.

A second disadvantage to cable television has recently emerged, ironically due in part to its phenomenal growth and success, as well as to the federal deregulation of the cable industry. Because cable companies are awarded franchises by the municipalities they wish to serve, they have, in effect, no competition once the franchise is granted. In addition, deregulation provides cable companies with what amounts to free rein in determining viewer subscription fees. Thus, absence of competition, the ability to charge whatever they wish, and widespread viewer appeal have combined to make cable companies very attractive corporate acquisition targets. A number of such acquisitions in major cable markets, often necessitating enormous debt on the part of the buyer, have resulted in sharp increases in subscriber fees – as much as 53 percent – largely to help finance the high cost of the acquisition. This unfortunate trend is of concern because such increases could eventually conspire to price cable television out of the reach of many low-income earners.[9]

Technical Problems

On the technical side, television and videotape have two inherent disadvantages: linear access and small screen size. Unlike the random access afforded by computers, compact disc players, and optical disc systems, the linear access aspect of videotape requires that the recorded images be read only in the order in which they were taped, from beginning to end. Thus, if viewers wish to locate particular image sequences whose video information is stored part way into the videocassette's wound tape supply, they must employ the play or fast-forward function in order to advance the tape supply to the location of the desired image sequences.

In terms of screen size, television monitors and receivers have rarely exceeded the 20- to 25-inch range, due to the screen resolution limitations imposed by the 525-line NTSC standard currently in use in the United States. Although big screen TV of 4- to 5-feet has been available in the consumer electronics market for a number of years, the unattractive graininess and poor definition of its images have served to restrict its appeal overall. Although, for most purposes, small screen sizes are more than adequate, the relative smallness of most TV screens has historically precluded or at least hindered classroom or other applications that require well-defined, big screen images like those available from 16 or 35 mm films.

Lack of Television Literacy

What is perhaps the greatest disadvantage of television and videotape, however, results neither from their content nor from their means of transmission. Instead, the primary disadvantage is the fact that our society has never learned how to use them to their best advantage.

In a culture that devotes great effort to the process of inculcating the intricacies of print-based literacy, it is ironic that we have ignored the teaching of the "grammar" of the video-based image, especially in the face of its nearly complete penetration of American society. Until relatively recently, many librarians, educators, print journalists, and social commentators, rather than studying and seeking to understand the language and culture of the video image so that they could in turn guide society in its optimal use for education, information, and entertainment, have simply turned their backs on television and its potential, preferring instead to laud the superiority of print. Even public television, although it did provide all the necessary programming links with formal and informal education, failed to provide sufficient guidance to viewers in how to select, understand, and best utilize television content for their own optimum benefit.

The growing information literacy movement within the library and education professions, which seeks to teach the skills of print literacy, computer literacy, and television literacy in the broader context of an overall critical evaluation of information in all its forms, represents a change to this mode of thinking. This new appreciation, we hope, will lead to a broader realization that each emerging information, entertainment, or education technology has its own unique language and culture. Each communicates with the human mind in ways that are neither better nor worse than the ways in which previous, more established technologies do; they are simply different, having different strengths and different weaknesses.

PROBLEMS OF INFORMATION ACCESS

Because videotape technology, by its very nature, enables its users to capture, retain, and display broadcast, cable, and satellite signals at will, many program producers, such as film studios, TV networks, and cable programmers, have articulated their deep concern regarding the implications of such uses in the context of U.S. copyright law. Indeed, one program producer, Universal Studios, filed suit against Sony Corporation of America, maker of the Betamax, in an effort to block the technology's introduction to the American consumer out of fear that home video recording of aired programming would ultimately damage the studio's profit-making potential. The Supreme Court, however, did not agree, and ruled in 1984 that VCR owners could indeed record commercial broadcast TV without copyright infringement, provided it was for home use only. Further clarifying the issue, Section 107 of Title 17 of the U.S. Code – the fair use clause – states in part that "the fair use of a copyrighted work, including such use by reproduction in copies or phonorecords or by any other means ... for purposes such as criticism, comment, news reporting, teaching (including multiple copies for classroom use), scholarship, or research, is not an infringement of copyright."[10]

Through the fair use clause, home viewers, in essence, are permitted to time shift programming as they see fit, as long as it is for their own private use and that use falls within the boundaries set forth in Section 107. *The Copyright Primer for Librarians and Educators*, by Mary Hutchings Reed, is an excellent introduction to the regulations that apply to the taping of copyrighted programming.[11]

Though copyright restrictions can prove vexatious to those wishing to use videotaped materials for a variety of purposes, it is helpful to remember that copyright exists to ensure that artists, writers, film- and videomakers, composers, and other creative personalities are rewarded for their efforts in a way that encourages them to continue their creativity. Without the protection and incentive to create that the principle of copyright affords, there would be little left to videotape.

The problem of gaining intellectual and physical access to material that has been transmitted via broadcast, cable, or satellite television constitutes one of the most significant impediments to the fruitful use of televised materials. In the world of print, readers gain access to information contained in books and periodicals by employing catalogs, indexes, and bibliographies that have been organized by subject, title, author, and other appropriate categories. If a local library does not hold the book or periodical required, readers can request that the library obtain the desired material through interlibrary loan. In this way, they are able to locate and borrow most published materials.

In the world of television, however, gaining access to the content of 50 years' worth of broadcast, cable, and satellite television transmissions is extremely difficult. In terms of intellectual access, the two principal comprehensive and encyclopedic works on TV programming are *Total Television* by Alex McNeil[12] and *The Complete Encyclopedia of Television Programs, 1947-1979* by Vincent Terrace.[13] The programs included in these works are indexed only by program title, featured performer or other person involved in the production, and, in *Total Television,* broad program category, such as "dramatic series." Only for such programs as national newscasts is the informational content of specific installments provided. Major sources include the *ABC News Index,*[14] the *CBS News Index,*[15] and the *Television News Index and Abstracts.*[16]

Obtaining physical access to videotapes or transcipts of individual program installments can be a challenge as well. Although Vanderbilt University's Television News Archive, which publishes the *Television News Index and Abstracts,* will duplicate either specific newscasts or overall news coverage of a topic, the cost to the requester can be prohibitive, even with a differential pricing structure that favors researchers or others from nonprofit educational institutions.

While many program producers, from large networks to small cable public access channel programmers, retain archival copies of their programming, many of them are reluctant to release transcripts or videotaped duplicates of their programs. A few video archives – most notably the American Television and Radio Archive at the Library of Congress – are available to researchers, but, for the average viewer, televised material not captured by the home VCR or available on commercial videocassette is very difficult to access.

Physical access to information stored on videotape can also be complicated by the fact that videotape itself is subject to deterioration. After approximately 100 uses, the magnetized oxide particles that contain all the video and audio information become less stable and begin to decay. Happily, one of the properties of videotape technology is ease of image transfer; the content can simply be transferred to a new tape when it becomes necessary.

ALTERNATIVE TECHNOLOGIES

In terms of accomplishing the goal of displaying moving visual images, there currently exist two primary alternatives to television and videotape: film and videodisc. Although technically a rival, film has played a vitally important role in the success of television and videotape by ensuring an almost endless supply of feature films and other programming that can be shown on television or transferred to videotape for commercial rental or sale. In addition, many television programs and made-for-TV movies are first shot on film and then transferred to videotape because of the resulting sharper and more attractive image. The primary disadvantage of film compared to videotape is the labor-intensive, costly, and time-consuming nature of shooting on film.

Introduced in 1978, videodisc technology fell into two categories: stylus-read and laser-read. Stylus-read videodiscs were grooved and functioned in much the same fashion as audio records; however, the hardware is no longer marketed in the United States. Laser-read videodiscs are grooveless and offer random access, enabling viewers to choose from an array of functions, which include image enhancement and frame manipulation. Unlike the VCR, the videodisc player is not able to record off air; this factor, more than any other, makes the videodisc a poor contender for home use in the face of the VCR's sophisticated recording and time-shifting capacity.

Interestingly, however, videodiscs have not faded away. They are being used successfully in education, business, and industry, as an alternative visual medium for everything from repair manuals and physics experiments to promotional advertisements. They record paintings, photographs, film clips, and endless combinations of sound, sight and motion, in either an analog or digital form as required by the application. Indeed, the 12-inch (300 mm) reflective optical videodisc marketed by Philips as LaserVision and used with computers has instigated a videodisc resurgence, especially in the context of Apple Computer's hypermedia software, which allows users to link concepts in textual, audio, and video format, thus integrating information from various sources in varying media. Hypermedia is discussed in more detail in relation to CD-ROM in chapter 7.

Optical videodiscs are read by shining a laser onto the surface of the disc and interpreting the variations in the light reflected back to the player. In an analog recording, the pattern of reflected light varies in direct relation to the material recorded. A digital recording uses a binary code of reflection or no reflection; a computer then translates it back into an analog pattern for playback. Digital recording is more expensive than analog recording, but unlike analog recordings, digital recordings can be manipulated by a computer as part of a hypermedia system.

A double-sided videodisc can store up to 108,000 still images or two hours of continuous play, depending on the technique used to rotate the disc during recording and play. There are two methods of disc rotation, and they produce significantly different output results.

Constant angular velocity (CAV) uses the same principle on which record players work: the disc spins at a constant speed, but the speed of the laser (or the stylus of a record player) through the track varies, depending on the position of the track on the disc. As the laser gets closer to the center of the disc, its speed through the track decreases as the rotations become shorter in length. The most significant result of using CAV is that it always takes the same amount of time for the laser to play one rotation of a track regardless of the track's length during that rotation. By storing one frame per rotation (up to 54,000 frames per side), it is possible to play a single rotation of track continuously to reproduce a still image on the screen.

With constant linear velocity (CLV) the speed of the disc varies in order to keep the speed of the laser through the track constant. CLV allows for more overall playing time than does CAV: 60 minutes per side, compared to 30 minutes per side. With CLV, however, single frame access is impossible because each rotation contains multiple frames. Videodiscs use CLV to store complete motion pictures, but CAV to store and retrieve many types of media in combination (sound, print, and motion video).

Videodisc can provide three different levels of interaction with the user, depending on the software and hardware. The first level is noninteractive use, where the user's control is limited to slow motion or freeze frame effects on a continuous playback of material. This level is most commonly seen in repeating demonstrations and commercially produced motion pictures for home viewing.

At the second level, the videodisc player is combined with an internal microprocessor that allows frame by frame random access of CAV-recorded videodiscs. This level of interactivity is most often applied to the storage and retrieval of still images. This type of storage has recently been applied to archival materials as an alternative to microfilm, and as a video catalog at the Library of Congress.

Third-level interaction between user and videodisc requires an external computer. The computer can combine the material on the videodisc with other data it has stored in its memory through the use of hypermedia. Hypermedia can link any digitally recorded item to any other digitally recorded item: text, data, graphics, still image, motion, and sound. This level of interaction makes the videodisc incredibly flexible and powerful.

Through the use of authoring systems, non-computer-trained people can program the interactive system to perform in virtually any desired fashion. For example, recorded sound can be compared with graphic representations of that sound, or different texts can be compared side by side. Complex simulations can be used for diverse training programs for pilots, physicists, doctors, or mechanics. Educational applications allow students to proceed at their own pace and to test their comprehension of the subject as they move along. Situations that are too rare, dangerous, or expensive for a normal classroom environment can be simulated again and again, much to the users' benefit.

A number of authors have described the development of the videodisc in relation to other optical disc technologies.[17] These other technologies – write once-read many (WORM), compact disc-read only memory (CD-ROM), compact disc-interactive (CD-I), and digital video interactive (DVI) – are discussed in chapters 6 and 7. They employ digital as opposed to the analog signals that are used in current television and videotape recording.

HIGH-DEFINITION TELEVISION

Now a common term in U.S. parlance, high-definition television (HDTV) has come to mean any of a half dozen or so proposed television systems that are currently competing to raise the present NTSC television transmission standard from 525 horizontal scanning lines to at least 1050, and the aspect ratio from 4:3 to at least 14:9.

Although still in the planning and prototype stages in the United States and Europe, HDTV in Japan – whose national public broadcasting service, Nippon Hoso Kyokai (NHK), has been researching HDTV since 1971 – is now underway, with limited broadcasting of HDTV programming via satellite to over 100 HDTV receivers installed in Japanese department stores, train stations, and other high foot-traffic locations.

At its core, HDTV (or advanced television, as it is sometimes called), in all its current and projected incarnations, seeks to provide a sharper, clearer, more colorful, and more intense television picture by at least doubling the amount of video information collected by the television camera and displayed by the receiver, by increasing the screen's aspect ratio to very nearly that of a motion picture, and by delivering sound that approximates compact disc quality. For its biggest sensory impact, however, HDTV needs to be viewed on 4- to 5-foot screens; otherwise, the viewer, at a normal viewing distance of seven screen heights from the set, would not perceive improvement in a 20-inch or smaller receiver.

Because of the vastly increased amount of video information required to construct the far more detailed HDTV picture and sound signals, a correspondingly large segment of the electromagnetic spectrum must be allocated in order for TV broadcasters to transmit the additional signal information. But therein lies the rub: the current FCC-mandated frequency allocation for broadcast TV is only 6 MHz per station, while HDTV of 1125 lines or more requires at least 8 MHz, one-third more than the present allocation. Thus, HDTV signals could not be received by the 200 million or so NTSC standard television sets now in use in the United States, nor could videotapes recorded in HDTV be read by existing VTRs or VCRs. However, even if the hardware were replaced at a rapid rate with HDTV equipment, the problem of the already crowded and nonexpandable electromagnetic spectrum would remain. The only option, increasing the current 6 MHz per station spectrum allocation to 8 MHz, would ultimately reduce the number of television stations allowed to broadcast.

Standards

In response to the dilemma, the FCC has issued a ruling that mandates that the HDTV system to be selected, which will set the new standards for signal transmission, must be compatible with existing NTSC television receivers. In essence, the ruling insists that current TV sets must be able to receive HDTV signals although not displaying them in high definition, of course, in the same way that black and white sets can receive color TV signals, while not displaying them in color. Thus, this FCC ruling echoes the spirit of its past rulings on UHF signal reception and the introduction of color television: that the airwaves belong to the people, and that even the much ballyhooed prospect of HDTV must give way to the more important goal of ensuring that millions of viewers do not become instantly disenfranchised when the HDTV revolution takes place and they cannot afford to buy a new $3000 HDTV set. For the present, the FCC plans to study, test, and compare the several competing systems; a decision on the winning system is not expected until 1992.

Of the handful of systems under consideration by the FCC, the three major contenders are Advanced Compatibility Television (ACTV) from the David Sarnoff Research Center; Spectrum-Compatibility HDTV designed by Zenith Electronics Corporation, the only remaining U.S.-owned TV manufacturer; and the original 1125-line HDTV system developed by NHK of Japan.

Currently the front runner, the ACTV system would be divided into two phases: ACTV-I and ACTV-II. ACTV-I would involve an initial move from the 525-line standard to 1050 lines. Called enhanced-definition television (EDTV), rather than full HDTV, this first phase would allow EDTV signals to be received on both NTSC and HDTV receivers, with the higher definition images apparent only on the HDTV set.

After several years – long enough for most people to have purchased new sets in the normal pattern of appliance replacement – ACTV-II would be implemented, with the full 1125-line screen or true HDTV, by broadcasting the additional video and audio information on a second channel. While such an arrangement would allow continued NTSC reception, the number of TV stations would need to be reduced as a result of the increased spectrum frequency required to broadcast on the second channel.

Spectrum-Compatibility HDTV would also require additional spectrum space. However, the system's designers have proposed the use of the "taboo" frequencies that separate broadcast channels, rather than annexing space currently used by other stations.

Although the Japanese NHK system was originally thought to be eliminated by the FCC ruling on NTSC compatibility because of its high spectrum allocation demands, NHK now has reportedly developed a means by which to deliver a less than full HDTV signal that is compatible with NTSC. Thus, for the moment, NHK remains in the running.

Potential Developments and Economic Issues

Innovative uses appear to be developing rapidly, which will have important economic consequences. Industry analysts have estimated that the long-term, worldwide HDTV market will create from $50 to $250 billion in economic activity, with up to $70 billion being spent by U.S. consumers.[18] The crystal clear images offer a wide range of military, educational, and medical applications, as well as entertainment.

For example, one of HDTV's great advantages is its ability to create spectacular special effects by seamlessly blending two pictures into one – a technique that does not work particularly well with normal TV cameras, yet is inexpensive to achieve with HDTV. Progress is also being made in transferring HDTV to film. New facilities for this process have opened in England, California, and New York, in addition to the one operating in Tokyo.

It is estimated that HDTV will eventually be anywhere from 12 to 25 percent cheaper than film and considerably faster to edit, saving up to 25 percent in studio and location time as well as postproduction time. Producers of commercials have predicted that filmed advertisements with lots of special effects may be able to save up to 50 percent in production time.[19]

Industry Response

HDTV technology relies heavily on sophisticated computer chips. Proponents argue that HDTV will be a "technology driver" to revitalize the U.S. electronics industry.[20] Others have expressed concern about the economic consequences of a de facto Japanese HDTV standard in the

United States, as Japanese electronics manufacturers stand ready to enter the American market with HDTV sets and VCRs, as well as the $3 to $8 million in equipment that will be required by each television station to convert to the HDTV transmission signal. As William Schreiber, director of the Massachusetts Institute of Technology's Advanced Television Program, observed recently, "HDTV isn't about beautiful pictures. It's about jobs and money. . . . If we create a new high-definition system in the U.S. and all of the equipment comes from overseas, we're going to get poorer, not richer."[21]

In response to such economic predictions, the Commerce Department, the Defense Department, and the U.S. electronics industry are considering the creation of an American HDTV consortium composed of key American electronics, telecommunications, and computer industry representatives and funded in part by the U.S. government. The purpose of the consortium would be to develop and manufacture American HDTV production, transmission, and reception technology and products.

Such a consortium would follow the lead of the pan-European electronics consortium, Project Eureka, which was founded in 1986. Through Project Eureka, European electronics manufacturers, universities, and broadcasters have joined together to research and develop economically strategic technologies to ensure that European interests are served in design and manufacturing. Toward that end, Project Eureka has recently established its own HDTV transmission system of 1250 scan lines and a rate of 25 frames per second. This standard is incompatible with the Japanese NHK system and with all of the proposed U.S. HDTV systems.

Cable, Satellite, and VCRs

For cable- and satellite-delivered television, the technological issues are somewhat less complex, since both cable and satellite transmission systems are sufficiently flexible to transmit the more detailed HDTV signals with relative ease. Unlike broadcast television, which must utilize the finite electromagnetic spectrum, cable and satellite TV systems are expandable, with negligible reduction in overall capacity. Thus, although cable and satellite TV providers would have to replace their production and transmission equipment for HDTV implementation, they are poised to introduce HDTV technology to their subscribers without the bureaucratic and regulatory complexities that currently vex broadcasters.

Similarly, HDTV VCRs will be able to record HDTV set-delivered programming, as well as play HDTV videos once they are commercially produced. Japanese firms, which will soon be marketing HDTV sets and VCRs in the United States, have already expressed interest in purchasing United Artists/MGM studios, for the eventual value their stock of films would provide in promoting HDTV and its related products. HDTV VCRs will not, however, be able to play current NTSC-standard videocassettes, a troublesome drawback when one realizes that millions of commercially prerecorded and home-recorded videos will become obsolete with the introduction and projected expansion of HDTV.

ISDN

From the proverbial left field, the telephone companies constitute a wildcard in the HDTV signal delivery debate. Although currently barred from entering the video transmission business, Bellcore, the research and development wing of the regional Bell Systems, has been experimenting with fiber-optic video signal transmission. Additionally, the ban on the Bell Systems' participation in transmitting–but not producing–video signals is reportedly being reconsidered.[22]

If the ban was rescinded, the telephone companies could easily challenge broadcast, cable, and satellite television transmission systems alike with the development of their integrated services digital network (ISDN), which was described in chapter 1. When fully implemented, ISDN will utilize fiber-optic technology to deliver voice, computer, and video data in digitized form. Because fiber optics are capable of carrying an enormous amount of signal information as a matter of course, the telephone companies could deliver HDTV signals directly to each home or office wired for phone service. In the meantime, however, such a prospect is decidedly visionary, since a regulatory ban on entry into the video transmission business is not the only impediment faced by Bell; the final cost of the full installation of the ISDN system in the United States is expected to exceed $400 billion.

Long-Term Considerations

In the midst of all the rhetoric that currently abounds in the debate over HDTV, two essential questions remain to be answered: whether there should be HDTV, and why there should be HDTV. It seems inevitable that the FCC will eventually select one of the competing HDTV standards as the new U.S. standard for television transmission; nonetheless, the proponents who so zealously seek the adoption of a new HDTV standard based on its technical sophistication are surprisingly silent regarding the substantive contribution HDTV would make to the life of the television viewer–the ultimate arbiter of the HDTV debate.

In truth, it appears that most HDTV proponents have simply taken widespread viewer enthusiasm as a given; after all, what TV viewer wouldn't spend $3000 on a new 4- or 5-foot HDTV set to view the vibrant, clear, and colorfully luminous picture and hear the crisp, "you-could-hear-a-pin-drop" compact-disc-quality sound that a move to HDTV would afford? The viewer's answer to that question, however, may very likely be, "It depends on the picture, and it depends on the sound."

In other words, it could well be the quality of HDTV programming, and not the technical beauty of the HDTV image, that proves to be the deciding factor in HDTV's success or failure. If HDTV promoters do not provide programming that meets the needs and wants of increasingly sophisticated and assertive viewers, the advantages afforded by HDTV's vastly improved screen resolution may largely be moot, and its possibilities as a credible information technology may be as circumscribed as those of current broadcast television.

With an insight into the current HDTV debate so incisive that it could have been written yesterday, Donald Fink and David Lutyens – in 1960 – observed, "There are many people who eye further development of TV with suspicion and regret, and who regard it as little more than a softener of the brain. Certainly, to use TV purely as a form of entertainment for killing time and masking a fundamental boredom with life would be a gross prostitution of the scientific skill and inventiveness which have produced this marvel. But there are many constructive uses of TV, and it is perhaps not unduly pompous to say that someday, when it becomes woven into a world-wide network of communication, TV may prove a decisive influence in helping different nations to understand and tolerate each other."[23]

Perhaps the most significant result of the current HDTV debate lies in the fact that it is providing a forum in which we as a society can begin to reexamine what the medium of television is, and what it could be. If HDTV can be used to meet the genuine needs and wants of its viewers for entertainment, information, and education through the provision of Fink and Lutyens's "constructive uses," it will have earned its place in American society.

NOTES

1. Erik Barnouw, *The Tube of Plenty,* rev. ed. (Oxford and New York: Oxford University Press, 1982), 148.

2. Bureau of the Census, *Statistical Abstracts of the United States, 1989,* 109th ed. (Washington, 1989), 544.

3. Marie Winn, *The Plug-In Drug* (New York: Viking Press, 1977).

4. Bureau of the Census, *Statistical Abstracts,* 544.

5. Ralph Negrine, ed., *Satellite Broadcasting: The Politics and Implications of the New Media* (London and New York: Routledge, 1988), 7.

6. Bureau of the Census, *Statistical Abstracts,* 544.

7. Mark R. Levy and Barrie Gunter, *Home Video and the Changing Nature of the Television Audience* (London: John Libbey, 1988), 73.

8. Office for Research, American Library Asociation, *ALA Survey of Public Library Services: A Summary Report* (Chicago: American Library Association, 1987), 2.

9. Geraldine Fabrikant, "In Free Rein of Cable TV, Fees Are Up," *New York Times*, 11 December 1988, 1.

10. United States Code, title 17, section 107, Limitations on Exclusive Rights, Fair Use, 1988 ed., printed 3 January 1989, 30-34.

11. Mary Hutchings Reed, *The Copyright Primer for Librarians and Educators* (Chicago: American Library Association; Washington, D.C.: National Education Association, 1987).

12. Alex McNeil, *Total Television: A Comprehensive Guide to Programming from 1948 to the Present*, 2d ed. (New York: Penguin Books, 1984).

13. Vincent Terrace, *The Complete Encyclopedia of Television Programs, 1947-1979*, 2d ed., rev. (South Brunswick, N.J.: A.S. Barnes, 1979).

14. *ABC News Index* (Woodbridge, Conn.: Research Publications, 1986–).

15. *CBS News Index* (Glen Rock, N.J.: Microfilming Corp. of America, 1975–).

16. Vanderbilt Television News Archive, *Television News Index and Abstracts* (Nashville, Tenn.: Vanderbilt Television News Archive, 1972–).

17. These include the following:
Crawford, Walt. *Current Technologies in the Library: An Informal Overview* (Boston, Mass.: G.K. Hall, 1988).
Forrest, Charles. "Technological Convergence: A Brief Review of Some of the Developments in the Integrated Storage and Retrieval of Text, Data, Sound and Image." *TechTrends* 33 (November-December 1988): 8-12.
Hessler, David. "Interactive Optical Disc Systems: Part 1: Analog Storage." *Library Hi Tech* 8 (Winter 1984): 25-32.
Rivott, Mike. "Videodiscs and Digital Optical Discs." *Journal of Information Science* 13, no. 1 (1987): 25-34.

18. National Association of Public Television Stations, *Washington Update*, 28 December 1988, 2.

19. Bernice Kanner, "On Madison Avenue–I want my HDTV," *New York,* September 1989, 28-32.

20. "Antiquated Policies Threaten High Technology, Study Says," *Seattle Times,* 20 November 1989, p.F11

21. Mark Levine, "You Are What You Scan," *American Way,* 1 January 1989, 25.

22. Calvin Sims, "F.C.C. Weighs Shift So Phone Companies Can Offer Cable TV," *New York Times,* 21 July 1988, p.A1.

23. Donald G. Fink and David M. Lutyens, *The Physics of Television* (Garden City, N.Y.: Anchor Books, 1960), 152-53.

▪ 5 ▪

Teletext and Videotex

Nancy D. Lane

Teletext and videotex, two technologies that bring up-to-date textual and graphic information to home television sets, have created greater interest in Europe, the industrially advanced countries of Asia, and Australia than in the United States. Nonetheless, a succession of pilot programs and business investments in the United States continues, despite the lack of a major consumer market.

Both technologies were lauded when first established in the mid-1970s to early 1980s. Numerous books were written that described their operation and potential.[1] Commentators made rosy predictions about their acceptance and penetration. For example, John O'Connor, the *New York Times* television critic, commented that by 1990 teletext would have become an integral part of the television experience.[2] The developers of an experimental videotex service in Ohio also predicted that by 1990 the distribution of electronic information would have become a common consumer service, generating $10 billion per year in revenue.[3]

These predictions and many others have not come to pass. French Teletel is the only national public videotex system that has truly taken off; other public systems operated by national telecommunications authorities such as Britain's Prestel continue their slow growth or have reached a plateau. Nonetheless, there are numerous videotex success stories on a much more limited scale – in particular, corporate in-house systems serving staff, affiliates, or customers, and private or government-backed public systems catering for strong vertical markets such as finance or agriculture.

TELETEXT TECHNOLOGY

Teletext is the transmission of textual and graphic information, either broadcast over the air waves or carried by coaxial cable, for reception on home television sets. Such information is transmitted in the same way as television images are, without interfering with normal reception. In fact, the frames or pages (in effect, "screensful") of information are transmitted in the section of the signal that does not normally appear on the screen.

Regular television transmission uses analog techniques, in which an electronic representation of the picture is created by a camera, converted to radio frequency for transmission, and reconstructed by the receiver using interlaced scanning for display on the screen, as described in chapter 4. The digital teletext information is inserted, or multiplexed, into the vertical blanking interval (VBI), the unused portion of the analog television signal.

In the United States, a television image comprises 525 scan lines, of which 483 to 499 may be viewable, depending on the television set. In Europe, an image comprises 625 scan lines, of which 563 to 587 may be viewable. The VBI comprises the scan lines that are not being used for the television picture field and occurs when the electron gun that creates the image moves from the bottom of one screen to the top of the next.

Some of the scan lines in the VBI are already devoted to other functions, such as vertical synchronization pulses and test signals. Although the number of scan lines available and the amount of data that can be transmitted per line are limited, teletext works because the textual and graphic information can be transmitted very quickly, in short bursts. For example, on the British 625-scan line television system, the data transmission rate is nearly 7 Mbps (megabits per second). Data is transmitted in bursts of 0.0001 of a second, 50 times per second.

Retrieval

A special decoder must be incorporated into or added to a television set in order to read the digital information transmitted and to convert it into its graphic form on the television screen. Decoders are required for videotex as well and are described in greater detail later in the chapter. As a full frame cannot be transmitted at once, the decoder stores portions of the frame until it is complete, then displays it. Approximately four complete frames of teletext can be transmitted per second.

Teletext is menu-driven, so the procedure for requesting a frame of information is very simple. Viewers use a keypad to switch back and forth from normal programming and to select the information they want from the teletext service. When a viewer first accesses the system with the keypad, a menu frame appears, listing the options from which to choose. The option is selected by number, leading either to another menu, which breaks that option down into more detailed options, or to the information itself. This type of hierarchical or branching structure is used for retrieval by videotex as well and is explained more fully later in the chapter.

A television station transmits its teletext frames in a continuous cycle. It takes 22 to 25 seconds to send about 100 frames. When a viewer selects a frame, it is "grabbed" from the cycle by the decoder and then saved on the screen for as long as the viewer wishes.

Thus, retrieval time can become lengthy with more than 100 or so frames – up to about 20 seconds. This time is reduced by the repetition of the most popular frames, such as the menus, weather, and sports scores, several times during each cycle. Other techniques to reduce retrieval time include the automatic linking of frames for local storage, and various forms of data compression.

Content and Services

Teletext services typically comprise from 100 to 400 frames of information, including the menus from which the specific information frames can be selected. These frames are called a *magazine* and supply information relevant to a particular local or regional viewing community: news headlines, weather forecasts, forthcoming events, restaurant and hotel guides, airline arrivals and departures, and so on. Television stations linked into network arrangements can insert their own frames into nationally distributed magazines.

Other teletext services include captions for the hearing-impaired or subtitles for foreign language programs, which are superimposed over the normal programming. Teletext handles closed captioning and subtitling easily from a technical viewpoint. The difficulty lies with converting speech to print in real time.

Other services that may be offered include a newsflash facility, which allows viewers the option of choosing to see teletext newsflashes cut into the normal programming as they are transmitted; continuous scrolling of information such as news headlines either up or across the screen; and telesoftware, the broadcasting of computer programs and data to television sets equipped with a microprocessor, or to personal computers (PCs) with a teletext decoder.

Teletext has continued to develop along several lines. Teletext enhancements include fine-line graphics and full-color, photographic-quality pictures. Digital information such as stock market updates is being multiplexed into FM radio, as well as television signals. Feedback channels can be provided so that viewers can send opinions or instructions using a touch-tone telephone number pad. Teletext on cable television can also be equipped for interactive feedback. Finally, security codes can be added to teletext frames so that only selected television sets can receive them; this is of potential value to groups such as doctors or the police.

DEVELOPMENT OF TELETEXT

Teletext originated in the United Kingdom. In 1972 the British Broadcasting Corporation (BBC), in conjunction with representatives from the independent television stations (ITV) and the semiconductor and television manufacturing industries, established a committee to develop standards for teletext. These were first published in 1974 and revised in 1976. The specifications established the format for the teletext frame (24 rows by 40 characters per row), as well as coding techniques and data transmission rates.

During 1973 and 1974, the BBC began its trial CEEFAX service (the name is reputed to have emerged as a cross between *BBC* and *see facts*), while ITV began its ORACLE service (standing for Optional Reception of Announcements by Coded Line Electronics). CEEFAX became fully operational in 1976.

The early pattern of teletext use in Britain varied markedly from the use of television as an entertainment medium. Although studies showed that typical teletext use averaged about two hours per week, it was made up of several short viewing sessions lasting one to ten minutes, comprising four to five frames at a time. The bulk of the viewing was carried out in the early evening. The most popular services based on initial surveys were news, sports, games and puzzles, financial information, weather, and travel news.

The French teletext system uses the same packet structure for transmitting digital information whether it is broadcast within a television signal or sent over a cable or a telephone line. It was designed by the Centre Commun d'Etudes de Télévision et de Télécommunications (CCETT), which had also been given the task of designing the packet-switched network.

The French system uses a display coding scheme called ANTIOPE (Acquisition Numérique et Télévisualisation d'Images Organisées en Pages d'Ecriture). It offers improvements to the British system in its single packet structure and its ability to display different colors. However, it also requires a more complex decoder.

The initial teletext service, which began in 1977, was aimed at the financial community. Called ANTIOPE-Bourse (stock exchange), it provides reports on over 2000 stocks to brokers and money managers. Rather than using the VBI on an existing television channel, it has its own channel so that many more scan lines are available for carrying signals. Such an operation can ultimately carry between 5000 and 10,000 pages of broadcast teletext with reasonable average waiting periods in the paging cycle.

The first teletext system in Japan was developed under the direction of Nippon Hoso Kyokai (NHK), the Japanese national broadcasting corporation. By 1971, the Japanese were developing a television set that would receive both teletext and videotex. The first experimental broadcasts began in 1978.

The Japanese faced the technical problem of designing a teletext system that could display as many as 3000 to 4000 different characters in their Kanji, Hiragana, and Katakana character sets. Thus, instead of building character generators into their decoders as do the English and French, the Japanese employ bit-mapping—that is, they treat the television screen as a matrix of dots and describe digitally the pattern of dots that creates the required characters. Although this system permits fine-line graphics in addition to characters, the memory required to hold the patterns of dots is 50 times that required of the British teletext decoders. These alternative methods of creating graphics on screen are also applicable to videotex and are described in more detail later in the chapter.

The Canadian teletext system, Telidon (from the Greek *tele*, meaning far away, and *idon*, meaning I saw), is an offshoot of the Canadian videotex system of the same name. Telidon trials began in 1980. The Canadian Broadcasting Corporation provides separate teletext magazines in French and English, which are distributed nationally by satellite.

Several local television stations throughout Australia broadcast teletext. Most were initiated in the early 1980s, but it has taken several years to build up a consumer market. The Brisbane, Queensland, station BTQ7 may have the distinction of being the first commercial service to make a profit on teletext. Brief advertisements appear on most of their pages, and in the early 1980s it was already reported that advertising revenue was exceeding their cost of operation.[4]

In the United States, the first wide-scale simulation of teletext was Chicago's Channel 32 "Night Owl" service in 1981. Later Time, Inc., experimented with a cable channel devoted entirely to teletext, then canceled the project. Another experiment, KeyFax National Teletext Magazine, was broadcast by cable station WTBS. The subscription price of $20 a month for decoder and access may have contributed to its lack of success. Experience elsewhere has shown that viewers are more likely to use the service if there is no access charge, with profits to broadcasters coming from information frames paid for by advertisers.

VIDEOTEX TECHNOLOGY

To the casual user, videotex may seem very similar to teletext. Using a keypad, viewers select textual and graphic information supplied by a remote computer to display on a television screen or a PC. However, there are major differences. With videotex the signal is usually received by telephone line rather than by broadcast signal or coaxial cable; the information service is two-way, or interactive; and the number of frames that can be selected is much greater—up to several hundred thousand.

The largest videotex services are set up as national public systems, such as those in Great Britain, France, and Australia. In such systems, the government telecommunications authorities (sometimes referred to as PTTs, originally an acronym for post, telephone, and telegram) manage the distribution function. They provide the telecommunications network and the central computer facility, as well as the public menus that bring together data from all the information providers. They also sign on new subscribers, send accounts, and, in some countries, provide additional services such as supplying training for information providers or publishing printed indexes for subscribers.

Closed user groups (CUGs) can be designated within public videotex networks. This allows only specified persons to view certain information frames. Such CUGs are of potential interest to private companies and industry associations such as banks, travel agents, doctors, and stock brokers.

There are a number of charges that telecommunications authorities may impose for videotex use. There may be a monthly or annual subscription fee; the charge for a long distance or local phone call every time the system is accessed; and a connect-time charge per minute, which may vary depending on the time of day and the day of the week that the system is being used. There may also be a small charge per frame levied by some information providers. Frame charges are normally not levied on menu frames.

There are also numerous private videotex systems, even in countries with national public systems. Some of these private systems are run exclusively for company staff or members of industry associations, while others are available to any interested individuals willing to purchase the necessary equipment and pay the ongoing subscription fees. For example, in Australia the Aftel system was set up originally as a service available only to travel agents, while Elderlink, which provides more than 150,000 pages of commodities reports, agricultural information, and farm management techniques, is available at reasonable cost to any interested subscribers.

Types of Services

The main types of services usually offered on public videotex systems include the following:

1. *Information call-up.* Information offered on videotex is organized into databases, which are separate computer information files. Such databases cover news and current affairs headlines; current rates for banks and stockbrokers; rural and agricultural information; educational, health, and medical information; government, public interest, and consumer affairs; tourism, travel, and accommodation; local entertainment; airline, bus, and train

timetables; sports scores and background statistics; and classified advertising.

2. *Telephone directory service.* Provision of a directory service was the reason for initiating the French videotex system. Inexpensive terminals are provided free to French households to replace the printed telephone directory. This system is described in more detail later in the chapter.

3. *Messaging.* Subscribers can send messages to the mailboxes of other subscribers, to be accessed as soon as they sign on. Messages are usually charged at a per-frame rate, and some services offer preformatted "greeting cards" sent on the screen.

4. *Transactions.* Shopping, banking, and other transactions can be carried out online. Items such as wine or small appliances can be purchased by billing to a credit card. Transferring of funds between accounts, checking on account balances, paying bills, and so on can also be accommodated by telebanking. Some of these transactions are handled by using the terminal as a gateway to the computer controlled by the service provider.

5. *Response frames.* Messaging and transactions are sometimes facilitated through the use of response frames. These are preaddressed to service providers and require selection of items or services in a way similar to using a menu. Users of response frames may also need to fill in credit card information for billing or home and business addresses for delivery of items purchased.

6. *Gateways.* Access to third-party computers for a range of activities is carried out through gateways. The videotex system provides the protocols to "tap in" to the external computer system. Banking, airline, and travel booking, as well as access to online information retrieval, can be accommodated through gateways.

7. *Telesoftware.* Telesoftware permits the downloading of programs from information providers through the central videotex computer into the memory of a subscriber's PC. These telesoftware programs can then be executed or stored on disk.

8. *Telemonitoring.* Telemonitoring is the remote surveillance of a home or business in order to detect fire or break-ins immediately and send an alarm, or to minimize energy output by controlling lighting, heating, and air-conditioning. Videotex can also be used as a medical alerting service by the ill or elderly.

9.   *Games and personal services.* These are perhaps the most controversial area of videotex services. Computer games are usually charged by the frame, and some parents have discovered to their regret that their children could rack up very high bills in a very short time. Personal services can range from the quite legitimate introduction and dating services to the not quite so legitimate "escort" and pornographic message services. Indeed, the French messaging service has been dubbed "the electronic singles bar." Personal services constitute a large percentage of use, particularly of the French videotex system.

Information Providers

The information on national public videotex systems is supplied by independent information or service providers, which include private corporations such as banks or stockbroking firms, airlines, educational institutions, professional associations, government departments, and companies set up specifically for supplying games or shopping facilities on videotex. These information providers supply and edit their own information, and update it as often as necessary. For example, news and stock market reports may be updated almost continuously, while other types of information may be changed only when it has lost its novelty or currency for subscribers.

   In addition to full-service information providers, there are also umbrella information providers. These are database providers who sublet frames of their databases to other individuals or organizations for a fee. The umbrella service is responsible for the design and maintenance of the sublet database. This is an ideal arrangement for professional associations, educational institutions, or other groups who want to make information available on videotex without having the responsibility for creating and maintaining a complete database.

   Each information provider supplies information in a separate database. It is important to realize that sometimes similar types of information may be provided by more than one information provider. For example, in some systems, each airline may have its own database of timetables, so that users may need to check several databases to get the necessary details for an extended trip.

Structure

Videotex databases are set up using a hierarchical or branching structure, which is built on a number of levels. Each level is essentially a further breakdown or specialization of the one above it. Access between the levels is by selection of numeric choices. An example of a simplified community services database is shown in Figure 5.1. Some of the frames are used for setting up menus that help guide users through the database. In this example, these are at levels 1 and 2. Other pages are used for holding the information users are trying to reach. In this example, these are at level 3.

Figure 5.1. Community Services Database

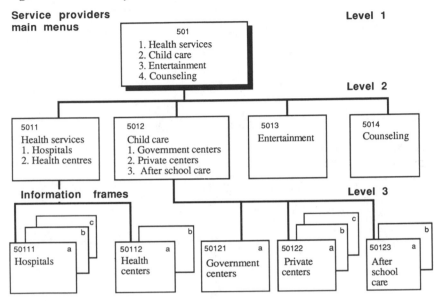

Using a videotex system is essentially the same as using teletext. The system is menu-driven, so that users continue to make a choice from each menu screen, each screen becoming more specific in focus, until they reach the topic they are seeking. A sample of two menu pages similar to those which appear on the Australian Viatel system are shown in Figure 5.2. However, because videotex has much more information than teletext, users may have to make many more choices to get to the information they want. Furthermore, because the information providers each create their own menus within their databases, the access terms may differ from database to database.

In addition to menu-driven topical branching, most systems also provide alphabetical indexes online. Access to these indexes is also menu-driven. Users select the appropriate initial letter of the alphabet on their first frame, and combinations of letters starting with that initial letter on subsequent frames, until they reach the index term they are after. The frame number where the information is located is shown following the index term.

Ideally, information providers should offer menu choices that are unambiguous, complete, and mutually exclusive. The textual information

Figure 5.2. Sample of Menu Frames Similar to the Australian Videotex System (Viatel)

VIATEL MAIN INDEX
---

1. BUSINESS & FINANCE News, Banking, Stocks, Professions, Agriculture

2. TRAVEL, TOURISM & TRANSPORT Tours, Holidays, Airlines, Accommodation

3. MAGAZINE News, Amusements, Advice, Entertainment, Food & Drink, Viatel Advertiser

5. MICROCOMPUTING Downline loading of telesoftware

6. MAILBOX, TELEX & TELESERVICES Electronic Mail, Shopping, Booking, Orders, Banking

7. ALPHABETIC INDEXES Subjects & SPs

8. HOW TO USE VIATEL

9. NEWS HEADLINE BAE estimates cost of EEC to Aust.agric – 5@5c

---
BUSINESS AND FINANCE
---

1. BUSINESS NEWS Financial, Economic Specialist News, Current Affairs

2. BANKING AND FINANCIAL SERVICES Loans, Savings, Investments

3. STOCK MARKETS Stocks, Commodities, Futures, Overseas Shares, Indices

4. AGRICULTURE News, Prices, Finance, Commodities, Extension, Machinery

5. FINANCIAL & ECONOMIC INFORMATION Statistics, Interest Rates, Trade

6. PROFESSIONS & ORGANIZATIONS For the professions and business community

7. GOVERNMENT INFORMATION For business

8. MONEY WATCH Stock prices, broking. Company reports & statistics

frames should contain no more than about 100 words, avoiding unnecessary abbreviations and using symbols that can be easily understood. In the best-designed frames, the number of colors is restricted to three for ease of reading, with lighter colors providing greater clarity.

The means of directing users from one page in a database to another is known as *routing*. Routing information is usually shown at the bottom of the screen, and usually three or four options are given. These may include moving to other pages in the database that may be of related interest; returning to the previous lower-level menu, the main information provider menu, or the main public videotex menu; or quitting.

Equipment

The equipment required for videotex is more expensive than for teletext, but then, the amount of information and the interactive services available are far greater. Most users will already own a telephone and a television set. This set must be adapted to communicate with videotex using an electronic interface or decoder, which normally contains the following components:

1. Linc isolator, which protects the telephone network from high voltages present in the television

2. Auto-dialer, for dialing the host computer and identifying the calling terminal automatically

3. Modem, which converts the analog telephone signal to a digital signal, and vice versa

4. Memory, which stores data for display. The size of memory will depend on the type of display (character generator or bit-mapped) and the number of frames to be stored simultaneously

5. Processing logic, which interprets the incoming signals and constructs the appropriate memory store

6. Input device, which permits a user to interact with the system. For a basic terminal, this is a numeric keypad, which can also serve as a TV controller. Other terminals require a full alphanumeric input device, such as a keyboard.

Teletext and videotex decoders have the last three elements in common. In addition, teletext decoders incorporate a frame-grabber. The decoder components can be packaged separately or together as a single unit and can be attached either inside or outside of the television set. Integral modems tend to be designed solely for videotex, whereas external modems can also be used for other telecommunications functions.

Unfortunately, none but the top-of-the-range decoders can store or download information, and their capacity is very limited. Nor does the television console itself have a memory as a computer does. However, printers can be attached to the converted TV set so that information can be printed out.

Other options for interacting with videotex include videotex terminals, computer phones, and PCs. Videotex terminals are dedicated to videotex system use only. No other equipment is needed as the necessary modem and software are built into the set. The advantage of videotex terminals is that they have built-in memory facilities and so downloading and storage of information are possible. They also have good picture resolution and are aesthetically compact units. Manufacturers include Sony and Philips. Most computer phones also contain the necessary modem and software to receive videotex.

In order to turn a PC into a videotex terminal, however, users must purchase a modem and appropriate software. Basically the software is required for three purposes: to access the videotex system through direct dial or auto-dial; to convert the videotex signals to those that can be interpreted by the PC and activate the PC monitor so the message can be displayed; and to regulate the transmission speed. Table 5.1 outlines the features that should be considered when selecting videotex software.

Table 5.1. Features to Consider in Purchasing Software for Connecting PCs to Videotex

Visual display features
Ability to download information to store on disk
Ability to download telesoftware programs
Ability to play back stored information
Ability to transmit stored information to a word processor
Capability to filter out certain colors, if the word processor is unable to cope with graphics
Auto-dial, if an auto-dial modem has been purchased
Save files
Input files
Speed regulator

Many PCs have color graphics built in as a standard equipment component. However, for PCs without this capacity, a color graphics card that allows the PC to receive and interpret such signals may have to be purchased. Instructions are always transmitted for color terminals, although videotex can be received on a monochrome monitor. Simple videotex systems permit characters to be displayed in eight different colors. These correspond to color television's three electron guns – red, blue, and green – being on or off in any combination.

Screen Displays

As indicated earlier in the section on teletext, there are different standards and methods used for constructing screen displays from the coded signals. In Europe, the European Conference for Posts and Telecommunication (CEPT) unified the British and French standards; while in North America, the Canadian and United States standards associations approved the North American Presentation Level Protocol Syntax (NAPLPS). These standards continue to be updated as the technologies advance.

Character Generation

Character generation, used by the British Prestel and the French Teletel systems, creates the least sophisticated level of graphics, but in turn, requires the least expensive receiving terminals. In character generator displays, each character is constructed in a fixed-size character rectangle made up of a number of dots. There are normally 40 characters per row, with 20, 24, or 25 rows per frame, depending on the standard being used.

Characters may include alphanumerics (conventional computerized character sets, including punctuation marks) or block graphics. The block graphics comprise three rows of two squares; each square may be colored or not, resulting in 64 possible block graphics characters. Low-resolution screen graphics are built up from these block graphic characters, creating a mosaic image. Hence, this type of display is also referred to as *alpha-mosaic.*

The rows are formed by contiguous character rectangles; adjacent rows are also contiguous. Thus, spacing between letters and rows is incorporated as part of the character rectangle. In addition to the use of color, a number of techniques can be used to make the frames easier to read and more interesting visually. For example, alphanumeric characters can be doubled in height; individual character rectangles can be made to flash on and off at a regular frequency; and a succession of screen images can be linked to give the impression of animation.

The shape of each possible character rectangle is permanently stored in read-only memory (ROM) in the receiving terminal. Instructions specifying what is to be displayed on a frame are transmitted as a series of numbers, each corresponding to a unique character shape. These are stored in random access memory (RAM). When all the instructions needed to create a frame have been received, the data stored in RAM are used as an index to access the equivalent character shapes stored in ROM in order to construct the screen image.

Developed by the Canadian Telidon system, Picture Description Instructions (PDIs) are another method used for the construction of screen images. Instead of a mosaic of small squares, a range of graphic elements is available: points, lines, arcs, polygons, and rectangles. As these codes are essentially geometric, this approach is also known as *alpha-geometric*. PDI provides greater image detail, but also requires greater complexity in the circuitry of the television receiver than does alpha-mosaic.

Bit-Mapping

There is also a finer resolution, photographic level of screen display available on various systems, created by a method called *bit-mapping*. In systems using bit-mapping, the terminals are more expensive because they require more memory for storage, but they are highly flexible in what they can display.

A television image is composed of thousands of dots called *picture elements* or *pixels*. A normal U.S. television set can resolve about 240 by 320 pixels. Such an image can also be bit-mapped, that is, described digitally by computer.

The Canadian Telidon system, for example, uses four bits to describe each pixel, including the color of the dot and other characteristics. Telidon terminals interpret instructions and display data to whatever degree of resolution has been incorporated into the design of the terminal. For example, on terminals capable of displaying up to 960-by-1280 pixels, a very high quality image is created; on typical home television receivers, the image is slightly courser than the regular television image.

The British photographic quality screen display is called PhotoVideotex. It complements the alpha-mosaic screen display such that the two can be combined on one screen. For example, a picture and text may be displayed as two layers, with the text beside or superimposed onto the picture. Where a terminal is not capable of presenting the photographic data, the host transmits only the text layer.

In the Japanese CAPTAIN system, the screen image comprises an array of dots: 240 columns by 192 rows. This relatively high-resolution picture requires an increased data transmission rate of up to 4800 bits per second (bps). This compares to the norm of the host transmitting at 1200 bps and terminals responding at 75 bps.

DEVELOPMENT OF VIDEOTEX

The first public videotex system, Prestel, was developed by British Telecom in the early 1970s. It was originally known as viewdata. The Prestel pilot trial began in 1976, and full service began in late 1979. Acceptance and use of the service by the viewing public was not nearly as rapid as had been projected. The contributing factors included high equipment and access costs, poor marketing, and inadequate initial databases. Nonetheless, Prestel has been the stimulus for much of the videotex development throughout the rest of the world, as the British have marketed their videotex technology widely.

Many Prestel users are joining the system not for information call-up, but for services such as telebanking, electronic shopping, and electronic mail. Whereas in 1982 home users accounted for 14 percent of Prestel terminals, by 1986 they accounted for 45 percent. By 1986, gateways were used in 25 percent of Prestel accesses and were expected to have risen to 40 percent by 1990. The major information providers and subinformation providers include the travel sector, publishers, airlines, banks, insurance companies, and government agencies.[5]

The Canadian Telidon system was first demonstrated in 1978, and field trials began in 1980. The first commercial service, Grassroots, provided information services for farmers, including commodities reports, weather, and livestock prices. The early government-supported service, Cantel, provided descriptions of government programs and services, addresses of local and regional government offices, Canadian travel information, and a national employment database listing hard-to-fill jobs.

The French government developed its videotex system, Teletel, as part of a major campaign to modernize and expand its telephone system. In addition to the use of adapted television sets as terminals, the government has backed the development of an inexpensive, stand-alone terminal with a small monochrome screen, called the Minitel.

The French have an installed base of over 3 million terminals. Statistics in mid-1987 indicated that each terminal was used an average of 3.7 minutes per day.[6] Despite the availability of over 3000 databases, approximately half of the traffic was for messaging, online dating, and similar services. According to Martin White, "The Teletel services have become an integral part of French business and society. . . . Overall the French service has only the problems of success to overcome."[7]

Australia, although a late entrant, has been rapid in its adoption of videotex. Since 1984, several systems have been launched nationwide, including Aftel and Elderlink. Viatel, Australia's public utility operated by Telecom, started in early 1985 and gained as many users in three months as Britain's Prestel service had in its first year, despite a very much smaller population base. The number of corporate in-house systems has grown exceptionally rapidly.

Numerous videotex experiments and launches have occurred in the United States. Many of them have concentrated on single applications, such as electronic banking or shopping. The first public (but nongovernment) system was launched in 1983 in Miami by Knight-Ridder and was known as Viewtron. A number of such services have come and gone including Viewtron, which lost $50 million; the Times-Mirror Company's Gateway, which lost $30 million; and Centel Corporation's KeyFax, which lost $25 million.[8]

At the same time, a number of nationally available, interactive computer database systems have been established. These are the major competitors of videotex because they contain similar types of information. These systems, however, require a personal computer rather than a modified TV set and keypad to communicate, a much more expensive proposition for anyone contemplating going online. They also tend to cater to specialist markets, such as computer buffs and investors, rather than the general public. Furthermore, they are not as "beginner-friendly" as videotex, which was purportedly designed for an intelligent four-year-old!

The Source, founded in 1979, provides city-to-city airline schedules, an employment database, news updates, games, electronic shopping, and other services. CompuServe, owned by H. and R. Block, has similar types of information, with numerous forums providing electronic interchanges among users based on their computer hardware and software, their professions, or personal interests as diverse as tropical fish, ham radio, model airplanes, comic books, and religion. Dow Jones/News Retrieval provides up-to-the-minute stock market prices and is used primarily by the finance and investment professions.

Prodigy, owned by the IBM Corporation and Sears, Roebuck and Company, was launched in 1989. This system differs from the others in that it sets a low monthly subscription but no connect-time charges. Profits are expected from advertisers who pay a fee based on the number of subscribers who see the message, plus a percentage of from 5 to 20 percent on products purchased through Prodigy.[9]

The U.S. Videotex Industry Association estimated that in mid-1987, there were 40 consumer-oriented videotex/public computer database services established.[10] Total annual revenue for these interactive database systems in the United States was estimated at $300 million in 1988, up from $7.5 million in 1981. As of September 1988, CompuServe had approximately 520,000 subscribers; Dow Jones, 270,000; GEnie, 110,000; QuantumLink, 80,000; and The Source, 50,000. The total number of users of these services was estimated at fewer than 2 million.[11] In addition, however, there are hundreds of noncommercial electronic bulletin boards set up by computer buffs to exchange information, as described in chapter 3.

Other major national public videotex systems include Bildschirmtex (BTX) in Germany and CAPTAIN in Japan. Videotex services or trials have now been conducted worldwide. Table 5.2 indicates the countries where videotex developments have been reported in the English-language literature.

Table 5.2. Countries that Have Carried Out Videotex Trials or Established Services

Australia	Italy
Austria	Japan
Belgium	Luxembourg
Brazil	New Zealand
Canada	Norway
Denmark	South Africa
Finland	Spain
France	Sweden
Germany	Switzerland
Great Britain	The Netherlands
Greece	United States
Hong Kong	Venezuela
Ireland	

LIBRARY APPLICATIONS

Libraries can and have utilized teletext and videotex services in several ways, as outlined below:

1. *User self-service.* Trials in both public and special libraries have shown that patrons will make use of videotex services available from the library as a service point. To a certain extent, initial interest may be aroused because of novelty value. As with all new technologies, staff time must be allowed for promotion and basic user training, despite the accessibility of most systems. Monitoring may also be required, so that the system is used for information retrieval, rather than for games. A budget will need

to be allocated for access time, as well as for patron use of information with frame charges, such as financial data.

Initial market trials were carried out in the library at the University of Aston in Birmingham, England, in 1978. Searches were undertaken for users by library staff for reasons of economy and security. Financial and company information was accessed most often; typical searches lasted about 10 minutes and averaged a reasonable 70 pence.[12]

2. *Reference desk access.* A videotex system can serve as one of the librarian's most important ready reference tools, especially for local information and information that is updated rapidly. The system can be interrogated from the reference desk to answer in-person or telephone queries.

3. *Provision of library-related information.* Library-related information such as subject bibliographies, new book lists, catalogs, and audio-visual holdings can be mounted relatively inexpensively on a videotex system, especially if it is already in machine-readable form. The primary requirements are the formatting of information frames and the addition of index frames.

In the early Online Computer Library Center (OCLC) experiment with videotex in Columbus, Ohio, called Channel 2000, the public library catalog of 300,000 items and the text of the *Academic American Encyclopedia,* along with banking and other services, were made available online to residents in their homes. Later, the American Library Association contributed book reviews to the Centel Corporation's KeyFax videotex system.

Of the respondents surveyed in the Channel 2000 experiment, 46 percent indicated that it saved them time getting books from the library (books requested were mailed directly to the viewers' homes); 41 percent thought that their knowledge of library services had increased; and 16 percent stated that they spent more time reading books than before the experiment.[13] For catalogs in particular, however, the access rate was low relative to the memory required for storage.

4. *Interlibrary loan.* Location of titles on a videotex library catalog is enhanced when these titles can be ordered immediately and then delivered as part of the service. One such system set up in a provincial capital in France showed that use of a school district's centralized audio-visual collection was increased greatly when

items could be identified on videotex, ordered on a response frame, and delivered the next day by the school district's courier service.

5. *Creation of local databases.* Libraries can also create databases of local interest, not necessarily related to the library itself. For example, as a class project, library school students in Australia created the Community and Library Information for Canberra (CLIC) database, which provided information on community services in the national capital. This was set up experimentally as part of a closed user group, under the auspices of an umbrella information provider. [14]

6. *Communication among professionals.* Videotex is potentially the simplest and the least expensive means of sending electronic mail among users with similar interests, but who may not have ready access to other computer networks. For example, the Royal Australian Institute of Architects encouraged their members to purchase terminals to use for communicating with headquarters and each other. The Elderlink system, mentioned earlier, provides a ready means of communication among isolated farmers and graziers.

CONCLUSION

Teletext and videotex have yet to become mass market technologies. Although growth has been continual, it has not proved exponential as has the market for video recorders and compact audio discs. It is still computer buffs and corporate users who are in the vanguard. Many of the PTTs are concentrating more on vertical markets (for example, the more lucrative financial services) than on horizontal markets catering to the general public. There is a shake-out in the hardware market, particularly in dedicated terminals, as well as in software. Early information providers who have not realized their initial profit projections are also pulling out.

According to Antone F. Alber, videotex suffers from the "chicken and egg" problem:

> The real issue isn't whether videotex will take off but rather when. No one will offer a videotex service and manufacture decoders in volume until a market for them exists, but no one will pay inflated prices for a decoder that has limited use because of a lack of available service.[15]

Videotex and teletext have potential as the means for information retrieval, electronic services, and communication for a mass audience. Industry analysts have suggested that incorporating videotex into a value-added network (VAN) as one of a range of services could provide the needed impetus. Experience to date, however, has shown that acceptance has come only with the free or inexpensive availability of equipment; pricing policies that depend on profits raised from advertisers rather than subscribers, or which are calculated on a low monthly fee rather than a connect-time charge; and databases with timely information such as stock market share prices or airline timetables that cater to narrow vertical rather than mass horizontal markets.

NOTES

1. These include the following (the list is far from comprehensive):
Rudy Bretz, *Media for Interactive Communication* (Beverly Hills, Calif.: Sage, 1983).
Dmitris N. Chorafas, *Interactive Message Services: Planning, Designing and Implementing Videotex* (New York: McGraw-Hill, 1984).
Sam Fedida and Rex Malik, *Viewdata Revolution* (London: Associated Business Press, 1979).
David Godfrey and Ernest Chang, eds., *The Telidon Book* (Toronto: Press Porcepic, 1981).
Information Technology on Screen: New Approaches in Viewdata, Teletext and Cable (London: Library Association, 1982).
James Martin, *Viewdata and the Information Society* (Englewood Cliffs, N.J.: Prentice-Hall, 1982).
Vincent Mosco, *Pushbutton Fantasies: Critical Perspectives on Videotex and Information Technology* (Norwood, N.J.: Ablex, 1982).
Efrem Sigel, *Videotext: The Coming Revolution in Home/Office Information Retrieval* (White Plains, N.Y.: Knowledge Industries, 1980).
Rex Winsbury, ed., *Viewdata in Action: A Comparative Study of Prestel* (London: McGraw-Hill, 1981).

2. As reported in Richard H. Veith, *Television's Teletext* (New York: North Holland, 1983), 1.

3. *Channel 2000: Description and Findings of a Viewdata Test* (Dublin, Ohio: OCLC Online Computer Library Center, 1981), 3.

4. "Teletext: The Only Thing Cheaper Is the Test Card," *Communications Australia* 2, no. 2 (July 1983): 24-25.

5. Martin S. White, "Videotex Services in Europe," in *Videotex International Proceedings* (London: Online Publications, 1986), 3-4.

6. Andrew Pollack, "Ruling May Not Aid Videotex," *New York Times,* 15 September 1987, 37.

7. White, "Videotex," 6.

8. Mark Lewyn, "Their Gamble May Set Pace for Videotex," *USA Today,* 20 September 1988, p.1B.

9. Lewyn, "Their Gamble," 2B.

10. Pollack, "Ruling," 37.

11. Lewyn, "Their Gamble," 1B.

12. Reg Carr, "Prestel: What's in It for Librarians?" *American Libraries,* January 1981, 13-16.

13. *Channel 2000,* 18.

14. *An Investigative Report on Videotex and the Construction of the CLIC (Community and Library Information for Canberra) Database on Viatel* (Bruce, ACT: Canberra College of Advanced Education, 1985).

15. Antone F. Alber, *Videotex/Teletext, Principles and Practices* (New York: McGraw-Hill, 1985).

■ 6 ■

Micrographic and Optical Disc Technologies for Document Management

Duncan MacKenzie and Andrew Link

Micrographics combines the science, art and technology by which information can be quickly reduced to the medium of microfilm, stored conveniently and then easily retrieved for reference and use.

—Joe Hardy

An Introduction to Micrographics

HISTORY OF MICROGRAPHICS

The birth of micrographics probably occurred in 1839 at Manchester, England, when John Danzer, an optician, produced the first microphotographs on daguerreotype plates. In 1859, a Frenchman, Rene Dagron, took out the first microfilm patent for the development of a method of producing microdots, based on Danzer's technique.

In 1871, as Paris lay under siege during the Franco-Prussian War, microfilmed messages (using Dagron's patented method) were strapped to the legs of courier pigeons and flown over the German lines into Paris. The "pigeon post" successfully delivered some 2.5 million messages during the course of the war.

It was 1928 before microfilming became a commercial reality. George McCarthy, a banker in New York, invented a camera to film checks before they were returned to depositors, thus providing a fast means of maintaining bank transactions and assisting in the prevention of fraud.

In the 1930s microfilm, with all the benefits it offered, was recognized as having great potential for use in libraries. In 1938, Eugene Power founded University Microfilms, with the aim of filming rare books so that they might be accessible to scholars around the world.

World War II saw the introduction of microfilm to millions of U.S. servicemen. Mail from relatives and friends of overseas servicemen was reduced on microfilm for shipment (called V-mail), and at its destination was enlarged and made into readable paper copies. The war was also responsible for the development of the aperture card (described later in this chapter) for military use, and for the microfilming of captured archival documents. However, it was not until the late 1950s and 1960s that microforms were widely accepted as a viable processing, retrieval, and dissemination tool for information Today, microforms are still an efficient and cost-effective means of storing and retrieving large amounts of information.

ADVANTAGES

The wide acceptance of micrographics has created a billion-dollar industry, owing in the main to its flexibility. For nearly every application or requirement, there is a system and a microform to meet the need. The effective marriage of micrographics with computer, laser, optical, and digital technology has ensured its long-term future in the information-processing field.

There are numerous advantages of micrographic systems over existing paper-based systems. These include:

■ Regardless of the size of an original document, images can be reduced to fit standard microform dimensions for convenient handling. Microform records require only 2 percent of the space occupied by the same records on paper.

■ Computer-recorded data can be transferred to microform in a fraction of the time and cost required for printing on paper.

■ Microform records are not vulnerable to erasure or memory loss caused by power failure or computer downtime.

■ Information can be indexed by computer and retrieved in seconds, even from a database of millions of documents.

■ If required, paper copies of the original documents or computer-recorded data can be produced in seconds from the microform images.

■ Microform records can be easily duplicated at a nominal cost and sent to other locations. Mail distribution is far less expensive than for hardcopy documents.

- Microform records are legally accepted on the same basis as paper documents.

The use of micrographic systems are so widespread that they touch many facets of our lives almost daily, although often we do not realize it. Governments at federal, state, and local levels are major users, as are libraries and educational institutions; medical, legal, and consumer services; and banking, insurance, engineering, aeronautics, and other businesses and industries. All of these users, and many more, rely on their micrographic systems to provide information quickly, accurately, and at a reasonable cost.

DISADVANTAGES

Many of the early perceived disadvantages of microforms were attitudinal, and these have changed with the advances in micrographic and computer technology. Likewise, the medium's present acceptance with regard to legality and archival preservation has meant that other legitimate concerns about microforms have been overcome. There are, however, a number of disadvantages associated with the use of microforms, and these must be considered before a decision is made to substitute microforms for paper records:

- Records cannot be altered. Once a paper record has been committed to microform, the filmed image cannot be annotated or updated.

- To read a microform image or obtain a paper copy of the image, specialized reading and retrieval equipment is required.

- If a simultaneous comparison is required between two or more microform pages, two readers would be required or a paper copy of one of the images would need to be created.

- If true archival preservation is required, microforms must be stored under controlled environmental conditions.

- Many users find it difficult to browse through microform records or to sustain long periods at a reader; they prefer to use bound or individual paper records.

MICROFORM PRODUCTION

There are basically four stages in the production of microforms. These stages are illustrated in Figure 6.1.

Figure 6.1. The Stages of Microform Production

Micrographic Systems

There is a microform system that can be designed to meet your specific application. This chart brings these various component parts together to show the logical flow of a total micrographic system.

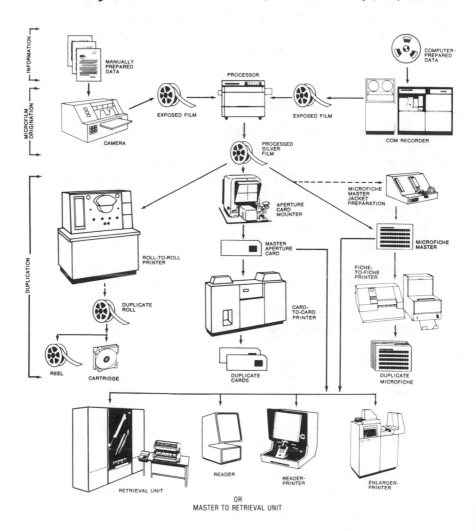

Reprinted from Joe Hardy, *An Introduction to Micrographics* (Silver Springs, Md.: National Micrographics Assn., 1980), 76, with permission from AIIM (Association for Information and Image Management).

First, there must be an information source, which may consist of existing written or printed material on paper, or digital information contained on computer tape or disk.

The second stage is converting that information to a microform image. This is achieved by using specialized cameras, such as rotary or flow cameras (16mm), where the documents pass through the camera; planetary cameras (16mm and 35mm), where documents remain stationary during exposure; or step-and-repeat cameras (105 mm), where microfiche is produced directly from original material. During processing, the latent images are developed and fixed on the film.

In the case of digitized data from a computer, a sophisticated device called a computer output microfilm (COM) recorder is utilized. The COM recorder converts the digitized data directly into microform images. The recorder can be either offline or online to the computer, and models to produce alphanumerics and graphics are available.

The third stage, if required, is the loading of the processed microform into its container (an open spool, cartridge, aperture card, or jacket). Depending on the system requirement, an intermediate stage may be the duplication of the microform. In the fourth stage, the microforms are ready for retrieval and reading, using appropriate equipment. The images may also be converted to paper copy if required.

FORMATS

The wide range of microforms in current use are appropriate to an even wider range of applications. These forms and some of their applications are described below:

1. *16mm roll film (open-spool or reel)*: The roll was the first to be used for the microfilming of office records. Of all the microforms, it is the least expensive to create and duplicate. Roll microfilm features high storage density and file integrity. Information is recorded in a fixed sequence, which guards against misfiling, alteration, or loss. In most cases, roll microfilm is used for records that are maintained in some logical sequence. There are other sophisticated microform systems available that allow for the random filing of data.

    The major drawbacks to open-spool roll film include its susceptibility to dust and scratching. The fact that open-spool film must be hand-threaded on to the retrieval device makes it less convenient to use and tends to increase search time.

    This form is most convenient where large volumes of records with low reference potential are to be stored for legal, security, or archival reasons. Roll microfilm lends itself well to applications such as purchase orders, invoices, correspondence, various accounting records, checks, and general office documentation.

2. *Cartridges*: Cartridge microfilm is produced by loading 16mm roll film into a cartridge. It has all the advantages of open-spool film, and the fact that the film is encased in a plastic housing provides protection when handling and storing and enables it to be used with high-speed automatic retrieval systems.

3. *35mm roll film (open-spool or reel)*: 35mm roll film is used for large documents such as engineering drawings, maps, plans, aerial photographs, newspapers, government archives, radiographs, library materials, and graphics. It is generally kept in roll form when the application is for low reference, security, or archival purposes.

4. *Aperture cards*: The aperture card is normally a Hollerith, or data-processing-size, card containing a single frame of 35mm film. The finished card is created either by photographing documents on 35mm roll film, then cutting and mounting individual frames of film onto preindexed cards; or by the direct filming and processing of premounted film cards.

   The original use of aperture cards was more or less restricted to *unitized* data–where one microform is related to one document or drawing for retrieval purposes–such as engineering drawings requiring high resolution. Today it is not unusual to find this microform being used outside of the engineering environment. In libraries aperture cards are useful for storing microform versions of maps, drawings, and so on. Ease of indexing, low-cost duplicating, and low-cost readers make aperture cards a viable microform for many applications.

5. *Microfiche*: A microfiche, or "fiche," is a flat sheet of film, approximately 4 inches by 6 inches (105 mm by 148 mm) in size, containing multiple microimages in a grid pattern. Microfiche may be created by filming with a step-and-repeat camera for source documents; by COM recorder for computer-generated data; by duplicating previously created jackets (described later in this chapter); or by stripping up (cutting roll film to approximately 6-inch lengths, coating with an adhesive, and sticking to a transparent sheet of film) and duplicating.

   Microfiche may contain from a few to several hundred images in a number of available reduction ratios. *Ultrafiche,* filmed at very high reduction ratios, permits thousands of images per fiche. Microfiche are widely available, particularly those created as COM-fiche. In libraries, they are used for source documents such as technical reports, journals, and theses and for bibliographic tools such as catalogs and union lists.

Microfiche generally permits unitized data storage and updating and is easily duplicated for mailing, security, or reference purposes. It is designed to permit either manual retrieval with an identification legible to the unaided eye at the top of the fiche or high-speed automated retrieval. Unlike roll and cartridge formats, however, it provides a lesser degree of file integrity, as individual fiche may be mislayed or misfiled. This is particularly evident in high-volume systems.

6. *Jackets*: The jacket represents a combination of the roll microfilm and microfiche concepts. It is a transparent acetate film holder containing channels into which strips of 16mm or 35mm roll film (or both) are inserted. Unlike microfiche, jackets can be updated or revised by adding or removing individual microfilm images. Images may be copied or read directly from the jacket without removing the film. Jackets can be visibly titled for quick, easy file reference. However, the jacket is one of the more expensive formats to create.

Microfilm jackets lend themselves well to applications in which smaller amounts of related data must be stored together as a unitized record. Medical and personnel records are two applications where jackets have, in the past, found favor. However, jackets are generally recommended for any situation where it is desirable to maintain complete files by single subjects and where additional data is added from time to time.

7. *Updatable microfiche*: Updatable microfiche allows images of records to be added or deleted on an original master microfiche over a long period of time. This capability allows greater flexibility in the design of micrographics applications for more active information. In addition to the other advantages of microfiche, an updatable system offers the flexibility and open-ended characteristics of conventional paper files. However, the equipment and materials required are more expensive than the more traditional formats.

RETRIEVAL

After the microform is produced, the information contained on it must be retrievable—when, where, and in the form required by the user. To achieve this, a number of coding and indexing techniques have evolved to suit the various formats.

There is a wide range of microfilm storage and retrieval systems available: manual, semiautomated, and automated. These range from a file drawer, to systems involving computers, local and remote data transmission, and high-speed, automatic display/printing capabilities which provide enlargements, indexed data, and selected retrieval.

Computer-assisted-retrieval (CAR) techniques, for example, are especially helpful in applications with constant requests for information, large data banks storing hundreds of thousands of documents, or dissemination of information to dozens of locations. A comparison of CAR with optical disc systems is made later in this chapter.

The availability of a wide variety of microforms and retrieval systems is one aspect that gives micrographics systems flexibility beyond the scope of paper systems. Primary factors to consider in selecting the appropriate micrographic system are listed in Table 6.1.

Table 6.1. Considerations in the selection of the type of microform and the retrieval system

- The format of the input

- The nature of the information to be stored

- The speed and ease of retrieval required

- The system cost

- Single- or multiple-site requirements

- The need for and cost of duplication

- The frequency of file changes or updates

- The need for file integrity

- The type of indexing required

- The number of users and frequency of retrieval from the system

- Users' needs and wants

- Compatibility with other information systems, such as word processing, optical disc, data processing, etc.

READING DEVICES

A variety of devices is available for viewing microforms. The choice will depend on the environment in which they will be used, user needs, the specific micrographic system in use, and cost. Basic types of readers include the following:

1. *Portable readers*: Portable readers are designed for compactness and personal use at field sites or while travelling. These can be hand-held or lap viewers, or readers designed to be folded or inserted into a case similar to a typewriter case or briefcase. Most lap and other portable readers offer the option of electric current, battery, or 12-volt (through a car's cigarette lighter) operation.

2. *Stationary readers*: Stationary readers are designed for use on a desk, table, or stand, or as stand-alone, self-contained units.

3. *Reader/printers or enlarger/printers*: Reader/printers are designed for both viewing and producing hardcopy reproductions from microforms. Enlarger/printers are not generally used for viewing, but for producing high volumes of hard copy.

PRESERVATION

In determining preservation requirements for microforms, it must first be established how they are to be used and the retention period required. There are three basic types of film used in the production of microforms, each with different characteristics and uses. These are silver halide, diazo, and vesicular microfilm. Diazo and vesicular films are generally used as working copies and for short-term storage, generally up to 25 years. They are not archival and cannot be utilized for long-term storage.

Silver halide film, however, if manufactured, processed, and stored to archival standards, can last for several hundred years – as long, in fact, as the finest-quality rag papers. Most silver halide films manufactured today meet archival standards, but users should refer to the manufacturer's specification sheet.

The most important step in processing silver halide film is the washing process. To be considered archival, the film must be washed until 0.007 gram or less of fixer (thiosulphate) remains per square centimeter of processed film (ANSI Standard PH1.28-1973). The archival storage requirements (ANSI Standard PH1.43-1976) specify that maximum temperature should not exceed 21 degrees centigrade and that relative humidity should be between 30 and 40 percent. There are other factors affecting the stability of the storage of archival microform, and reference should be made to the relevant standards for detailed specifications.

APPLICATIONS IN LIBRARIES

The information-processing industry is the largest and most rapidly developing industry in the world today, and will remain so for the foreseeable future. When compared with the computer, micrographics may seem to be the poor cousin, but consider the following factors:

- Microform is still the cheapest information medium in relation to creation, storage, and retrieval of images.

- Microform's proven credentials as a viable information medium are much older than the computer's or that of any other of today's information technologies.

- There have been more international standards established for micrographics than for any other information technology.

- Microform, properly processed and stored, can last for hundreds of years – a true preservation medium.

In the library, these factors have been enough to ensure that micrographics has been, and will remain, a dynamic management tool.

The past decade has seen a marked decline in the acquisitions and operating budgets of libraries, but at the same time, there has been a dramatic increase in the demand for library and information services. The ability of micrographics to fill this economic gap has resulted in a sharp rise in the provision for microforms in acquisitions budgets, and over 80 micropublishers now service this section of the library market.

A library's microform holdings can be developed by one of the following three methods:

1. Acquisition of microform material from outside sources, such as other libraries, research institutes, or universities, or from institutional or commercial micropublishers and microrepublishers. (Micropublishing is the issuing of multiple-copy microform for sale and distribution to the public of previously unpublished material that has been edited or reformatted. Microrepublishing is the similar issuing of material that has been published previously or is being published simultaneously in hard copy.)

2. The production of microforms in-house. This involves the formation of a department within the library to film, process, duplicate and maintain quality control of microforms. An in-house microfilming system is very expensive to set up and maintain, and a detailed cost justification should be carried out beforehand to prove the long-term viability of such an operation.

In-house filming is generally carried out for the preservation of newspapers, historical documents, or rare or fragile works. Such a program may also be used to satisfy external requests for purchase of unique material held by the library or as a common method of fulfilling interlibrary loan requests, particularly for theses.

3. The use of an outside commercial microfilm bureau to film all of the material that would normally have been done by an in-house operation as described above.

The choice between an in-house operation or outside bureau is generally based on economics and the expected volume of throughput (material to be microfilmed). A bureau will work to standards set by the library, so it is often better to give the headaches of production to others, sit back, and accept a quality, finished product at a competitive price. This then means that the library need only be concerned with the management of its microform collections and the provision of hardware and services for the retrieval and viewing of those collections.

Table 6.2. Examples of Microform Applications in Libraries

- Abstracting services
- Archives and manuscripts
- Bibliographies
- Catalogs
- Conference proceedings
- Educational documents
- Interlibrary loans
- Journals and serials
- Large microform sets
- Magazines and periodicals
- Maps, plans, and drawings
- Monographs
- Newspaper-clipping files
- Newspapers
- Out-of-print books
- Programmed learning material
- Research materials
- Subject collections
- Technical reports
- Theses
- Union lists
- University handbooks

Since the initial application of microforms in libraries during the early 1930s, the science of micrographics has radically changed the manner in which librarians develop and manage their collections and provide services to their end users. The microform applications listed in Table 6.2 in use in libraries throughout the world are indicative of the impact and penetration that micrographics has had in libraries.

The ability of the micrographic industry to keep pace with the rapid growth and diversification of information technology–through the merging of technologies–has resulted in an expansion of the industry. Rather than displace micrographics, the new technologies, such as optical disc, are integrating with micrographic systems to produce solutions that previously would not have been justified by cost or practical as stand-alone solutions for either technology.

In deciding which technology best suits users' requirements, cost will always be a prime factor. In this area, micrographics remains a front runner.

BACKGROUND OF OPTICAL DISC

The optical disc (also referred to as a laser disc) was initially introduced in the late 1970s in the form of videodisc. Videodisc provides a way of storing and playing back analog video information, such as video movies, as described in chapter 4. Special WORM (write once-read many) videodisc systems are also available for applications requiring the storage and retrieval of photographs or graphic images. In these systems the graphic information can be written to the disc and retrieved as required.

The audio compact disc (CD) was released in Japan in 1982 and in the United States in 1983 after joint development efforts by Philips and Sony. Compact discs offer a high-quality alternative to LP records for storing music. The same principle of laser optics is used in compact disc players and videodisc players, but the way in which information is stored on a compact disc is significantly different. On a compact disc, the analog information (music) is converted to digital information (binary 1s and 0s) and then stored on disc in digital form. On a videodisc, however, the information (moving or still images) is stored directly on the disc in analog form.

As a result of the success and acceptance of the compact disc, the technology was employed by the computer industry to store computer-readable data. Hence compact disc-read only memory (CD-ROM) was developed. Since the compact disc already stored information in digital form, it lent itself very well to the storage of computer digital data.

Both CD and CD-ROM are read-only forms, and the technology is designed for distribution of information, whether it happens to be music, computer data, or publications. Since the discs are mastered by special equipment and copies are "stamped" for mass distribution, CD and CD-

ROM discs do not allow users to store their own information without special mastering, which is cost prohibitive.

WORM optical discs were developed in the early 1980s to allow users to write their own information to a disc once and then read it back as many times as required. WORM systems use laser optics and digital information storage as does CD, but users are able to write information to the disc on their own system, without having to use special mastering systems and processes usually confined to mass production environments. As a result, WORM technology has allowed optical disc to be used in a wide range of applications other than mass distribution.

Various forms of optical media are now available or becoming available. Other prerecorded formats are compact disc interactive (CD-I) and digital video interactive (DVI), which are discussed in chapter 7. Erasable optical disc is now available for users to read and write on, and optical memory cards for write-once storage are on the horizon. Figure 6.2 shows the relationships among the most common types of optical media.

Figure 6.2. Relationship among the Most Common Types of Optical Media

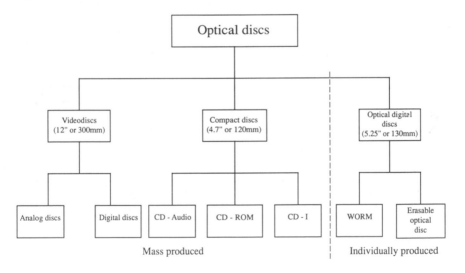

ACCEPTANCE OF OPTICAL DISC

Currently the most widely accepted optical disc on the consumer market is the audio compact disc. In the United States alone, 150 million CDs have been purchased since 1983, and predictions indicate that another 200 million will sell by the end of 1991. Figures show that 11 million CD players were sold in the United States between 1984 and 1988.[1]

Optical disc technology is slowly gaining acceptance in the corporate and government sectors, with the majority of growth and acceptance expected to occur in the five years from 1989 to 1994. At present, optical disc technology is being used in the following applications:

1. Publishing and distributing of information and software (CD-ROM).

2. Archival storage of computer data (WORM).

3. Online storage of computer data (erasable optical disc and WORM).

4. Storage and retrieval of files and documents (WORM).

The different applications of optical disc technology have gained variable degrees of acceptance. For those listed above, it should only be a matter of time before the technology is widely accepted. This will occur as more people become aware of the uses and benefits of the systems and as more cost-effective systems become available.

HOW OPTICAL DISC TECHNOLOGY WORKS

The term *optical* relates to the process of recording information on and reading it from the disc. Although the exact techniques may differ, in general, CD-ROM and WORM discs are recorded, or "written to" by a focused laser beam. This laser beam physically alters the surface of the disc, forming holes called *pits;* the surfaces remaining between the pits are called *lands.* The pits have different light-reflective characteristics, enabling a lower power laser beam to detect the differences in transferring between pits and lands (a binary 1 or 0) when reading the disc. The surface of the disc is protected by a transparent coating, which does not affect reading by the laser beam. Figure 6.3 shows how digital data is stored on a disc.

There are two major advantages in using laser technology to store and retrieve information: very high storage densities can be achieved, and no physical contact exists between the pickup and the disc surface. This lack of contact eliminates any degradation of the disc information, even after thousands of reads. A 4.72-inch (12 cm) compact disc can store around 600 megabytes of data on one side. A 12-inch WORM disc can now store 6.5 gigabytes of data (3.25 gigabytes per side). This equates to a storage capacity of about 150,000 one-page digitized document images on one side of a 12-inch disc! Higher storage densities are constantly being developed.

Figure 6.3. Optical Disc Storage

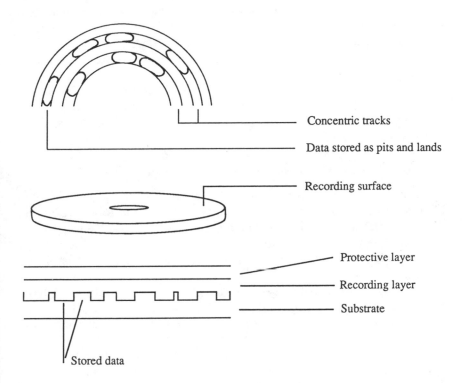

Concentric tracks

Data stored as pits and lands

Recording surface

Protective layer

Recording layer

Substrate

Stored data

APPLICATIONS

Applications requiring large amounts of digital data storage are particularly well suited to optical disc, especially when the information needs to be kept for a number of years. Magnetic media such as hard disk and computer tape do an excellent job for shorter-term storage and backup of computer data, but they are subject to information deterioration after a few years or even earlier. This is why only the latest "live" information is usually kept online in a computer system, and other longer-term information is stored in hard copy, such as paper or microfiche.

Magnetic tapes are used for information backup, but generally they are not suitable for longer-term storage (that is, more than two years) because of susceptibility to magnetic fields, temperature, and longer-term deterioration. This is why tapes are often cycled through data backup procedures and are generally replaced after repeated use to ensure integrity of backed up data. Since optical disc technology provides high-volume storage of data, long-term stability (currently to 100 years safe life), and no degradation no matter how many times it is read, it is well suited to permanent storage of important data.

WORM discs offer storage solutions in two main areas: archival storage of computer data, and storage of paper files and documents in digitized image form. The latter is often referred to as document management. WORM discs are particularly well suited to document storage and retrieval because generally, when a document is saved, it does not need to be altered. In fact, it is desirable in most document storage applications that documents cannot be altered or tampered with for legal reasons and document integrity. This is why WORM discs will continue to be used for permanent storage of document images, even though erasable optical disc is now available.

Document Management Systems

Although it is unlikely that paper-based communications will ever become obsolete, storing document images in electronic form offers a viable alternative with numerous benefits. Paper communication can be inexpensive and convenient when manageable; however, it can present a number of problems when large numbers of documents and regular retrieval are involved.

Document management systems are basically very effective filing systems. They can be thought of as "electronic filing cabinets." Benefits offered are the ability to decrease storage space for filing documents, reliable document retention life (no data degradation within 100 years), and easier retrieval and distribution of documents. Also, these systems can perform important tasks other than the filing and retrieval of documents, including automatic electronic transmission of a document, audit reporting, simultaneous access of the same document by several users, and production of paper copies on request.

There are two main operations in a document management system: filing a document and retrieving a document. The equipment required for these processes is illustrated in Figure 6.4. The central computer (for example, a personal computer or PC) controls the operation of the whole system with special software.

Filing a Document

Filing a document begins when the user types a command on the PC and then places a document on the scanner. The document is electronically scanned (not unlike the way a fax machine or photocopier scans), and the electronic document information is sent to the PC and displayed on the high-resolution visual display unit (VDU) screen. The user can then verify that the document was correctly scanned (neither too light nor too dark). If necessary, the document can be rescanned darker or lighter for optimum quality. The document is then saved to the optical WORM disc after document indexing information is entered. Once the document is stored on optical disc, it cannot be erased or written over. To scan and display a one-page document generally takes from 2 to 20 seconds, depending on the type of system used.

Indexing information (such as name, address, date of letter, and subject matter) allows accurate retrieval of the document or file at a later date. This information is entered while the document is on the screen. In the case of a file consisting of multiple documents, indexing information may be entered only for the first page, and the following scanned pages would also be retrieved using this indexing information.

Figure 6.4. Basic Optical Disc Filing System

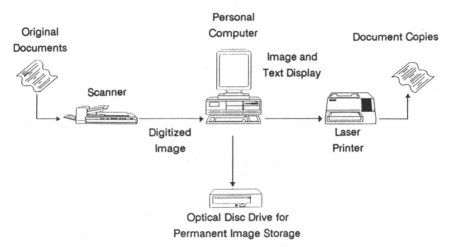

Retrieving a Document

To retrieve a document, the user enters the index information (such as name and date), which causes the appropriate document reference information to be displayed on the screen once it has been found by the computer. The user verifies whether that is the required document by reading the screen fields (such as subject matter) and presses the document retrieve key, which causes the document to be fetched from optical disc and displayed on the screen. If no disc is present in the drive, or the wrong disc for the desired document is in the drive, the system prompts the user to load the correct disc, and the desired document is then displayed. The user can then scroll and view subsequent pages (if a multipage file has been retrieved), or print one or more pages on the laser printer.

Thousands of documents and files can be stored in this way, and the power of accurate retrieval is evident by the ability to retrieve selectively by name, date, or subject matter and print many documents in a matter of minutes. The retrieval process for a one-page document normally takes from 5 to 10 seconds if the correct disc is already loaded. Printing takes from 5 to 30 seconds per page, and the quality of the copy closely matches the original. In some cases, the digitized copy can be enhanced to appear better than the original.

Multiuser Systems

Figure 6.4 illustrated an entry-level filing system. Larger multiuser systems are also available and can include the following features:

1. Multiple scanning and viewing stations for several people to scan or view documents simultaneously. These can be connected through a local area network (LAN), as discussed in chapter 2.

2. Central high-speed printer where users can route print requests.

3. Facilities for connection and communication to existing company computers for system integration and special database access.

4. Several optical disc drives online for automated access to more documents. An optical disc jukebox can also be used for this purpose, allowing, for example, up to 99 optical discs to be loaded in and out of drives automatically as required.

5. Special software and configurations to allow documents to be automatically routed throughout different departments of an organization. Various actions can be performed on the document, and the document can even be combined with supporting documents from various departments.

Cost

Prices for document management systems start at around $20,000 for a basic single-user system. Such systems can typically store 20,000 pages of information on each 5 1/4-inch optical disc. Multiuser systems are generally $100,000 and above, with larger systems reaching several million dollars. Configurations and system sizes vary considerably depending on the application.

COMPARISON OF OPTICAL DISC AND MICROGRAPHICS CAR SYSTEMS

Optical disc document management systems are being used successfully in a variety of organizations, as listed in Table 6.3. There are numerous benefits to be gained from their use. These include:

1. Lower cost of maintaining files, as less time is spent filing and retrieving files.

2. Faster and more accurate retrieval of documents.

3. File integrity, with fewer lost files.

4. Improved customer service.

5. Greater staff productivity.

6. Space savings, as documents can be stored off site or destroyed.

Nevertheless, micrographics CAR systems have been available for a number of years and will continue to be available to solve document management problems. As with optical disc systems, CAR systems range from single-user configurations to large multiuser configurations. CAR systems do offer an alternative to optical disc systems in document management applications. In many cases, it may be cost-prohibitive to use optical disc because of the sheer volume of documents, and CAR systems can often address the application at a more cost-effective price. Table 6.4 lists specific advantages of each type of system over the other.

Systems are available that combine micrographic and optical disc technologies. These systems make sense in applications in which a large number of backlog documents exist and documents in current use also need to be captured. Microforms can be used to store the backlog, and optical discs can be used for the current documents. One central computer can manage both the microform and optical disc portions of the system. This approach provides a more cost-effective way to capture and index the backlog information, while giving the advantages of optical disc for the current ongoing, and presumably more relevant, documents.

Table 6.3. Types of Organizations and Typical Applications of Optical Disc Document Management Systems

Type of Organization	Application
■ Insurance companies	Policy files
■ Government departments	General correspondence
	Application forms
■ Patent offices	Patents and trademarks documents
■ Hospitals	Patient records
■ Wholesalers/suppliers	Delivery dockets and invoices
■ Financial institutions	Customer records
■ Freight companies	Proof of delivery documents

Table 6.4. Comparison of Optical Disc and Micrographics CAR Systems

Advantages of CAR Over Optical Disc Systems

- Equipment and labor costs are lower, particularly in high-volume document capture applications, as cameras are generally faster than scanners.

- At present, microfilm is a legally accepted medium to store documents.

Advantages of Optical Disc Over CAR Systems

- Documents can be controlled centrally while being made available to several users simultaneously. This is because documents are in electronic form and therefore can be transmitted easily to multiple users.

- The quality of a document image (quality control) is easier to maintain.

- The equipment is more reliable since solid-state technology is used.

- Better control is maintained in routing of documents throughout an organization.

- More documents can be held "online" by using jukeboxes.

Library and Archive Applications

In the past, microform was the only true archival medium available to preserve documents for extended periods of time. Since there are WORM discs available that now guarantee data integrity for at least 100 years, this technology also has the potential to preserve valuable manuscripts or books. In a library application, this would be useful particularly for fragile or rare books that may be deteriorating through age or regular use. Once scanned onto an optical disc system, document retrieval could occur without ever having to disturb the original, which would be preserved for posterity.

Optical disc technology is equally valuable for archives storage. In particular, computer data is often printed out in large quantities on paper or microfiche. Large quantities of computer paper can prove difficult for distribution and storage, and even more difficult and time-consuming for searching and retrieving information. Microfiche can provide a more cost-effective solution, particularly when daily, weekly, and monthly information needs to be quickly produced and distributed to several locations. Microfiche has traditionally also been used for longer-term offline storage of accumulated printed data.

However, WORM optical disc can also be used for this purpose. Computer print data can now go directly from the computer to optical disc in a print file format. This means that the information is stored in a human-readable report form on optical disc, as it would appear on paper or microfiche. Huge amounts of print information can be stored this way, providing an efficient method of storing much of the computer output that is generated every day, without tying up valuable online magnetic disk space. Indexing information is automatically extracted from the print information coming from the computer, thus providing a way for the information to be retrieved from optical disc at a later date. This is an attractive benefit, as no additional key entry for indexing purposes is required.

Although this type of storage can be considered archival, WORM technology allows several users to access the main computer system to retrieve archived information whenever necessary, effectively making archival data available online.

Optical disc provides another way to store document images or computer data. In certain circumstances, optical disc will lead the way in solving information storage problems. However, many applications will still demand the use of paper, microfilm, magnetic media, and other storage media, to address the vast requirements of communication and management of today's information.

NOTES

1. "The Final Days of Vinyl?" *Compact Disc Yearbook 1989,* no. 2: 4.

SUGGESTED READING

For standards, books, and other publications relating to micrographics, request a catalog from the Association for Information and Image Management (AIIM), 1100 Wayne Avenue, Suite 1100, Silver Spring, MD 20910.

Monographs

Cinnamon, Barry. *Optical Disc Document Storage and Retrieval Systems.* Silver Spring, Md.: Association for Information and Image Management, 1988.

Costigan, Daniel M. *Micrographics Systems.* 2d ed. Silver Spring, Md: National Micrographics Association, 1980.

Helgerson, Linda W. *Introduction to Optical Technology.* Silver Spring, Md.: Association for Information and Image Management, 1987.

Saffady, William. *Micrographics.* 2d ed. Littleton, Colo.: Libraries Unlimited, 1985.

_____. *Optical Disks vs. Micrographics as Document Storage and Retrieval Technologies.* Westport, Conn.: Meckler, 1989.

_____. *Optical Storage Technology 1989: A State of the Art Review.* Westport, Conn.: Meckler, 1989.

Journals

IMC Journal, published by the International Information Management Congress.

Inform, published by the AIIM.

International Journal of Micrographics and Optical Technology, published by Pergamon Press.

∎ 7 ∎

CD-ROM and Multimedia Publishing

Nancy D. Lane

Whereas many sophisticated optical disc technologies for document storage require mainframe computers and specialized equipment for access, compact disc-read only memory (CD-ROM) technology is likely to emerge as a standard peripheral for the personal computer, as common as a printer. CD-ROM can replace floppy and hard disks to store text, data, or images; however, because CD-ROM is prerecorded, the stored information cannot be added to, deleted, or changed. According to Carl Stork of Microsoft, the growth of the CD-ROM market will depend on affordable hardware, readily available through retail outlets; agreed-upon standards; and low-cost, high-interest titles for a horizontal or mass market. At present, much of the development is in vertical or specialist markets.[1]

One of the major strengths of CD-ROM is that it can hold a wide range of digital formats: data, text, graphic, image, animation, video, and sound. The relative storage capacity of these formats is shown in Table 7.1. With the availability of this range of media formats, one of the challenges for the developer will be to integrate successfully the options available for the purpose required.

Data is stored and retrieved differently in CD-ROM compared with magnetic disks. The two types of storage and retrieval mechanisms correspond to the two types available on videodisc, constant angular velocity and constant linear velocity, as discussed in chapter 4. In magnetic disks, data is recorded in sectors arranged on concentric rings called tracks. Each disk has a specified number of tracks and sectors, cut like pieces of a pie. They spin at a constant rate, or CAV.

CD-ROM discs, however, have sectors arranged in a continuous spiral, similar to a phonograph record. They spin at varying speeds—faster when reading the inner sectors and slower when reading the outer sectors—so that the data sectors pass the reading head at a constant speed, or CLV. Average rotation speed is 200 to 500 rpm, with an average access time of one to two seconds.[2]

Although this configuration allows greater storage density than magnetic disk, it results in slower retrieval time. This is because the reading head must travel along the spiral track to reach the right sector; to do so the disc must be slowed down or speeded up, a mechanical process. However, the data transfer rate from disc into memory is approximately 150K bytes per second, which falls between the rate for floppy disks (31K bytes per second) and hard disks (625K bytes per second).

Table 7.1. CD-ROM Storage Capacity for Various Media Formats

540-600 megabytes of data

270,000 pages of text (A 20 volume encyclopedia with an index to every word would fill approximately one-quarter of the disc space.)

1800 digitized images (200 dots per inch, 12-to-1 compression)

18,000 pages of computer graphics

1,500 floppy disks (5 1/4-inch)

74 minutes of music

4,500 hours of digitized voice

RANGE OF CD-ROM PRODUCTS

A decision to purchase CD-ROM products should be based on a real need, and not just a desire to jump on the technology bandwagon. Considerations should include existing online and manual usage, document backup, cost comparisons, and availability and compatibility of equipment. Reviews in publications such as *CD-ROM Librarian* [3] should always be consulted before purchase, as such reviews alert potential purchasers to problems as well as alternatives.

When choosing between discs available from different producers but with similar content (for example, machine-readable cataloging [MARC] records, serials directories, government documents, or MEDLINE citations), decisions should be based on factors such as the disc's search software and what it can do, relative response times, costs, and the hardware on which it operates. In addition, some discs offer interfaces to various library systems, in particular for acquisitions or cataloging, and this may be a major consideration.

The types of CD-ROMs of greatest interest to libraries are described more fully below, with examples given for each type. A guide to discs is published in UNESCO's *Guide to CD-ROM,*[4] and a regular update of discs available is published in *CD-ROM Review.*[5] *CD-ROMs in Print,* published by Meckler (Westport, Conn.) lists the following for each CD-ROM title: data provider, distributor, players, search software, software producer, microcomputers, minimum memory, peripherals, update frequency, and price, as well as an annotated description. Indexes are available by title, subject, data providers and distributors, and players.

Abstracting and Indexing Services

Numerous print and online abstracting and indexing services also supply CD-ROM discs. These include MEDLINE, Applied Science and Technology Index, National Technical Information Service (NTIS) covering U.S. government-sponsored research, Educational Resources Information Clearinghouse (ERIC), Psychological Abstracts (PSYCLIT), Infotrac magazine index, Public Affairs Information Service (PAIS), AGRICOLA covering agriculture and related fields, and MLA Bibliography covering language and literature. Some of the more popular databases such as MEDLINE and ERIC are available from more than one vendor, with different search options and software as well as pricing policies.

The H.W. Wilson Company offers a wide range of its indexes on CD-ROM, some of which are important for bibliographic control such as Bibliographic Index, Book Review Digest, Vertical File Index, and Biography Index, as well as other general and specialized journal indexes in the humanities, social sciences, and sciences. The Newsbank Electronic Index provides subject indexing of articles from a wide range of U.S. newspapers on current issues and events, business, people, film and television, and the arts. The articles themselves are available on microfiche.

Cataloging Records and Public Access Catalogs

A number of CD-ROM publishers have used MARC records as the basis for their products. BiblioFile, which was introduced in 1985, comprised four discs containing 3 million records. General Research Corporation's LaserQuest provides more than 4 million records and adds about 150,000 records to the database in each cumulation. Both the Online Computer Library Center (OCLC) and the Western Library Network (WLN) offer CD-ROM databases that complement their online systems. The British Library General

Catalogue of Printed Books to 1975, representing over 8.5 million volumes, is being published and released progressively by Saztec Europe.

In 1985 Brodart introduced LePac, the first CD-ROM public access catalog system. The system can store 1 million MARC records on a single CD-ROM disc, along with cross-references, with access by author, title, and subject. If required, the system can support up to four disc drives for access to 4 million records. Marcive was the first company to develop write once-read many (WORM) discs for a library public access catalog.[6]

Interestingly, a number of developing countries are in the forefront of CD-ROM technology for their library catalogs. The library of Papua New Guinea's University of Technology converted from computer output microfiche (COM) to CD-ROM in late 1987 using the LePac system. The catalog includes all books added to the library service since 1983, when the original COM catalog was developed.[7] The University of Mexico has also developed a Spanish-language CD-ROM system for its new acquisitions, which was demonstrated at the International Book Fair in Guadalajara in 1988.

Acquisitions

The Books in Print Plus system from R. R. Bowker includes listings for over 850,000 current and forthcoming books. The search software permits searching by author, keyword, publisher, subject, language, price, publication year, International Standard Book Number (ISBN), grade level, and other characteristics. The Tacoma Public Library, for example, uses it for bibliographic verification, automated ordering, compilation of bibliographies, and reference.[8] The Library Corporation's LaserSearch includes 1.5 million records for U.S. books in print, the names and addresses for approximately 20,000 publishers, and an automated acquisitions module that converts the data into a purchase order for printing or sending to a vendor electronically.

Ulrich's Plus provides access to more than 100,000 serial titles as well as an index to current and former International Standard Serial Numbers (ISSNs). The Faxon Company and EBSCO Industries have also developed serials databases. A number of companies have developed modules within their library automation packages to link such databases into the acquisitions modules.

Reference

Grolier's Electronic Encyclopedia holds the full text of the 20-volume *Academic American Encyclopedia* – over 30,000 articles. McGraw-Hill publishes an electronic reference work based on its printed science and technology dictionary and encyclopedia.

Microsoft's Bookshelf is described as a tool for serious writers and works in conjunction with most major word-processing software. (Word-processing is described in more detail in chapter 8.) It includes several standard reference works, including a dictionary, thesaurus, style manual, almanac, dictionary of quotations, and zip code directory. Access is seamless; the cursor is placed on the word in the text to be looked up, and is selected from the on-screen menu.

Compact Disclosure provides financial information for over 12,000 public companies in the United States, which is updated every two months. Reports contain data from corporate annual reports, proxy statements, and Securities Exchange Commission filings. The Classification and Search Support Information System (CASSIS) is a patent information data service supported by the U.S. Patent and Trademark Office. The database also includes the full text of the *US Patent Classification Manual.*

Microsoft's Small Business Consultant includes information from 220 publications, including many available through the government's Small Business Administration. Contents cover planning, finance, management, and marketing. Microsoft's StatPack includes the *Statistical Abstract of the United States,* as well as statistics covering public lands, business, wages, and agriculture. It includes spreadsheet files that feed into Lotus 1-2-3 or Excel. (Spreadsheets are explained in more detail in chapter 8.) Slater Hall Information Products offers an array of statistical data series, including business indications, census of agriculture, and population statistics.

Similar types of sources are available internationally. For example, the Australian Business Connections database contains an extensive range of marketing data about Australia's top 20,000 companies. The companies are ranked by size, and information includes types of business, sales volume, types of computers, names and positions of senior officers, and other characteristics. Australia on Disc is an enhanced telephone directory containing millions of Australian business names, addresses, and phone numbers. Residential directories are also included for Australia's two largest cities, Sydney and Melbourne, and for the national capital, Canberra.

Document Delivery

Document delivery via CD-ROM is being tested by 10 leading European publishers and the Commission of European Communities through the Adonis project. The trial involves 217 biomedical serials from the publishers' own lists, selected because they were requested most frequently for interlibrary loan (ILL). The full text of all issues published in 1987 and 1988 are indexed and stored digitally in bit-mapped mode (discussed in chapter 5, and again later in this chapter). When requests are received for these materials, the appropriate CD-ROM disc is searched, and the item is printed out immediately. The printouts are equal to high-quality photocopy standard and include half-tones, graphs, and tables.[9]

Educational Materials

The Electronic Map Cabinet and Webster's Ninth New Collegiate Dictionary from Highlighted Data make use of both graphic and audio capabilities. Map Cabinet enables users to zoom in from an overview and select a close-up map of any region in the United States. Webster's features recorded pronunciations of all entry words, in addition to the full text and graphics of the print edition. The dictionary can be displayed on-screen in 18-point typesize, making it the world's most comprehensive large-print dictionary for the visually impaired. The Visual Dictionary, which is published by Facts on File and Canada's Quebec/Amerique, includes 1000 images, 10,000 terms, and audio pronunciation in English, French, and Spanish.

The Whole Earth Learning Disc is an interactive electronic catalog compiled from the most useful books and tools appearing in the *Whole Earth Catalog* over the last 20 years. For example, users can access mail order catalogs of blues music with listings of recording artists. A click on a sound button plays a representative sample from the album selected. Or users can find a book review of a field guide to birds, view an excerpt card with text and an illustration of a bird, and click to hear its call.

Xiphias's Time Table of Science and Innovation covers 6000 important events in the history of scientific development, using text, graphics, and sound. The software allows users to select any word in the articles as a search term, and to link personal information and notes to key words in the articles using a hard disk.

In addition to these commercial ventures, several universities are undertaking major development projects. Boston University and Harvard University have collaborated on the Perseum Project, which integrates 100 megabytes of text with 10,000 images that pertain to the history, politics, languages, art, and philosophy of ancient and classical Greece. The University of Southern California's Project Jefferson, based on the U.S. Constitution, has combined curriculum development with online retrieval and hypermedia (discussed in chapter 4 and later in this chapter).

Megazines and Source Databases

Megazine is a word coined to describe a disc that has a variety of source materials combined with bibliographies or indexes, usually related to a particular topic. These often cater for special user groups and comprise almost a library in themselves. Source or knowledge databases contain information organized for immediate retrieval, with no need for referral to printed or other resources.

For example, the Medical Publishing Group's Compact Library on AIDS is aimed at the medical market. Contents include the San Francisco General Hospital Knowledge Base on AIDS, the full text from selected journals, and selected citations and abstracts from MEDLINE. Micromedex Computerized Clinical Information Services contain full-text drug information dealing with poisons and drugs, including toxicology information, identification, and therapy; drug dosage, interactions, and clinical use; and drugs in acute care.

Diversified Data Resources' CD-ROM Sourcedisc includes a glossary of CD-ROM acronyms, current essays and articles about CD-ROM, the full text of Microsoft's CD-ROM publications, and marketing information on over 250 commercially available CD-ROM titles in print. Many of these titles include a demonstration of the search software and contents.

Other Products

In addition to the range of products of interest to general and special libraries, there are products of value to a number of professions and specialist groups. This range seems to be limited only by the imaginations of the developers. Examples are listed in Table 7.2.

Table 7.2. Range of CD-ROM Products

Text	*Image*
Conference proceedings	Architectural drawings
Contracts	Circuit diagrams
Government regulations	Digitized artwork
Legal reference	Document archives
Mailing lists	Engineering drawings
Membership directories	Fingerprint files
Patents	Graphics primitives
Product catalogs	Medical images
Research grants	Musical scores
Technical documentation	Photograph banks
Telephone directories	Satellite photographs
Yellow pages	Visual catalogs

Numeric and Data	*Audio*
Cartographic systems	Lectures
Credit card verification	Music
Econometric databases	Sound effects libraries
Geological data	Speeches
Government statistics	Talking books
Invoices and purchase orders	Transcriptions
Meteorological data	
Navigational systems	*Multimedia*
Oceanographic data	Education
Payroll data	Entertainment
Rate tables	Expert systems
Scientific research data	Training
Software publishing	
Time series	

Source: Thomas M. Lopez, "The CD-ROM Solution: Solving Business Problems with CD-ROM Applications," *Optical Information Systems* 6, no. 2 (March/April 1986): 122-24.

ADVANTAGES AND DISADVANTAGES OF CD-ROM

The major advantages of CD-ROM include the following:

1. *Versatility.* With the range of media that can be integrated on a disc, as well as the capabilities of the search software available, CD-ROMs can be designed to fulfill numerous roles in information retrieval, education, mapping, art and creative design, and numerous other fields. This wide range of data is readily available for reading into memory and subsequent data manipulation.

2. *High storage density.* CD-ROMs can store 540 to 600 megabytes of information per side, 1000 to 1500 times as much as a 5¼-inch floppy disk. For other comparisons, refer to Table 7.1.

3. *Ease of use.* Producers and manufacturers are attempting to make CD-ROMs more user friendly through menu-driven options, availability of routing information at the bottom of each screen, use of color, and other features.

4. *Durability.* CD-ROM discs are less prone to damage from scratches or spills than floppy disks because of their plastic coating. Furthermore, data cannot be accidentally erased or destroyed as can occur with floppy disks if their write-protect stickers are missing or with hard disks should they crash.

5. *Fixed-cost searching.* Once purchased, databases on CD-ROM can be accessed without paying telecommunications or connect-time charges.

There are also a number of disadvantages to CD-ROM. These include the following:

1. *Cost.* Initial costs are relatively high. These include the equipment, as well as the subscription costs for databases and reference materials.

2. *Access limitations.* In a library setting, either separate terminals are required for each CD-ROM disc; or, if there is only one terminal, the CD-ROM disc, and in some cases the search software on floppy disk as well, need to be changed each time a new database is required. Furthermore, only one person can search a database at a time on a terminal, whereas with printed indexes, several people can use the resource at once as they search over a range of dates.

3.   *Currency*. CD-ROMs are not updated as often as online databases. Thus, an online search is still required for users who want the most recent material.

4.   *Response time*. CD-ROMs have a slower response time than hard disks for searching online or retrieving information. [10]

5.   *Lack of standardization*. Not all discs nor all equipment conforms to the same standards; subsequently, not all discs can be played on all equipment. Philips and Sony developed the physical standards for CD-audio, often referred to as the "Red Book," before the launch of CD-audio players in 1982. Similarly, they developed standards for the physical format of CD-ROMs, the "Yellow Book," in 1983.

What they did not do was define the logical format for CD-ROM, namely, the types of information to be stored (including data, text, graphics, audio, and video); the means of encoding or compressing this information; and the logical layout of the information on the disc (for example, where to store the directory, how to identify files, and how to open a file). This situation has improved markedly, however.

A group of vendors calling themselves the High Sierra Group got together in 1985 to develop such a standard. It became a de facto standard immediately and was subsequently approved with minor changes as ISO 9660: Volume and File Structure of CD-ROM Information Interchange. Difficulties occur primarily for equipment or discs purchased before the standard was introduced or purchased from developers who have not conformed to the standard.

PRODUCTION OF CD-ROMS

The production of CD-ROMs is similar to the production of CD-audios. If not already in machine-readable form, the information database is keyed in or optically scanned. Directories and indexes are built up to work in tandem with the search software used in the application. The database and indexes go through a premastering step in which special codes are integrated into the data to permit location and reading of the data by the CD-drive.

The premastered data is transferred to magnetic tape for disc production. It is written onto a glass master by a laser, which burns the microscopic pits onto the surface of the master, as described in chapter 6. Sophisticated error detection and correction techniques are used to ensure the integrity of the data. The quality control is exceptional: approximately one error per 2,000 discs.

From this master, a stamper is created that is used to replicate the injection-molded CD-ROM discs. The discs are coated with a protective layer of lacquer. The duplication of the discs is relatively inexpensive, as low as $3 per disc depending on the production run. However, the high prices charged relate to one-off costs of initial data capture, indexing, premastering, and mastering, which must all be included in the costing. Manufacture of CD-ROMs has led to some awe-inspiring statistics, listed in Table 7.3.

Table 7.3. Some Compact Disc Statistics

The spiral track on an average compact disc is 2.8 miles long.

The track's width is 1.2 micrometers, one-sixtieth that of the groove in a long-playing record.

Each disc contains approximately five billion pits that contain the disc's information. If each pit were magnified to the size of a grain of rice, the CD would be 1.3 miles in diameter. If each pit were magnified to the size of a footstep, the track would equal some 300,000 miles, a journey to the moon and halfway back.

If the five billion pits were compacted together, the total volume would be 0.5 cubic millimeters – about the size of a pinhead.

As a storage medium, the CD can hold 15 billion bits of data.

Source: "Laser Disk Technology (A State-of-the-Art Report for Librarians): Part 3," *Kansas Library Automation News,* no. 12 (January 1986).

EQUIPMENT REQUIREMENTS

In order to set up a CD-ROM workstation, the following equipment is necessary:

1. A microcomputer with a minimum of 512K bytes of random access memory (RAM), and preferably more, with associated hard disk or floppy disk drives, depending on the requirements of

the software. IBM, Apple, and a number of other manufacturers provide equipment that can support CD-ROMs.

2.   CD-ROM drive. Options include internal drives, which fit into conventional personal computer disk drives; stand-alone drives, which can be front loading or top loading; multidrives, which combine up to four drives in a combined unit; and jukeboxes, which swap discs like jukeboxes for phonograph records. Drive manufacturers include Philips, Sony, Hitachi, DEC, Denon, Toshiba, Amdek, and Apple. Drives are reviewed from time to time in *CD-ROM Review*.[11]

Apple CD SC drives, introduced in 1987, provide desk accessory software and an audio chip set that allows the drive to play commercial compact audio discs. The CD SC does not tie up the computer's operating system while playing compact discs, so users can listen to their favorite music while they work at their terminals – so long as they do not need to access a CD-ROM!

As standards are not yet universal, libraries and other purchasers should choose drives that are compatible with the CD-ROM products they plan to use. In particular, there can be problems in trying to use more than one disc per drive as the disc requirements may be incompatible. Even if the hardware is not a problem, separate search software may still be needed for each CD product, which means a reboot to change discs. Assuming all discs run on the same software, there could still be a problem monitoring the users when they change discs – more one of theft than damage.

3.   Controller/interface, including cabling. This is needed to connect the drive with the microcomputer. The choice is primarily between the PC-BUS to connect IBM PCs and compatibles, or the Small Computer Systems Interface (SCSI) bus to connect a range of other microprocessors. In addition, software is now normally provided through Microsoft Extensions, which is being shipped with the drives. Drives purchased early may need to buy Extensions separately.

4.   Keyboard or other input device such as a touch screen, mouse, or joystick.

5.   Monitor. More and more CD-ROM products are available in high-resolution color, so it is worth considering whether to purchase a monitor with the necessary color capacity or to upgrade an existing monochrome monitor with the appropriate graphics cards. For example, monochrome display screens deliver

images whose resolutions may range from 70 to 150 dots per inch, while many CD-ROM images are now being stored at resolutions of 200 to 400 dots per inch.

6.   Printer. A low-cost dot matrix or inkjet printer saves users time at the terminal, particularly if they are copying down index or catalog information. Laser printers, although more expensive, may also be worth considering, as their costs are coming down.

7.   Modem for online searching, to update information located on CD-ROM disc, if applicable.[12]

In the first few years of CD-ROM availability, many disc publishers sold their products bundled with equipment purchase or rental. Now that many more discs are available and discs and equipment are more standardized, libraries may want to purchase equipment separately. Configurations can include one database per workstation, two or more databases per workstation, a modem for conversion to online searching, integration with related computer software, and integration with other automated library systems, including online public access catalogs (OPACs).

Equipment problems are much fewer now than in the past, but they can still exist, particularly if users are trying to make use of older equipment. These problems can include lack of compatibility among the computer operating system, the CD-ROM drive, and the interface card; discs using pre-High Sierra, High Sierra, and ISO 9660 standards; drives lacking Microsoft Extensions; IBM compatibles that are not 100 percent compatible; earlier versions of DOS; and older drives that may not work with faster computers (greater than 6 Mhz). Furthermore, the minimum RAM stated according to requirements may result in slow response times, and more RAM may be required for efficient public operation.

In addition, most application discs come with their own search software on floppy disk, which must be loaded before the CD-ROM discs can be searched. There are more than 30 companies which now manufacture such software.[13] The better search software offers a number of features, which are listed in Table 7.4.

HYPERTEXT

Hypertext is also being used for CD-ROM retrieval. It allows the linking of concepts associated in any number of ways, not just through the relatively rigid cross-referencing structure found in subject headings lists and thesauruses used in library catalogs and periodical indexes. In effect, a body of information can be referenced within itself.[14] Hypertext is a personal information retrieval tool, which allows developers as well as users to navigate their way through the contents of a database and link it as they wish.

Originally available on the Macintosh computer as HyperCard, various versions are now being written for MS-DOS machines. Hypertext is being promoted as the fourth generic category of software – along with word processing, spreadsheets, and database management systems, which are discussed in chapters 8 and 9 in this book.

Table 7.4. Software Capabilites to Consider in Selecting CD-ROMs

Boolean searching using AND, OR and NOT

Ability to search multiword phrases as adjacent terms

Reasonable response times, even from relatively complex search statements

Thesaurus capabilities

Truncation or "wildcard" searches, including single or multiple characters as a prefix or suffix

Nesting (indication of the order of performance of operations through use of parentheses)

Postings (statement of number of documents containing the search term)

Highlighting of search terms within documents

Option of menu-driven or command-based searching

Option of printing or saving retrieved files to disk

Option of transferring search online

Option of saving search parameters to use again later.

Source: Linda Stewart, "Picking CD-ROMs for Public Use," *American Libraries* (October 1987): 738-40; and Anneli Heimburger, *Guide to CD-ROM* (Paris: UNESCO, 1988), 24.

Although hypertext is used primarily for linking concepts to each other in PC databases, developer Bill Atkinson indicated that he had the concept of CD-ROM firmly in mind as he created HyperCard. His intent was to provide seamless integration – that is, the ability to move in and out of a range of applications effortlessly and without interruption to the work flow, preferably with one click of a mouse.[15] The Electronic Encyclopedia, Xiphias's Timetable of Science and Technology, and the Whole Earth Learning Disc described earlier in this chapter are some of the applications that take advantage of hypertext.

Hypermedia is the extension of hypertext, in which the linked concepts can be text, graphics, speech, audio, still images, animation, and video. The journal *Hypermedia*[16] provides a forum for research and discussion on hypermedia, although not specifically in relation to CD-ROM. The first issue contains a bibliography giving an overview of the developments in this emerging field.[17]

MANAGEMENT OF CD-ROMS IN THE LIBRARY

Unlike online searching, which normally requires an intermediary, users can search CD-ROM databases themselves. This availability to users requires adequate planning and budgeting, promotion, training, monitoring, and maintenance.

With planning and budgeting, it must be recognized that equipment and discs are not a one-off cost; many discs are available on subscription, which must be paid each year in order for discs to be updated. It may not be possible for costs to be met from a decrease in online searching, as several early studies have shown little drop-off in online activity with the availability of CD-ROM. There are also hidden costs such as paper, ribbons, and other maintenance, which in one study cost $2000 per printer per year.[18]

Managers have used various methods to promote CD-ROM products. Posters, articles in newsletters or newspapers, and mailing of announcements to selected groups bring in the curious. Demonstrations can be organized as part of library orientation or bibliographic instruction programs, or as special public relations exercises. Videotape programs illustrating some searches can cater for large groups in a lecture situation. However, the best source of promotion is usually word of mouth: satisfied users tell their friends.

The acquisition of CD-ROMs must be incorporated into the collection development policy of the library, especially for reference, curriculum support, and megazine discs. There are particular problems of accessibility to the megazine discs, which, for example, might include journal articles, conference proceedings, and monographs. A decision must be made whether to catalog the disc at all; to catalog the disc as an entity; to catalog individually some of the contents of the disc, such as monographs and conference proceedings; or to catalog individually all of the contents.

Some CD-ROM indexes are limited by date and do not include early materials. Users may be unaware of this and assume their search has been comprehensive. The decision must also be made as to whether printed copies of these indexes should be retained, especially if there are space problems. In addition, looking forward, a decision must be made as to whether continued duplication of print and CD-ROM copies is affordable, or whether the purposes served by each are so different as to require both versions.

User Access and Training

Many users, particularly those who have used OPACs or who have home computers, are pleased to experiment with CD-ROM and require little if any training. Early studies of user acceptance showed that from 80 to 95 per cent of users in university and special library settings needed little or no training for simple index discs such as InfoTrac. However, many librarians attending continuing education seminars on CD-ROM have indicated that for the more complex discs, training would help users feel assured that they were getting maximum output from the disc.

Training can take many forms, including integration with formal bibliographic instruction, demonstration sessions based on sign-up, individual point-of-use instruction, quick reference cards or instructions at the terminal, tutorials for self-instruction on the disc itself as part of the main menu selection, or reliance on help screens. Problems occur, not so much in using simple systems like InfoTrac, but, in particular, when users encounter differences in searching procedures among different discs. For advanced users, differences between command-driven modes for discs and online retrieval modes for the same database can cause confusion. Furthermore, some CD-ROMs have dropped data elements that are included in online searches.

Problems have occurred because of insufficient terminals to serve the number of users who wish to take advantage of the systems. The physical space requirement may need to be greater than expected, as people tend to wait in line for terminals during busy periods. Some libraries have had to limit searching sessions to 10 to 15 minutes maximum; others have developed a system of signing up on schedule sheets. Other libraries have limited the number of items users can print out.

A reference librarian may need to be stationed in the vicinity of the terminals to answer questions and ensure equal opportunity of access for users. With an increasing amount of time on the reference desk dedicated to point-of-use instruction, other regular activities may be affected.

Licensing

Normal licensing agreements are usually single site, for a single terminal with individual users. Other uses, such as downloading of data for editing and multiple distribution, servicing multiple users through networked terminals, or time-sharing or similar arrangements, may require specific written consent and appropriate supplementary payment.

Licensing agreements are becoming more important as CD-ROM is integrated into local area networks (LANs), discussed in chapter 2. For example, Information Access Reference Center offers up to 8 terminals, with access to 16 CD-drives, 8 videodisc players, and dial-out access to remote databases. Meridian Data has announced CD Net for smaller LANs and CD Server for medium- to large-size LANs, which allow for the integration of multiple CD-drives and databases. Apple File Server and Apple Talk software allow multiple-terminal access to a single CD-drive and "incompatible" systems to share files, CD-ROMs, and other peripherals.

CD-ROM IN COMPARISON WITH RELATED TECHNOLOGIES

Similarly to videotex as described in chapter 5, images may be stored digitally in two ways: character-based or bit-mapped. Character-based information is represented electronically in bytes, one byte per character. Data captured as characters are represented in the computer as characters, and can be searched as characters. Bit-mapped information, however, stores data as a picture comprising tiny dots that make up the image of the data. The number of dots per inch (dpi) that make up the picture determine its resolution – how distinctly the picture is described, and hence, stored or displayed.[19]

Each dot is represented in the computer by a bit. A page of information scanned at 300 dpi requires over 1 million bytes of storage. Depending on the amount of white space per page, it can be compressed to about 100,000 bytes. The image-based representation is significantly more data-intensive than a character-based representation of the same page, by a ratio of more than 50 to 1.

CD-ROM overlaps many other technologies, and in the future, may vie with more and more of them. These include microform, magnetic storage media, and videodisc.

As described in chapter 6, microforms are well established, and computer-assisted retrieval (CAR) applications allow for rapid document retrieval. However, many users are not satisfied with the image quality and the reader/printers available. Although not yet as cost-effective, CD-ROM may soon start to challenge computer output microfiche (COM) library catalogs, providing more rapid and interactive retrieval. Linked to hard disk systems, library catalogs can be kept completely up to date, with seamless interfaces or transfers between CD-ROM and hard disk.

The CD-ROM can store approximately 25 times more data than a 20-megabyte hard disk. However, although mainframe magnetic storage is more expensive, retrieval is also faster. But because of the vast amount of storage required, for image storage to a greater degree than for text storage, the potential for CD-ROM is immense.

A videodisc incorporating analog information can carry 54,000 images versus a few thousand for CD-ROM. Thus, videodisc can readily handle motion picture sequences, up to 30 minutes, while CD-ROM cannot. (The reasons for this are discussed later.) Such analog images, however, cannot be processed or manipulated by computer.[20]

In summary, CD-ROM is an appropriate choice of medium when the database contained on it is large, has wide distribution, can benefit from enhanced searching capabilities, is a workstation application, and is historical or infrequently updated.[21]

COMPACT DISC INTERACTIVE (CD-I)

In 1986, Philips and Sony announced another standard (the "Green Book") for the development of compact disc interactive (CD-I). CD-I is not a computer peripheral like a CD-ROM drive, but a self-contained system. It is aimed at the mass consumer market for entertainment and education and is intended to be as user friendly as a typical home appliance.

The CD-I player incorporates both a monitor and input device and includes decoder chips for graphics, video, sound, and text. All discs will be interchangeable, to play on all CD-I machines. The discs incorporate their own retrieval software, so a separate floppy disk is not required for operation. The equipment also plays existing CD-audio discs.

Philips publicly demonstrated its first fully functional CD-I disc in 1987, soon making its developmental apparatus – authoring systems, software tools, prototype players, and demonstration discs – available to hardware and software industries. A range of software products is currently in production for the CD-I player.

The standards for various CD-I options are outlined in Table 7.5. These options create the potential for diversity in the design of CD-I products. The highest level video option allows for a capacity of up to 7,000 photographic-quality pictures. There are 16 million color variations possible, with 32,768 available for user-manipulated graphics. CD-I also allows the use of single-plane visual effects, such as cuts, scrolls, pans, and mosaics, and of two-plane effects such as wipes, dissolves, and transparent color keys and mattes.

With 16 parallel audio channels available, albeit at the lowest sound quality, the CD-I is ideal for multilingual applications, allowing producers to create parallel soundtracks in different languages. For example, a Philips demonstration disc features narration synchronized with a series of still pictures in three languages: English, Spanish, and Dutch. More than 19 hours of audio are possible on a single disc.

A full-motion digital video image can occupy up to one-ninth of the screen. With some quality loss, a video image at 12 frames per second with accompanying sound can occupy over 51 percent of the screen in NTSC (the U.S. television standard) and 42 percent in PAL (the European and Australian standard).

Table 7.5. CD-I Standards and Options

Video resolution
Normal (360 by 240 pixels), equivalent to U.S. television receivers
Double (720 by 240 pixels)
High (720 by 480 pixels), in anticipation of high definition television

Video quality levels (coding standard indicated in parentheses)
Photographic-quality pictures (Delta YUV)
User-manipulated graphics (RGB 555)
Sharp graphics and text (CLUT 8)
Animation (Run-length encoded)

Digital video
High-quality full-motion digital video, occupying up to one-ninth of
the screen
Lower-quality full-motion digital video, occupying up to one-half of
the screen

Audio (a channel is equivalent to a maximum of seventy minutes
continuous playing time)
CD digital audio, stereo, one channel
High-fidelity music, stereo or mono, two or four channels
(approximately FM radio standard)
Mid-fidelity music, stereo or mono, four or eight channels
(approximately AM radio standard)
Speech, stereo, or mono, eight or sixteen channels (approximately
telephone quality)

Source: "Fully Functional CD-I Disc Unveiled Publicly at Microsoft CD-ROM
Conference," press release, Philips International B.V., 1988.

CD-I applications are expected to fall into the categories shown in Table
7.6. The terms *edutainment* and *infotainment* have been coined to describe
these applications, which are aimed at learning as well as leisure activities.

Whether or not CD-I becomes a mass-market success will partially depend
on the cost of the hardware and the quality and availability of the software.
Hardware prices are expected to be in the $1,000 to $2,000 range.

Production of CD-I discs requires extensive research, scripting, design, filming, and graphics work, easily exceeding $1 million per title. These development costs will in turn require high-volume sales in order for unit costs to be acceptable to consumers. However, corporate strategy in the product launch, coupled with the tastes and interests of the target market, may ultimately determine whether CD-I takes off like CD-audio, or languishes like videodisc.[22]

Table 7.6. Types of CD-I Applications

Education and training
  Do-it-yourself
  Home learning
  Reference books
  Talking books

Entertainment
  Music plus (with text, notes, pictures, etc.)
  Action, strategic, and adventure games
  Simulations of sports and travel

Creative leisure
  Drawing, painting, and animation
  Filming
  Composing

Travel
  Maps
  Navigation
  Tourist information
  Language learning

Work
  Document processing
  Information retrieval

Source: Bert Gall, "CD-I: A Powerful Interactive Audio/Video System," *Bulletin of the American Society for Information Science* 13, no. 6 (August/September 1987): 18–20; and R. Bruno and M. Mizushima, "New Developments in Optical Media," *Optical Information Systems* 6, no. 4 (July, August 1986), 319.

DIGITAL VIDEO INTERACTIVE (DVI)

The General Electric Company, RCA Laboratories, and the David Sarnoff Research Center in Princeton, New Jersey, are creating a new technology that takes advantage of the digital storage capacity of CD-ROM to provide high-quality motion video that differs from and exceeds the CD-I standard. This development is called digital video interactive (DVI). Although DVI can work with all types of audio-visual materials in digital form – still images, audio, graphics, computer data, or text – it is in video that its techniques are primarily of value.

DVI has the ability to display approximately one hour of full-screen motion video from compressed digital data stored on a single, standard CD-ROM disc. DVI motion video can be combined with foreground video objects, text, dynamic graphics, and multitrack audio, all under the user's control. This technology is expected to fill a market niche for realistic simulations for education and training; video tools such as animation, editing, titling, and special effects; presentation preparation and display; marketing, especially at point of sale; and scientific imaging.

Producing digital-based video is a complex process that requires a large amount of data storage. To convert a standard frame of analog video (512 by 400 pixels) into digital form requires about 600 kilobytes. Thirty frames of video must be displayed each second in order to portray full-motion effects. A standard CD-ROM disc holds about 540 megabytes of data, and thus can store only about 30 seconds of digital video. However, because CD-ROM reads data out at the rate of 150 kilobytes per second, it is not fast enough to show video at its real-time speed. Thus, it would take more than one hour to read out 30 seconds of full-screen digital video!

DVI is solving these problems through special techniques of data compression and decompression. Before a master is made of the compact disc, the digital video is compressed so that fewer bits are required to represent each second of display. The compression process uses complex algorithms that require large computer capacity; however, this compression is done only once and not in real time.

When the CD-ROM video is played, the compressed data must be decompressed, in real time. DVI uses a very large scale integration (VLSI) chip set called a video display processor (VDP) to perform the decompression and display. The pixel processor is capable of processing 12.5 million instructions per second, many in parallel. The output display processor allows for the level of resolution (from 256 to 768 pixels horizontally and up to 512 pixels vertically) and choice of color (up to 16 million different options). This wide color selection permits DVI to bring television-quality pictures to the computer screen.

DVI is also of value in storing still images. The compression capability of DVI can save storage space (decreasing it by approximately ten times) and improve the speed of reading stills from storage. Decompression of stills, even at high resolution, is completed in a fraction of a second. DVI can store up to 7000 stills at high resolution (768 by 480 pixels); 10,000 at medium resolution (512 by 480 pixels); and 40,000 at low resolution (256 by 240 pixels).

To date, a number of demonstration and pilot discs have been made. These include a flight simulator, complete with three-dimensional models of terrain and video-mapped buildings, authentic sounds, and instrument panels; a guide to Palenque, the Mayan ruin in Mexico, which provides 360-degree panoramic views and multitracked background sounds; a Sesame Street wordbook, which uses multiple video sequences for words that begin with the same letter and incorporates stock footage from the television show; a design and decorating package, which allows users to "furnish" a room with three-dimensional models of furniture and photographs of fabrics, wallpaper, and carpets used to cover the walls and floors; and a dynamic text tool kit, which allows users to create, edit, animate, change color, preview, and perform other operations on text and bit-mapped images.

Although these demonstration discs indicate the potential for DVI, there are still major hurdles to overcome before the process is commercially viable. For the types of applications envisaged, it will be necessary to retain picture quality and integrity, while at the same time achieving compression ratios of more than 100 to 1. The extensive processing required may preclude cost competitiveness for years to come. Commercial development, however, should eventually be achieved, as Microsoft, Lotus, and Intel have publicly announced their support for the DVI standard.

FUTURE TRENDS

As CD technologies – and the links between the technologies – become even more sophisticated, the potential for creative applications will grow. At present, CD-ROM is a format standard for placing digital data on a compact disc; it does not specify what kind of data, only how the data is to be arranged. It is the underlying structure used by both CD-I and DVI. CD-I is a specification for an interactive, multimedia product for the mass consumer market, relying on stand-alone, user-friendly hardware. DVI is a technology relying on sophisticated data compression to deliver motion and still images more compactly.

It is hard to predict future trends because of the uncertainty with which the mass market will accept these products. However, among the trends that have been predicted are the following:

1. CD-ROM will be used widely as an adjunct to the personal computer at home and in the office. This will occur as prices for information discs drop.

2. Sales of equipment will no longer be so strongly linked with software. There will be less bundling of hardware and software packages.

3. The growing horizontal and vertical markets should decrease the cost of most discs.

4. There will be an increase in the audio and visual features of what have to date been primarily text-based discs.

5. There will be new types of uses, including software, clip art, clip sounds, and multilingual interfaces.

6. Value-added search software will proliferate–for example, to generate mailing labels from directories or to manipulate statistical data by integrating it into spreadsheets.

7. Market leaders, and thus informal standards, will emerge in search software.

8. CD-ROM will become more prevalent in the LAN environment, using jukeboxes and multidrives. Although response time in a LAN environment can now be slow depending on the number of simultaneous users, advances in technology and applications software should improve this problem.

9. There will be growing, innovative uses of hypermedia linking textual, visual, and sound retrieval.

10. There will be greater compatibility among technologies, allowing the linking of CD-ROM, OPACs, and online searching from a single terminal.

Although the acceptance of the technology has been very high, researchers have found that most users are not aware of nor do they make use of the very powerful and flexible search capabilities built into CD-ROM databases and search structures. Librarians will need to design better learning opportunities so that users can incorporate this new technology, which has been with us only since 1986, into their information-seeking skills.

NOTES

1. Carl Stork, addressing the Microsoft Third International Conference on CD-ROM, 1 March 1988, Seattle, Wash., as reported in Nancy D. Lane, "Future Shock," *Incite* 9, no. 4 (25 March 1988): 1.

2. Hugh Marlor, "Data Structures for CD-ROM," *Bulletin of the American Society for Information Science* 13, no. 6 (August/September 1987): 18-20.

3. *CD-ROM Librarian* is published by Meckler, 11 Ferry Lane West, Westport, CT 06880.

4. Anneli Heimburger, *Guide to CD-ROM* (Paris: UNESCO, 1988).

5. *CD-ROM Review* is published by IDG Communications /Peterborough, 80 Elm St., Peterborough, NH 03458.

6. Norman Desmarais, "Laserbases for Library Technical Services," *Optical Information Systems* 7, no. 1 (January/February 1987): 57-61.

7. Bernard J. S. Williams, "Document Delivery and Reproduction Survey," *FID News Bulletin* 38, no. 6 (1988): 45-47.

8. Dalia L. Hagan, "The Tacoma Debut of Books in Print Plus," *Library Journal* 112, no. 14 (1 September 1987): 149-51.

9. "ADONIS: A Glimpse into the Future," *National Library of Australia News* no. 4 (June 1989): 1-2.

10. Linda K. Appel, *Optical Information Systems '86: On the Road*, (Portland, Or.: Fred Meyer Charitable Trust Library and Information Resources for the Northwest, 1987), 4.

11. *CD-ROM Review*, address as per note 5.

12. David C. Miller, "Online CD-ROM: Moving Graphic Images," *Inform* 1, no. 3 (March 1987), 28-33, 45; Heimburger, *Guide to CD-ROM*, 19.

13. Janet M. Tiampo, "The Search Is On," *CD-ROM Review* 2, no. 2 (June 1987): 26-31.

14. T. J. Byers, "Built by Association," *PC World* 5, no. 4 (April 1987): 244-51.

15. Bill Atkinson, addressing the Microsoft Third International Conference on CD-ROM, 2 March 1988, Seattle, Wash.

16. *Hypermedia* is published by Taylor Graham Publishing, 500 Chesham House, 150 Regent St., London W1R 5FA, England.

17. Jakob Nielsen, "Hypertext Bibliography," *Hypermedia* 1, no. 1 (Spring 1989): 74-91.

18. Tim Miller, "Early User Reaction to CD-ROM and Videodisc-based Optical Information Products in the Library Market," *Optical Information Systems* 7, no. 3 (May/June 1987): 205-8.

19. David C. Miller, "Text as Image," *Inform* 1, no. 2 (February 1987): 26.

20. David C. Miller, "Text as Image," 33.

21. Shannon Smith Saviers, "Reflections on CD-ROM: Bridging the Gap Between Technology and Purpose," *Special Libraries* 1, no. 4 (Fall 1987): 288-94.

22. Gary Herman, "CD-I: A New Solution Looking for the Problem," *Inter Media* 17, no. 1 (January 1989): 35-39.

SUGGESTED READING

Eaton, Nancy L., Linda Brew MacDonald, and Mara R. Saule. *CD-ROM and Other Optical Information Systems: Implementation Issues for Libraries.* Phoenix: Oryx Press, 1989.

Heimburger, Anneli. *Guide to CD-ROM.* Paris: UNESCO, 1988.

Lambert, Steve, and Suzanne Ropiequet, eds. *CD-ROM, the New Papyrus: The Current and Future State of the Art.* Redmond, Wash: Microsoft Press, 1986.

Oppenheim, Charles, ed. *CD-ROM: Fundamentals to Applications.* London: Butterworths, 1988.

Roth, Judith Paris, ed. *CD-ROM: Applications and Markets.* Westport, Conn.: Meckler, 1988.

■ 8 ■

Personal Computer Software

Linda Main

The major impact of the computer has been on the way we structure, process, access, and present information. It can be argued that just as the printing press had an immense impact on the distribution and availability of information, so the computer–and especially the personal computer–has had an immense impact on the ease, cost, and convenience of using information.

It is important to stress that the term *information* implies meaning, not just facts. Facts are isolated bits of data without context, e.g., two inches of snow fell in Cheyenne last month. What does it mean? Is two inches a lot or a little? Did it cause a disruption? Was it a single storm? To assign meaning requires more information to organize what we have, and it is this organization that computers have a talent for. With the appropriate software a computer can take large collections of facts and convert them into comparisons, graphs, and so on, and thus assign meaning.

Using a software program requires no programming experience. The user need only learn the particular software program commands. This may take a few minutes or several hours, depending on the complexity of the program. Software is either menu-driven, command-driven, or a combination of both. Menu-driven software is easier to use and less intimidating for a beginner; command-driven software requires that the user learn the commands necessary to work the program. Command-driven software, however, is faster and more efficient.

Software is divided into general-purpose software and specific software (i.e., software that will only perform a particular application). General-purpose software is more popular as it offers greater flexibility and can be customized to particular professional needs rather than conforming to a predetermined format. General-purpose software encompasses, among other things, word processing, spreadsheets, database management, integrated software, communications, graphics, including business graphics, and desktop publishing. This chapter concentrates on word processing, spreadsheets, business graphics and desktop publishing; database management is covered in chapter 9.

It is important to realize that software and hardware cannot be divorced. Before moving onto a discussion of software, it is worth mentioning current trends in hardware that have had and continue to have an effect on software development:

1. Extremely fast central processing units (CPUs), the heart of the computer, capable of processing millions of instructions per second.

2. The move towards parallel processing, that is, using multiple CPUs to do different pieces of a problem, in chunks.

3. Increased memory capacity. Until recently, computers could hold only 640K bytes in their internal memory. This translates into approximately 640,000 characters, made up of the software program and the work done by the user with the software program. Computers can now hold up to 32 megabytes in their internal memory. This translates roughly into 32 million characters and means that software developers can build bigger programs capable of more tasks.

4. An ability to link to CD-ROM drives and discs, thus acquiring access to huge volumes of stored information.

5. An ability to link to optical scanners, which will read information into the computer.

Finally, it is worth briefly mentioning artificial intelligence (AI). AI is that area of computer science concerned with making computers "smarter." More specifically, it is a collection of techniques that permits a computer to mimic the human reasoning process. Artificial intelligence is discussed in more detail in chapter 10.

The developments in hardware outlined above will make it possible for AI to affect all types of general-purpose software. The process is already beginning. The term used to describe this process is *embedded artificial intelligence*, and the process makes software more flexible, easier to use, more responsive, and more powerful. For example, in a word-processing program, the software might ask basic questions to help you structure your thoughts, or in a business graphics package, the software could suggest ways to make a graph better.

WORD PROCESSING

Any organization is made up of people and people communicate using words. The mastery of words can make the difference between a sale and no sale, between clarity and confusion, between communication and misunderstanding.[1]

Word-processing software allows the user tremendous flexibility in creating, editing, sorting, and printing all types of documents – letters, memos, articles, reports, and manuscripts. Insertions and deletions can be made, words and paragraphs quickly moved, misspellings corrected, and several revisions of the original text saved. Once the document is complete it can be printed out in a variety of ways by defining margins, spacing, and justification.

The origins of word processing are found in the text-editing programs used by data-processing personnel in the late 1950s. The actual term was coined with the introduction of the first magnetic card typewriter in 1964. Although slow and limited by present standards, the magnetic card typewriter spurred the development of many similar products over the next five years, and the notion of a word-processing department began to replace that of the typing pool.

In the early 1970s, word-processing systems based on small microcomputers with video screens were introduced. The first word processing system suitable for business and professional use on a minicomputer was introduced in 1976. Today word processing is the most commonly used of all software applications for personal computers, and there are thousands of word processing programs available. The most popular are listed in Table 8.1. Some are available for either IBM-compatible or Apple Macintosh equipment, including *WordPerfect* and *Microsoft Word,* while others are marketed for just one type.

Features

All word-processing programs tend to have similar basic structures. They have a writing (or input) mode or function, an editing mode, and a printing (or output) mode. A program with just these limited functions is a simple text editor. At the other end of the scale are programs with capabilities such as right-justified type, underscoring, superscripts, multiple options for formatting, sequential merging of addresses with form letters, spellcheckers, indexes, thesauri, and a capacity for creating footnotes, tables of contents, and outlines.

Table 8.1. Some of the More Popular Word-Processing Programs and Their Publishers

Display Write, IBM Corporation, White Plains, N.Y.
Lotus Manuscript, Lotus Development Corporation, Cambridge, Mass.
MacWrite, Claris, Cupertino, Calif.
Microsoft Word, Microsoft Corporation, Redmond, Wash.
MultiMate, Ashton-Tate, Torrance, Calif.
PC-Write, Quicksoft, Seattle, Wash.
PFS Professional Write, Software Publishing Corporation, Mountain View, Calif.
Sprint, Borland International, Scotts Valley, Calif.
Total Word, Lifetree Software, Monterey, Calif.
WordPerfect, WordPerfect Corporation, Orem, Utah.
Wordstar, Wordstar International, San Rafael, Calif.

With the more sophisticated programs, indexes can be based on a concordance file containing a list of words to be indexed throughout the document, eliminating the need to mark each occurrence of each word for indexing. The quality of the outlining function varies greatly from program to program. A true outliner will allow the user to develop a hierarchical structure of headings and subheadings containing body text. The outliner should not only number headings automatically according to a specified numbering scheme, but also allow the user to collapse and expand headings to any level in the hierarchy and to hide or redisplay body text. It should be possible to restructure the outline, including body text, by moving headings around.

The sophisticated word-processing programs let you open several documents at one time, import material from other programs into your word-processing program, and export material from it to other programs. They also have stylesheet features. Stylesheets allow the user to record combinations of formatting commands, fonts, and type styles under a style name; the same style can then be reinvoked at will either elsewhere in the same document or in other documents.

There are two aspects of using word processing on the Apple Macintosh that should be taken into account. One is the Mac's reliance on the mouse, an input device that is moved around the desktop while its movements are duplicated on the screen. Users can select commands and text by clicking a button on the mouse. The mouse can slow the fastest typists by requiring that they remove their hands from the keyboard to maneuver the mouse pointer.

Microsoft Word offers key sequences that can move the pointer around the documents without the mouse, but it is necessary to use a combination of three or four keys simultaneously. It is possible to buy an optional Macintosh keypad with cursor and numeric keys which helps with this problem. The second aspect that affects word processing on the Macintosh is its small screen, which makes it hard to get a feel for the document. It is possible to obtain larger screens for the Mac – 12- or 13-inch monitors – and this makes word processing much easier.

The amount of learning involved with word-processing software varies according to the complexity of the program and whether it is menu- or command-driven. *Microsoft Word* uses a unified menu approach, available at the touch of the escape key. *WordPerfect* follows the school of thought that the screen should emulate a blank sheet of paper; it just sits there and awaits your commands. Different commands are assigned to all function keys in their unshifted state, as well as in combination with the shift, control, and alt keys, giving 40 key combinations.

Graphics

One of the big trends in word-processing software is the ability to include graphics, derived from standard drawing, painting, and charting software, in the text. The latest versions of *WordPerfect, Microsoft Word,* and *Wordstar,* for example, let the user set up columns and graphic boxes. Charts, pictures, graphs, and so on can be imported into these boxes. Text can be made to flow around the boxes and, depending on the type of printer, use can be made of different fonts and type styles. *WordPerfect, Wordstar, Microsoft Word,* and *PC-Write* can produce *Postscript* output on a suitable typesetting system (discussed later in this chapter with desktop publishing and printers).

With the better software it is possible to see exactly what a page is like before it is printed; true fonts, true layouts, and true text attributes such as bold, italics, and underlining can be shown. This is in contrast to earlier versions of *WordPerfect, Wordstar,* and *Microsoft Word,* and to the less sophisticated programs, which use embedded codes to mark bold, underlining, and other attributes. It is also possible to set up facing pages side by side to see how the spacing will look before they are printed.

In acquiring a word-processing program with these desktop publishing features, it is necessary to ensure that the program can indeed bring in charts, graphs, and so on from a variety of other sources. Many word-processing programs require the original graphic application to be turned into a print file (i.e., print to disk) before it can be imported into the program. However, many graphic applications cannot produce print files. Even if you succeed in importing your graphic application as a disk file, you will have very little control over the file – no positioning or editing functions, and possibly no page preview to see how the document will look.

It is important also to remember that it is necessary to have a graphics adapter in order for the monitor or screen to be able to display the layout, and to print graphics it is necessary to have a graphics printer. The word-processing program must also be able to tell the printer when to switch fonts. These concerns are the same as with desktop publishing software and are discussed more fully in that section.

Comparison with Desktop Publishing

It would seem from the above that word processing and desktop publishing are starting to merge. However, this has not happened as yet, and it may not happen. None of the word-processing programs currently available gives the same control over the page as a desktop publishing software program. They may never do so. Many people who use word processing do not want to publish per se; they merely want to use graphics to illustrate the text of a document, and they want to put it all together as quickly and easily as possible. The term *compound document* is being used to describe this process, which is essentially keeping the input of text as a pure process and adding graphics and page makeup features.

First and foremost, word-processing software is still a tool for enabling the computer to organize text for output on sheets of paper. There is a current concern with the design of the page and with how the information will look, but, essentially, word-processing software provides an easier method for putting words on paper. It is to be hoped that possibilities offered with embedded artificial intelligence will enable us to move from paper, which forces us into a one-dimensional perception of information, toward a true electronic document, structured not to fit the confines of paper, but to fit our ideas – multileveled, cross-referenced, and annotated in an interactive way.

SPREADSHEETS

An electronic spreadsheet can be used much like a financial ledger sheet to record figures or expenditures and to make calculations. It can be said that spreadsheets manipulate numbers the way word processing manipulates words. But just as word-processing software on the computer gives more options than a typewriter, so electronic spreadsheets give more options than a financial ledger sheet.

The first electronic spreadsheet was developed in 1979 by Dan Bricklin and Bob Frankston while they were at Harvard Business School. During a study of marketing surveys, they came up with the idea of an electronic blackboard and electronic chalk. The first spreadsheet, designed for the Apple II, had 5 columns and 20 rows and required only 20K bytes of random access memory (RAM). It neither printed nor performed division, and the replicate function did not work. However, Bricklin and Frankston formed a company called Software Arts and presented their program—which they called *VisiCalc*—to the National Computer Conference in New York in 1979. *VisiCalc* and Apple Computer both grew at an amazing rate, and for many years *VisiCalc* was the best-selling spreadsheet for personal computers, although it is no longer being manufactured. Currently the market is dominated by the spreadsheets listed in Table 8.2.

Table 8.2. Prominent Spreadsheet and Business Graphics Software

Spreadsheets and Related Software
  Kwikstat, Mission Technologies, Cedar Hill, Texas.
  Lotus 1-2-3, Lotus Development Corporation, Cambridge, Mass.
  Lotus HAL, Lotus Development Corporation, Cambridge, Mass.
  Microsoft Excel, Microsoft Corporation, Bellevue, Wash.
  Multiplan, Microsoft Corporation, Bellevue, Wash.
  Quattro, Borland International, Scotts Valley, Calif.
  Supercalc, Computer Associates, San Jose, Calif.
Business Graphics
  Execuvision, Prentice-Hall, Englewood Cliffs, N.J.
  GSS Plottalk, Graphic Software Systems, Beaverton, Ore.
  PFS Graph, Software Publishing Corporation, Mountain View, Calif.
  Adobe Illustrator, Adobe Systems, Mountain View, Calif.
  Byline, Ashton-Tate, Torrance, Calif.

Features

Spreadsheets are widely used, not just by businesses, but by anyone who needs to analyze numerical data. The main part of a spreadsheet program is called the worksheet, illustrated in Figure 8.1., p. 207. The worksheet is really a large grid, divided into columns and rows. The intersection of a column and a row is called a cell. The columns are usually labeled with letters of the alphabet (a notable exception is *MultiPlan,* which uses numbers). Columns from 27 on are labeled AA, AB, and so on. The rows are usually labeled with numbers. This makes it possible to refer to each cell by its address, which is a combination of the letter of the column and the number of the row that the cell is in.

Spreadsheets can have hundreds of thousands of cells; the only practical limitation is the memory size of the computer. Thousands of cells, however, cannot be placed on a computer screen at one time. Approximately 8 columns and 20 rows of most spreadsheets can appear on a screen at one time; most of the spreadsheet is in the computer's memory.

Each cell of a spreadsheet is able to hold one of three types of information: numbers, called *values*; text, called *labels*; and formulas, used to set up mathematical relationships between the contents of two or more cells. Formulas are stored in cells, and if any entry on which a formula depends is changed, the program automatically recalculates and redisplays the new values.

Formulas

Spreadsheets offer shortcuts in the writing of formulas. Common ones are built into the spreadsheet programs as predefined automatic functions. They can be invoked simply by using the function name whenever the desired value needs to be calculated. Functions can be arithmetic, such as sum, average, or square root; trigonometric, such as sine, cosine, or tangent; and so on.

Spreadsheets are capable of taking advantage of similarities between formulas to avoid wasteful duplication of effort. A formula may be entered once and copied to other cells requiring one of similar form. This may be implemented in one of two ways:

1. *Adjustment of relative formulas.* The spreadsheet interprets all formulas representing cell addresses in terms of the relative distance from the cell in which the formula is actually stored. Some spreadsheets refer to the creation of new formulas from an existing formula as copying, while others refer to it as replication.

2. *Absolute formulas.* On some occasions a spreadsheet may contain one or more formulas that must remain unchanged. In order to assure that these formulas are not changed during copying, the user must designate them as absolute, instead of relative formulas.

Templates and Macros

Spreadsheets can be customized by designing templates and macros. A template is a partially completed spreadsheet that contains headings and formulas already filled in. All the user has to do is supply the appropriate numbers. Many user groups and independent companies supply or sell spreadsheet templates.

A macro is a way of automating things done often, or a way of not having to remember how to do something complicated. The procedure is to work out how to do something once, write the actions in a macro, then remember only a single keystroke to call up the macro. There are two main kinds of macros:

1. *Keystroke macros*. A set of keystrokes used to do such things as select options from the menu, enter data, and so on is stored for repeated use.

2. *Program macros*. These can be considered a complete programming language contained in the spreadsheet, so that doing loops and making selections between options can be performed.

Additional Requirements

Features that should be looked for in spreadsheets include the following:

1. Error protection. It should be possible to protect a cell in order to prevent the accidental erasure of information stored in that cell.

2. A command to check the accuracy of the formula.

3. A command to print out a list of all the cells and their interdependencies.

4. Printing. Printing out a large worksheet can be a problem. Does the program offer compressed printing? It is often necessary to print out the spreadsheet by using another program, such as *Sideways*.

5. Ability to link spreadsheets. Smaller spreadsheets use less memory and are easier to manage. When they are linked, it is possible to accomplish just as much as with one giant spreadsheet. When spreadsheets are linked, a change in one should update all the others.

6. Ability to sort or identify records that meet certain criteria, e.g., sort a personnel file by name, within departments, and extract the records of those within a particular age bracket.

7. Graphics capability. A graphics capability is built into many spreadsheets and is the basis for what has become known as business graphics. The numbers in the spreadsheet are the basis for the graphical presentations. The graphs are automatically altered as the spreadsheet numbers are altered or recalculated. *Lotus 1-2-3* offers an excellent graph capability. *Excel* benefits greatly from the Macintosh interface and is able easily to change font styles and sizes of graphs. *Kwikstat* offers three-dimensional graphs. It is necessary to have a graphics printer to print the graphs.

Embedded AI

Spreadsheets lack a feature that users of word-processing programs take for granted, that is, the ability to search for characters, words, or phrases and replace them with others. *HAL,* an embedded AI program that works with *Lotus 1-2-3,* lets the user accomplish this and much more besides. *HAL* lets users run the *Lotus* spreadsheet by typing commands in English phrases such as "Graph Jan thru Mar" instead of going through the numerous steps required from the command menu at the top of the screen. Users can concentrate on what they want *Lotus* to do, not how to get *Lotus* to do it. For instance, typing "total all columns" will cause *Lotus* to draw a dashed line at the bottom of each column, create a formula for each column to obtain the sum, then execute the formula. The program understands 2,000 words describing spreadsheet functions. It can be taught about 10,000 other words, ideal for creating special applications using their own vocabulary. *HAL* needs a minimum of 512K bytes of memory to run.

Projection Capabilities

Spreadsheets may be used for simple or complex record-keeping tasks, but their real power lies in projection capabilities. With a spreadsheet it is possible to set up the coming year's budget based on projected formulas, such as a monthly sales increase of 15 percent. If the first month's sales figures are changed, the entire spreadsheet will change to make adjustments for this new figure. In this way a spreadsheet is a very handy tool for playing the "what if" game of projection.

As the use of CD-ROM for storing vast quantities of information continues to develop, the projection capabilities of spreadsheets will become more and more important. Using CD-ROM and spreadsheets, users could create their own "what if" scenarios using real data. For example, it would be possible to collect raw business data from primary sources covering a long period of time – possibly all the commodity exchanges in the country – and store the data on CD-ROM. Using a spreadsheet, any user could uncover trends or patterns that are genuine, not statistical possibilities, because the spreadsheet is using the actual transaction information accumulated over a long period of time.

BUSINESS GRAPHICS

People want to understand information at a glance. As the realization grew that computers could manipulate all kinds of information – not just information in the form of words – there has been a shift toward using graphics both as an enhancement of other applications such as word processing or spreadsheets, and as an application in its own right.

The great growth of business graphics began in the early 1980s. A 1984 University of Minnesota study revealed that 90 percent of the companies surveyed used computer-created business graphics, yet less than one-third of these companies had done so before 1981.[2] It has been projected that between 1986 and 1991 business graphics software will account for 40 percent of the software market, compared with 25 percent in 1985-86.[3]

Business graphics software has two primary purposes: to create charts and graphs from files of numbers for presentations, and to summarize and compare volumes of data to give a quick grasp of a situation or to help explore the relationship among numbers. *Lotus 1-2-3* made people aware of the capability of business graphics, and all good business graphics programs should have the ability to automatically use data files generated by spreadsheet programs as input to their graph or chart drawing functions.

Business graphics programs can be a little overwhelming. Some packages offer over 400 colors and color patterns, over 10 styles of charts and graphs, animation, clip art, and many type styles and fonts. It is important for the user to understand a little about the design process in order to select the best chart format for a particular situation. Bar and line charts represent the changing nature of data over time; pie charts are used to compare values that represent part of a whole (many programs will let you "explode" pie charts to direct attention to the most important pieces of information); and line charts connect data points on a grid, allowing you to graph interpolated and extrapolated data and describe trends.

Programs range from the very sophisticated, such as *Execuvision,* which contains 19 collections of symbols, graphs, and charts, to the very simple, such as *PFS Graph,* which can graph only four series or data sets with 36 data points in each. *GSS Plottalk* is an example of a business graphics program with embedded artificial intelligence. It is a software version of a live graphic artist. The program accepts orders in English–for example, "Make a chart with a blue background."

The quality of the graph or chart possible with business graphics software is dependent on the type of screen or monitor being used; the quality of the output is dependent on the type of printer. These issues are discussed in detail in the next section on desktop publishing, as the same concerns apply to both categories of software.

DESKTOP PUBLISHING

Desktop publishing refers to the application of a microcomputer, a laser printer, and various software programs (all used in combination) to the entire range of the publishing process, from the typing in of the author's original copy to the final printing. Documents produced by desktop publishing can be anything from a single page of text to advertisements, pamphlets, magazines, and books.

Although computer-aided publishing has been available since the early 1970s, desktop publishing as a function of personal computers became possible on a broad scale only in 1985 with the introduction of the first relatively inexpensive laser printer producing letter-quality type and visuals with a printing resolution of 300 dots per inch. It was in 1985 also that Paul Brainerd coined the term "desktop publishing." He was president of Aldus Corporation, the firm that produced *PageMaker,* one of the first programs capable of composing and formatting text merged with graphics on a microcomputer for subsequent output to the new laser printers. Since 1985 there has been a dramatic rise in the popularity of desktop publishing. The Sierra Group, a market research firm, found that, in 1988, 62.6 percent of companies surveyed had purchased desktop publishing software compared to 18 percent in 1987.[4]

Features

The basic equipment needed for desktop publishing is a microcomputer, a laser printer, software that includes a page description language (to translate the image on the computer screen into a set of digital instructions that the laser printer can follow), and a composition program to drive the entire system. The technical features of the software should include the capacity to "paste up" pages electronically; merge text with graphics; use several different fonts and typefaces in a single page or column; move text or images inside a predefined layout; allow for sizing, editing, and pagination; and create WYSIWYG images on the screen. WYSIWYG (*What You See Is What You Get*) means that what you see on the computer screen is roughly what you will get when the information is printed out.

Desktop publishing programs allow text to be imported from word-processing programs – the text automatically flows around any graphics, page design, etc. With programs like *Ready Set Go,* it is possible to type the text directly into the program, thus eliminating the need for a word-processing program.

Table 8.3. Major Desktop Publishing Software
> *PageMaker,* Aldus Corporation, Seattle, Wash.
> *PFS First Publisher,* Software Publishing Corporation, Mountain View, Calif.
> *Ready Set Go,* Letraset USA, Paramus, N.J.
> *Ventura Publisher,* Xerox, El Segundo, Calif.
> *XPress,* Quark, Denver, Colo.

Text and graphics can also be scanned into many programs using a scanner. A scanner simply digitizes text and graphics and stores them inside the computer's memory where they can be edited or changed and integrated into a page. Desktop publishing programs increasingly allow scanned material, as do some word-processing and business graphics programs. It is important to remember that scanners use a lot of memory.

As with all categories of personal computer software, desktop publishing software ranges from the simple with limited features to the complex with many and varied features. The major desktop publishing packages are listed in Table 8.3. Software Publishing Corporation's *PFS First Publisher* is probably one of the easiest programs to learn; *Byline* from Ashton Tate is a little more complex. The top programs are currently Letraset's *Ready Set Go, Adobe Illustrator, Ventura Publisher,* and Aldus's *PageMaker.* Aldus has also brought out *Snapshot* and *Freehand* for use with *PageMaker. Snapshot* captures live recorded images from video sources, including video cameras, VCRs, TV monitors, still video cameras, or videodiscs. *Freehand* is a drawing program that incorporates color and advanced text-handling capabilities. It allows users to draw freehand sketches and modify individual letters.

Equipment Requirements

With desktop publishing it is very important to have the correct monitor and printer, and to understand how they work. This is true also for business graphics and for the desktop publishing features of word-processing software.

Monitors

Monitors are also called visual display units (VDUs) or visual display terminals (VDTs). For any kind of serious graphics or desktop publishing work it is necessary to have a high-resolution monitor. The resolution refers to the monitor's ability to display clear sharp pictures. Each computer-generated image is composed of rows and rows of tiny dots or rectangles of light called picture elements (pixels). The greater the number of pixels, the higher the overall resolution. Not being able to distinguish subtle differences in type faces, type styles, and detailed illustrations can result in a poor product.

Another item to consider is the graphics adapter. Macintosh and Amiga computers come with their own monitors and adapters as part of the basic system. If using an IBM or IBM-compatible, it is necessary to have a graphics adapter in the computer. The Hercules Monochrome Graphics Adapter (HMGA) lets you add some graphics to black and white or one-color text. It offers a high resolution of 720 by 384 pixels (that is, 720 horizontal by 384 vertical pixels) and supports many–but not all–graphics programs. A Color Graphics Adapter (CGA) gives 4 different colors on the screen at a time out of 16 available hues. The resolution is 640 by 200 pixels. An Enhanced Graphics Adapter (EGA) gives 16 colors on the screen simultaneously with 64 tints, tones, and hues. Resolution is upgraded to 640 by 350 pixels, and if a super-EGA is used, to 800 by 600 pixels.

Video Graphics Array (VGA), built into the new IBM PS/2 computer, gives 256 colors on the screen at any one time with 262,144 choices of tints, tones, and hues. To use all of these, however, resolution is reduced to 320 by 200 pixels. Resolution can be pushed up to 640 by 480 pixels by limiting the number of colors to 16. High-level VGA adapters will give resolution as high as 1280 by 960 pixels.

A final thing to consider regarding the monitor is the size. For desktop publishing it is best to pay more and get a 17-, 19- or 25-inch screen, so that a full page is visible at a time.

Printers

For desktop publishing, a laser printer is the only choice unless a connection directly to a typesetter like Linotype, which has a page resolution of 1,693 dots per inch, is possible. This is because laser printers support proportional spacing. With proportional spacing, narrow letters such as *i* or *I* are made to occupy less space than wider letters such as *m* or *w*. Unsightly white spaces are eliminated. Combined with justification of the right- and left-hand margins, this gives the work a professional look.

Laser printers have their own memory where instructions from the computer are stored and translated. Desktop publishing software such as *PageMaker, Ventura Publisher,* and *Ready Set Go* integrate the typesetting instructions with the layout of the page. The laser printer must be told where to put the dots or blank spaces that comprise the page. To aid in this process a special computer language called *Postscript* has been created by Adobe Systems and is built into many laser printers.

Factors to consider with a laser printer are how fast it produces a page, how long it takes for the instructions to be fed from the computer to the printer, and how large the memory buffer is. The memory buffer acts as a holding tank, where the printer stores the words, illustrations, and type specifications it has received from the computer. The buffer can often hold up to two megabytes of information at a time, making it possible for laser printers to mix several text sizes, faces, fonts, symbols, and illustrations on a single page.

Much work is being done in the area of output options for desktop publishing. For example, Quark (the makers of *XPress,* a desktop publishing program for the Macintosh) has developed a version of *XPress* that will feed into a color separation system developed by Scitex (Herzlia, Israel). The result is a greatly improved color publishing process.

Use

Desktop publishing should not be approached in a casual fashion. A certain amount of thought and skill is necessary. Learning desktop publishing is not simply a matter of loading the software and going through the tutorial. It is essential to have a familiarity with publishing practices and to understand the basic rules of good page design. Otherwise, one can end up with what is often called "the ugly document" syndrome. In too many cases, an individual can become intent on using every conceivable feature rather than on creating an attractive, effective document. Putting Michelangelo's brushes into the hands of a hobbyist would not create a masterpiece because it is the skill of the individual – and not the tools – that creates attractive results.

The answer may be to incorporate a computer-based expert system in the desktop publishing product to help get around obvious design faults. The expert system would have its own set of design rules – for example, knowing the correct ratio of text to white space for a given typeface. It would warn the user when design rules were being broken.

Although desktop publishing software is based on the concept of the printed page, it may eventually release us from the necessity of having to adhere to the structure of the printed page. In the future, desktop publishing will be used to bring text and data to the consumer using multimedia techniques – for example, combining computerized data and video projection systems to create new kinds of business presentations. The output of a desktop publishing program can also be distributed via telecommunications without going to paper. This will free us from the need to produce one-dimensional output to fit onto paper.

There are no typical desktop publishing users because all organizations need printed documentation. There are, however, three main impacts of desktop publishing: it gives the choice of what is to be published back to the author; censorship is harder; and specialist or minority books can be easily published.

APPLICATIONS IN LIBRARIES

Personal computers have had an immense impact on libraries and librarianship, concerned as libraries are with the information process. Initially simply a tool to help meet changing needs in libraries, technology has become a driving force in itself. It has been difficult for many librarians to reconcile the humanistic essence of librarianship with modern information technology and to accept that they must use machinery in order to manipulate information. In short, technology has become a professional requirement for librarians, and in the process it has changed librarianship from a specific area of study to a specific kind of work.

Word Processing

Word processing has been heavily used in all areas of librarianship for some time, primarily for report writing. Some library systems make efforts to choose a particular software package as a standard in order to make training easier. *Wordstar, WordPerfect,* and *Microsoft Word* tend to predominate, but many other word-processing software packages can be found in libraries.

Word processing has posed an interesting dilemma for many librarians. The trend is for administrators to give librarians a microcomputer and a word-processing software package and expect them to turn out professional-looking reports. Gone are the days when librarians drafted a report in rough and gave it to a secretary or word processor to handle. Librarians are arguing that they do not want to be word processors; another difficulty is that they do not use complex, command-driven programs like *WordPerfect* regularly enough to become truly familiar with them.

Spreadsheets

Spreadsheets can help librarians develop a clear picture of what is happening in the library for a whole range of management activities including budgets. Spreadsheets can deal with the question of what kind of staffing, hours, and money are needed to perform present or desired services. They work well with managing by objectives (MBO) and zero-based or other formula-based business principles in order to give different cost configurations. Budget figures can be categorized by factors such as service, type of user, or staff. Thus, the effective cost of various programs or activities (e.g., event programming) can be analyzed.

Circulation figures are often kept on spreadsheets so that the librarian can see present use and can calculate predicted use by age range, loan period, number of copies, type of patron, discipline, and so on. Reference fill notes can be controlled by spreadsheets and *Output Measures for Public Libraries*[5] published by the American Library Association can be adapted to spreadsheet format. In short, any measurement of library service that can be clearly categorized is a candidate for spreadsheet operation.[6]

Desktop Publishing

Desktop publishing is beginning to have a major impact on all kinds of libraries. The pragmatic reality for most libraries and information centers is that whatever printed information is produced will compete with many other graphically appealing products for a library patron's time and attention. Desktop publishing gives a library the opportunity to produce eye-catching publications in-house. It can be used for a wide range of library publications, including brochures, handouts, reports, newsletters, memos, instruction guides, forms, announcements, signs, small posters, bibliographies, help lists for senior citizens, children's newsletters, and local history publications.

Potentially desktop publishing could have a wider implication for libraries in terms of collection policy and bibliographic control. As more people produce their own books and as small runs of many different publications become commonplace, libraries will find it increasingly more difficult to keep track of publications.

Computers for Patron Use

There is one final issue that should be mentioned in connection with personal computer software in libraries, and that is whether libraries should make personal computers and personal computer software available for patrons' use in the library. The trend is toward providing computers in the library since they are information-producing devices, but the following concerns are very real:

1. *Training.* The question of training has two aspects. Library staff have to be trained in the use of the computers, but how much training should library staff provide for patrons?

2. *Software.* Should patrons be allowed to bring in their own software? If libraries provide software, what kind of software? Should it include computer games? Many libraries feel that the answer should be yes. The library does, after all, provide fantasy and escapist literature. Should software circulate? If it does, how can the library protect against viruses (programs inserted into the software by vandals and designed to destroy data, disrupt processing, and replicate into other software)?

3. *Location.* Where should the computers be located to allow for privacy, but also to protect against noise, vandalism, and theft?

APPLICATIONS IN PUBLISHING AND JOURNALISM

The introduction of desktop publishing technology has meant radical changes for the printing and publishing industries, where it is referred to as *micropublishing.* It offers greater flexibility in fixing mistakes and making last-minute changes; it also offers the possibility of cost-effective small runs. Small presses and self-publishers have been at the forefront of micropublishing, representing as they do small specialized sectors of the book market.

Ted Nace of Berkeley, California, founded PeachPit Press in 1986 and published *Laserjet Unlimited,*[7] now in the second edition, and *Ventura Tips and Tricks.*[8] Arthur Naiman, also of Berkeley, produced *The Macintosh Bible*[9] by micropublishing. Since he is his own publisher he has a freedom he would not enjoy with a large publishing house. He takes advantage of this freedom by offering two free updates with each purchase of *The Macintosh Bible*. Crystal Clarity Publishers has produced more than 20 specialized books using Aldus *PageMaker* and a laser printer. The company prints between 2,000 and 5,000 copies of a title and then revises or refines it.

Larger publishing houses are beginning to move towards micropublishing. Collins published *A Day in the Life of the Soviet Union*,[10] *A Day in the Life of America*,[11] and *Christmas in America*[12] on an Apple Macintosh. In *Christmas in America*, black and white versions of the pictures were scanned in as an aid to visualizing layout. Color pictures were pasted in later. Addison-Wesley is producing several of its computer books by micropublishing, including the *Inside Macintosh* series. John Wiley and Sons uses micropublishing for in-house newsletters and author bulletins, and recently for children's books and cookbooks tailored to regional tastes. It seems likely that this trend toward micropublishing will continue with the increasing competition from nonprint media.

Micropublishing has also marked the beginning of a trend towards distributed processing in publishing. Coupling personal computers to laser printers and digitizing scanners and using excellent desktop publishing software enable a publisher to carry projects through the editing, composition, and page makeup stages at one location and send them via telecommunications to another location for printing.

Journalism has been greatly affected by the personal computer and by software applications for the personal computer, especially word processing. Journalism has now embraced the concept of the electronic newsroom, consisting of video display terminals, computer keyboards, and high-speed printers.

Text manipulation has transferred the entire writing process for journalists. Corrections are made by overtyping, and sections of text can be added, deleted, or moved around the screen without difficulty. It is interesting to note, however, that simple word-processing programs that are easy to learn seem to be preferred over the mighty *WordPerfect*, *Wordstar*, or *Microsoft Word*.

Most systems allow the screen display to be split so that journalists are able to write their stories on one half of the screen and read the latest news agency message on the other. A built-in dictionary lets writers check spellings. The most obvious advantage to computerization of the newsroom is speed. Instead of waiting for copy to be delivered, journalists can call up the story from an incoming agency and begin the task of editing.

Macintosh II computers are being used with Compatible Systems Engineering's *Newslink*, a text editor that automatically codes text for transmission to an Atex minicomputer system, used by many newspapers.

The Macintosh II and *Newslink* are easy to use and prevent journalists from having to deal directly with the minicomputer.

U.S. News & World Report uses a personal-computer-based system that allows the magazine's editors, artists, and feature editors to preview photographs taken at different locations. The photos are digitized and stored in the computer using a video camera and an image software board. They are sent by telecommunications to another location, complete with captions and other supporting information. They can then be edited or changed using programs such as *MacDraw* from Apple or *Cricket Draw* from Cricket Software. *USA Today* goes even further and scans the photographs into desktop publishing software. *USA Today* produces much of the paper by micropublishing as does *Spy*.

Lotus 1-2-3 is being used for newsroom budgets. Associated Press has begun sending Macintosh-generated business graphics, including bar graphs and pie charts, to many of its newspaper clients.

Agencies involved with public relations are making heavy use of desktop publishing software. Particularly important for them is the ability to make last-minute changes. *PageMaker* with *Freehand* and *Adobe Illustrator* seem to be extremely popular. Public relations agencies are also experimenting heavily with three-dimensional images for maximum effect.

NOTES

1. Peter A. McWilliams, *The Personal Computer in Business Book* (Los Angeles: Prelude Press, 1983), 39.

2. John A. Lehman, Doug Vogel, and Cary Dickson, "Business Graphics Trends," *Datamation*, 15 November 1984, 119-22.

3. Karen Sorenson, "Presentation Graphics Show the Big Picture," *InfoWorld*, 16 December 1988, 27-28.

4. Sierra Group, *Desktop Publishing Software Survey* (Unpublished report, Tempe, Ariz., 1988).

5. Douglas Zweizeg and Eleanor Jo Rodger, *Output Measures for Public Libraries* (Chicago: American Library Association, 1982).

6. The following are useful for libraries:
   Auld, Larry. *Electronic Spreadsheets for Libraries*. Phoenix: Oryx, 1986. (Second edition in progress).
   Clark, Philip. *Microcomputer Spreadsheet Models for Libraries*. Chicago: American Library Association, 1985.

7. Ted Nace and Michael Gardener, *Laserjet Unlimited: Edition II* (Berkeley, Calif.: Peachpit Press, 1988).

8. Ted Nace, *Ventura Tips and Tricks* (Berkeley, Calif.: Peachpit Press, 1989).

9. Arthur Naiman, *The Macintosh Bible.* 2d ed. (Berkeley, Calif.: Goldstein and Blair, 1988).

10. Rick Smolan and David Cohen, *A Day in the Life of the Soviet Union* (San Francisco: Collins, 1988).

11. Rick Smolan and David Cohen, *A Day in the Life of America* (San Francisco: Collins, 1986).

12. David Cohen, Rick Smolan, and Mark Rykoff, *Christmas in America* (San Francisco: Collins, 1988).

Figure 8.1. A Spreadsheet and Its Components

A. What is a Spreadsheet?

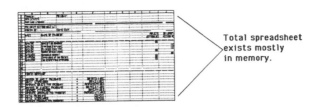

Total spreadsheet exists mostly in memory.

Portion of spreadsheet visible on screen.

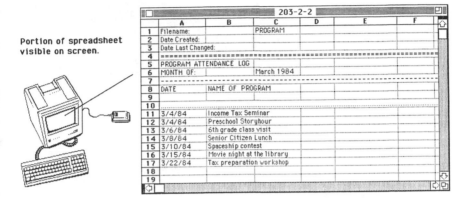

	A	B	C	D	E	F
1	Filename:		PROGRAM			
2	Date Created:					
3	Date Last Changed:					
4	==
5	PROGRAM ATTENDANCE LOG					
6	MONTH OF:		March 1984			
7	--
8	DATE	NAME OF PROGRAM				
9						
10						
11	3/4/84	Income Tax Seminar				
12	3/4/84	Preschool Storyhour				
13	3/6/84	6th grade class visit				
14	3/8/84	Senior Citizen Lunch				
15	3/10/84	Spaceship contest				
16	3/15/84	Movie night at the library				
17	3/22/84	Tax preparation workshop				
18						
19						

B. Spreadsheet Matrix

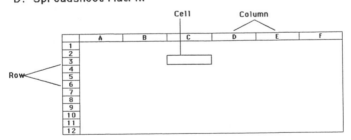

Cell   Column

Row

	A	B	C	D	E	F
1						
2						
3						
4						
5						
6						
7						
8						
9						
10						
11						
12						

C. Spreadsheet Example of Functions and Formulas

	A	B
1	Number 1	1234
2	Number 2	4567
3	Number 3	789
4	Number 4	2222
5	Number 5	1111
6		
7	SUM(B1:B5)	9923
8	COUNT(B1:B5)	5
9	AVERAGE(B1:B5)	1984.6
10	MAX(B1:B5)	4567
11	MIN(B1:B5)	789
12	SQRT(B7)	99.614256007863

▪ 9 ▪

Database Management Systems

Terrence A. Brooks

Database management systems (DBMSes) are used to store information and retrieve it easily and effectively. There are numerous advantages to using a computer database system instead of a paper file system: for example, computer indexes can be searched quickly and comprehensively, computer input can be monitored, privileged information can be shielded behind passwords, and different kinds of output can be created from the same information. Computer database systems will continue to evolve along two lines: increased user friendliness, and more powerful ways to manipulate and interpret information. It is possible that future DBMSes, allied with artificial intelligence programs, may be able to interpret simple English queries and apply a set of rules to the database to infer information not explicitly expressed.

While database management and relational database design are currently recognized as academic disciplines, the origin of the modern DBMS was in practical business applications and military intelligence work, not the research laboratory. At this time database management is being advanced by computer science research, human factors research, and modern management theory. It is research in management information systems especially that has encouraged the perception that information, as well as capital and labor, requires careful control and development. A well-designed and responsive business database will help in both allocating scarce resources (what is our most productive sales region?), and supporting company decision making (which employees can speak French?).

Data independence is a primary advantage of the modern DBMS. Early database systems did not support independence between the user's manipulation of the data and the machine requirements of the database. Consequently, any change in the computer hardware, or any reconfiguration of the data, input requirements, or output formats, required some additional programming, or at least the recompilation of the database program. The data independence of a modern DBMS shields the end user from changes in the manner in which data are actually stored or accessed by the database system. This is called *physical data independence*. The best of the modern DBMSes can support many views of a database, respond to unanticipated queries, and produce many different output formats, all without reference to the conceptual representation of the data in the database. This is *logical data independence*.

The second advantage of the modern DBMS is reduced duplication of data. It is common in paper systems for the same data to reside in several independent files. Such information duplication has meant extra expenditures in both gathering and maintaining the data. Data duplication can lead to problems such as contradictory records – that is, different records each purporting to store the same fact expressing different values simultaneously. A second major problem is the special effort necessary to ensure that uniform changes are made in all the locations where a particular fact may be stored in the database. Modern DBMSes are designed to minimize information duplication so that, ideally, a fact is recorded only once in the database. Ultimately, the reduction of data duplication represents a cost savings in the storage of information in a database and an increase in the reliability of the database's information.

TYPES OF DATABASE MANAGEMENT SYSTEMS AND FEATURES

The most characteristic feature of a database management system is its *record structure*. A record structure represents the database designer's choice of a uniform storage strategy for all the information in the database. It is by handling information in a uniform manner that DBMSes exert power over thousands of disparate facts in a database. While each record may express different information, all the records of a particular file have the same characteristics. Deciding on the characteristics of a record structure is one of the first decisions in the database design process. A record structure is defined in terms of *fields*, a field being the minimum unit of information in a database. Examples of possible fields are "Lastname," "Firstname," and "Initial" of a "Person" record. A *file* is composed of many instances of the record structure holding different information.

There is some artful strategy to the definition of a record structure. For example, it is possible to define a record structure as one large field and use it as an information dump. In terms of the example in the last paragraph, there would be just one "Person" field without separate fields for the elements of a person's name. This is the strategy followed by text-oriented DBMSes. These systems are called *electronic file cabinets* and can host any type of information in one file. While this may seem to be an easy solution to the database design problem, there is a price to be paid for such convenience.

The absence of separate field definitions means that text-oriented systems suffer a limitation in the manipulation of information. One cannot, for example, ask that a list of last names be produced if the database does not have a field containing those data exclusively.

In contrast, a file manager supports the interrogation of only one record structure at a time. An example would be the name/address records of a subscription list. A database management system hosts more than one type of record structure and permits the interrogation of several types of records simultaneously. An example would be a database system supporting modern library functions. In a modern library database, the file of bibliographic records might be the most important file, but it would be surrounded by many associated files. Some of those other files would have no other purpose than to provide linkages among several files. For example, circulation or acquisitions files might link the bibliographic files to other files listing the library users and library book suppliers. Ad hoc queries could be put to such a library database system requiring the collection of parts of the response from several files.

There are advantages and liabilities to all types of file managers and database management systems. For example, file managers are often very inexpensive and easy to use, but suffer limitations of power and adaptability to unique demands. A common experience is choosing an inexpensive file manager and then discovering later that a desired report cannot be created. Database management systems are more expensive and offer a full range of powerful functions such as the capability of producing almost any report. The price of using a powerful database system, however, is learning some programming and writing your own applications. If this seems daunting, you can choose a text-oriented system that can serve as an electronic file cabinet.

Data Dictionaries

The structure of a database is so important to its efficient use that *data dictionaries* were invented to broadcast the structure of the database to the user community. Data dictionaries can range from simple paper lists of the fields of the record structure to elaborate online systems that account for each field in each record across hundreds of files. A data dictionary acts as a database about the database, supplying information about the nature of the information in the database. Data dictionaries can also perform sophisticated functions such as maintaining statistics on use, aiding in data validation, and providing database security. Sophisticated DBMSes have automated data dictionaries that permit programmers to manipulate a data definition language that will supply field definitions, ranges of legitimate values, and occurrences of any field across the many files of a database.

Conceptual Frameworks

Database management systems can be distinguished by their conceptual frameworks or logical schemas. There are three major database conceptual frameworks:

1. A *hierarchical* database system provides the conceptual view that information resides in pyramidal data structures. In a conceptual pyramid one record can lead to several associated subrecords, each of which can lead to more associated subrecords, and so on.

2. A *network* database system is an elaboration of this pyramidal view of information. It supports the conceptual view that information resides in a web of preprogrammed links. These links act as pathways among associated records at levels both higher and lower in the conceptual hierarchy of the database.

3. A relational database system supports the conceptual view that information resides in flat, two-dimensional tables where there are no preprogrammed links to other tables. Information in different relations are associated at the time queries are processed with the nature of the query determining the manner of connection.

Hierarchical Model

Early DBMSes used the hierarchical model as a conceptual schema. This model portrays database records as having parent/child relationships. For example, a department may have several employees, each of whom may be assigned to several workstations. To access the workstation information at the bottom of the conceptual hierarchy, it is necessary to start at the top of the conceptual pyramid with the department information. This is an efficient search if information is normally accessed in the department/employee/workstation pattern.

Other patterns, however, can create some processing inefficiencies. Suppose the program has to gather information across all the records of the database about the workstations. It cannot jump from one workstation record to another without first traversing each of the department hierarchies, an obviously inconvenient process. While the hierarchical model works well in situations that lend themselves to parent/child relationships, there are many other situations that must be distorted to fit this model. Some database situations call for an equality among records, perhaps a parent/parent relationship for example, and are poorly served by the hierarchical model.

Network Model

The network model is an elaboration of the hierarchical model and permits an element to have several parents or children. In finding information in a network model, the database user has been likened to a navigator traveling the various links among pieces of data throughout the database.[1] The dominant influence in the development of the network model has been a series of proposals issued by the Data Base Task Group (DBTG) of the Conference on Data Systems Languages (CODASYL), the group responsible for the programming language COBOL. The CODASYL approach was the basis for I-D-S (Integrated Data Store), the first commercially successful DBMS.

The network database model has been criticized for lack of physical data independence. The advantage of the network model is that the designer can program links between records and therefore maximize processing efficiencies. These very advantages, however, become disadvantages if an unanticipated request is put to the network database. An unanticipated request may prove to be difficult, perhaps impossible, to process. Many database applications, however, have constrained designs where all possible queries can be anticipated. For example, an airline ticket reservation system has a database system devoted to a limited series of tasks that can be fully specified beforehand. The network model serves very well many of the modern mainframe DBMSes that support high-speed, high-volume applications.

Relational Model

The relational model is the first database management model to achieve physical data independence. The relational model is conceptually the simplest of the three structural models, describing data as if they resided in flat, two-dimensional tables in the database. In 1970 E. F. Codd proposed a simple tabular representation of information that permitted database theorists to use mathematical concepts to describe the functions of the database.[2]

Three motivations drove the development of the relational model: data independence, communicability, and set processing. Codd argued that the relational model went further than the network model in separating the logical manipulation of data from concerns about physical storage on a computer.[3] The relational approach also facilitates communication about the database design. Unlike network configurations, which can be complex, tabular presentations are an easy medium for designing and manipulating data. Finally, there is a well-developed body of mathematical theory describing the manipulation of sets that could be transferred to the manipulation of data. The relational model incorporates relational algebra and relational calculus, notational systems that permit researchers to make abstract statements about large sets of data.

The relational model's elegant brevity and easy comprehension by nonprofessional users was quickly employed by the many microcomputer DBMSes that became available in the last decade. It can fairly be said that the relational model has come to dominate the microcomputer DBMS market. It is the model that is used in theoretical database work. Arguments have even been advanced that every database application should be designed first in terms of well-formed relations (described later in this chapter) before being programmed in other database models.

HISTORY

Database management has roots in the late 1950s with the development of generalized sorting routines and early report writers such as *RPG II* and *MARK IV*. COBOL, a computer language for business applications, was also developed in this early period. The data division of a COBOL program provided the first independent data definition of a database. *I-D-S,* which was built by Charles Bachman at General Electric in 1964, is often considered to be the first significant database manager. It was the direct ancestor of many later systems, and the source for many ideas for the CODASYL family of programs.

Relational database design, as introduced by Codd, heralded a new era in the design of database systems. Thus was begun a schism between academic, research database work, which tended to focus on relational concepts, and the application of commercial systems, which tended to focus on the CODASYL model. A detailed history of the database families of machines and programs is available in Fry and Sibley's article.[4]

During the early 1970s the commercial DBMS market developed with several commercially successful products such as *I-D-S* at Honeywell, *DMS 1100* at UNIVAC, and *EDMS* at Xerox. Other well-known DBMSes were *IMS/VS* (Information Management System/Virtual Storage) from the IBM Corporation, *IDMS* (Integrated Data Management System) from the Cullinane Corporation, and *ADABAS* (Adaptable Database System), which originated in West Germany at Software AG. By the middle 1970s there was a general recognition that modern business must employ database management with its advantages of making information more accessible, making updates more convenient, and reducing data duplication. Modern database management came of age at this time with the growing awareness of information as a resource to be managed and controlled.

By the end of the 1970s, research projects were demonstrating the possibilities of relational DBMSes, data dictionaries had emerged as stand-alone ancillaries to mainframe DBMSes, and the database administrator emerged as a person who might occupy a vice-presidential position in a modern business firm. During the early 1980s, the first commercial relational products such as *Oracle* from Oracle Corporation and *INGRES* from Relational Technology International were offered. The microcomputer database management market became dominated by *dBase* products from Ashton-Tate. Every year microcomputer products increased their capabilities. There was speculation about fourth-generation languages (4GLs), which would permit unskilled users to program their own applications.

By the middle 1980s, products were offered that operated identically, as far as the end user was concerned, in both microcomputer and mainframe environments. Structured Query Language (SQL) became an industry-standard database query language. Research work continued on the marriage between artificial intelligence programs and database management, one well-known offspring being expert systems. By the early 1990s, near-term developments will make DBMSes more "intelligent" by anticipating user requests and using sets of rules that bring more semantic meaning to the processing of the information in the database.

It is conceivable that in the near future anyone will be able to buy a microcomputer database management system that will permit database applications to be created in artificial intelligence languages such as PROLOG or LISP. CD-ROM applications will make vast stores of information available at every workstation. Many database applications await the development of programs that can index visual and sound materials.

Database systems are reviewed in articles by Atkinson[5] and Huffenberger and Wigington.[6] Shneiderman gives some personal insights into the history and development of database technology by recalling the early debates between the advocates of the network and relational systems.[7]

MAINFRAME DATABASE MANAGEMENT SYSTEMS

The largest share of the mainframe DBMS market is held by IBM's *IMS (DL/1)*, which uses a hierarchical model for environments that require a high volume and high performance. Another leader of the mainframe market is Cullinet's *IDMS/R*, a CODASYL database system that is enhanced to support relational operators, an integrated data dictionary, and 4GL. Four other products have noteworthy places in the mainframe DBMS market: *Datacom/DB* from Applied Data Research, which supports relational interfaces; *TIS/XA-Supra* and *Ultra*, which are relational systems from Cincom Systems; IBM's *DB2* and *SQL/DS*, which are also relational systems; and *ADABAS* from Software AG, which has an inverted record structure and supports relational operators. This brief listing leaves out about 30 other viable commercial products in the mainframe market. The best sources of information on current mainframe database products are industry reviews and computer review journals.

DATABASE SOFTWARE FOR PERSONAL COMPUTERS

Selected database products and sources for personal computers are listed in Table 9.1 and discussed in the following sections. Information concerning the features of current file managers and database management systems is available in various journals and rating services such as *Software News, Software Digest Ratings Newsletter,* and *PC Magazine.*

Table 9.1. Selected Database Products and Sources

Product	Source
Clipper	Nantucket Corp., Los Angeles, Calif.
Cornerstone	Infocom, Cambridge, Mass.
dBase IV	Ashton-Tate Corp., Torrance, Calif.
dBMassN	VersaSoft Corp., San Jose, Calif.
dBXL	Wordtech Systems, Orinda, Calif.
FoxBase	Fox Software, Perrysburg, Ohio.
FYI3000	FYI, Austin, Texas.
Oracle	Oracle Corp., Belmont, Calif.
Paradox	Borland International, Scotts Valley, Calif.
PC-File	ButtonWare, Bellevue, Wash.
PCFile	TexaSoft, Dallas, Texas.
PowerBase	Compuware Corp., Farmington Hills, Mich.
Q & A	Symantec, Cupertino, Calif.
Quicksilver	Wordtech Systems, Orinda, Calif.
R:base for DOS	Microrim, Redmond, Wash.
Reflex	Borland International, Scotts Valley, Calif.
Revelation	Cosmos, Seattle, Wash.

File Managers

File management programs exist at the lower end of the spectrum in the database market. They are usually hosted in a personal computer and serve a limited number of uses such as for name/address files. Despite these simple purposes, there is a great variety of file managers available, ranging from shareware products (which users may copy, try out, and pay a nominal registration fee to the developer if they want to receive updates and documentation) to products costing hundreds of dollars. This excludes a product such as *Lotus 1-2-3,* a spreadsheet program originally designed for the manipulation of accounting or financial data, which some users employ as a file manager.

There are several outstanding file managers. *PC-File Plus,* a well-known shareware product from ButtonWare that permits the definition of long text fields, supports some limited relational capability, and has strong query and reporting functions. In its latest manifestation, *PC-File:dB,* it can also import a *dBase* file. Thus even the most humble database products are becoming increasingly powerful over time and challenging their more expensive database rivals.

Q & A from Symantec has an "Intelligent Assistant," which accepts plain-English instructions. This is an example of an artificial intelligence application in the database management field. It can be expected that future database products will be able to translate loosely constructed instructions into commands in the database system.

Reflex: The Analyst from Borland International is an example of a spreadsheet product that has strong file management features as well. Its particular strength is in creating graphs, cross tabulations, and other quantitative reports of data. This brief review ignores at least 50 other viable microcomputer file management products.

Text-Oriented Data Managers

Text-oriented data managers are programs that manage heterogeneous bodies of text. Unlike file managers, which demand that information be organized in fields and records, text-oriented managers treat information as a single body of text. The purpose of these programs is to provide an index to a collection of fragments of text. This is accomplished by either indexing each word, except the most frequent articles and prepositions, or identifying each text fragment with a series of keywords.

PCFile from TexaSoft is an example of a text-oriented data manager that has two fields per entry: a field for keywords and a field for the text. The text field can be created with a word processor and can host any sort of information in nearly any format. Each entry can be searched with its associated keywords. *FYI3000* from FYI indexes every word in its entries except the most common articles and prepositions. The strength of text-oriented systems is their versatility in accepting any text fragment, indexing it, and retrieving it. Their weakness is that by accepting text uncritically, they are unable to analyze information and manipulate it as finely as other database products.

Relational Databases

Microcomputer relational databases have, at minimum, the ability to extract information from two separate files simultaneously. While this is a very marginal definition of a relational database, it passes for one in the world of personal computers. The market for microcomputer databases has been overwhelmed by relational products, almost to the exclusion of products featuring any other conceptual model.

Relational database programs in the microcomputer market, however, are not all of one type, but can be divided into those with programming languages and those without. The advantage of a programming language is that local application programs can be created by nonprogrammers. This potentially gives the microcomputer user of a product such as *dBase IV* every advantage enjoyed by the users of a mainframe product. Those relational database programs lacking an applications language, on the other hand, may offer some attractive feature such as extensive menus.

Nonprogrammable Relational Databases

Nonprogrammable relational systems include *Cornerstone* from Infocom, a system that features menus for data entry and analysis. It can use information from two files at once by defining some fields in one record to be filled with data from another record. This awkwardness is typical of these less-powerful products. Even *PC-File Plus,* mentioned above as a file manager, permits data from two files to be output in a single report format. *PowerBase* from Compuware Corporation is one of the most powerful relational database systems that lacks a programming language. Files are tied together with a "zoom" feature that calls up a structure diagram of the second file and permits the user to select a common field.

Programmable Relational Databases

Programmable microcomputer DBMSes, perhaps the family of products that affects the greatest number of computer database users, is dominated by Ashton-Tate's *dBase.* Since 1981, more than 2 million copies of various generations of *dBase* have been sold. The latest manifestation is *dBase IV,* which has been designed for both OS/2 and MS-DOS environments. It features networking capabilities and a dBase/SQL language. The latter enhancement gives *dBase IV* a powerful applications development environment rivaling mainframe systems.

The dominance of *dBase* is evidenced by the fact that it has a large aftermarket of associated products such as *Clipper* and *Quicksilver,* compilers that translate a program written in *dBase*'s programming language into a set of machine language instructions. As might be expected, these products advertise the speed of execution of their coding and their great convenience for the user. There are also a host of *dBase* clone products such as *dBMan* and *dBXL Diamond Release.* A group of vendors of *dBase* add-on products and *dBase* replacements has attempted to codify the *dBase* programming language. Ashton-Tate declined to join this group in an effort to keep its *dBase* programming language proprietary.

There are a number of other outstanding products in the programmable database management market. *Advanced Revelation* from Revelation Technologies has an applications generator, a procedural language, and a screen painter for easy creation of input screens. *FoxBase Plus* from Fox Software is one of *dBase*'s most serious rivals. It does very well in speed comparison tests because it maintains as much of the application as possible in random access memory. It can use files created by *dBase* without modification. *Paradox* from Borland International is based on a table concept that should be familiar to spreadsheet users. Data are stored in tables, commands are stored in temporary tables, and even the results of queries are stored in tables. *R:base for DOS* from Microrim is divided up into various modules for forms definition, applications definition, reports generation, and so on. It has some limited SQL implementation.

As an indication of the turbulent price and features competition in the programmable database management market, a new product, *1 on 1 = 3!!,* can be bought for less than $50, compared with the norm of $400 to $800. It is a product that is based on *FoxBase* and is attempting to rival *dBase* in execution speed and features. New software products are being developed that are portable to any kind of computer environment. *Oracle* from the Oracle Corporation is an example of a product that runs identically across mainframe, minicomputer, and microcomputer environments. It is a relational system with a comprehensive implementation of SQL. There are approximately 30 other noteworthy programmable relational DBMSes not mentioned here.

DATA ANALYSIS

The first step in the successful application of any database management system is an analysis of the data of the enterprise. All of the many systems reviewed in the preceding paragraphs must be regarded, not as ends in themselves, but merely as tools to facilitate the ultimate creation of a well-designed database. Historically, this has been an unappreciated part of database management falling under the shadow of the more spectacular software systems development. A process of data analysis prior to applications programming will enhance the usefulness of the final database design by uncovering the fundamental data resources of the organization, creating flexible data structures amenable to any possible future application, and achieving an understanding of the database data across the organization.

Until recently there have not been many tools to use in modeling the data of an organization. Analysts have often attempted to use a hierarchical or relational model directly. There was a need for formal data analysis systems, more generalized than the hierarchical or relational models, that could be a preparatory step in the database design process. Data analysis diagrams could then be translated into hierarchical, network, or relational models.

The Entity-Relationship (E-R) Model

Chen's entity-relationship (E-R) model is perhaps the best-known data analysis system.[8] Chen proposes three parts for his data analysis system: entity sets, relationship sets, and properties of entities and relationships. A database entity is any named thing that has an existence in the real world. It is the charge of the database administrator to identify the entities that are most suitable for the *enterprise*, or part of the real world that is represented in the database. While appearing to be a simple process, the entity identification task can be quite complex because the same data elements may have independent existences under several synonyms in various parts of a large organization. Achieving the minimum set of important enterprise entities may require some tough negotiation and artful compromise.

Entities also exhibit various relationships with each other. Entities can exhibit a one-to-one relationship; for example, a person has one identity number. One-to-many relationships occur when an entity relates to several other entities; for example, a department has several employees. Many-to-one relationships occur when several entities relate to the same entity; for example, several employees may receive the same rate of pay. Many-to-many relationships occur when several entities relate to several other entities simultaneously; for example, several suppliers can deliver the same part, and several parts can be delivered by a single supplier.

Diagrammatically, Chen represents an entity set by rectangular boxes and each relationship set by a diamond-shaped box. These are joined together with a notation for each of the four types of relationships. The computer program, *The E-R Designer,* automatically models data in an entity-relationship diagram and can also produce normalized relations (discussed in the next section). Alternative systems have been suggested by numerous other people such as Davenport[9] and Ross.[10] Ross's highly developed system distinguishes between categories of entity types: people, places, things, organizations, concepts, and events.

Needless to say, the relationships among entities are not without their own ambiguities. It is also quite possible that an enterprise may regard the relationship of two entities to be of more interest than either of the two entities themselves. For example, a marriage bureau may be interested in the relationship "marriage" rather than information about the particular bride or groom. These complexities illustrate the potential difficulty of the data analysis process and the need for simple but powerful conceptual tools for laying the foundation of a database design.

The Normalization Process

Normalization results in the creation of well-formed relations, a design step that is integral to the use of a relational database system. It can prove useful in rationalizing the design for any database or file management system.

Relations are commonly presented as flat, two-dimensional matrices of rows and columns, or "tables" of data, especially in textbooks and articles where only a small fragment of a complete database is presented. The table metaphor is not exactly appropriate, even though it is widely used. Rows (or tuples) and columns (or attributes) in a relation have no fixed positions. Any column can appear first in a relation, and the rows of data in a relation can be sorted in any manner. A table presentation, however, is fixed in time and deceives by presenting rows and columns in a fixed relationship. Presenting relations as tables, however, is a convenient shorthand used in explanation.

Normalization is the analytical process of breaking up large relations into smaller ones based on the functional dependencies, or relationships, that exist among the data elements – that is, if A has only one associated value of B, then A is a determinant of B, and B is said to be functionally dependent on A. For example, my name is functionally dependent on my social security number. Names can be rather common, but a social security number is unique. Given my social security number, you could retrieve one individual with a rather common name. But given only my name, you would find numerous individuals, each with a different social security number.

One of the first jobs of a database designer is to codify the enterprise rules of a potential database (in the data analysis step above) and then use these rules to create well-formed relations. The enterprise rules of an organization describe the manner in which information is consistently used by that organization. Consider the example of a relation hosting two attributes, "Social Security Number" and "Name." The social security number attribute would serve to identify unique rows in the relation. Each tuple would describe one instance of the entity of the relation. In terms of the example above, each tuple would describe a single individual.

Each relation needs at least one attribute with unique data. This is the ultimate method of distinguishing among the tuples of the relation and, by extension, the various examples of the entity that the relation is describing. Such an attribute is the key for the relation. In the example above, the key attribute of the relation is "Social Security Number"; the nonkey attribute is "Name."

The impetus for the normalization process is the assumption of a rapidly updated information environment. This assumption is most appropriate in an enterprise with a large throughput of information in the database, where, for example, orders are received, invoices processed, and shipments sent out daily. The normalization process creates relations so that high-frequency operations such as additions, deletions, and updates can occur without the loss of necessary information and without being inhibited by the database design.

Figure 9.1. A Relational Design for an Information Retrieval Database

CITATION	<DOC #, TITLE, DATE, PUBLICATION, VOLUME, NUMBER, PAGES>
ABSTRACTS	<DOC #, ABSTRACT>
INDEX	<TERM, DOC #, WEIGHT>
THESAURUS	<TERM 1, TERM 2>
AUTHORS	<DOC #, NAME>
DIRECTORY	<NAME, ADDRESS>
SOURCE	<PUBLICATION, PUBLISHER>
KEYWORDS	<DOC #, KEY>

Source: Robert G. Crawford, "The Relational Model in Information Retrieval," *Journal of the American Society for Information Science* 32, no. 1 (January): 52-54.

Applications of the Relational Model

C.J. Date's *An Introduction to Database Systems* is a fundamental text detailing relational database design.[11] There are also many examples of applications of the relational model in the computer science, information science, and business literature. An example of a relational design for an information retrieval database is shown in Figure 9.1.

This design has eight separate relations. DOC# serves as a device that links most of the relations together. This design eliminates unnecessary duplication of data by recording PUBLISHER only once in the SOURCE relation. Reference to the PUBLISHER is made by PUBLICATION being duplicated in the CITATION relation. Having achieved such a design, a database designer would check that it satisfied all enterprise information, computer, and political requirements. The designer might then implement this database design with one of the relational software systems reviewed previously. This design can be used directly to define a relational database.

The wide application of the relational model has been tempered, however, by the recognition that some enterprises do not have rapidly updated information environments. Libraries, for example, often add data to their databases, but infrequently delete from them. In recent years, there has been a growing recognition that the relational model may not be completely suitable for every application, particularly when dealing with document storage and retrieval.[12] Nonetheless, Beiser illustrates numerous programs written in *dBase* to accomplish library tasks such as creating bibliographies, abstracts, serials control, and library catalogs.[13] Indeed, Matthews lists several commercial products for acquisitions, cataloging, and serials control that have been developed using *dBase*.[14] It is an unanswered question at this point whether or not the relational model is the best approach to use with bibliographical data.

Applying the Normalization Process

In applying the normalization process, a data designer begins with first-normal form (1NF), then proceeds to second-normal form (2NF), and so on. There are five normal forms, although for most database purposes 3NF is considered sufficient. Higher normal forms subsume lower ones: a relation in 3NF must already be in 2NF form, and so on.

First-normal form is a formatting convention and concerns the shape of the record. A relation is in 1NF if there is one data element at the junction of each row and column, thus excluding all repeating field elements from a relation. Consider this example:

Key = PERSON, EMPLOYER

PERSON CODE	ADDRESS	EMPLOYER	EMP.ADDRESS	POSTAL
Susan	BigTown	ABC Widgets	OverThere	123
Jeff	BigTown	DEF Tools	CloseBy	456

A relation achieves 2NF if each nonkey attribute depends on the whole key of the relation. Common violations of 2NF have a nonkey attribute modifying only part of the key. In the above example, ADDRESS modifies just PERSON, which is only a part of the complete key of PERSON, EMPLOYER. Similarly, EMP.ADDRESS and POSTAL CODE modify just EMPLOYER, the other part of the key. Second-normal form can be achieved in the above example if it is decomposed into two relations, as follows:

```
Key = PERSON
PERSON          ADDRESS
Susan           BigTown
Jeff            BigTown
Key = EMPLOYER
EMPLOYER        EMP.ADDRESS      POSTAL CODE
ABC Widgets     OverThere        123
DEF Tools       CloseBy          456
```

Third-normal form is violated when a nonkey attribute modifies another nonkey attribute. The PERSON/ADDRESS relation above is in 3NF, but the EMPLOYER/EMP.ADDRESS/POSTAL CODE relation is not. One of the enterprise rules of this example is that POSTAL CODE modifies EMP.ADDRESS and not EMPLOYER. Consequently one nonkey attribute is modifying another. Third-normal form is achieved when every nonkey attribute is dependent on the whole key and nothing but the key of the relation. This can be achieved by another decomposition:

```
Key = EMPLOYER
EMPLOYER        EMP.ADDRESS
ABC Widgets     OverThere
DEF Tools       CloseBy
Key = EMP.ADDRESS
EMP.ADDRESS     POSTAL CODE
OverThere       123
CloseBy         456
```

Pushing the normalization process to its limits shows that it is as much an art as a science. C.J. Date discusses the problems of overnormalization, which occurs when data elements have been broken down so finely that extra retrieval operations are required to rebuild the information that was unnecessarily fragmented.[15] In this case, the opposite process of normalization, *denormalization*, can be used to reconnect relations to facilitate faster processing. The irony of this reverse process, in view of the fact that normalization is a design process that originated in part from the desire to abandon hardware considerations, is the introduction of hardware processing speed requirements as a guide to normalization.

FUTURE TRENDS

Research continues on several fronts with the aim of increasing the utility, power, and flexibility of database systems. Particularly interesting is the potential connection between database management and expert systems. Expert systems, discussed in detail in chapter 10, emulate a human expert's ability to make decisions about some limited domain of knowledge. They work by combining the idea of a database and rules that can be applied to information in the database.

Artificial intelligence programming languages like PROLOG facilitate the creation of such databases. Except for the formatting conventions, a PROLOG predicate such as "color" is very much like a database relation:

color(red, grapes).
color(purple, plums).
color(red, apples).

An artificial intelligence program may have many such predicates recording many different facts. A set of rules governs the manner in which the facts relate to each other. The facts and rules together form a knowledge base.

H.L. Berghel reports marrying a *dBase* database with a PROLOG artificial intelligence system.[16] He argues that PROLOG is a superior query mechanism because more meaning can be captured from the database by introducing new rules that do not require restructuring the database. He also finds PROLOG queries to be more powerful and easier to use than SQL commands. Lucas surveys several expert systems and argues that shortcomings in PROLOG can be overcome by combining it with a relational database system.[17]

Fuzzy relational systems represent another line of future research. Database management systems respond to queries by finding exact matches; thus conventional systems force users to retry specific queries repeatedly with minor modifications until they find an exact data match. Zemankova-Leech and Kandel believe that relational systems would be more useful if they were able to respond to inexact, or fuzzy, queries.[18] They believe that future database systems could be individualized so that users match their perceptions through processes such as term weighting or fuzzy set theory.

NOTES

1. Charles W. Bachman, "The Programmer as Navigator," *Communications of the ACM* 16, no. 11 (November 1973): 653-58.

2. E. F. Codd, "A Relational Model of Data for Large Shared Data Banks," *Communications of the ACM* 13, no. 6 (June 1970): 377-87.

3. E. F. Codd, "Relational Database: A Practical Foundation for Productivity," *Communications of the ACM* 25, no. 2 (February 1982): 109-17.

4. James P. Fry and Edgar H. Sibley, "Evolution of Data-Base Management Systems," *Computing Surveys* 8, no. 1 (March 1976): 7-42.

5. Malcolm P. Atkinson, "Database Systems," *Journal of Documentation* 35, no. 1 (March 1979): 49-91.

6. Michael A. Huffenberger and Ronald L. Wigington, "Database Management Systems," in *Annual Review of Information Science and Technology*, vol. 14, ed. Martha E. Williams (White Plains, N.Y.: Knowledge Industries, 1979), 153-90.

7. Ben Shneiderman, "Design, Development and Utilization Perspectives on Database Management Systems," *Information Processing & Management* 13 (1977) : 23-33.

8. P-S. C. Chen, "The Entity-Relationship Model–Toward a Unified View of Data," *ACM Transactions on Database Systems* 1, no. 1 (March 1976): 9-37.

9. R. A. Davenport, "Data Analysis for Database Design," *Australian Computer Journal* 10, no. 4 (November 1978): 122-37.

10. Ronald G. Ross, *Entity Modelling: Techniques and Application* (Boston, Mass.: Database Research Group, 1987).

11. C. J. Date, *An Introduction to Database Systems* (Reading, Mass.: Addison-Wesley, 1986).

12. Ian A. Macleod, "Is the Relational Model Suitable for Document Storage and Retrieval?" *Journal of the American Society for Information Science,* forthcoming.

13. Karl Beiser, *Essential Guide to dBase III in Libraries* (Westport, Conn.: Meckler Publishing, 1987).

14. Joseph R. Matthews, *Directory of Automated Library Systems* (New York: Neal-Schuman, 1985).

15. C. J. Date, *Relational Database: Selected Writings* (Reading, Mass.: Addison-Wesley, 1986).

16. H. L. Berghel, "Simplified Integration of Prolog with RDBMS," *Database* 16, no. 3 (Spring 1985): 3-12.

17. Robert Lucas, *Database Applications Using Prolog* (New York: John Wiley, 1988).

18. M. Zemankova-Leech and A. Kandel, *Fuzzy Relational Data Bases –A Key to Expert Systems* (Koln: Verlag TUV Rheinland, 1984).

▪ 10 ▪

Artificial Intelligence and Expert Systems

Donald E. Riggs

Artificial intelligence (AI) is a subfield of computer science that focuses on understanding and performing intelligent tasks such as reasoning, learning new skills, adapting to new situations, and problem solving. AI is concerned with the concepts and methods of symbolic inference by a computer and the symbolic representation of the knowledge to be used in making inferences.

Seeds for development of AI were planted shortly after World War II. Norbert Wiener's pioneering work with cybernetics set the stage for the evolvement of AI. In 1950, Alan Turing's proposed test for determining if machines could "think" marked the true beginning of the creation of machines capable of emulating the thought processes of the human brain. The 1956 Summer Institute on AI at Dartmouth College was one of the first meetings that encouraged significant AI research. The 1960s are known as the time of development and redirection in AI research. Chess programs and robotics became tests for certain principles of AI.

Techniques (heuristics) for limiting search strategies and building in shortcuts in order to get the correct answers as quickly as possible played a major role in the advancement of AI use. AI programming languages have made it possible to accommodate the specialized requirements for symbol manipulation and implementation of strategies for searching alternative paths. The two most popular languages are LISP and PROLOG. LISP (from LISt Processing) is the language commonly used in the United States, and PROLOG (standing for PROgramming in LOGic) is used by Europeans and Japanese. PROLOG is a higher-level language, but LISP allows for more flexibility.

Greater specialization evolved in the application of AI principles during the 1970s – for example, the creation of knowledge-based systems. Expert systems became more aligned with specific knowledge domains in the 1980s.

As a subset of artificial intelligence, an expert system is essentially an intelligent computer program that uses a knowledge base and inference procedures (described later in this chapter) to solve problems that are difficult enough to require significant human expertise for their solution. The knowledge base necessary to perform at such a level, plus the inference procedures used, can be thought of as a model of the best practitioners in the field.[1] A true expert system should be able to "think" as well as the human expert. It has to solve problems, ask intelligent questions, explain its reasoning, and justify conclusions.

The remainder of this chapter focuses on expert systems in libraries. The expert system is a rather new phenomenon in libraries, but the potential for these knowledge-based systems is unlimited. No technology thus far implemented in libraries has had as much potential to change library services so dramatically.

BUILDING EXPERT SYSTEMS

Very few library expert systems can be purchased; most of the systems found operating in libraries are homegrown. During the early stages in expert systems construction, the librarian should work with a systems engineer. The engineer can offer helpful suggestions in designing the system to support intelligent problem solving. Hayes-Roth et al.[2] give five steps in a methodology for building expert systems:

1. *Identification.* Identifying the problem area and its scope must come first before the goals and objectives can be clearly delineated for the expert system under consideration. Resources must be determined and a commitment made to provide personnel and computing resources.

2. *Conceptualization.* During this step it is necessary to organize "think-tanks" in order to discuss critical aspects of the proposed expert system. Many questions need to be addressed during this step, including the following: Is the expert system necessary? Can the goals and objectives be achieved better by using existing practices? Who will use the expert system? Who is going to train the users? What will be the cost benefits of the expert system?

3. *Formalization.* Formalizing the process is the linchpin between conceptualization and implementation. During this step a decision is made on which strategies, equipment, and program language to use. The systems engineer will bring valuable expertise to the methodology during formalization.

4. *Implementation.* This step determines how well the expert system meets user demands. Feedback from users is crucial in the refinement of the system. Users will tell the librarian and systems

engineer if the knowledge base is too small and if the interface with the machine is smooth and effective.

5.   *Evaluation.* What went right? What went wrong? These are the types of questions that the librarian and systems engineer need to ask during the evaluation phase. A terrible expert system is worse than no expert system. Regular evaluation has to take place to determine if the users' needs are being satisfied. High standards of excellence in performance are necessary if the library expects expert systems to sustain credibility with users.

Components of Expert Systems

An expert system has four basic components:

1.   *Knowledge base.* Facts in the subject domain are represented in the knowledge base, unquestionably the most important part of the expert system. The most complex challenge in building an expert system is the construction of an effective knowledge base. An expert system's performance is related directly to the function and size of the knowledge base. Most library expert systems developed thus far address narrowly defined subject domains. This is because in order for the expert system to be effective and credible it must be able to give correct answers to all questions it is asked. Therefore, it is easier to choose a specific subject domain and develop a reliable expert system than to try the near-impossible task of creating a knowledge base on all topics in the universe. A knowledge base has several features that play an integral part in representing expert knowledge. Fenley[3] describes them as follows:

A. *Semantic network.* This network is a graphical representation of properties and relationships of objects, situations, and concepts in the knowledge base. The network consists of points called *nodes* connected by links called *arcs,* which describe the relationships between the nodes. An example of a semantic network is indicated in Figure 10.1.

B. *Predicate logic.* In predicate logic a proposition consists of objects, persons, and concepts (*arguments*) about which something is stated (the *predicate*). For example, the proposition "A component of a cataloging record is the series area" might be stated in the form of predicate logic as "has component (cataloging record, series area)" where "cataloging record" and "series area" are the arguments and "has component" is the predicate, which in this case expresses a relationship between the arguments. Predicate logic lends itself well to inferences.

Figure 10.1. An Example of a Semantic Network Designed in a Hierarchical Manner

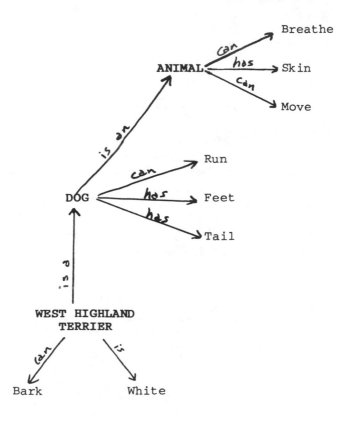

Relationships are given between the nodes (animal, dog and West Highland Terrier). The lines connecting the nodes are commonly called arcs.

C. *Frames.* Frames assemble the information about an object, act, or event into a recognizable entity. As with semantic networks, relationships are expressed between these entities. Frames are versatile data structures; they are subdivided into slots that execute specific procedural changes. For example, in a cataloging expert system, the appearance of the word "proceedings" on a book's title page would cause the expert system to select the "conference" frame and fill in the slots accordingly.

D. *Production rule.* This method is the most commonly used technique for knowledge representation. Production rules normally occur in the **IF-THEN** mode where the **IF** portion describes a condition, evidence, antecedent, or situation, and the **THEN** portion describes the resulting action, conclusion, or consequence.

A production rule from the knowledge base of an expert system in cataloging might read:

"**IF** forms of a name vary in fullness,

THEN choose the form most commonly found."

2. *Inference engine (the reasoning mechanism).* This component is responsible for applying the facts in the knowledge base in order to arrive at an answer to the question or problem under consideration. It is the structure that controls, organizes, and executes the processing and searches and interprets the knowledge base.

    Two strategies are included in the expert system for control purposes:

    A. *Forward chaining* (or data-driven or bottom-up control) starts with known facts and matches them with other facts in the knowledge base; when such matches occur, new facts are inferred. This process continues until no new conclusions can be reached.

    B. *Backward chaining* (or goal-driven or top-down control) starts from a potential goal and works backward through the search tree seeking facts that support that goal. If the available facts do not support the goal, the search fails, at which point another potential goal is selected, and the search is tried again.[4]

3. *User interface.* If the expert system is to be successful, then the interaction between the human and machine should be a high priority in the construction of the system. A two-way message track has to exist: the expert system sends messages to the user, and the user communicates effectively with the system. Menus and preformulated questions can assist in the search of the knowledge base. One of the major weaknesses in current library expert systems is the inability of the user to interrupt or modify dialogue with the system.

4. *Explanation mechanism.* Users are entitled to know why the expert system reached a particular conclusion. Thus, along with the user interface, a complete expert system will include an

explanation mechanism. For credibility, it is important that the user knows the "thinking" process used by the system to arrived at its conclusion. The system's explanation mechanism should display a list of steps taken in arriving at its conclusion or recommendation.

Shells

It is no longer necessary to be an expert about expert-system software. Skeletal systems, known as *shells*, can be purchased. A shell is a software package designed for the creation of specific expert systems. Shells are designed to handle a large number of rules presented in the IF-THEN mode. More than 50 expert system shells geared to run on personal computers are currently available. Examples include Tiny Einstein, 1st Class, Guru, and KnowledgePro; prices range from $100 to a few thousand dollars. Features to consider when buying a shell should include:

1. *Operating environment.* Will the shell run on your equipment? Is the shell networkable? Is it compatible with DOS?

2. *Recommended configuration.* Is it geared for hard disk? Floppy disk only? What is the random access memory (RAM)?

3. *Application types.* Is it designed for library applications? What about decision-process applications? Will it support more than one application?

4. *System type.* Is it a stand-alone shell?

5. *Experience required.* Is programming experience required? If so, which? Pascal? C? LISP? Other?

6. *Interface.* Is it menu-driven or command line? Or both?

7. *Logic types supported.* Which of the following applies: Forward chaining? Backward chaining? Procedural coding that tells a system what to do (e.g., multiply A times B then add C)?

8. *Rules.* Is the number of rules limited by disk capacity?

9. *Data types.* Are "yes" and "no" statements included? Will the shell accommodate graphics? What about multiple choice, numeric, or character string input statements?

10. *System development.* Does the package include an editor, compiler, and a mechanism that will find the IF-THEN rules? Is a custom interface included? Can certain programs be modified or deactivated, that is, are run-time versions available?

11. *Import/export capabilities.* Are the import or export measurement and control data derived from a scientific apparatus? Are export data in ASCII, *dBase III,* or *Lotus 1-2-3* formats?

12. *Support.* What type of support is provided: Online help? Tutorials and manuals? Free phone support?

13. *Price.* Does the price include a run-time disk? Is an authoring package included in the price? Is a license required? Are there special items (e.g., a compiler) that are required but not included in the base price?[5]

LIBRARY APPLICATIONS

The application of expert systems to library activities remains in the infancy stage. Several experimental projects involving librarians and patrons, however, are underway. There is much optimism on the part of enthusiasts that expert systems can be applied in most areas of the library. The current main drawback is the limited knowledge base that can be developed. For instance, an expert system can be created for a particular area of reference service, but it is not possible at this time to create a knowledge base to accommodate all aspects of reference service.

What are the reasons for implementing expert systems in libraries? First, expert systems improve the daily work of librarians. For example, an expert system will assist the librarian in realizing an improvement in productivity (e.g., processing more books, conducting more online searches, and serving more users each day). A well-programmed expert system will also improve quality. An expert system, for example, will be less likely to make human errors in answering questions and be more consistent in providing the same information time after time. Library areas that are candidates for the application of expert systems include cataloging, database searching, indexing, management, and reference.

Cataloging

Since much of cataloging is rule-based, it is an area that can benefit greatly in consistency and quality from an expert system. Fenley[6] believes that the most promising opportunities for the application of expert systems at the Library of Congress include the development of a series consultant and a subject cataloging consultant.

Series work has been described as one of the most problematic aspects of descriptive cataloging at the Library of Congress. Series encompass rules and procedures that are complex and numerous, and the practices of handling series have undergone significant changes making it more difficult to work with them. The proposed series consultant would specifically assist the cataloger in dealing with a new series and resolving complex problems and questions pertaining to the way it is presented, including the interpretation of ambiguous information. Expertise in series work is scarce and is frequently lost with a change in personnel.

The proposed subject cataloging consultant would benefit the Library of Congress by enhancing the productivity of the subject cataloging operation, providing greater consistency, and retaining complex knowledge and scarce expertise even after a human expert leaves. Subject cataloging requires substantial expertise due to the complexity of interpreting and applying correct subject cataloging policy and practice for subject headings and classification using a large body of documentation. These complicated aspects of the work entail symbolic reasoning and heuristic decision making.

A past dream of a cataloger would include having had an expert system during the implementation of the second edition of the *Anglo-American Cataloging Rules (AACR2)*. Many days were spent teaching the proper use of *AACR2*. If the technology had been available, an expert system could have saved a tremendous amount of time in instructing the cataloging staff on the new rules. Consistency and quality control would also have been enhanced by a knowledge-based system.

Figure 10.2. An Example of the EMYCIN Shell Applied to Cataloging

IF   – The item is not a work of personal authorship,

             – The item is not a work emanating from a corporate body,

             – The item is not a work or collection of works produced under editorial direction, and

             – The item is a work of unknown or uncertainauthorship

THEN   – It is definite that the title proper of the item is the main heading under which the item is entered in the catalog.

Source: R. Hjereppe, B. Olander, and K. Marklund, *Project ESCAPE – Expert Systems for Simple Choice of Access Points for Entries: Applications of Artificial Intelligence for Cataloging* (Linkoping, Sweden: Linkoping University, Department of Computer and Information Science, June 1985).

Hjerppe, Olander, and Marklund contend that *AACR2* may be too complex to be accommodated by current expert systems.[7] To compound the situation, *AACR2* has many variations and inconsistencies. For example, terms are poorly defined, rules are not precise, exceptions to the code appear to have been made on an ad hoc basis, and the relationship between general rules and specific rules is not sufficiently understood. Special attention should be given to these concerns prior to planning an expert system for existing and future editions of *AACR*.

Hjerppe, Olander, and Marklund are pioneers in researching and testing the adaptability of *AACR2* for expert systems.[8] They performed research on the feasibility of using an expert system for testing rules presented in chapter 21 ("Choice of Access Points") of *AACR2*; this project is often referred to as ESSCAPE (Expert Systems for Simple Choice of Access Points for Entries). Two shells were used in this project–EMYCIN and Expert-Ease. An example of EMYCIN is shown in Figure 10.2.

Database Searching

Online database searching can be enhanced by using expert systems. An expert system can assist the library user by:

1. Ascertaining the user query.

2. Identifying potential databases.

3. Identifying the conceptual components of the query.

4. Expressing the conceptual structure in terms of the fields of the selected databases, keywords, descriptors, and Boolean logic.

5. Accessing the database using the necessary communication protocol.

6. Entering the search logic.

7. Analyzing the search results.

8. Revising the search strategy.

9. Broadening the search, if too few hits resulted.

10. Narrowing the search, if too many hits resulted.

11. Ending the search and communicating the results to the user.

Much work remains to be done in designing effective front-end expert systems for database searching. Users normally have the most difficulty in properly accessing the databases. The ideal front-end system would draw a user profile, select the type of search required, identify the appropriate databases, and then quickly delineate the primary terms for the topic to be searched. The ideal system would enable the user to ask for and receive an explanation at any time in the search process. Micco and Smith describe the ideal front-end expert system as:

> ... one that has access to all resources available in a library or information center, namely the online catalog, the circulation records, OCLC's interlibrary loan system ... the addition of specialized databases that would provide access to the Library of Congress authority file, and a full-text version of *Books in Print*... It would also be connected to a whole range of commercial databases with the ability to automatically dial through to the required database and provide the necessary passwords and hand shaking.[9]

Research is being conducted on how and why searchers select specific search keys during online database searches. Results from this type of research will be helpful in designing expert systems that act as expert intermediaries between the user and databases, as they represent the searching behaviors of expert human intermediaries who have developed certain rules of thumb. A number of expert systems used to aid online searching are described in chapter 11.

Indexing

Automation has been used for some time in performing certain aspects of indexing. The intellectual part of indexing is not yet automated; however, efforts are underway in applying expert systems. For example, Susanne Humphrey at the National Library of Medicine is directing the Indexing Aid Research Project. The purpose of the project is to develop and test a prototype knowledge-based expert system providing computer-assisted indexing of the medical literature in the MEDLINE database.

> The system has been encoded in frames and is designed to interact with trained MEDLINE indexers using prompts, menus, and simple commands. The indexers enter subject terms as slot values in filling in document-specific frames that are derived from the knowledge-base frames. The automatic application of rules associated with the knowledge-base frames produces a set of medical subject heading (MeSH) keyword indexes to the document.[10]

We will begin witnessing greater use of expert systems in the indexing of journal articles. The intelligent characteristics of an expert system will assist the indexer by:

1. Identifying concepts discussed in the journal article.

2. Translating the concepts into verbal descriptions.

3. Translating the verbal descriptions into subject descriptors and their subdivisions.

4. Applying the appropriate rules governing the assignment of subject descriptors.

5.   Assigning subject descriptors, including subdivisions, to the article.

Management

Few, if any, management expert systems are currently being used by library directors. Nevertheless, this scenario will gradually change until directors are consulting management expert systems via their personal computers on a daily basis. There is a void in this area that will be filled when expert systems become a regular part of the manager's decision-support system.

Areas that are appropriate for library management expert systems include:

1.   Personnel planning and recruitment.

2.   Collection development.

3.   Construction of new buildings.

4.   Utilization of existing space.

5.   Accounting and general budgeting.

6.   Strategic planning.

For-profit organizations have already found expert systems to be indispensable; millions of dollars are being invested in decision-support expert systems each year. Significant returns are being reaped from these investments. For example, time for resolving management issues has been reduced from two or three days of work spread over a few weeks to half an hour. "Intelligent" machines have finally been accepted as valuable companions in the business world. They will likewise be accepted in library management within the next few years.

Reference

At first glance, one might surmise that a reference department could be replaced with expert systems. This is not possible in the near future, and it may never be possible to replace librarians with machines. Reference service is a very complex endeavor. The interaction between the reference librarian and the user carries with it many unanticipated challenges and human anomalies. Nevertheless, as expert systems and other products of artificial intelligence become more sophisticated in library practices, they will become a significant component of the reference librarian's workday. Dowell and Crews project several advantages for using expert systems in reference service:

1. Reference service can be provided even when a reference librarian is not available for consultation because the library is not open, the reference desk is not open, or the reference librarian is too busy.

2. Depending upon the expert system architecture, reference service can be provided at a number of locations throughout the library – not just at the reference desk.

3. Expert systems can be designated to provide library instruction, thereby taking a large amount of drudgery work away from the reference librarian.

4. A typical reference librarian possesses a vast amount of knowledge about the library collections, reference clientele, the institutions they work for, productive search strategies, and out-of-the-way but useful reference sources. Expert systems can be designed to capture this knowledge so that it would not be lost when the librarian retires or resigns.

5. Expert systems can serve more patrons, especially at peak hours, resulting in more user satisfaction without having to hire more reference librarians.[11]

Online Reference Assistance (ORA) is a reference expert system developed by James Parrott at the University of Waterloo Library. This system makes use of several color-graphic materials and a VAX computer that runs on a VMS operating system. Software used is Digital Equipment's Course Authoring System (CAS) whose command language is Digital Authoring Language (DAL). Its knowledge base contains forward and backward chaining structures. The Waterloo system was designed to suggest sources to answer factual questions and provide assistance with bibliographic instructional activities.

Another example of a reference expert system is the prototype PLEXUS, developed by Helen Brooks and Alina Vickery of the Central Information Service, University of London. PLEXUS has a well-defined subject domain focusing on gardening. This system refers users to resources about gardening, such as those found in guides to reference sources and in directories of online databases. Users interact with the system to develop an effective search strategy, search the database, and evaluate the results of the search. A list of annotated sources on a particular area of gardening is the final product.

Knowledge is represented in PLEXUS in four ways:

1. By a faceted classification scheme, which is not only a subject code but also an ordering system.

2. By task-oriented rule knowledge.

3. By the content of the referral sources (e.g., Walford's *Guide to Reference Material*).

4. By the semantic context of each dictionary term represented as the associated semantic category and its related frame structure (this is the term-oriented factual knowledge of the system).

The software of PLEXUS is mainly written in Pascal. It handles a knowledge base, user interface, database management system, and production rules. The system is implemented on a SIRIUS I microcomputer with 850K bytes of RAM and a 20-megabyte hard disk. PLEXUS is not a perfect system, as its creators admit, but it is an excellent example of a referral system that engages in intelligent problem solving with the user.

Other examples of reference expert systems include ANSWERMAN and POINTER. ANSWERMAN, developed by Sam Waters of the National Agricultural Library, is designed to help users find answers to ready reference questions. A series of menus helps delineate the question and identify the type of reference tool needed (e.g., atlas, dictionary or encyclopedia). ANSWERMAN serves as a consultation system and as a front end to external online databases and CD-ROM reference tools. Karen Smith's POINTER at the State University of New York at Buffalo directs users to government publications that will provide the answer to a particular question. Users make choices from menus, and the system responds with the names of specific reference sources, call numbers, and instructions.

WHY EXPERT SYSTEMS HAVE RISEN TO PROMINENCE

Expert systems should not be perceived as the panacea for all library and information science problems and shortcomings. Our current expert systems have some serious limitations, of which the primary one is the size of the knowledge base that can be constructed and maintained. In addition, it is difficult to sustain consistency among overlapping terms.[12]

Nonetheless, some of the reasons expert systems have made recent rapid progress on the international level are as follows:

1. There has been a gradual revolution at conceptual and operational levels from data processing–through information processing–to knowledge processing and management. All three technologies, however, continue to contribute to the decision support systems needed by workers today.

2. Artificial intelligence, the discipline from which expert systems have developed, has experienced a renaissance in the last 5 to 10

years. In a limited, well-defined domain, a computer program can perform as well as, and often better than, a human expert. Further, in many cases this expertise can often be encapsulated in a few hundred rules. On the other hand, what appear to be relatively easy tasks for humans, such as picking up a pencil, are extremely difficult to program into robotic or other mechanical devices.

3. Many major information-technology-related projects funded in America, Europe, and Japan include a substantial element of research directed at knowledge-based systems.

4. The commercial world has recognized that expert systems are revenue earners and cost savers. Success in a company involves considerable investment in skilled human resources. People leave organizations for better opportunities and they take their many years of training and expertise with them. Expert systems provide the opportunity to avoid, or make better use of, the large-scale investment involved in acquiring human expertise. It is clearly attractive, and the result has been a massive movement of venture capital to artificial intelligence and expert systems research.[13]

COMPARISON WITH ALTERNATIVE TECHNOLOGIES

AI development addresses the human thought process more than any other technology advances. "Intelligent" and "thinking" are often used when describing AI and expert systems. Emulating the mental processes of the human is the central thrust of this phenomenon. The question is no longer, "Can machines think?" It is now, "What will they think?" New advances like hypertext are not on the same level as AI; in a sense, as far as sophistication in new technology is concerned, AI and expert systems are lightyears ahead of the others.

Initially, expert systems could run only on mainframes; now they can operate efficiently on microcomputers. John P. Crecine believes there is a bright future for expert systems working on personal computers:

These new microcomputers will cost no more than fully configured versions of current microcomputers, but they will be five to 10 times more powerful, with 10 to 21 times the active memory and with the graphics capabilities previously available only on costly, specialized systems.

The next generation of personal computers will provide the most advanced professional design aids, document and graphic design tools, and knowledge-based systems (artificial intelligence programs, expert systems, and intelligent tutors) for $5,000 or $6,000. This includes the raw computational power that comes with a computer able to execute about 3-million instructions per second (MIPS) and 2-million or more bytes available in active memory. . . Thanks to a feature called "virtual memory," software developers need not worry about shoe-horning sophisticated programs into the particular memory constraints of a given personal computer, and users will have access to programs and databases limited in practice only by the size of their hard disks.[14]

Crecine paints an exceptionally rosy future for expert systems; others share this view. Every eight years computer technology has advanced in performance parameters by an order of 100 times. No other industry has enjoyed comparable advances.

IMPACT ON LIBRARY STAFF

Based on past experience, most library users will take to new technology like ducks to water. For example, users are finding the online catalog a great tool and, almost immediately after such a catalog is introduced, begin asking for more databases to be placed on the system. We can assume that the experience of users with expert systems will be just as rewarding.

The persons in the library who will "suffer" the most from the implementation of expert systems will be the staff, both professional and nonprofessional. The thought of being deskilled by a machine can be frightening for anyone. Some of the dehumanizing aspects associated with computers cannot be avoided.

Librarians should not jump to conclusions, however, about their being replaced by an expert system. This is not going to happen unless they are only performing clerical tasks. Similarly feared when it was first introduced, the Online Computer Library Center (OCLC) did not and will not drive catalogers into unemployment. Instead, the positive aspects of this new technology should be emphasized. Expert systems can make the librarian's life much better. They will enable librarians to use their time for more creative, job-related activities. After all, don't librarians want to devote more time to professional work and less time to tedious, repetitive tasks?

WHAT TO EXPECT NEXT FROM ARTIFICIAL INTELLIGENCE

Just when we are getting ready for expert systems to become more sophisticated in order to reap more benefits from them, a phenomenon known as *neural networking* is evolving. Researchers have tried for years to program computers to mimic the brain's abilities, but without total success. Now a growing number of designers believe they have the answer: if a computer is to function more like a person and less like an overgrown calculator, it must be built more like a brain, which distributes information across a vast interconnected web of nerve cells, or neurons.

Even with much of neural networking still in the conceptual stage, people have already begun thinking differently about artificial intelligence. Neural networking shares information among the interconnected neurons and performs tasks simultaneously; this two-dimensional approach works best at recognizing patterns. Instead of looking for patterns, expert systems distill the decision-making process used by human experts into rules of thumb. Neurocomputer researchers argue that neural networks will eventually prove superior because they can adjust more easily to changes in the nature of the problem to be solved. The trick is to use a combination of neural networks and expert systems to solve problems too tough for either to tackle alone.[15]

Now is the most exciting time in our civilization to be a librarian. And we can count on it becoming more exciting as we head for the year 2000. In 1964 Jesse Shera stated, "We can now build machines to do library work . . . the machines are ready for us . . . but we are still very far from being ready for machines."[16] After a quarter century, do we have any choice but to make ourselves ready for the opportunities provided by artificial intelligence?

NOTES

1. Paul Harmon and David King, *Expert Systems: Artificial Intelligence in Business* (New York: John Wiley, 1985), 3.

2. Frederick Hayes-Roth, Donald A. Waterman, and Douglas B. Lenat, eds. *Building Expert Systems* (Reading, Mass.: Addison-Wesley, 1983), 140-49.

3. Charles Fenley, *Expert Systems: Concepts and Applications,* Advances in Library Information Technology, no. 1 (Washington, D.C.: Library of Congress, 1988), 11.

4. Fenley, 13.

5. Steve Rosenthal, "You Don't Have to be an Expert to Use Expert Systems," *PC Week* 5 (19 December 1988): 97-109.

6. Fenley, 32.

7. R. Hjerppe, B. Olander, and K. Marklund, *Project ESSCAPE – Expert Systems for Simple Choice of Access Points for Entries: Applications of Artificial Intelligence for Cataloging* (Linkoping, Sweden: Linkoping University, Department of Computer and Information Science, June 1985), 5. (Paper for presentation at IFLA, Chicago, 18-24 August 1985.)

8. Hjerppe, 7.

9. H. Mary Micco and Irma Smith, "Designing an Expert System for the Reference Function Subject Access to Information," *Proceedings of the 49th ASIS Annual Meeting* 23 (1986): 204-10.

10. Susanne M. Humphrey and Nancy E. Miller, "Knowledge-based Indexing of the Medical Literature: The Indexing Aid Project," *Journal of the American Society for Information Science* 38(3):184-96.

11. Connie Dowell and Philip L. Crews, "Applications of Expert System Technology to Reference Service," 12. (Unpublished paper)

12. Donald E. Riggs, "Expert Systems in Libraries," *Proceedings of the International Symposium on New Techniques and Applications in Libraries,* (Xi'an, People's Republic of China: Xi'an Jiaotong University Press, 1988).

13. Forbes Gibb, "Expert Systems: An Overview," in *Expert Systems in Libraries,* ed. by Forbes Gibb (London: Taylor Graham, 1986), 3-5.

14. John P. Crecine, "The Next Generation of Personal Computers," *Science* 231 (28 February, 1986): 935-43.

15. "Putting Brainpower in a Box," *Time,* 8 August 1988, 59.

16. Jesse Shera, "Library of the Future," *Wilson Library Quarterly* 39 (November 1964): 43.

■ 11 ■

Research on Information Access

Raya Fidel

The new developments in information technology provide faster and better access to information. These developments are gradually introducing major and significant changes in our lives and, quite strikingly, in libraries and information systems. These qualitative changes are mostly caused by an important social development: with the new information technology, direct access to information is no longer reserved for a few trained professionals; instead, various information systems are accessed daily by most members of society, at work and at home.

Technology, however, caught information science unprepared. As a result, the new technological and social developments have had a qualitatively marked effect on research in information science. New areas of research in information science are emerging, and the focus of research in the traditional areas has shifted significantly.

The new areas of research are well represented in this book, with each chapter addressing the application of a new technology or issues that are a direct result of these applications. Although not always apparent, the need for these new areas of research is strongly motivated by the fact that the use of information technology is now widespread.

Consider expert systems, for example. The technological developments that are associated with artificial intelligence made these systems possible. But the task of an expert system is specific: to act like an expert in a certain field. Clearly, the need for such systems was not urgent when the use of information systems was reserved for experts only. Today, however, when information systems are made available to the public, this subject is of supreme importance.

The shift in the focus of research in traditional areas is more subtle. To trace it, one needs to examine research about one of the oldest and most established branches of information science, retrieval from bibliographic databases. This chapter summarizes the trends in information retrieval research since it first encountered computerized systems and online bibliographic databases, through online catalogs, to CD-ROM and expert systems. It shows that the focus of research is gradually shifting from the study of retrieval performance to the study of users' searching behavior.

INFORMATION NEEDS AND RETRIEVAL TOOLS

First, a delineation of the topic is required. The process of retrieving information typically consists of two stages: users first identify the information that will answer their information needs, and then they retrieve the relevant information.

Reality, however, is much more complex than this description. More important, information need is an elusive concept: even if a real and precise need for information exists in an objective sense, it is difficult to determine it accurately. Asking users to define their information needs requires them to describe in exact terms what they do not know—a situation that is most often contradictory in nature.[1]

For the purpose of this discussion, however, we assume that what is expressed by users of libraries when they want to retrieve information are information needs that *are* clearly defined. We also assume that most of these needs are subject related: users want to find information about a certain subject. Further, users' requests include an additional aspect: the purpose of the request. For example, a request for information about CD-ROM systems by a library patron who wishes to learn how to use such systems is essentially different from the one raised by this author who needed a literature review on the subject.

Users can employ two types of retrieval tools when they search subject-related requests: the library catalog, or abstracting and indexing (A&I) services. Traditionally, users have been expected to use the card catalog and the printed volumes of the A&I services on their own with the librarian available on call. Today, a growing number of libraries provide access to their collections through online catalogs and most A&I services can be accessed online via search systems such as ORBIT, Dialog, and BRS, which were discussed in chapter 3. In addition, there is a steady and rapid growth in the number of databases that are available for searching through CD-ROM systems, discussed in chapter 7.

The first search systems that provided access to A&I services (now called bibliographic databases) were geared to the professional librarian. Online catalogs and most CD-ROM systems, on the other hand, were always designed for direct user searches.

Library catalogs and A&I services, whether manual or computerized, organize information in a manner that is useful for retrieval. The construction of retrieval tools involves the creation of subject indexes. For printed tools, subject indexes include index terms–descriptors or subject headings–taken from an authority list of controlled vocabulary. A thesaurus is such a list of controlled vocabulary terms that are used both for searching and for indexing (assigning descriptors or subject headings to bibliographic items). Indexing can be performed either by humans or by computers (automated indexing).

In addition to thesauri, computerized tools provide subject indexes that list all the meaningful words in the bibliographic citations and in their abstracts. Such indexes are generated by the computer and do not require manual indexing or the construction of a thesaurus, and users search them with free-text terms. In recent years, databases have been created that provide the complete text of documents in a machine-readable form. Such full-text documents as journal articles, textbooks, or chapters in an encyclopedia can usually be searched with both free-text terms and descriptors.

ONLINE BIBLIOGRAPHIC DATABASES

Research about information retrieval from computerized systems had begun in the late 1950s, before such systems were commonly used. Anticipating the new capabilities that computerized systems offer, in particular free-text searching, a few investigators examined the effect that the then-new technology would have on information retrieval. Most noted are the Cranfield studies which tested retrieval performance of a variety of index languages–including free-text searching.[2] While the results are still controversial, the Cranfield studies established the procedure for retrieval experiments and the measurements to use: precision (what proportion of the citations retrieved are relevant) and recall (what proportion of relevant citations have been retrieved).

Searching bibliographic databases was first possible in the batch mode only. During that period, the use of computerized databases was limited, and various researchers replicated the Cranfield studies with some variations. When in the late 1960s databases became accessible online, however, their use spread rapidly and with this change came a shift in research interest.

The results of these early studies were not considered when the first online bibliographic databases were designed. These databases were simply computerized versions of the printed A&I services. In fact, even today, many A&I services are publicly available in both printed and computerized versions which are often identical in content and structure. More important, the first search systems for bibliographic databases were designed for professional searchers, mostly librarians. Their use required expert knowledge, training, and experience.

Characteristics of Searchers

Research in online searching began in the 1970s with two large-scale studies that focused on users' attitudes, satisfaction, and success.[3] Most of the research that followed, however, concentrated on the attributes of a "good searcher": those personal characteristics a librarian should possess to become successful online. Experience in online searching,[4] type of training,[5] personal traits such as creativity,[6] and cognitive abilities[7] are among the characteristics examined. No conclusive results have been found, and most investigators observed that the large individual variability among searchers impeded their studies.[8]

The method used in online searching studies is well established today. Briefly, an experiment is set up in which the searchers, known as subjects in experimental studies, are assigned to a group, depending on their score on the tested characteristics (e.g., experience, cognitive style) or variables. All subjects are asked to search a given set of requests, and their search processes and results are analyzed and compared. These analyses employ a well-established set of measurements. The search process is evaluated by the number of commands used, number of search terms entered, length of search, and similar measurements. Search results are evaluated by precision, recall, and unit cost (the cost of each citation).

Why did these studies fail to produce conclusive results? There are several possible reasons, but what immediately comes to mind is that the personal characteristics (the variables) that have been tested do not affect the quality of online searching. Unfortunately, such a generalization contradicts common sense: it is common knowledge among librarians that experienced searchers perform better than novices and that training is important for online searching. Therefore, one conclusion is that the measurements that have been used are inadequate. This conclusion was substantiated when 10 librarians with almost identical subject background, training, and experience scored very differently from one another on search process measurements.[9]

Another impediment to obtaining conclusive results is the experimental setting in which variables that are not studied are assumed to be controlled. In reality, however, a large number of variables affect online searching behavior,[10] and no single experiment can control all of them. Variables that were ignored in these experiments, such as the ability of a subject to perform a search without interviewing the user, may have stronger effects than the ones tested.

But it is more important to ask: why did researchers focus on the attributes of a good searcher? The answer is apparent if we consider the patterns in which information retrieval technology was used at that time. When the access to information is provided primarily by experts it is important to investigate and identify the characteristics of these experts – the training, knowledge, and experience that is required of them.

With the new developments, however, we gain a different perspective on the subject matter. While identifying the characteristics of a good searcher may at times help administrators to decide which employee should perform online searching in their libraries, the issue is of very little significance when online bibliographic databases are searched by library users themselves. The important issue is to discover the characteristics of a good search. Identifying strategies and moves that can enhance the success of online searches is beneficial to all users of all online retrieval systems.

The Search Process

Online searchers have long known the importance of the search process. Journals such as *Online, Online Review,* and *Medical Library Reference Quarterly* include many articles that describe useful strategies in certain databases and search systems.

Research in this area began in the 1980s, but it is still sparse and requires different research methods from those that attempted to identify attributes of good searchers. Based on the experience of librarians, Bates proposed a number of information search tactics that could be employed in online searches.[11] Tactics to use early in the search include an examination of information already found in the search ("trace"), and those to use later in the search include the rejection of items indexed by certain terms ("block").

Fidel analyzed search protocols and verbal protocols of seven experienced searchers performing approximately 90 searches as part of their regular workload. As a result, she listed the moves (changes in search strategies) that searchers made to increase or decrease the number of items retrieved, or to improve the search in other ways.[12]

Studying the search process is a complex task requiring the probing of phenomena that are not easy to observe or analyze. Nevertheless, user training and the design of useful online retrieval systems cannot be successful before this process is thoroughly understood.

User Searching

The idea that users can search bibliographic databases for their own requests is rapidly gaining popularity, particularly with the proliferation of CD-ROM systems. The interest in this idea, however, emerged earlier, when search systems and other commercial vendors started to provide gateway (front-end, or intermediary) systems such as Search Helper or Knowledge Index, which are supposed to mediate between the end user and online bibliographic systems. Such gateway systems do indeed provide a simple interface with search systems. They free users from having to learn a command language or deal with the idiosyncrasies of specific databases. This is especially important since most users are not likely to perform online searches frequently. Most of the current gateway systems, however, achieve their simplicity by providing users with a limited range of capabilities, thereby simplifying the search process itself.

While several in-house studies have been performed on gateway systems, studies of users searching their requests directly would have far more impact. The only example of such a large-scale study is a research project that examined 11 years of searching the databases of the National Library of Medicine (NLM) in the United States by pathologists and pharmacists.[13] The results of this study are many, but as yet not all have been published. Of particular interest here are the findings that users did not encounter many problems with the technique of searching but rather with the vocabulary and content of the system and that most performed simple searches. In addition, the major problems encountered were with the more sophisticated capabilities of the databases—problems that sometimes caused a substantive loss of citations.

Although this study examined a specific population, its results substantiate the findings of online catalog use studies, as described in the next section: the weakest point in patrons' doing their own searching is their inability to formulate successful strategies. Gateway systems do not provide help because they do not employ any of the sophisticated capabilities of databases—in fact, some even eliminate simple ones. But gateway systems do not employ sophisticated capabilities because research that can guide the design of such systems is still sparse. At present, the only source on which we can rely for search strategies is the community of experienced online searchers.

ONLINE CATALOGS

Online catalogs are designed for library users. Though libraries had prior experience with online retrieval through bibliographic databases, the introduction of online catalogs in the late 1970s and early 1980s marks the beginning of a new era in which users have begun to do their own searching. This new scenario has had an important effect on research in information science.

Unlike research in searching online bibliographic databases, studies in online catalogs focus on users' requirements. Major studies were set up to discover users' attitudes to and acceptance of the new catalogs by examining characteristics of both users and catalogs. Most studies, however, concentrated on the human-computer interface, that is, on how easy it is to "converse" with the computer. Only a few addressed the retrieval problem:

whether or not users are satisfied with the results of their searches, and what could be done to improve these results.

Further, studies in online catalogs are guided by an administrative approach that is essentially different from the approach taken by researchers of online searching in bibliographic databases. In studying online catalogs, researchers assume that the user population is a given and that features of the catalogs themselves need to be examined in order to eventually design an online catalog that is most useful. In contrast, research about retrieval from online databases assumes that the databases and the search systems are a given and focuses instead on the characteristics of the users (i.e., professional searchers) that are most suitable for online searching.

Surely, the difference in these research approaches stems from the reality of library decision making, which is determined by the use of technology. Librarians do not elect which patrons to serve, but they may want to design an online catalog and should be able to select the system that provides the best catalog for their users. In contrast, library administrators cannot change databases and search systems, but they can select from among a number of candidates those persons who would best perform online searches.

Nevertheless, the searching of bibliographic databases and of online catalogs is one and the same: searching for bibliographic information. There is a diminishing distinction between the database as a store of citations to journal articles, which can be manipulated with sophisticated techniques, and the online catalog as a store of information about monographs, which only provides for simple manipulation. The difference in research approaches is, therefore, an impediment to both areas of research: studies of online catalogs cannot rely on research that already has been performed in online searching, and vice versa.

User Interface with Online Catalogs

Online public access catalogs (OPACs) are a relatively new phenomenon in libraries. In the United States, the Council on Library Resources (CLR) funded in 1981-1983 a nationwide study of 17 online catalog systems (both in-house and commercial) in 29 libraries. While many articles about experience with online catalogs in specific libraries have been published, this first large-scale study provides most of our knowledge about OPACs.

The study was conducted by various agencies, and although numerous attempts to summarize and synthesize its results have been made (see, for example, Matthews and Lawrence's article[14]), more meaningful interpretation and integration of the vast amount of data are required before specific conclusions can be drawn.

CLR Study Methods

Typical of a large-scale study (although a novelty in research about online searching behavior), the study applied a variety of methods. A questionnaire survey of 8,094 users and 3,981 nonusers of online catalogs in 31 libraries was administered by various agencies. A summary of the data collected is provided by Matthews and his colleagues.[15] They point, for example, to demographic characteristics of users, the manner in which most users are informed about the availability of an online catalog, the persons to whom they address their requests for help, problems with the interface, and the rate of success and satisfaction perceived by users.

Focused-group interviews with library staff and patrons – both users and nonusers of online catalogs – were carried out in six libraries and were conducted through an open, in-depth discussion led by a moderator.[16] While such group interviews do not supply quantitative data, they can explore the degree of satisfaction and expectation of both patrons and staff. Among other things, these particular interviews revealed that while users of online catalogs are happy to use them, they have problems with subject access to information, and they expect online catalogs to provide more services than are currently available.

The results from the focused-group interviews were complemented by the results of individual and group interviews conducted among library staff at three research libraries.[17] These interviews supported the analysis of the questionnaires and addressed issues such as problems that users have in using the catalogs, possible system improvement, and the impact of online catalogs on the library staff and its patrons.

In addition, transaction log analysis, in which the protocols of individual searches are analyzed, were performed in seven libraries.[18] It was found, for example, that while there is a great variability in the length of searches and in their types (author, title, or subject searches), users tend to remain in the type of search that was initiated and to repeat their mistakes. These analyses also provided statistics about issues such as the rate of success (nonzero hits) in subject and author searches, frequency of commands used (in particular, "sophisticated" commands), and patterns of searches.

Feature analysis of 10 existing online catalog systems was also performed for the CLR study.[19] This was a functional analysis, documenting the functions and commands of each system, its interface capabilities, and the documentation available to users.

CLR Study Findings

The CLR study stimulated further analyses of the data, additional explorations, and considerations of possible implications. Cochrane and Markey showed how the results from focused-group interviews were useful in interpreting questionnaire findings,[20] and Borgman compared the study results with research findings in other areas of online bibliographic retrieval.[21] She concluded that more similarity existed in conceptual than in mechanical problems. Dickson, on the other hand, analyzed a sample of zero-hit author and title searches to discover reasons for failure and concluded that users have a conceptual model of the online catalog that is different from the one they have of a card catalog.[22] Last, a collection of articles assessed the impact of online catalogs on technical services, reference services, subject access, and library administration.[23]

In a summary of the CLR OPAC study, Matthews and Lawrence outlined the principal findings:

1. Experience with the library and its catalog is the most important factor in determining success and satisfaction in using the catalog.

2. Online catalogs should provide a variety of interfaces, depending on the type of search and the level of user experience.

3. Users adapt their attitudes to the capabilities and limitations of the online catalogs they use.

4. The form and nature of training and user assistance are important.[24]

These findings only substantiate common knowledge among librarians; they do not provide insight as to how to design online catalogs that are most useful.

Studies from Great Britain

The spread of online catalogs in Great Britain has been slower than in the United States. Nevertheless, much research has been conducted there, most of it sponsored by the British Library Research and Development Department. While only a few large-scale studies have been completed, researchers take a multifaceted approach: they study retrieval techniques and interface design, as well as the quality of the database. Controlled experiments are common, and most are based on theoretical developments in the area of bibliographic databases. In addition to direct use studies, researchers have conducted comparative studies – either before-and-after surveys or examinations of the performance of different systems – and created experimental systems to study the user-catalog interface.[25] Findings from these various projects (some of which are still incomplete) have yet to be integrated.

Subject Access in Online Catalogs

The importance of subject access to online catalogs was the most significant finding of the CLR study.[26] This is not surprising because early studies of catalog use (e.g., by Lipetz and by Bates[27]) showed that subject access in card catalogs was inadequate. With online catalogs – which are actually automated card catalogs – the issue assumes an even greater importance because library users who were not satisfied with subject searching in a card catalog *expect* to be more successful with online catalogs.[28] Here again, the CLR study only substantiated previous findings but did not provide guidelines for improved subject access.

Present online catalogs are more sophisticated than the early ones and stand ready to facilitate improved subject access. However, the various ways that users can actually be helped in subject searches are not yet known. A display of a classification scheme, for example, can help users to "browse" in a subject area.[29] It is not clear, however, which classification scheme is most suitable for this purpose: the Dewey Decimal Classification[30] or Library of Congress Classification.[31] Each scheme raises both conceptual and technical problems.[32]

Another approach to aid users is to provide online help in the use of the Library of Congress Subject Headings. Such assistance could include an alphabetical display of the headings with cross references or a display of related subject headings. In addition, searching keywords (i.e., free-text searching) in the titles of books[33] or even in their indexes and tables of contents[34] can improve subject access.

Researchers of online catalogs have only begun to consider subject access, and most of the literature in this area is limited to expert opinion about the direction online subject access should take.[35] An exception is provided by the European research community. Several projects have begun to experiment with methods to improve subject access: the use of a thesaurus to suggest narrower terms if the user retrieves many references or broader terms if too little is retrieved; the development of automatic stemming techniques such as removing word suffixes to improve recall; and the preliminary design of an expert system that derives classification numbers from natural language terms, to name a few.[36] It remains the task of future research to integrate the results of these projects, most of which are ongoing.

With the development of more powerful online catalogs, subject searching becomes more similar to subject searching of bibliographic databases. For example, CITE – the online catalog at the NLM – can also access the NLM databases.[37] All in all, research in subject access to online bibliographic databases is more developed, and studies of online catalogs can draw on its experience. It is clear, however, that while current technological capabilities provide for improved subject access, research in this area is lagging behind.

CD-ROM SYSTEMS

The use of CD-ROM technology in libraries is spreading fast, and any statistics about this use are bound to be outdated by the time they are published. At present, libraries acquire CD-ROM software and hardware primarily for searching bibliographic databases, even though this technology enhances access to various types of databases, such as image or voice databanks.

Typical of an innovative technology, CD-ROM systems immediately introduced a qualitative change in libraries: because searching time is not a factor in the cost of online retrieval, users can search their own requests for free or at a low cost. Thus, while most CD-ROM products for bibliographic databases are designed for both users and professional searchers, most interest and research is focused on user searching.

As a result, the introduction of CD-ROM systems to libraries accelerated the emergence of users' searching behavior as a focus of research in information science. But while the technology is already in use and the importance of such research is widely recognized, actual research in this area has barely begun.

One problem typical of the new pattern in which this technology is used is the simple, unsophisticated manner in which users conduct their searches. A number of studies of end-user searching revealed that users carried out very simple searches, ignoring the sophisticated capabilities that are available to them. Moreover, there is an indication that, given a choice, simple systems (those that are commonly not powerful) would become more popular than sophisticated ones.[39]

Nonetheless, studies of users' searching show that CD-ROM users indicate a high rate of satisfaction (e.g., see Karp and Kleiner[38]): users believe most of the time that their searches are successful. Moreover, having retrieved information from the computer, they often assume that the search is complete and that there is no need to search other databases—whether printed or online. This tendency was even spotted among advanced students in a library school.[40]

The trade-off between sophistication and ease of use is not surprising, but it is alarming when users are not aware of this trade-off and when they are generally satisfied with the results of simple searches. This problem was clearly demonstrated in the CLR studies of online catalogs. These studies found that user satisfaction levels were surprisingly high given the relatively high error rates.[41]

There are two approaches to resolving the situation: to provide adequate training to users before–or even during–their searches; and to design systems and interfaces that are powerful and sophisticated, yet easy to use.

Training

Training is an important factor. Although CD-ROM products are tailored to end-user searching, and some even claim that no training is needed for their use, experience shows that no matter how simple a system is, some training is always needed.[42]

Furthermore, training seems to be a promising approach because there is evidence that users' training has a great effect on their searching. A study at Drexel University, for example, found that students followed closely the instruction they received in a short training session when they selected databases and search strategies.[43]

To complicate matters further, training sessions are usually short because most library patrons are infrequent users and are not willing to spend long hours on training. As a result, these brief sessions tend to emphasize the mechanics of a search or the technical aspects of searching because these are the basics necessary to access and search databases. In contrast, a number of studies revealed that end users encounter very few problems in learning the technical skills, but found it difficult to formulate search strategies. This difficulty was found across a variety of user groups, from highly trained pharmacists[44] and physicians[45] to high school students[46] searching in an academic library.[47]

Clearly, preparing users for searching CD-ROM databases is a complex task: the trainer must explain the basic technical features, as well as the "art" of constructing effective search strategies, and all in a short period of time. Training for online searching is performed today on an ad hoc basis, depending on the resources available. Furthermore, there is no agreed-upon understanding of what should be included in such training. This is not surprising. User searching is a new phenomenon and librarians have not yet acquired enough experience to know what problems users face in searching. As with general bibliographic instruction, training of users for online searching will become more effective in time. However, conducting research to uncover the problems and difficulties that users encounter when searching is necessary to achieve this goal.

Such research should reveal the features–both technical and conceptual–that are most important to effective user searching. At present, only a few studies of actual CD-ROM searching have been reported in the literature. In addition, most of these studies are surveys in which users are asked to rate their satisfaction and provide some kind of demographic data. A number of studies examined the effect of CD-ROM searching on searching activities in libraries. For instance, a study in a medical school's library found that while users searched CD-ROM systems more frequently than online systems, the introduction of CD-ROM systems to their library did not change the number of mediated searches, i.e., those performed by a librarian.[48]

While such surveys are important to the general management of online services, they rarely illuminate the problems users encounter in searching. A few attempts to discover these problems have already been made, however. One example is the study of students at Drexel University that examined actual search strategies,[49] and another is a study of searching behavior of elementary school children while searching a full-text electronic encyclopedia on CD-ROM.[50] As first studies of this kind, however, they provide only tentative observations about problems encountered in searching. Much research in searching behavior is still needed before training effectiveness can be improved.

Systems Design

Another approach to help users to improve their searches is to design CD-ROM systems that are powerful and sophisticated, yet easy to use. At present, the development of these systems is guided by a "seat of the pants" approach, rather than by drawing from systematic studies of user searching.[51] Moreover, a number of fundamental issues are not yet resolved.

A viable example here is the issue of standardization: the development and use of a common standard for all bibliographic retrieval systems. There are two opposing views about whether or not standardization would be useful for searching CD-ROM systems. On one hand, some software designers claim that their creativity would be inhibited by the enforcement of a standard. On the other hand, such a standard would be extremely helpful because it would enable users to learn how to use only one system and to move freely and easily from one database to another.

In reality the National Information Standards Organization (NISO) issued a proposed standard for common command languages (CCL),[52] but CD-ROM producers exercise their creativity, each designing their own command language. In fact, a study of 20 databases provided by 10 different CD-ROM system producers showed that the system varied greatly in the search capabilities they offer, in their ease of use, and even in their use of function keys.[53]

Only research into the searching behavior of CD-ROM system users can determine whether or not a standard is needed. Moreover, such research could determine which standard would be most effective. By extension, using the results of research about searching behavior, software producers will be able to spot the problems in searching–and learn how to resolve at least some of them–when they have both a description and an evaluation of searching behavior with current systems. They could then design more useful interfaces and more powerful systems than are available today.

Thus, as is the case with bibliographic databases and online catalogs, CD-ROM systems are already in use, but the research that can facilitate both effective training and the design of powerful and useful interfaces has just begun.

INTERMEDIARY EXPERT SYSTEMS

It is believed that an increasing number of users prefer to interact directly with online bibliographic retrieval systems. Although no statistics exist as yet to support this assumption, a large amount of effort is being invested by software producers and search system vendors in developing systems, such as SciMate or Colleague, that facilitate online bibliographic retrieval from users' offices or homes. It is also believed that users will very likely search their own requests online when search processes are simplified or made friendlier. The prevailing approach to providing such user-system communication is to develop intermediary systems designed to mediate between users and complex information retrieval systems – online bibliographic databases, online catalogs, or CD-ROM systems.

With intermediary expert systems, users should be able to present their requests to a system, which would then make expert decisions about the search process (that is, make decisions about the databases to search and the search strategy to employ). Such systems should interrogate users to elicit request characteristics, but would use their own expertise to make decisions about matters that are beyond the knowledge of users. For example, an intermediary expert system should ask the user whether high recall or high precision is required, and then use this information to decide which search strategy would provide the best results.

Various intermediary systems are already available for public access, such as CITE,[54] while others are prototype systems being tested in experimental settings. Examples of the latter are CANSEARCH, PLEXUS, EP-X, and CoalSORT, each covering a limited subject domain and searching a single database.[55] Through such systems, users are freed from encounters with the numerous peculiarities of databases and search systems – such as ORBIT, Dialog, or BRS – and yet can benefit from a large range of capabilities.

In particular, an intermediary system allows users to enter a request in a loosely structured format, preferably in natural language, using a sentencelike expression. The system then processes the request terms, displays information to users, and asks for feedback. The information displayed may be in the form of a list of subject areas, databases, search keys, or actual citations from which users are asked to make a selection, possibly in ranked order. Interaction of this nature usually proceeds until the user terminates the session.

Helper vs. Expert Systems

Some intermediary systems are actually helper systems: they provide menu-driven interaction that frees users from learning the command language while still requiring them to make most of the decisions during a search process, or they drastically simplify searching by reducing the number of options to a minimum. CITE, for example, leaves the selection of search keys to the user. It displays a list of search keys that can be used for a request concept – both descriptors and free-text terms – and asks the user to select the terms. In contrast, CONIT – which provides an interface with a number of databases covering a variety of subjects – simplifies the selection of search keys because it searches each search key as a free-text term and, under certain circumstances that depend on the search system rather than the request, also searches each as a descriptor.[56]

Intermediary expert systems, on the other hand, attempt a more powerful form of user assistance: they replicate the performance of an expert in online bibliographic retrieval by incorporating the knowledge of an expert with rules for making inferences on the basis of this knowledge. As such, they have attracted attention and controversy.

Most researchers agree about the nature of intermediary expert systems, even though a variety of definitions for expert systems currently exist. Studies examining users searching their own requests with no intermediary assistance show repeatedly that users need intermediary expertise mostly for formulating search strategies, while they seem to master the command language with no difficulties. Therefore, every intermediary expert system that is being developed today must include a component that supports decisions about search strategies.

Requirements for Intermediary Systems

Daniels, Brooks, and Croft, among others, delineate the requirements for such intermediary systems.[57] One such requirement is that an intermediary expert system should be able to take into account request (and user) characteristics that are beyond the topical description of the search. Existing intermediary expert systems, however, are unable to account for such characteristics because their knowledge is derived primarily from the information stored in bibliographic databases.

For example, to users who ask for information about online catalogs, such a system may suggest that they search under the term "OPAC," because this new term appears in the titles and abstracts of many items indexed with the descriptor "Online Catalogs." Deriving its knowledge only from the stored text, however, prevents the system from considering aspects that are not directly related to the subject of a request. For instance, the system would not "know" that it is useful to find out what level of material is required: introductory and instructional material, or data about recent research.

Although the debate about whether knowledge for expert systems should be derived from human experts or from other sources is not yet settled, some attempts have been made to extract knowledge from librarians. Among the first steps in this direction is a project supported by the British Library that produced a model of the search process[58] and a list of moves to improve search results[59] with a decision tree that guides decisions about whether to enter free-text terms or descriptors.[60] In fact, a few prototype systems such as PLEXUS and EP-X are already based on such knowledge. In addition, in the area of indexing, two institutions in the United States, the American Petroleum Institute and the NLM, have used indexers' knowledge and practice to develop expert systems to aid in-house indexing.[61]

Research on intermediary expert systems is in its early years, even though various attempts have already been made to design such systems. Our short experience indicates, however, that the most promising approach to the creation of knowledge bases is to model searching behaviors. Thus, the technological developments that made expert systems possible also direct research to focus on users' searching behavior.

CONCLUSION

The application of new technology has a significant effect on the retrieval of information; access to information and the capabilities to manipulate information for retrieval have undergone revolutionary changes. Research to support these new possibilities, however, has just begun.

In a report about a recent study on information seeking and retrieving, Saracevic and his colleagues conclude their summary of the review literature with the observation:

> It is most indicative that an identical conclusion appears in every one of these reviews despite different orientation of the review and different backgrounds of the reviewers. They all conclude that research has been inadequate and that more research is needed. In the words of Belkin and Vickery: ". . . research has not yet provided a satisfactory solution to the problem of interfacing between end-user and large scale databases." Despite a relatively large amount of literature about the subject, the research in information seeking and retrieving is in its infancy. It is still in an exploratory stage.
>
> Yet, the future success or failure of the evolving next generation of information systems (expert systems, intelligent front-ends, etc.) based on built-in intelligence in human-system interactions depends on greatly

increasing our knowledge and understanding of what is really going on in human information seeking and retrieving. The key to the future of information systems and searching processes (and by extension, of information science and artificial intelligence from where the systems and processes are emerging) lies not in increased sophistication of technology, but in increased understanding of human involvement with information.[62]

Technology is racing ahead and is being applied at a rapid pace, but research that is needed to guarantee the useful exploitation of the new applications is lagging behind. This disadvantage, however, can be turned into a significant advantage. Because new technological developments are already applied – indeed, some are becoming common – it is possible to study the use of new information systems as it actually happens in real life. For instance, researchers do not have to simulate the use of CD-ROM systems; they can go to the many libraries that provide CD-ROM searching and investigate searching behavior in reality.

Clearly, exploring information seeking and retrieving as it regularly occurs is a powerful approach to improving our understanding of users' searching behavior. In effect, the applications of information technology have opened a new and exciting avenue for research in information science.

NOTES

1. N. J.Belkin and A. Vickery, *Interaction in Information Systems: A Review of Research from Document Retrieval to Knowledge-Based Systems,* Library and Information Research Report 35 (London: The British Library, 1985).

2. C. W. Cleverdon, *Report on the Testing and Analysis of an Investigation into the Comparative Efficiency of Indexing Systems* (Cranfield, England: College of Aeronautics, ASLIB Cranfield Research Project, 1962).

3. F. W. Lancaster, *Evaluation of Online Searching in MEDLARS (AIM-TWX) by Biomedical Practitioners,* Occasional Paper no. 101 (Urbana: University of Illinois, Graduate School of Library Science, 1983); and J. Wanger, C. A. Cuadra, and M. Fishburn, *Impact of Online Retrieval Services: A Survey of Users, 1974-1975* (Santa Monica: Systems Development Corp., 1976).

4. C. H. Fenichel, "Online Searching: Measures that Discriminate among Users with Different Types of Experience," *Journal of the American Society for Information Science* 32, no. 1 (1981): 23-32.

5. J. Wanger, D. McDonald, and M. C. Berger, *Evaluation of the Online Process* (Santa Monica: Cuadra Associates, 1980).

6. T. Bellardo, "An Investigation of Online Searcher Traits and Their Relationship to Search Outcome," *Journal of the American Society for Information Science* 36, no. 4 (1985): 241-50.

7. N. N. Woelfl, *Individual Differences in Online Search Behavior: The Effect of Learning Styles and Cognitive Abilities on Process and Outcome* (Ph.D. diss., Case Western University, Cleveland, Ohio, 1984).

8. C. H. Fenichel, "The Process of Searching Online Bibliographic Databases: A Review of Research," *Library Research* 2, no. 2 (1980): 107-27.

9. R. Fidel, "Moves in Online Searching," *Online Review* 9, no. 1 (1985): 61-74.

10. R. Fidel and Dagobert Soergel, "Factors Affecting Online Bibliographic Retrieval: A Conceptual Framework for Research," *Journal of the American Society for Information Science* 34 (May 1983): 163-80.

11. M. J. Bates, "How to Use Information Search Tactics Online," *Online* 11, no. 3 (1987): 47-54.

12. Fidel, "Moves in Online Searching."

13. W. Sewell and S. Teitelbaum, "Observations of End-User Online Searching Behavior over Eleven Years," *Journal of the American Society for Information Science* 37, no. 4 (1986): 234-45.

14. J. R. Matthews and G. S. Lawrence, "Further Analysis of the CLR Online Catalog Project," *Information Technology and Libraries* 3, no. 4 (1984): 354-76.

15. J. R. Matthews, G. S. Lawrence, and D. K. Ferguson, eds., *Using Online Catalogs: A Nationwide Survey,* Report of a study sponsored by the Council on Library Resources (New York: Neal-Schuman, 1983).

16. K. Markey, "Thus Spake the OPAC User," *Information Technology and Libraries* 2, no. 4 (1983): 381-87.

17. D. Ferguson, *Public Online Catalogs and Research Libraries,* Final report to the Council on Library Resources (Stanford: Research Libraries Group, 1982).

18. R. R. Larson, "Users Look at Online Catalogs: Results of a National Survey of Users and Non-users of Online Public Access Catalogs," in *Interacting with Online Catalogs,* Part 2 (Berkeley: University of California, Division of Library Automation and Library Research and Analysis Group, 1983); and J. E. Tolle, "Understanding Patrons' Use of Online Catalogs: Transaction Log Analysis of the Search Method," in *Productivity in the Information Age, Proceedings of the 46th ASIS Annual Meeting,* ed. R. F.

Vondran, A. Caputo, C. Wasserman, and R. A. V. Diener (White Plains, N.Y.: Knowledge Industries, 1983), 167-71.

19. C. R. Hildreth, *Online Public Access Catalogs: The User Interface* (Dublin, Ohio: OCLC, 1982).

20. P. A. Cochrane and K. Markey, "Catalog Use Studies since the Introduction of Online Interactive Catalogs: Impact on Design for Subject Access," *Library and Information Science Research* 5, no. 4 (1983): 337-63.

21. C. L. Borgman, "Why Are Online Catalogs Hard to Use? Lessons Learned from Information-Retrieval Studies," *Journal of the American Society for Information Science* 37, no. 6 (1986): 387-400.

22. J. Dickson, "An Analysis of User Errors in Searching an Online Catalog," *Cataloging and Classification Quarterly* 4, no. 3 (1984): 19-38.

23. J. R. Matthews, ed., *The Impact of Online Catalogs.* (New York: Neal-Schuman, 1986).

24. Matthews and Lawrence, "Further Analysis of the CLR Online Catalog Project."

25. J. Kinsella and P. Bryant, "Online Public Access Catalog Research in the United Kingdom: An Overview," *Library Trends* 35, no. 4 (1987): 619-29.

26. K. Markey, "Subject-Searching Experiences and Needs of Online Catalog Users: Implications for Library Classification," *Library Resources and Technical Services* 29, no. 1 (1985): 34-51.

27. B. Lipetz, "Catalog Use in a Large Research Library," *Library Quarterly* 42, no. 1 (1972): 129-39; and M. J. Bates, "Factors Affecting Subject Catalog Search Success," *Journal of the American Society for Information Science* 28, no. 3 (1977): 161-69.

28. Matthews, Lawrence, and Ferguson, *Using Online Catalogs: A Nationwide Survey.*

29. E. Svenonius, "Use of Classification in Online Retrieval," *Library Resources and Technical Services* 27 (January/March 1983): 76-80.

30. K. Markey and A. Demeyer, *Dewey Decimal Classification Online Project: Evaluation of a Library Schedule and Index Integrated into the Subject Searching Capabilities of an Online Catalog,* Final Report to the Council on Library Resources (Dublin, Ohio: OCLC, 1986).

31. L. M. Chan, "Library of Congress Classification as an Online Retrieval Tool: Potentials and Limitations," *Information Technology and Libraries* 5, no. 3 (1986): 181-92.

32. P. A. Cochrane and K. Markey, "Preparing for the Use of Classification in Online Cataloging Systems and in Online Catalogs," *Information Technology and Libraries* 4, no. 2 (1985): 91-111; and J. S. Hill, "Online Classification Number Access: Some Practical Considerations," *Journal of Academic Librarianship* 10, no. 1 (1984): 17-22.

33. G. S. Lawrence, "System Features for Subject Access in the Online Catalog," *Library Resources and Technical Services* 29, no. 1 (1985): 16-33.

34. Markey, "Subject-Searching Experiences and Needs of Online Catalog Users: Implications for Library Classification."

35. E. Carson, "OPACS: The User and Subject Access," *Canadian Library Journal* 42, no. 2 (1985): 65-70.

36. R. M. Jones, "Online Catalogue Research in Europe," *Journal of the American Society for Information Science* 40, no. 3 (1989): 153-57.

37. T. E. Doszkocs, "CITE NLM: Natural Language Searching in an Online Catalog," *Information Technology and Libraries* 2, no. 4 (1983): 364-80.

38. N. S. Karp, "ABI/Inform on CD-ROM: A First Look," *Laserdisk Professional* 1, no. 1 (1988): 28-34; and J. P. Kleiner, "InfoTrac: An Evaluation of System Use and Potential in Research Libraries," *RQ* 27, no. 2 (1987): 252-63.

39. M. D. Bonham and L. L. Nelson, "An Evaluation of Four End-User Systems for Searching MEDLINE," *Bulletin of the Medical Library Association* 76, no. 1 (1988): 22-31.

40. J. M. Day, "LISA on CD-ROM–A User Evaluation," in *Online Information 87; 11th International Online Information Meeting* (Medford, N.J.: Learned Information, 1987), 273-83.

41. C. L. Borgman, "Information Retrieval from CD-ROM: Status Quo or a Revolution in End-User Access?" *Canadian Journal of Information Science* 12, no. 3/4 (1988): 43-53.

42. Karp, "ABI/Inform on CD-ROM: A First Look;" J. A. Capodagli, J. Mardikian, and P. A. Uva, "MEDLINE on Compact Disc: End-user Searching on Compact Cambridge," *Bulletin of the Medical Library Association* 76, no. 2 (1988): 181-83; and Borgman, "Information Retrieval from CD-ROM: Status Quo or a Revolution in End-User Access?"

43. L. A. Wozny, "College Students as End User Searchers: One University's Experience," *RQ* 28, no. 1 (1988): 54-61.

44. Sewell and Teitelbaum, "Observations of End-User Online Searching Behavior over Eleven Years."

45. J. G. Marshall, "The Perceived Complexity of Database Searching among End-Users: A Multivariate Analysis," *Canadian Journal of Information Science* 12, no. 3/4 (1988): 89-97.

46. D. Barlow, B. Karnes, and G. Marchionini, "CD-ROM in a High School Library Media Center: A Research Project," *School Library Journal* 34, no. 3 (1987): 66-72.

47. Wozny, "College Students as End User Searchers: One University's Experience."

48. F. A. Brahmi, "The Effect of CD-ROM MEDLINE on Online End User and Mediated Searching," *Medical Reference Services Quarterly* 7, no. 4 (1988): 47-56.

49. Wozny, "College Students as End User Searchers: One University's Experience."

50. G. Marchionini, "Information-Seeking Strategies of Novices Using a Full-Text Electronic Encyclopedia," *Journal of the American Society for Information Science* 40, no. 1 (1989): 54-66.

51. J. H. Sweetland, "Beta Test and End-User Surveys: Are They Valid?" *Database* 11, no. 1 (1988): 27-32.

52. National Information Standards Organization (NISO), *Proposed American National Standard for Information Science – Common Command Language for Online Interactive Information Retrieval* (Gaithersburg, Md.: National Bureau of Standards, 1987).

53. Tian-Zhu Li, "Generic Approach to CD-ROM Systems – A Formal Analysis of Search Capabilities and Ease of Use," Paper presented at the Midyear Meeting of the American Society for Information Science, San Diego, May 1989.

54. Doszkocs, "CITE NLM: Natural Language Searching in an Online Catalog."

55. S. Pollitt, "CANSEARCH: An Expert Systems Approach to Document Retrieval," *Information Processing & Management* 23, no. 2 (1987): 119-38; A. Vickery and H. M. Brooks, "PLEXUS – The Expert System for Referral," *Information Processing & Management* 23, no. 2 (1987): 99-117; D. Krawczak, P. J. Smith, and S. J. Shute, "EP-X: A Demonstration

of Semantically Based Search of Bibliographic Databases," in *Proceedings of the 10th Annual International ACM SIGIR Conference in Research & Development in Information Retrieval*, ed. C. T. Yu and C. J. Van Rijsbergen (New York: ACM, 1987), 263-71; and I. Monarch and J. Carbonell, "CoalSORT: A Knowledge-Based Interface," *IEEE Expert* 2, no. 1 (1987): 39-53.

56. R. S. Marcus, "An Experimental Comparison of the Effectiveness of Computers and Humans as Search Intermediaries," *Journal of the American Society for Information Science* 34, no. 6 (1983): 381-404.

57. P. J. Daniels, "Cognitive Models in Information Retrieval–An Evaluative Review," *Journal of Documentation* 42, no. 4 (1986): 272-304; H. M. Brooks, "Expert Systems and Intelligent Information Retrieval," *Information Processing & Management* 23, no. 4 (1987): 367-82; and W. B. Croft, "Approaches to Intelligent Information Retrieval," *Information Processing & Management* 23, no. 4 (1987): 249-254.

58. P. W. Williams, "A Model for an Expert System for Automated Information Retrieval," in *Proceedings, 8th International Online Information Meeting* (London: Learned Information, 1984), 139-49.

59. Fidel, "Moves in Online Searching."

60. R. Fidel, "Towards Expert Systems for the Selection of Search Keys," *Journal of the American Society for Information Science* 37, no. 1 (1986): 37-44.

61. E. H. Brenner, J. H. Lucey, C. L. Martinez, and A. Meleka, "American Petroleum Institute's Machine-Aided Indexing and Searching Project," *Science and Technology Libraries* 5, no. 1 (1984): 49-62; and S. M. Humphrey and N. E. Miller, "Knowledge-Based Indexing of the Medical Literature: The Indexing Aid Project," *Journal of the American Society for Information Science* 38, no. 3 (1987): 184-96.

62. T. Saracevic, P. Kantor, A. Y. Chamis, and D. Trivison, "A Study of Information Seeking and Retrieving. I. Background and Methodology," *Journal of the American Society for Information Science* 39, no. 3 (1988): 161-76.

▪ 12 ▪

Information Policy and Information Technology: An International Context

Peter J. Judge

Information policy remains "a piece-meal, half-hearted creature," according to Representative Sherwood L. Boehlert of New York. He complained that almost no one in government talks about information policy, and few government leaders recognize the enormous role the federal government has played and must continue to play in the generation, collection, and dissemination of scientific and technical information.[1] Why should this matter?

DEFINITIONS

The definition of information policy has been a rock on which many well-intentioned submissions to governments have foundered in the past. For example, an Australian government Task Force on Departmental Information made the plaintive comment in 1980 that "It was put to the Task Force several times that the Government ought to have a publicly expressed 'information policy.' The proposed content of the policy varied with the interests of the person making the case. To some extent, the expressed concern would be answered by the passage of the Freedom of Information legislation. Others bore largely on the development of a nationally coordinated library system, which the Task Force judged to be outside its terms of reference."[2]

In the early days of national and international discussions on information policy in the latter half of the 1960s, the meaning of the word *information* was often restricted to scientific and technical information (STI–often now STIM, to explicitly include medical information). Since then, policy discussions have also been largely concerned with information destined for the print and electronic media and with information aimed at the community, explaining government actions or the citizen's rights and obligations.

This chapter deals at times with all of these, and with any other kinds of information that can be stored in some accessible format (paper, electronic, or whatever). It tries to distinguish between them if and when the distinction matters, but sometimes these boundaries become very fuzzy and can only be made explicit through examples. It is concerned with the practical information that is generally carried by information services, which is the stuff of policy discussions, and will not become at all embroiled in a discussion of information as an abstract concept.

Given these disparate kinds of information, a single catch-all national information policy may not be feasible, meaningful, or desirable. A government may certainly need some general principles by which it disseminates the information that it generates. But it may need to look differently at the information it puts out to inform its citizens from the information it publishes, say, as products of its statistical compilations or its scientific research. The latter products, in the right context, may be salable commodities; the former is unlikely ever to be profitable. Also, in most Western nations, governments do not try to interfere with the private sector's information business: the information industry. However, they may make government-produced tradable information available to information vendors in the private sector for sale in value-added packages. They may provide development funding, venture capital, or tax relief to encourage the private sector to invest in particular kinds of information activity.

The word *policy* will generally be used here in the sense of Richard Titmuss's definition: "Principles that govern action directed towards given ends."[3] Titmuss argues that "the concept denotes action about means as well as ends and it therefore implies change: changing situations, systems, practices, behaviour . . . the concept of policy is only meaningful if we believe we can effect change in some form or other." Hence, when the Australian Labor Party (the party in government since 1983) resolves from year to year that "all Australians are entitled to free access to information and library services. . . . The right to know, to be informed, is basic to every person. In our society access to information . . . should not be concentrated in the hands of the rich,"[4] by the Titmuss definition, this resolution will become a statement of policy only when the government begins to do something about it, to make it reality. In fact, the government began to do something about it in 1984–the Labor Party Caucus instigated an Interdepartmental Working Group on National Information Policy, convened by the Department of Science. Unfortunately, the Department of Science disappeared in a restructuring of the Public Service in 1987, and with it the Working Group before it could report to Cabinet.

HISTORICAL BACKGROUND

International recognition of the need for a government policy (i.e., government support) for scientific and technical information services is often dated from 4 October 1957, when the first Sputnik took the world by surprise and shocked Western scientists and administrators. A part of the shock came from the realization that it need not have been a surprise – that the Soviet achievement could have been predicted from freely available reports in the scientific and technical literature. A part of the reaction was the determination to bring this literature into more effective control and use, so that such shocks could not recur.

As it happened, the Soviet Union already had a working scientific and technical information policy. As far back as 1913, Lenin had been advocating a centralized system of libraries. In 1921 he had taken the initiative of formulating a foreign publications acquisition policy and setting up the organization to carry it out, with the aim of exploiting the findings of capitalism to fight capitalism. Lenin had an action-oriented approach to policy – he asked "Chto delat'?" ("What is to be done?")[5]

Alvin M. Weinberg, Director of the Oak Ridge National Laboratory, provided a clarion call to the U.S. administration in 1963 in a landmark report to the president's Science Advisory Committee, *Science, Government and Information*.[6] In this he stated unequivocally that "each Federal agency concerned with science and technology must accept its responsibility for information activities in fields that are relevant to its mission," and made it clear that he was talking about dissemination to other scientists and to society, and not merely about the gathering of information.

Weinberg's was not the first call for a national information policy in the United States: it followed the 1958 Baker Report, the 1960 report of a joint Congressional and Senate subcommittee, and the 1962 Crawford Report.[7] But the Weinberg Report had far-reaching repercussions and is still widely quoted. It became the key document, launching international discussions on information policy, when it was used in late 1964 as a basis for the proposal by the U.S. delegation to the Science Policy Committee of the Organisation for Economic Cooperation and Development (OECD) to set up a Scientific and Technical Information Policy Group. This embryonic group was instructed to examine the need for information policies and, if appropriate, to promote the development and application of compatible information policies (and hence, of compatible and coordinated information services) in OECD member countries.

Only a quarter of a century later it is difficult to appreciate how revolutionary this was. Prior to the 1960s, a government developed its policy on a particular knotty question as the situation demanded. It did not commonly make general statements about fields that did not require its immediate attention. Economic policy was becoming a respectable subject for study, but the idea of a government science policy was still two or three years down the track. Science was not yet widely accepted as a proper field for government intervention, except where "big science" needed huge sums of public money for vast projects in, say, nuclear physics or space. It was feared that government meddling with scientific research planning would threaten academic freedom. The concept of information policy was even more outlandish: the term translated awkwardly into other European languages and seemed to have vague connotations of espionage.

The Information Policy Group (IPG) prospered for about 10 years. During this time it promoted practical action among OECD member countries in:

- Formulating some principles of government information policy in relation to science and technology policies on one hand, and economic and social development on the other.[8]

- Examining the economics of technical information.

- Preparing cost-benefit analyses of information services.

- Implementing international cooperative information services.

- Studying information networks.

- Comparing national technical information and technology transfer services for industry.

- Forecasting manpower and training requirements.

- Studying member country STI systems, specifically the national reviews of information policy in Canada, Ireland, Spain, and Germany.

A few years after the IPG's birth a sister group on Computer Utilization was set up, and in 1975 the two groups were merged into an Information, Computer and Communications Policy Group, which later became an OECD Committee (the ICCP Committee) in its own right. The work of the IPG contributed in the 1960s to the development of information policy thinking in Eastern Europe and in other countries that were not members of OECD. It also had a strong input into the work of UNESCO (the United Nations Educational, Scientific and Cultural Organization), of which more is said later.

As we enter the 1990s, a quarter century after the birth of the IPG, information professionals around the world are still animatedly discussing information policy and are enthusiastic to see it develop in their countries. This enthusiasm of the professional community is not often shared by governments. With rare exceptions, governments have failed to develop and implement a broad national policy for information. Indeed, some which began to set up ambitious policies in the 1960s have since largely dismantled them. They have preferred to tackle the information issues (as the opening quotation put it) in a piecemeal way, as specific problems arose in their countries in some of the areas related to information activity, which are described below.

In this dilemma, we have to ask, "Who is right?" Is the failure by most governments to act in this area really a failure, and if so, does it matter? Is the aim of a broadly conceived national information policy still valid, or is it–has it always been–an intellectual will-o'-the-wisp, which will remain just beyond our grasp? Can we safely leave the problem (if there is a problem) to the marketplace, with perhaps some occasional ad hoc government action as required to support national needs and objectives?[9]

GOVERNMENT POLICIES

Essentially, all governments must come to terms with John Gray's "three common elements of policy"[10]: identifying the information needs of the nation; devising ways of meeting these needs; and promoting effective use of the resulting services.

However, governments in different countries face up differently to issues of information policy, depending on their conviction (or lack of it) about the importance of these issues, their political ideologies, and the means available to them. An expansion of Gray's three elements might lead to questions such as:

■ Is there to be a government commitment to support information services in the country?

■ Should there be a statement of national policy, setting national objectives, with the government providing leadership?

■ Should there be a national plan for information services?

■ What parts in such a plan should be played by different levels of government (federal, state, county, municipal)?

- Should government fund and maintain the national information resource (libraries and information services) and ensure that mechanisms exist for the collaborative activities necessary to achieve successful resource sharing?

- How can government create an awareness in the community of people's needs for information and the means of satisfying those needs?

- Should government make explicit its approach to interactions with, and practical support for, the private sector information industry, including technical publishing and the print and electronic media?

- Does the national education system train a sufficient number and variety of information specialists to support the national objectives relating to the postindustrial information society, and educate its citizens to use the benefits of this society for their personal development?

- Is government ensuring an adequate level of research and development in information fields, so that the country can contribute to technological development and make effective use of technology that may be developed elsewhere?

- What about copyright, including the protection of electronic media (sound, video recordings, and software)?

- Will the government respect the international conventions regarding customs duties and sales tax on cultural materials (i.e., treating electronic media and software no differently from print media or films)?

- What is the policy regarding transborder data flow?

- What about freedom of information? and privacy?

- Is government to promote development of the information technology industries in the country?

- Are the means of communication adequate for the developing needs of the information users?

- Is government to provide the internationally compatible national standards to ensure connectivity of the information structures within the country and with countries overseas?

- Does the country have a commitment to supporting developing countries that may be geographically or historically related to it?[11]

United States

In most countries, legislative activity continues in information-related areas, not always recognized as such by the professional communities concerned. To take just one large example, Chartrand[12] comments that in the 95th, 96th, and 97th U.S. Congresses some 200 public laws were enacted in the categories of telecommunications, broadcasting, and satellite transmissions; information disclosures and confidentiality/right of privacy; government records, documents, and paperwork; information inventories, programs, or clearinghouses; dissemination of information; new information systems or computerized databases; and library policies, procedures, and assistance.

All this without a formal national information policy! And yet there is continuing criticism from many of those concerned with library and information services that the government has been backing off from the idea of such a policy since the early 1970s![13] Such people remember the demise of the State Technical Services Act and the problems that the National Commission on Library and Information Science (NCLIS) had a few years ago in obtaining the operational budget that it needed; they may not be asking how things have changed and what new opportunities are arising.

Malaysia

An example of a country that is newly coming to terms with these issues is Malaysia. A recent publication details their national situation, the approaches that are being considered, and the steps they would like to take.[14] In the four years since a UNESCO-supported planning seminar was held, a task force has prepared a formal information policy proposal, which has now been submitted to government. But as the national librarian of Malaysia points out, "Policy by itself will have little effect if it is not backed by the allocation of resources, both human and material ... and libraries must demonstrate their contribution to national development."

UNESCO

It may be convenient at this point to mention briefly the UNESCO achievements in the fields of library and information developments, some by influencing government policies, some by direct action. In the 1950s and

1960s UNESCO assisted in setting up libraries in several disadvantaged countries. In some cases these flourished after the withdrawal of UNESCO support, but in other cases they failed because of lack of funding from the national government.[15]

This is always the dilemma of national or international aid policies: establishing and equipping an institution is fine so far as it goes, but if the donor agency does not also pay for the salaries and the consumable stores, there may be copying machines standing idle for lack of toner or paper, and printing machines with no ink. Moreover, once staff members have been trained overseas at the expense of the donor agency, they may be overqualified for the intended job and promoted to do something quite irrelevant to the aid project (or simply disappear and refuse to return home).

In 1969 UNESCO held the first UNISIST Conference. (The name UNISIST is not an acronym, although many people have tried to interpret it as such. However, it gives the flavor of a "United Nations International System for Scientific and Technical Information," which was the program's early goal.) The conference was based on two years of planning in collaboration with the International Council of Scientific Unions and was aimed at promoting ideas of information policy worldwide, in contrast with the OECD activity, which was limited largely to its 26 member countries. It called for the 150 or so UNESCO member countries to set up official agencies at the national level to promote the development of information resources and services. Twenty years later, only about half have done so. Some confusion arose because in another department of UNESCO there were library, documentation, and archives development programs under the acronym of NATIS, which for a time seemed to run in competition with the UNISIST activities.

In 1976 UNISIST and NATIS were merged into a General Information Programme (usually abbreviated to its French initials, PGI) with five main themes:

1. Promotion of the formulation of information policies and plans (national, regional, and international).

2. Promotion and dissemination of methods, norms, and standards for information handling.

3. Contribution to the development of information infrastructures.

4. Contribution to the development of specialized information systems in the fields of education, culture and communication, and the natural and social sciences.

5. Promotion of the training and education of specialists in, and users of, information.

Current information about PGI developments can be obtained from the *UNISIST Newsletter,* available gratis from UNESCO, Paris.

UNESCO does not have a monopoly on international or regional policy promotion, although it is the largest intergovernmental body in the information field and can draw on World Bank funding for specific projects to extend the range of its operations. Other United Nations agencies such as the Food and Agricultural Organization in Rome, the World Health Organization in Geneva, and the International Atomic Energy Association in Vienna have developed major international bibliographic services and the worldwide organization, through their member governments, to exploit these services.

Scandinavia

The four Scandinavian countries have long had a common information policy and a history of cooperation in this field. Coordination was originally ensured by a body called Nordforsk established in 1972, whose secretariat rotated among the capital cities; it became Nordinfo in 1977. Each country also has its own national policy body. Nordinfo has prompted a regional scheme among the major libraries, Scandiaplan, to share subject responsibilities among specialized collections and centers of excellence, subsidizing some of them where necessary to maintain high standards.

However, the Scandinavian packet-switched network Scannet is under strain. Denmark is a member of the European Economic Community (EEC) and has supported Euronet (a telecommunications network described later in this chapter) since June 1981, leaving Sweden as the main user of Scannet. In March 1982 the Swedish network Telepak also signed up on Euronet, followed by Finland in November 1982. In these circumstances it is not surprising that one of the objectives of Nordinfo is now the coordination of developments in the information field with those in Europe and the United States, and that this complementary and rationalizing approach is considered as important as the coordination of the Scandinavian and separate national policies.

FID

The Scandinavian countries very nearly have the advantage of sharing a common language. So too do the South Americans, who have been using the International Federation for Information and Documentation's regional Commission for Latin America (FID/CLA) as a very effective basis for cooperation.

FID (the International Federation for Information and Documentation) has its origins at the turn of the century, in the early days of applying the Dewey Decimal Classification (DDC) in Europe. Its early goal was to modify the DDC to the Universal Decimal Classification or UDC, making it a more useful tool for documentalists. FID has developed over the past 80 years with the intention of becoming a federation of professional societies. However, many of its 70 or so national members are in fact government bodies of one kind or another, and it is not clear what its impact has been in recent years on these members. Like UNESCO it has a medium term plan, but little seems to have emerged apart from the proceedings of its biennial congresses. It is still the custodian of the UDC and its multifarious revision committees, but with the all-pervasiveness of computers in library and information work UDC is becoming rapidly less important.

INFORMATION AT LARGE

If you are working in a library, you are likely to understand information services as the work of the readers' help desk, which draws from the indexes and catalogs of the library's collections, as well as the references or data obtained from internationally or locally produced computer-based information services. The latter are looming ever larger, raising policy questions of budget and cost recovery. It is easy to suppose that such online services are very big business; they are often said to be "a billion dollar industry."

They are indeed big business, even if perhaps only a quarter of a billion worldwide, but we should put the electronic services used in libraries into perspective, in relation to other kinds of online information activities. A 1985 analysis by the journal *Monitor*[16] showed that the sum total of the activities of all the familiar, mainly text-based, online services (Mead, Dialog, Pergamon-Infoline and the like) amounted collectively to only a small fraction – perhaps one-tenth – of one of the big-league online data communications activities, such as airline booking systems, Reuters, the banks, or American Express.

The online text-based services we see in libraries are now often called the elite services, to emphasize their high-cost, small market and relatively low usage. Only a handful are economically viable in their own right. These economic constraints have important policy implications when governments are setting priorities for funding. Governments generate a significant proportion of the information that goes into these elite services, but they also have much larger information-related programs in other areas.

For example, the Department of Science in Australia calculated that the Australian federal government spent $1.25 billion dollars on its major information activities in 1985/86,[17] but the elite services component forms only a small part of this, perhaps around $100 to 200 million. Moreover, the Australian government spent heavily on other information-related but quite different activities, such as communications infrastructure, computer services, computer equipment, research and development, education and training, and museums. The total for all this came to over $8 billion, or 11.5 percent of budget outlays. If we cynically suppose that the government will put its policy emphases where it can get the most votes, which areas are likely to attract attention – and to obtain increased funding?

This is not to play down the importance of community information services. They have a fuzzy common boundary with the information services aimed at small business or with agricultural extension services, and they all have economic implications and hence policy significance. The requirement of cost recovery (if that is a normal part of the government's policy) is generally waived, since this category of services is tied to specific policy objectives in welfare, health, or whatever. Such services tend to be relatively unsophisticated at their user interface; generally they rely on face-to-face contact and a dialogue with the users to ensure that the questions and answers have been properly understood. Databases in these services, if present at all, generally give technical support to the information or extension officers.

SCIENTIFIC AND TECHNICAL INFORMATION (STI)

Information policy discussions began in the STI area because of its economic and strategic importance and because much STI is a product of direct or indirect government funding. Fortuitously, also, a number of OECD member countries, such as the United Kingdom, Canada, France, and Denmark, already had technical information services in operation. Representatives of these technical information services had earlier been meeting to exchange their experience under the aegis of the OECD.

The STI literature had the advantages of being well structured and of using well-understood terminology, and therefore being easier to specify and exchange compared with the literatures of the social sciences or the humanities. A number of very big subject indexes to the scientific and technical literature existed, and three or four of these had begun to print their indexes with the aid of computers and make the resulting database tapes available for information retrieval. This retrieval was relatively slow because the tapes had to be run from end to end to search them, a question at a time. Hence, the operators preferred to provide the users with Selective Dissemination of Information (SDI, not to be confused with STI) on a regular weekly or monthly basis, looking only at the latest additions to the tape.

OECD

This was the situation in 1966, by which time the initial principles of information policy had been worked out in the OECD Information Policy

Group and the practical expansion of computer-based information services began. The first of these was MEDLARS, produced by the U.S. National Library of Medicine (NLM), which was then available in Europe through only two agencies: the Karolinska Institute in Stockholm and the National Lending Library for Science and Technology (now the British Library Document Supply Centre) in Boston Spa, Yorkshire, whose tapes, in those pioneering days, had to be run on the nearest available computer, 70 miles away at Newcastle University.

OECD also set up a Chemical Information Committee to promote the use of *Chemical Abstracts,* which was produced by the nonprofit American Chemical Society (ACS). *Chemical Abstracts* was prepared to license its tapes to all subscribers able to meet its stringent conditions. The members of the Chemical Information Committee eventually found its meetings had become so useful to them that, when its life in OECD was over, it began a separate existence outside and broadened its mandate to cover all computerized information, under the name of EUSIDIC (the European Association of Scientific Information Dissemination Centers. A similar body then existed in the United States called ASIDIC).

The OECD activity added one new European MEDLARS center, the German Institute for Documentation and Information (DIMDI) in Cologne. A couple of years later MEDLARS was the first in the world to begin regular commercial online operation, and the distance of the users from these medical information centers became less important.

When the IPG was negotiating the increased availability of specific information services, even though the NLM and ACS were not-for-profit, was this a legitimate international policy activity, or was the United States making use of the OECD for commercial purposes? At the time, there were complaints from those information services, like INSPEC (produced by a not-for-profit society) and Excerpta Medica (then produced by a semicommercial publisher, but soon to be taken over by the commercial publishing giant Elsevier), that did not benefit from the treatment accorded to MEDLARS and *Chemical Abstracts*. INSPEC was invited to give a presentation before the IPG, but thereafter the IPG members (most of whom did not have local information services to promote) complained that the IPG program was interrupting its policy discussions in order to market particular information products, and the series came to an abrupt end.

In OECD, this promotion was seen as a worthwhile and necessary action to ensure international awareness of these big information investments and to develop the national and regional resource sharing for which IPG had been started.

Germany

The next development, national support for the development of subject information centers, was most evident in Germany. A statement issued in 1974 by the Federal Ministry for Research and Technology proposed that there be 16 subject information centers (in German, *Fachinformationszentren* or, popularly, FIZs) and four special-purpose systems, coordinated by a central body with some research capability, the Society for Information and Documentation (*Gesellschaft für Information und Dokumentation* – GID).[18]

By 1986, 12 FIZs had been set up, but the centralist nature of the program was being vigorously criticized, and the private sector complained that these subsidized services were undercutting its efforts to develop an indigenous information industry. In consequence the program was radically changed in the direction of promoting a better interface between government and the private sector, adjusting government support for these FIZs in response to the demand for their services, and promoting their use by more effective marketing.[19]

At the end of 1987 the GID was dissolved. The professional journal *Nachrichten für Dokumentation (NfD)* remarked that this came as no surprise: the GID had started under an unlucky star, with no clear purpose, and was never adequately supported.[20] Most of its functions went to the Society for Mathematics and Data Processing (*Gesellschaft für Mathematik und Datenverarbeitung* – GMD), and the rest to the private sector, but the GMD is not thought to be able to perform what the GID was intended to do. The loss of the GID therefore leaves Germany with no central infrastructure facility, and it seems to be agreed that, if the development of the information society is a social process, this function cannot be left to the private sector. What Germany needs, thinks the *NfD*, is something like the GID restored, with a mandate to provide sympathetic oversight, planning, coordination, cooperation, and other informal functions.

France

Since setting up the Documentation Center of the National Scientific Research Center (CNRS) in 1941, the French government has been involved in the provision of scientific and technical information. Once the IPG discussions began in 1965 the French government paid closer policy attention to STI, initially through the General Delegation for Scientific and Technical Research (DGRST), then in 1972 through the National Office for Scientific and Technical Information (BNIST). In 1979 BNIST was elevated to an Interministerial Mission for Scientific and Technical Information (MIDIST), responsible to the prime minister through the secretary of state for research.

BNIST, and later MIDIST aimed at a range of sectoral databases, in chemistry, toxicology, health, patents, standards, information for industry, and others, often through supporting new or existing initiatives in the public or private sectors. For a while MIDIST was seen as a model policy development, even by many critics of government intervention in information matters.[21] Its philosophy recognized the fragility of the online information sector: facilities are expensive to set up and have a low short-term profitability. Through its substantial budget (about $10 million in 1983, 15 times greater than the budget of BNIST when it started in 1972), MIDIST was able to offer subsidies or contracts to help developers through their difficult first stages. It also awarded growth contracts through the Ministry of Industry, where more substantial sums could be made available for from three to five years. This aimed to encourage larger firms to diversify into information activities, rather than to create a host of small new information businesses. If the project succeeded, the award was retained; if not, it had to be returned.

MIDIST was the government representative in discussions on the establishment of the national online network, based on the QUESTEL division of the private firm Télésystèmes, and funded jointly through MIDIST and the French national telecommunications authority. By 1983 QUESTEL already had 24 public databases and some private ones, and it continues in business. However, the French online industry appears to have problems common to many online activities. In 1986 it had some 200 publicly accessible databases, but its professional association released some very depressing figures for its members. As the *Monitor* commented, "If French figures conform to the general pattern, one can expect ten or so of the 200-plus databases to be doing moderately well, another ten to be doing respectably, and the rest to be losing money hand over fist."[22] Two-thirds of these databases were created out of public funds, so their losses were carried by the taxpayers in support of their government's policies. Such perpetuation of money-losing databases through public subsidies always infuriates the private sector, although on occasions it may be justifiable and inevitable.

In fact, MIDIST lost its mandate at the end of 1984, under something of a cloud. According to the *Monitor*, it was said that MIDIST's "strongly left-wing, government-will-do-everything flavour" became unpalatable and that its staff ruffled a lot of feathers, particularly in industry, by being too stubbornly idealistic and militantly intransigent.[23] A few months later, the *Monitor* was reporting that MIDIST's dissolution was delayed pending investigation into its financial dealings.[24] The government auditors were accusing it of exercising insufficient control in spending its funds, in choosing which projects to aid and in evaluating these projects, and of awarding large sums of money to fund general operating expenses of many organizations that were not directly part of MIDIST's responsibilities. The major programs that MIDIST was supporting have subsequently continued in spite of this contretemps, but this appears to be another example of too much central planning being counterproductive.

Small Businesses and Manufacturers

How effective have government industrial information services been? The issue of technological information transfer to the small firm has been extensively studied by T. J. Allen and his collaborators, in Ireland, Spain, and Mexico.[25] His findings, which have been supported by work in other countries, are that "technology is found to flow principally through informal channels within industries . . . (documentation) plays a relatively minor role. Once again we find that technology is seldom transferred by the printed word. Hopefully, some day documentalists will hear this message, and governments will realize that the support of document storage and dissemination systems will not, by itself, solve the problems of technological development."

As Kjeld Klintøe, the Director of the Danish Technical Information Service, used to say, "To get results, you have to pay visits." This was usually illustrated by a cartoon showing two cats sitting cosily on a wall, followed by another cartoon showing the mother cat with a litter of kittens. A good document collection is only the foundation of an information service, and policy concerned with promoting innovation in industry must accept that this is still a people-intensive activity, not something that can be left to information technology (IT). Very many countries of Europe, South America, and Asia have established information services for small manufacturers, nearly all based on extension officers and direct personal contact. Their success appears to depend more on the enthusiasm and competence of the individuals concerned than on the size and funding of the parent organization.

This low-technology situation is, however, evolving rapidly. The people who are willing to actively seek out information form a relatively small group, and their access to information tends to improve, while the rest of the community fails to make use of the availability of this information. This was shown clearly in the 1960s in the United Kingdom, during a period when a variety of initiatives was being tried to bring technical information more widely to small manufacturers. Each new service was expected to bring in new groups of users, but it was found that those who had been benefiting from the old services were the most enthusiastic users of the new: they became increasingly well served and constituted a kind of information elite – one manifestation of a major policy issue, that of the information rich versus those at the grass roots who remain the information poor.

Efforts continue worldwide to bridge this gap for small business. For example, the 1984 Congress of FID, in a session on the use of information in industry, had reports from Nigeria, Hungary, South Africa, Bulgaria, and others. Lawrence Tagg, the business and technical librarian of the Newcastle-upon-Tyne City Libraries, which fulfill the role of a regional reference service, spoke of an interesting way to achieve success in spite of tight budgets. These libraries received government funding for three years to hire two young unemployed engineers to carry the message of the availability of practical information on demand to 800 small businesses, with good results. This is an isolated example, but by no means a unique one, of individual initiative achieving something worthwhile in the absence of policy support.

Developing Countries

This gap between the rich and poor has caused serious political (that is, policy) problems internationally. The developing countries of the Third World have accused the developed countries of keeping from them the information they need for economic development. The 1979 United Nations Conference on Science and Technology for Development brought this controversial topic in the North-South dialogue into sharp focus, and the problems it posed then have still not been resolved. It has not become so conspicuous a policy problem *within* most developed countries, because as soon as members of the information-poor grass roots recognize the need for personal development they have effectively left the grass roots behind.

The active elite users are better able to identify and define their problems, so that information or extension officers at the interfaces become less essential, and importantly they have the open minds needed to apply the solutions and change their former practices. These people are also more willing to experiment with new media and to interrogate directly services such as videotex, the Source, or QUESTEL. Government policy in these instances may be concerned with ensuring that the publicly available, subsidized services that they provide complement the services offered for a price by the private operators and that their information is made available where appropriate to private operators, with the necessary safeguards to ensure accuracy, timeliness, and completeness.

For unsophisticated users, a high-technology information service may seem threatening and incomprehensible, and so fail to yield results as planned. This was found in Australia with the Commonwealth Scientific and Industrial Research Organization (CSIRO, the large national research body active in most fields of science and technology). A survey of small manufacturers in Sydney from 1972 to 1974 found that "since most of (our respondents) believed themselves without the specialized knowledge to interpret CSIRO technical reports, they are also reluctant to approach scientists and research officers personally. For most types of small industry, CSIRO is, on our findings, not a source of information and advice."[26] Clearly, once an organization is perceived as unfriendly, no matter how unjust this perception might be, it may take many years to break down the barriers. Recent funding cuts for this service may have aggravated the situation.

The danger is that, because an organization exists, the government planners assign it a role, assume that it will take care of the problems, and then go on to other things. It may take a long time before the planners are aware that their perceptions may be faulty.

National Bodies

Other governments have set up large bodies to deal with STI. The most significant of these are:

- The British Library Document Supply Centre, formerly the National Lending Library for Science and Technology, at Boston Spa in Yorkshire, which has acquired something of a world role in providing hard-to-get material.

- The National Technical Information Service (NTIS) in the United States, formerly the Clearinghouse for Federal Scientific and Technical Information. This was set up initially under the Department of Commerce to handle U.S. government report literature, but has broadened its base over the years and aims at recovering its full costs from its sales. It is currently under discussion for privatization.

- The Canadian Institute for Scientific and Technical Information (CISTI), which comes under the National Research Council's responsibilities.

- The Japan Information Center for Science and Technology (JICST).

- The All-Union Institute for Scientific and Technical Information (VINITI) in Moscow, and its homologues in most of the Eastern European countries.

Many of these bodies also issue national bibliographical databases in their fields, the largest being *Referativniy Zhurnal* from VINITI and the *Bulletin Signalétique* from the Documentation Center of the CNRS in Paris (now renamed the National Institute for Scientific and Technical Information, INIST, and moved to Nancy). Since the big international scientific and technical information databases are produced in North America and Europe, why produce national databases as well? Is this just wasteful overlap? The answer for all countries has to be an emphatic *no*. The big databases select material for inclusion on a cost-effective criterion of what will be important to the majority of their readers. As was pointed out earlier, such giant databases suffer from expensive memory requirements and relatively small use, and they cannot afford to carry the costs involved in providing a comprehensive service to minority user groups overseas.

In Australia it was shown, for example, that only one-third of the items indexed for the Australian Road Research Board's purposes satisfy the criterion of international interest to be accepted for the OECD-based International Road Research Documentation, but the remaining two-thirds carry material of high relevance to local users in Australia. The same kinds of proportions were found in the educational research and earth sciences fields. The homegrown databases were effectively complementary to the international databases and were vital in providing access to the national literature. The situation may be exacerbated: Australian scientists publish about 70 percent of their work overseas, in internationally prestigious journals or in the specialized journals that are not available at home. If this material is not picked up by the big databases, it will probably be missed altogether. No doubt similar considerations apply in most other small countries.

RELATIONS WITH THE PRIVATE SECTOR INFORMATION INDUSTRY

A 1982 report by NCLIS, *Public Sector/Private Sector Interaction in Providing Information Services,* exposed many of the problems in this area.[27] The 25 recommendations out of 27 on which the 16 members of the NCLIS Task Force were almost unanimous may be summarized briefly:

Provide an environment to enhance competition in information
services.
Apply the First Amendment to information services.
Encourage Congress to be consistent in legislation affecting such
services.
Encourage government agencies to use efficient technologies.
Encourage voluntary standards.
Encourage education and research in library and information science.
Encourage statistical programs in information fields.
Assess the economic impact of federal information activities.
Identify and evaluate alternatives to federal information activities.
Develop libraries for public access to governmental information.
Eliminate legal barriers to new information services.
Encourage private enterprise to "add value" to government
information by repackaging and marketing it.
Encourage agencies such as libraries and bookstores to disseminate
government information.

Involve the private sector in national information planning.
Ensure that government information activity matches policies and
goals.
Give sufficient warning of new government information actions so that
the private sector can become involved.
Submit such actions to outside review before implementation.
Periodically review government information activities to see whether
they should continue.
Announce the availability of government information and maintain
registers of it.
Deposit government information where it may be examined at no
charge.
Waive copyright for domestic use of government information.
Expand existing libraries and information centers to distribute
government information, rather than create new ones.

There were two recommendations on which the vote was split. The first
was to encourage federal agencies to regard the dissemination of
information, especially through the mechanisms of the private sector, as a
high priority responsibility. Some members of the NCLIS Task Force thought
that the reference to the private sector should be omitted. The second was
not to arbitrarily restrict the federal government from enhancement of
information products and services, even if solely to meet the needs of
constituencies outside the government itself. The circumlocution here was an
attempt at compromise, accepting that some constituencies, e.g., the
handicapped or disadvantaged, might need special support from government.
The 27 recommendations were grouped into seven principles as follows:

Take a leadership role in creating a framework for information
service development and use.
Establish procedures to encourage private sector investment in
information services.
Not provide information services commercially unless there are
compelling reasons and the private sector is protected.
Protect private sector property rights in relation to government use of
private sector information.
Make government information available to the private sector, without
constraints on subsequent use.
Set its pricing policies so that these reflect true cost, and submit these
to independent review.
Use existing mechanisms, such as libraries, for distributing
information to the public, rather than set up new ones.

Compare these with the findings of the 1979 White House Conference on Library and Information Services, which believed that the elements essential to a comprehensive national library and information services program were those concerned with national leadership support; national library and information services resources; community library and information services; statewide library and information services; education and training; technical assistance for library and information services; and funding.[28] The major issues seem not to have changed.

A piece of U.S. legislation predating the NCLIS private sector recommendations provided a practical foundation for them. This had the innocuous title of the Paperwork Reduction Act of 1980.[29] It set up an Office of Information and Regulatory Affairs in the Office of Management and Budget (OMB), a Federal Information Locator System, which enables departments to see whether the information they need already exists, and new procedures for review and elimination of duplication. A consequent OMB document emphasized that information resources management encompasses the total information life cycle from collection to distribution, and that information is an economic resource that should be managed as such.[30]

Another OMB document, Circular A-76, sets down specific guidelines on which federal commercial activities should be managed in-house and which by private sector firms under competitively awarded contract. This circular explicitly includes information products and services. It is being used by the U.S. information industry (which has a very lively professional association, the Information Industry Association, IIA) to press its case for greater involvement in federal information activities, with cost effectiveness and quality of service as the main criteria for determining where the work should be done.

The question of cost effectiveness and full cost recovery came into prominence in 1983, in battles between the NLM and the Dutch service Excerpta Medica over whether MEDLINE database tariffs were being subsidized by the U.S. government in breach of normal fair trading practices.[31] This led to an inconclusive ruling requiring full costs to be recovered, but full costs may mean different things in different environments, and the U.S. Office of Technology Assessment upheld the NLM actions with the argument that if MEDLINE were discontinued there were no grounds for supposing that the private sector would recreate it, that the citations in MEDLINE and related databases do not exactly duplicate those in commercial databases, and that some diversity of biomedical data may be advantageous. It is now well established by practical experience in online retrieval that for a comprehensive output, it is essential to search several databases. The MEDLINE tariff was modified as a result of this legislation, although some questions remained.

In 1982, the European Information Providers Association published a report of its symposium, *Defining Public and Private Interests in the European Information Industry.*[32] This report, which again criticized the unfair competition from government-subsidized services, has to be placed in the context of the high activity among members of the EEC to counter the American dominance of the growing online market in Europe. Robert Maxwell, the chairman of Pergamon Press, commented in that same year that the European online database industry was dominated by the three leading American suppliers – Lockheed, SDC and BRS.[33] Economically, the market was but one-tenth of that in North America, at best about half a million searches a year. While the 36 host suppliers then linked to Euronet might be considered the basis for a competitive system, nearly all of them were heavily public-funded, highly specialized, and no real threat to the Americans.

Euronet had been a response to the European Commission's d'Avignon Report,[34] which urged EEC members to generate a climate of innovation, promote a European information industry, foster collaboration, and so on, and was a good example of the kind of action envisaged by the commission. It set a target for the European telecommunications authorities (the PTTs) to achieve common standards and tariffs in their national packet-switched services, after which Euronet as a separate organization would cease to exist, but would give way to the Direct Information Access Network for Europe (DIANE) service operating on the European PTTs' newly standardized network. The commission, as mentioned earlier, also provided incentive funding for entrepreneurs to establish new services in designated areas of high need and potential high profit and is promoting a series of imaginative experiments to facilitate access to documentation by electronic means. These include Docdel, a project to investigate the technical feasibility and economic viability of electronic transmission systems and to test user reaction to the services they provide; Apollo, a project to explore the potential of digital text transmission by satellite as a means of document delivery; and Artemis, a proposed system for document digitizing and teletransmission.[35]

ACCESS AND PRIVACY

The issues of freedom of information, confidentiality, and privacy are inextricably linked: your access to government records may turn up information that may harm me, as may your search of credit files or hospital records. It may well be that the credit file is part of a commercial service available to firms with whom I am doing business. Moreover, this file may be held on a computer in another country, operated by an agency in a third country. I may not even know that the file exists, let alone whether the information on it is accurate. If I am refused credit, it may be through an error that I would be unable to correct. Hence the importance of the legislation on access to files containing personal information, which has been, or is being, enacted in most developed countries of the world, and of the international convention on transborder dataflow introduced in the OECD and supported by most of the member countries.

In a brief account like this, it is impossible to do justice to the complexities of this subject on a country-by-country basis. All will be different in detail, and the situation is changing by the week. Jacob and Rings have brought together an immense amount of information, up to date in 1986, giving an overview of policy developments in more than 20 countries and a summary of the distribution of media services in nearly 100 countries.[36] Valuable though this is, much of it is already out of date, some before it was printed. For more recent information the reader should refer to journals like *Information Hotline, Monitor, Communication Technology Impact,* and *Information World Review.*

COPYRIGHT, SOFTWARE PROTECTION, AND DATA PROTECTION

The same caution has to be given with regard to copyright, software protection, and data protection. For example, between successive drafts of this chapter, the Australian government passed the 1989 Copyright Amendment Bill, with significant changes affecting educational libraries in particular. Most copyright legislation considers the nature of fair use and its implications and tries to do justice both to the author's rights and to the reader or user, but the details of, say, U.S., U.K., and Australian legislation are quite different. Most countries follow the convention that they accord the same rights and privileges to the publications of foreigners as to their own nationals, but in the past this has not been much reassurance for Western publishers who have seen their books and journals freely copied in those countries where all publications automatically become the property of the state.

The photocopying machine has freed the reader to indulge in what publishers see as blatant piracy. The ease with which sound and video tapes and computer software can also be copied has broadened the problem without changing its nature. In many Asian capitals it is possible to buy for a few dollars a software program and a well-bound photocopy of the manual, which would cost many hundreds of dollars if bought legally at home. In Australia and some other countries there is now a small tax levied on each virgin cassette tape, which is shared among the commercial cassette publishers whose interests may have been damaged by the wholesale copying of their works, but this does not apply to blank computer disks.

For the moment there seems no easy answer. The early attempts at software copy-protection generally required the user to insert the master disk before running the working copy of the program. This was a tiny challenge to computer hackers, whose underground speedily circulated the way to un-copy-protect each new program. Legitimately available commercial software could also bypass the copy-protection of most programs. Users of the programs who had paid the full price for them complained about the nuisance of having to boot with two disks instead of one. Most new software now has no such protection, although there may be other safeguards. In Australia, for example, copyright inspectors are liable to make spot checks of university campuses and other large software users to ensure that any software in use has been legally acquired.

There are certainly major policy questions here on the degree of control exercised over intellectual property, the way it is enforced, and the way compensation is paid to the property holder. However, the technical questions are just as great. For the moment, honest users are paying inflated prices for software to cover the losses caused by the pirates.

EDUCATION AND TRAINING

The education and training of library and information professionals in many countries are matters for the institutions of higher learning themselves, rather than for government policy, except to the extent that government approves the content and level of courses as a prerequisite for funding. In the same way, the continuing education of these professionals is often left to their professional associations on a self-funding basis.

Governments have been instrumental in many countries in ensuring the integration of IT into the primary and secondary education system, as a preparation for the "information society." This has caused problems in the early years because the teachers had not been trained to use computers, and there were difficulties in finding lifelike applications for teaching purposes. At the present time, much of the computer teaching is performed as a separate subject, rather than being integrated into the whole breadth of the curriculum. Until the schools are more lavishly endowed with equipment, it will be difficult to generate the level of computer literacy that can appreciate how IT reaches into every facet of human activity and can make use of this knowledge in everyday life.

INFORMATION POLICY AND TECHNOLOGY

In most countries information technology as such has not been a major component of national information policy as we have defined it, although as John Gray says, "This is where the most important boundary problems occur."[37] Gray points out that a country's motives for an IT policy are twofold: to promote applications of IT in all walks of life in order to get the maximum advantage from it as quickly as possible; and to stimulate the domestic IT industry.

Where there is conflict between an information policy and an IT policy, Gray believes that IT will win out because of the economic implications of decisions on IT developments. However, he points out that since the OECD's Information Policy Group was merged with its IT-based successor, the Information, Computer and Communications Policy Group, little of interest to information policy makers has resulted.

Gray also notes that "advances in IT have focused attention on other large stores of information held by governments: national and local collections of statistics, public records, company records, patents, trademarks and information published in press handouts, advisory leaflets, handbooks and so on.". The British government has an Information Technology Advisory Panel (ITAP) reporting to the Cabinet Office, in order to promote the development of IT manufacture and application in the country. In 1983 ITAP published a report, *Making a Business of Information*, which made an immediate impact on the information service sector in the United Kingdom.[38]

First, it introduced the notion of tradable information as a basis for increased export activity, looking closely at these large stores of information and their potential as a basis for value-added services. Second, it put forward the notion of an umbrella representative trade body, which was established in 1985 as the Confederation of Information Communication Industries (CICI). CICI has working parties on topics such as public affairs, legal affairs, technology and education.[39] It aims to provide a single voice by which the U.K. information industry can speak to government. This is an important development; the U.K. information industry had been as fragmented as in most other countries in the world, with the possible exception of the United States, which has benefited enormously from the early formation and strong leadership of the Information Industry Association.

AN APOLOGY TO THE READER

This has been a frustrating chapter to write. Most countries have many information problems in common, but because each country is different, so in detail are the solutions. Often it is those details that become fascinating, but there is no space in a short chapter like this to pursue them in any depth. In this respect, examining the policy of a single country is more straightforward than trying to skate across the globe. It is hoped the references will open up paths to identify the details when they are needed. Bear in mind that those details are changing with a rapidity that requires a daily newspaper rather than a book to keep pace with them.

NOTES

1. Quoted in *Information Hotline* 20, no. 7 (September 1988), 4.

2. Autralian Department of Prime Minister and Cabinet, *Task Force on Departmental Information Report, July 1980,* (Canberra: AGPS, 1982), paragraph 16.65.

3. Richard Titmuss, *Social Policy* (London: Allen & Unwin, 1974), 23.

4. *Australian Labor Party Platform, Resolutions and Rules* (Barton, ACT: ALP, 1986), 235.

5. From A. I. Mikhailov, A. I. Cherniy, and R. S. Gilyarevskiy, "Organization of Scientific and Technical Information in the Communist World," in *Foundations of Scientific Information* (Moscow: VINITI), in a 1965 English translation from the NTIS Clearinghouse, AD 627-802. More accessible may be J. Stephen Parker, *UNESCO and Library Development Planning* (London: Library Association, 1985), 16-24.

6. U.S. President's Science Advisory Committee, *Science, Government and Information: The Responsibilities of the Technical Community and the Government in the Transfer of Information* (Weinberg Report) (Washington, D.C.: Government Printing Office, 1963), 4.

7. For further information on these see D. E. Berninger and B. W. Adkinson, "Interactions between the Public and Private Sectors in National Information Programs," in *Annual Review of Information Science and Technology,* vol. 13, ed. Martha E. Williams (White Plains, N.Y.: Knowledge Industry Publications, 1978).

8. Organisation for Economic Cooperation and Development. *Information for a Changing Society – Some Policy Considerations.* (Piganiol Report) (Paris: OECD, 1971).

9. See Peter J. Judge, "Questions of Information Policy," *Journal of Information Science* 14 (1988): 317-18.

10. John Gray, *National Information Policies – Problems and Progress* (London and New York: Mansell Publishing, 1988), 3.

11. Adapted from Peter J. Judge, *National Information Policy,* Legislative Research Service Discussion Paper no. 2, 1985-86 (Canberra: Department of the Parliamentary Library, 1985).

12. Robert Lee Chartrand, "The Politics of Information," *Journal of the American Society for Information Science* 35, no. 6 (1985): 376-82.

13. Harold Wooster, "The Apparatus We Built in the 70's Has Been Carefully (If Not Lovingly) Dismantled. Where Do We Go From Here? Which Way Is Up? Who Cares? Some Funny Things Happened on the Way to 1984," in *Proceedings of the 47th ASIS Meeting,* vol. 21, (White Plains, N.Y.: Knowledge Industry Publications, 1984), 19.

14. Oli Mohamed, ed., *Formulating a National Policy for Library and Information Services: The Malaysian Experience* (London and New York: Mansell Publishing, 1988).

15. J. Stephen Parker, *UNESCO and Library Development Planning* (London: The Library Association, 1985). See especially pp. 174-87.

16. "Information – The Billion Dollar Industry," *Monitor,* no. 55 (September 1985), 3-5.

17. Australian Department of Science, Scientific Development Division, *The Commonwealth Government as an Information Provider: Statistics 1985-86* (Canberra: Department of Science, 1986), 6.

18. *The Programme of the Federal Government for the Promotion of Information and Documentation (I&D-Programme) 1974-1977* (Frankfurt am Main: The Federal Minister for Research and Technology, 1974). English translation published in 1976 by the Institute for Documentation, Frankfurt am Main.

19. *Programme of the Federal Republic of Germany for Specialized Information 1985-88* (Bonn: The Federal Minister for Research and Technology, 1985).

20. H. Samulowitz, "Das Ende einer Affäre – die Auflösung der GID kam nicht überraschend," *Nachrichten für Dokumentation* 39, no. 1 (February 1988): 20.

21. This section on France draws on Peter J. Judge, *National Information Policy,* and on the final *Rapport d'Activité 1983-1984* of MIDIST, (Paris: MIDIST, 1984). This final report is a special issue, which looks back on the actions of BNIST and MIDIST and provides valuable insights into the aspirations and achievements of these bodies.

22. "Become a Database Producer – and Guarantee Yourself a Tax Loss," *Monitor,* no. 65 (July 1986), 3.

23. "France – Crumbling MIDIST," *Monitor,* no. 51 (May 1985), 3.

24. "Report Criticizes Public Spending," *Monitor,* no. 53 (July 1985), 6.

25. Thomas J. Allen, Diane B. Hyman, and David L. Pinckney, "Transferring Technology to the Small Firm: A Study of Technology Transfer in Three Countries," *Research Policy* 12 (1983): 199-211.

26. Carmel J. Maguire and Robin Kench, *Information and the Small Manufacturer* (Sydney: School of Librarianship, University of New South Wales, 1974), 65.

27. U.S. National Commission on Libraries and Information Science (NCLIS), Public Sector/Private Sector Task Force 1982, *Public Sector/Private Sector Interaction in Providing Information Services,* Washington, D.C., NCLIS, February 1982. Cited in Dennis D. McDonald, "Public Sector/Private Sector Interaction in Information Services," in *Annual Review of Information Science and Technology,* vol 17, ed. Martha E. Williams (White Plains, N.Y.: Knowledge Industry Publications, 1982), 85.

28. Chartrand, "The Politics of Information," 380.

29. U.S. Congress, *Paperwork Reduction Act of 1980: Public Law 96-511,* 96th Congress, 2d Session, 1980. Cited in McDonald, "Public Sector/Private Sector Interaction in Information Services," 88.

30. U.S. Office of Management and Budget, *Improving Government Information Resources Management,* Washington, D.C., 1982. Cited in McDonald, "Public Sector/Private Sector Interaction in Information Services," 88.

31. Constance Holden, "Library of Medicine versus Private Enterprise," *Science,* 5 June 1981, 1125-26. See also *Information Hotline* 15, no. 4 (April 1983): 1.

32. *Defining Public and Private Interests in the European Information Industry.* A report of a symposium organized by EURIPA and held in Luxembourg, 26-27 January 1982. EURIPA, 79 Great Titchfield Street, London W1P 7FN, UK, 1982.

33. Robert Maxwell, "Data Retrieval Systems and International Publishing," *Aslib Proceedings* 34, no. 1 (January 1982): 38-45.

34. Commission of the European Communities, "European Society Faced with the Challenge of the New Information Technologies: A Community Response," (d'Avignon Report) COM (79) 650 final. Brussels, 26 November 1979.

35. For information on these actions, see the commission's quarterly newsletter in this field, *I'M (Information Market),* formerly known as *Euronet DIANE News,* published by the European Communities Directorate General XIII, Luxembourg.

36. M. E. L. Jacob and D. L. Rings, "National and International Information Policies," *Library Trends*, Summer 1986, 119-69.

37. Gray, *National Information Policies – Problems and Progress*, 50-52.

38. Cabinet Office, Information Technology Advisory Panel, *Making a Business of Information: A Survey of Opportunities* (London: HMSO, 1983).

39. *CICI Newsletter* is available from CICI, 90 Bedford Square, London WC1 3HJ. The journals *Aslib Information* (Aslib, London) and *Communication Technology Impact* (Elsevier, Amsterdam) also carry news of CICI.

Glossary

A&I Abstracting and indexing.

AACR2 *Anglo American Cataloging Rules,* 2d edition.

ABN The Australian Bibliographic Network, operated under the auspices of the National Library of Australia.

Access channel (cable television) See public access channel.

Access time The interval between the time data is requested from storage and the time the transfer of data is complete.

ACTV See advanced compatibility television.

Adonis A project being tested by European publishers to deliver journal articles in the biomedical field using CD-ROM.

Advanced Compatibility Television (ACTV) A high-definition television system designed by the David Sarnoff Research Center, with implementation planned in two stages to ensure continued reception by existing NTSC receivers. ACTV I will use 1050 scan lines, and ACTV II, 1125 scan lines.

Advanced television See high-definition television.

AI See artificial intelligence.

AIIM The Association for Information and Image Management.

Allocation The designation of particular frequencies in the electromagnetic spectrum for specific types of broadcast services.

Alpha-geometric An image displayed on a visual display unit using alphanumerics and shapes built from geometric instructions, such as picture description instructions.

Alpha-mosaic An image displayed on a visual display unit using alphanumeric and block graphic characters.

Alphanumerics The conventional computerized character sets comprising the 26 letters of the alphabet in lower- and upper-case, Arabic numerals, punctuation marks, and other special characters.

AM See amplitude modulation.

Amplification The use of specialised equipment to boost the strength of an electronic signal without changing its structure.

Amplitude modulation (AM) One of the ways in which an electrical signal in radio wave form is altered (modulated) so that information is coded into it. The strength of the signal is modified, as represented by an increase in the height of the sine wave above its midline.

Analog In communications, a signal whose form viewed as a wave can vary continuously. For example, the human voice can generate variances in frequency from a few hundred to several thousand hertz. Contrast with digital.

ANSI The American National Standards Institute.

ANTIOPE The French display code standard for teletext and videotex transmission. Acronym for Acquisition Numérique et Télévisualisation d'Images Organisées en Pages d'Ecriture.

Aperture card A standardized data-processing-size card into which has been inserted a microfilm document image indexed for retrieval. This format is most often used for maps and engineering drawings.

Applications software Programs to solve specific business or organizational problems. Typical examples are payroll, accounts receivable, and sales analysis.

Apollo European Commission project to explore the potential of digital text transmission by satellite as a means of document delivery.

Arc In an expert system, a link between nodes that indicates their relationship in a semantic network describing a knowledge base.

Argument (expert system) See predicate logic.

Artemis A proposed system for document digitizing and teletransmission, studied in 1980 for the European Commission by A. D. Little.

Artificial intelligence The field of study that explores how computers can be used for tasks requiring the human characteristics of intelligence, imagination, and intuition.

ASCII The American Standard Code for Information Interchange, a standard digital code for information exchange among computer and data communications systems and associated equipment. ASCII uses seven data bits to represent alphanumeric characters, typically with an eighth bit for parity checking. Contrast with EBCDIC.

Aspect ratio The relationship of horizontal to vertical units in a television image.

Asynchronous In data communications, the addition of control bits to indicate the beginning and end of each character being transmitted, as the time interval between individual characters being transmitted may vary. Contrast with synchronous.

AT&T American Telephone and Telegraph.

Attenuation The loss of strength as a signal passes along its transmission medium.

Attribute In a relational data model, a column in a relation or table. Contrast with tuple.

ATV Advanced television. See high-definition television.

Audiotext See voice mail.

Authoring system A high-level English-like language and procedures used by people without formal programming skills to create interactive videodisc, CD-ROM, or computer-assisted instruction software.

Auto-dial/auto-answer Features found in modems operating in dial-access mode that enable them to place data calls using telephone numbers or access codes stored in the computer or entered by an operator at a keyboard, and to respond automatically to incoming data calls from remote modems and connect them to a local computer system.

Automatic stepdown The process by which a transmitting FAX machine identifies and, if required, adjusts to the reception rate of the receiving FAX machine.

B channels The two 64-Kbps channels in the minimum standard integrated services digital network configuration in North America.

Backbone circuit That part of a multipoint circuit used by all the devices communicating on it.

Backward chaining In an expert system, the process of starting from a potential goal and working backwards, seeking facts that support that goal. Contrast with forward chaining.

Bandwidth The range of frequencies that, when aggregated, indicate the capacity of a communications channel.

Baseband A communications path capable of handling only one channel at a time. Frequently associated in local area networks with low-speed copper wire communications.

Batch mail Electronic mail messages transferred and processed as a group in order to eliminate the need to repeat command sequences for each message.

Batch mode A type of information retrieval in which searches are accumulated into groups and processed periodically.

Baud A unit of measure of information transmission speed, equal to the number of discrete conditions or signal events per second. Named for J.M.E. Baudot, the French inventor of the five-bit Baudot code still used in low-speed Telex systems. See also bits per second.

BBC The British Broadcasting Corporation, the state-owned radio and television broadcasting service.

BBS See electronic bulletin board system.

Bell-compatible Modems whose audio tones meet Bell Telephone standards. Variants of the term include Bell 103-compatible (standard for 300-bps modems) and Bell 212A-compatible (standard for 1200-bps modems).

Bibliographic database A database whose records comprise descriptions of books, journal articles, and other types of information sources. Fields comprise data elements such as author, title, publisher, and year of publication.

Bibliographic network A network comprising a central computer system with a large database of cataloging records, linked by telecommunications facilities to libraries. The network may provide services such as online cataloging, union lists and interlibrary loan messaging. Examples of bibliographic networks include OCLC, RLIN, WLN, UTLAS, and CLASS.

Bibliographic record See record.

Bildschirmtext (BTX) The West German public videotex system, meaning literally "picture screen text."

Binary A number system using base 2 mathematics. Binary mathematics assigns only two values, 0 or 1, to each place in a number, rather than the ten values, 0 through 9, which base 10 uses. Because these two values can be expressed in an on or off form, and can be combined to represent any number, binary mathematics is the heart of computing and digital communications.

Binary digit See bit.

Bit (binary digit) The smallest unit of digital information that can be handled by a computer or data communications signal. A binary unit corresponds electrically to off or on, represented as 0 or 1.

Bit-level protocol A protocol that uses a sophisticated mathematical algorithm to scan bit patterns and reject blocks of data that cannot be valid because of transmission errors. Usually associated with high bit-rate transmission. Contrast with character-level protocol.

Bit-mapping The process of treating an image as a matrix of dots and describing digitally the pattern of dots necessary to recreate the image.

Bit rate The rate of transmission of digital information, regardless of blocking factors or protocol. See bits per second.

Bit stream Refers to binary signal transmission without regard to grouping by character.

Bits per second (bps) The number of digital bits transmitted per second, sometimes mistakenly referred to as baud rate. Kilobits per second (Kbps) refers to the transmission rate per thousand bits; and Megabits per second (Mbps), per million bits.

Block In data communications, the application of controls to create a specified number of characters for synchronous transmission.

Block graphics Characters in the character-generation videotex display system comprising three rows of two squares each; each square may be colored or not, resulting in 64 possible block graphic characters. These characters are used to build mosaic images on the screen.

BNIST In France, the National Office for Scientific and Technical Information.

Boolean search Use of AND, OR, and NOT functions to combine search terms for selecting information during an online search.

Boot To load the computer's operating system into RAM from a disk.

Bps See bits per second.

Branching structure Arrangement of a database in a number of hierarchical levels, with each level as you move lower presenting information of increasing detail. Also known as tree structure.

Broadband A communications path capable of handling multiple simultaneous communications channels. Associated in local area networks with a high-capacity transmission facility such as shielded wire, coaxial cable, or fiber optics.

BRS Bibliographic Retrieval Services, New York.

BT British Telecom, the formerly nationalized telecommunications company that operates Prestel and BT Tymnet.

BTX See Bildschirmtext.

Buffer A temporary storage area in a computer system where small sections of data are stored during the transfer process.

Bulletin board See electronic bulletin board system.

Bundled Software sold in conjunction with hardware.

Bus A circuit board that transmits coded data in either parallel or serial mode between processors or other hardware components in a computer system; or a local area network topology in which all equipment is attached to a single, open-ended transmission medium, where equipment at the end passes messages back along the bus as required.

Business graphics A type of applications software that converts numbers in spreadsheet format into their equivalent representation as bar graphs, pie charts, etc.

Byte A sequence of binary digits or bits, whose length is the smallest accessible unit in computer memory. Eight bits is commonly equal to one byte, which can equal one character.

Cable television Television that transmits its programming via coaxial cable. Originally known as community antenna television or community access television (CATV).

Camcorder A portable videocamera/cassette recorder designed for home use.

CAPTAIN The Japanese national public videotex system, an acronym for Character and Pattern Telephone Access Information Network.

CAR (micrographics) See computer assisted retrieval.

Carrier A signal with a constant frequency that can be modulated to produce an information carrying signal; or a communications provider that offers data transmission service, such as a common carrier or a value-added network.

Carrier Sense Multiple Access/Collision Detection (CSMA/CD) A communications technique used in local area networks whereby a node waits until the line is clear before transmitting and checks after transmission to ensure that no other node is transmitting simultaneously.

Cartridge microfilm Microfilm that has been loaded into a specialized plastic container for storage and access by high-speed automatic microfilm readers.

CATV Community access television or community antenna television. See cable television.

CAV See constant angular velocity.

CBEMA Computer and Business Equipment Manufacturers Association.

CCETT Centre Commun d'Etudes de Télévision et de Télécommunications, the joint research establishment of the French PTT and the French national broadcasting authority.

CCITT Comité Consultatif International Téléphonique et Télégraphique, a worldwide representative body of PTTs and telephone service operators that deals with communications standards.

CCL See common command language.

CCTV See closed circuit television.

CD See compact disc.

CD drive See compact disc drive.

CD-I See compact disc interactive.

CD-ROM See compact disc-read only memory.

CEEFAX Broadcast teletext service operated by the British Broadcasting Corporation.

Cell A unique position in a spreadsheet matrix identified by a row and column location.

Central processing unit (CPU) Computer hardware that interprets and executes program instructions and communicates with the input, output, and storage devices. It consists of the control unit and the arithmetic/logic unit. The CPU is sometimes known as the central processor or processor.

CEPT European Conference for Posts and Telecommunications.

CGA Color Graphics Adapter. See graphics adapter.

Channel A much-used term that has shades of meaning depending on context. Generally refers to a communications path with discrete limits, controls, and information content.

Character A number, letter, or punctuation mark; in a computer, a sequence of bits. A character is usually represented by one byte. Kilocharacter refers to units of 1000 characters.

Character generation One of the systems used by videotex systems for displaying characters, in which the shapes of all possible characters are predefined and stored in the terminal's memory.

Character-level protocol Protocol that controls transmission and detects and corrects errors at the individual character level. Contrast with bit-level protocol.

Character rectangles In a videotex character-generation display, the matrix grid of 40 columns by 20, 24, or 25 rows per frame in which the characters to make up the display are incorporated. The character rectangle may comprise alphanumerics or block graphic characters, as well as spacing between the characters and rows.

Characters per second (cps) A measure similar to bps, but expressing the transmission or operating rate in characters rather than bits.

Chat Real-time online communication between users of an electronic mail, bulletin board, or other computer system, in a one-to-one or group mode.

Chip A device in which microscopic electronic circuitry (such as that forming a transistor or integrated circuit) is printed photographically on the surface of a tiny piece of semiconductor material (usually crystalline silicon).

CICI In the United Kingdom, the Confederation of Information Communication Industries.

Circuit A path along which signals move.

Circuit board A card, usually containing software or memory chips, that can be plugged into a computer to increase its processing abilities.

CISTI The Canadian Institute for Scientific and Technical Information, which comes under the National Research Council.

CLASS Cooperative Library Agency for Systems and Services, a bibliographic network.

Clip art Predesigned graphics that can be imported into a document from magnetic storage.

Clone Less well-known brand of computer that operates nearly identically to an industry-standard model such as an IBM.

Closed circuit television (CCTV) A cable television system self-contained within a building, used primarily for surveillance or viewing educational programming.

Closed user group (CUG) A videotex service to which only preidentified users have access.

CLR Council on Library Resources.

CLV See constant linear velocity.

CNRS In France, the National Scientific Research Center.

Coaxial cable (COAX) A transmission medium made of a single wire surrounded by copper mesh and sometimes an aluminum sheath, and wrapped with insulating plastic. Coaxial cable is the transmission medium for cable TV, because of its high data transmission speed and large bandwidth capabilities, and for many broadband local area networks.

COBOL Common Business Oriented Language, a computer programming language most often used for business applications.

CODASYL Conference of Data System Languages, a group of government and industry representatives interested in creating standardized programming languages. They are known principally for the development and standardization of COBOL.

Color graphics card See graphics adapter.

COM See computer output microform.

Command One of a number of coded instructions input to an online retrieval system, by which database searches are carried out and results displayed and printed.

Common carrier A provider of long-distance communications service accessed through the public switched (telephone) network. Some common carriers may also provide local carrier service.

Common Command Language (CCL) A standard developed for uniform search commands in information retrieval systems, being considered for adoption by the International Organisation for Standardisation.

Communications controller Computer equipment that manages the flow of information or signals from or between computers or telecommunications systems.

Communications software Software required by a microcomputer to interact through a modem over a telecommunications network with an external computer system.

Community access television See cable television.

Community antenna television See cable television.

Compact disc (CD) An injection-molded aluminized disc, 12 cm in diameter, which stores high-density digital data in microscopic pits and lands read by a laser beam.

Compact disc digital audio A compact disc containing digitized music, spoken word, or other sound that conforms to an industrywide audio standard (sometimes called the Red Book standard), ensuring exceptionally high fidelity.

Compact disc drive (CD drive) A device designed to read digital data from a compact disc to computer memory.

Compact disc interactive (CD-I) A technical specification, sometimes called the Green Book standard, for a self-contained compact disc multimedia system that allows simultaneous, interactive presentation of video, audio, text, and data.

Compact disc-read only memory (CD-ROM) A laser disc that is pitted with electronic data, usually text or graphics, and that has an ultra-high density storage capacity. The contents of the disc cannot be changed by the user.

Compile To translate instructions from a programming language into a machine code that can be read by computer.

Compound document The addition of graphics and page makeup features to text in word-processing software.

Compression See data compression.

Computer-assisted retrieval (CAR) A micrographics system linked to a computer that allows automated searching of index terms and subsequent mechanical retrieval of the microform images required from storage.

Computer output microform (COM) Any microform on which the contents have been recorded directly from digital data by a computer without a printout as an intermediate step.

Conference See online teleconference, videoconference.

Connect time The time spent online to a host computer while using a database, electronic mail, etc. Connect time, measured in fractions of a minute, is a common basis for billing.

Constant angular velocity (CAV) A drive mechanism that spins magnetic disks (and some types of videodiscs) at a constant speed, resulting in the inner tracks of the disk passing the reading mechanism more slowly than do the outer tracks. Sectors on a CAV disk radiate in uniform patterns from the disk's center, so they are smaller at the inner areas, with higher storage density. Contrast with constant linear velocity.

Constant linear velocity (CLV) A drive mechanism that rotates compact discs at varying speeds, moving data past the optical head at a constant speed. The drive must rotate the disc more slowly as the head moves from the inner tracks toward the outer perimeter. This design allows data to be stored on the disc at a constant linear density, but requires special tracking and sensing devices to slow down the disc as the head rotates. Contrast with constant angular velocity.

Contention A method of managing a multiterminal circuit in which the terminals request access to transmit signals (Contrast with polling); or the conflict or service problems that occur when two or more communications facilities attempt to pass an information signal to another facility at the same time, without having a prearranged management process.

Control character A character in a stream of data being transmitted that instructs a computer or control unit to perform an action on the rest of the data, such as conversion or screen formatting.

Controller A computer or circuit board that controls the flow of data between a computer and one or more memory devices, usually tape or disk drives. Controllers sometimes also perform channel and error correction coding and decoding.

CPB Corporation for Public Broadcasting.

CPE See customer premises equipment.

CP/M See disk operating system.

CPS See characters per second.

CPU See central processing unit.

CSIRO In Australia, the Commonwealth Scientific and Industrial Research Organization, the national scientific research body.

CSMA/CD See Carrier Sense Multiple Access/Collision Detection.

C-SPAN Cable Satellite Public Affairs Network.

CUG See closed user group.

Cursor The usually flashing indicator on a computer display screen that shows which character or space is currently being addressed.

Customer premises equipment (CPE) The communications equipment located within a home, building, or office and controlled by the customer.

D channel The single 16-Kbps channel used for managing the signals that flow on the B channels in the minimum standard integrated services digital network configuration in North America.

Database A collection of logically related records or files on a computer, which can be searched by keywords or other identifiers to retrieve the information needed; or a series of frames arranged in a hierarchical structure in a videotex system. The frames contain either information or menus to guide users to the information.

Database management system (DBMS) A set of computer programs that organizes, stores, and retrieves information from a database. The information in a DBMS is stored in various record structures so that it is not needlessly duplicated and so that several types of records can be searched simultaneously if required.

Data compression With digital images, the process of using mathematical algorithms to compact data based on the presence of large areas identical in color. With text, any technique that saves transmission cost or storage space by eliminating gaps, empty fields, redundancy, or unnecessary data. All compressed data must be expanded by a reverse operation called decompression.

Data communications equipment (DCE) The equipment, such as modems, multiplexers, and controllers, that sends and receives digital information. Contrast with data terminal equipment (DTE).

Data communications system A computer system that transmits data over communication lines such as telephone lines or coaxial cables.

Data dictionary A complete listing of the fields and their characteristics in the record structures across the files in a database management system—in effect, a database about the database.

Data independence In a database management system, the separation of the representation and storage of data from the input/output or hardware requirements, so that changes in one do not consequently require changes to the other.

Data radio A communications system based on radio-frequency transmission using radio transmitters and modems.

Data terminal equipment (DTE) The equipment that displays, prints, or provides operator input capabilities for data transmission. Contrast with data communications equipment (DCE).

DBMS See database management system.

DBS See direct broadcasting satellite.

DCE See data communications equipment.

DDC The Dewey Decimal Classification scheme.

Debug To detect, locate, and correct errors in a computer program.

Decoder A device that receives and processes transmitted signals, so that they can be displayed on a screen in their original form. Various types of decoders are used for the reception of cable and satellite television, and of teletext and videotex. Videotex decoders are also called adapters.

Decompression See data compression.

Dedicated line A voice-grade telephone line used in point-to-point or point-to-multipoint circuits, generally between a terminal and a central processing unit. Since dedicated lines are not switched, they are used solely for a single function or to provide communications between specific sites. See also leased line.

Demodulation Extraction of information from a signal that has been modulated.

Demodulator See modem.

Descriptor Generally used to indicate a preferred subject heading, but sometimes used to mean any substantive term in the title, abstract, or other fields of a bibliographic record.

Desktop publishing The use of microcomputer software and a laser printer to input, edit, format, illustrate, and publish documents, from single-page announcements to lengthy newsletters, magazines, and books.

Determinant (database management system) See functional dependency.

DGRST In France, the General Delegation for Scientific and Technical Research.

Dial access or dial-up access Use of the public switched (telephone) network or a value-added network to transmit digital data. Involves the use of a modem.

Dialog An online information retrieval system established commercially in 1972 by Lockheed and operated as a time-sharing service.

DIANE Direct Information Access Network for Europe, the information service operated on Euronet.

Diazo film (micrographics) A slow-print film used in recording microimages that is sensitized by a coating of diazonium salts. Diazo film generally produces nonreversed images; a positive image will produce a positive image, and a negative image will produce a negative image. Contrast with silver halide and vesicular film.

Digital In communications, a signal whose form can vary only by containing separate and discrete binary elements or pulses, which are represented by binary 0 or 1. Contrast with analog.

Digital video interactive (DVI) A technology using a special chip set and data compression techniques to provide a greater number of motion or still images on CD-ROM than other technologies provide at present.

DIMDI The German Institute for Medical Documentation and Information, in Cologne.

Diode See light-emitting diode.

Direct broadcasting satellite (DBS) A satellite designed to transmit broadcast, premium cable, subscription TV, or pay-per-view programming to subscribers of the service. Because DBS utilizes vastly increased power when it transmits signals back to earth, subscribers can receive clear transmissions using dishes that are much smaller and less expensive than those required to receive from standard-power satellites.

Directory A structure indicating the locations, or addresses, of files on a storage medium such as CD-ROM or floppy disk.

Disk drive A mechanical unit that may be built into a computer or added as a peripheral. It reads and records to and from the computer's memory and disk storage.

Disk operating system (DOS) Software that controls the flow of data between a computer system's internal memory and external disks. MS-DOS, CP/M, and UNIX are widely used operating systems.

Disk storage An external computer storage medium on which information is stored as magnetized dots on the surface of a disk. This kind of storage allows direct access to any data stored on it. See also floppy disk, hard disk.

Dissolve A video effect in which images from two different motion sequences blend gradually to produce a smooth transition from one scene to the next.

Distributed processing Decentralization of a computer system such that the computers carry out processing in various locations. These computers are connected to each other via telecommunications networks; frequently there is a central host computer to which minicomputers or microcomputers are connected.

Docdel A European Commission project to investigate the technical feasibility and economic viability of electronic transmission systems and to test user reaction to the services they provide.

Document Written or printed material containing information.

DOS See disk operating system.

Dot matrix printer Computer printer in which the shape of a character or component of a graphic is defined as a series of dots within a small grid.

Dots per inch (dpi) A measure of resolution, or the number of pixels per inch on a screen display or scanning device.

Downlink A transmission antenna contained in a satellite that conveys amplified video and audio signals back to earth for reception by any appropriately tuned earth station or dish.

Download To transfer information from the host computer into local computer storage.

Down time Time during which a computer or periphal device is malfunctioning or inoperative.

Dpi See dots per inch.

DTE See data terminal equipment.

Dumb terminal A terminal that acts as an input/output device only. Contrast with smart terminal.

Duplex The ability of a communications system to transmit information in both directions. Full duplex can transmit in both directions simultaneously; half duplex, in only one direction at a time. Contrast with simplex.

DVI See digital video interactive.

Earth station Terrestrial facility that sends and receives satellite transmissions.

EBCDIC Extended Binary Coded Decimal Interchange Code, IBM's eight-bit code for transmitting and processing digital information, used to represent 256 numbers, letters, and other characters. Contrast with ASCII.

EDC See error detection and correction.

EDTV See enhanced-definition television.

EEC The European Economic Community.

EGA Enhanced Graphics Adapter. See graphics adapter.

EIA Electronic Industries Association.

Electromagnetic interference (EMI) A form of interference that particularly affects unshielded metallic communications circuits. It can be caused by magnetic fields associated with electrical motors and generators, among other sources.

Electromagnetic spectrum The whole range of frequencies over which electromagnetic waves can be propagated, ranging through radio waves, microwaves, infrared radiation, visible light, ultraviolet radiation, and x rays.

Electromagnetic wave A moving disturbance in space produced by the acceleration of an electric charge, consisting of perpendicular electric and magnetic fields moving at the same velocity.

Electronic bulletin board system (BBS) A telephone-linked network formed by personal computer users that constitutes a public access message system. Messages can be sent continuously as part of a group conference, or one at a time as a chain of messages added to by users as they log on to the host.

Electronic file cabinet Common name for a text-oriented database management system.

Electronic mail (email) A system for transmitting, receiving, storing, and forwarding textual information and messages in electronic form. Some systems are available on local area networks; others, such as ALANET and On-Tyme, are accessed via value-added networks.

Email See electronic mail.

Embedded artificial intelligence The incorporation of artificial intelligence techniques into software applications programs to make them more flexible and easier to use.

EMI See electromagnetic interference.

Enhanced-definition television (EDTV) The first stage of advanced-compatibility television, in which the 1050-scan-line picture could be received by both NTSC and HDTV standard receivers, although the superior image would be apparent only on HDTV receivers.

Enhanced service providers A term used by the Federal Communications Commission to refer to value-added networks such as Tymnet and Telenet. See also value-added networks.

Enterprise The part of the real world about which data are stored in a database management system.

Entity A class of things that exist, which are related to other classes of things in a database management system.

Entity-relationship (E-R) model One of the best-known methods of analyzing data for a database management system, developed by P-S.C. Chen in 1976.

E-R See entity-relationship model.

Error detection and correction (EDC) In data communications the use of one of a number of techniques for examining the contents of a bit stream, identifying errors (generally through some mathematical computation), and then correcting the errors. Frequently, the correction involves having the incorrect portion of the bit stream retransmitted; or a technique that uses an error detection code and error correction code for identifying and correcting errors that occur during the transfer or recording of information on CD-ROM.

ETV Educational television.

Euronet A regional cooperative program of the European Economic Community, through which the European PTTs have developed common standards and compatible tariffs to facilitate information flow in the region.

EUSDIC The European Association of Scientific Information Dissemination Centers.

Execute To run a computer program.

Expert system Software package aimed at providing consultancy advice or assistance with problem solving, usually in a specialist field such as science, engineering, medicine, or business.

Export To move text, tables, or other data developed using one software program into documents using another. Compare with import.

Facsimile See telefacsimile.

FAX See telefacsimile.

FCC See Federal Communications Commission.

FDM Frequency division multiplexer. See multiplexer.

Federal Communications Commission (FCC) The U.S. regulatory body that promulgates the rules of broadcasting and telecommunications, sets tariffs for communications services, reviews and allocates the bandwidth spectrum for broadcasting, and performs other functions associated with electronic and broadcast communications.

Fiber optics Communications technology that uses very thin strands of glass fiber (optical fiber) to transmit information coded in pulses of light, frequently with a laser as the transmission mechanism. Fiber optics is rapidly becoming the preferred method for transmitting high volumes of information because it is immune to noise, suffers less attenuation, has very high bandwidth capacity, and is very secure.

Fiche See microfiche.

FID The International Federation for Information and Documentation.

FID/CLA The International Federation for Information and Documentation's regional Commission for Latin America.

Field A subdivision of a record.

File A collection of related records treated as a unit, for example patron file.

File maintenance The activity of keeping a file up to date by adding, changing, or deleting data.

File manager A software program that creates, maintains and retrieves records from a database.

File transfer The electronic transmission of text documents, databases, encoded computer programs, spreadsheets, or other data held in a computer file.

Fix In micrographics, to remove undeveloped chemicals from film by using a special solution. This creates a permanent image on the film negative and prevents further reaction with light.

FIZ In Germany, a specialized information center (Fachinformationszentrum).

Floppy disk (diskette) A magnetic storage medium that uses a flexible polyester (plastic) disk, usually 5 1/4 inches in diameter.

Flow camera See rotary camera.

FM See frequency modulation.

Font In printing and computerized character generators, the set of characters and special symbols available in one style and size of type.

Footprint The extent of geographic area in which appropriately tuned satellite earth stations or dishes can receive a given satellite's downlink transmissions.

Format To set out the instructions to a printer as to how a document should look on a page with respect to margins, justification, headings, fonts, etc.

Forward chaining In an expert system, the process of using known facts and matching them with other facts in the knowledge base to infer new facts. Contrast with backward chaining.

4GL Fourth-generation computer language.

Frame In telecommunications, a block of information in bit form, with its own control, sequence, and error-checking bits incorporated into the block; or, in video or television, a complete picture comprises 525 horizontal scan lines composed of two separate frames. The first frame consists of the odd-numbered lines, and the second, the even-numbered; or, in videotex, a screenful of graphic information; or, in an expert system, a device used to assemble information in a data structure and execute procedures based on this structure by filling in appropriate slots.

Frame-grabber The component of a broadcast teletext decoder that captures a predesignated frame as it is broadcast.

Free-text searching Online searching in which any substantive in a bibliographic record or document in a database may be used as a search term.

Frequency A measure of the number of times the cycle of a wave form is repeated in a second, expressed in cycles per second, or hertz. A short wavelength is equivalent to a high frequency.

Frequency division multiplexer See multiplexer.

Frequency modulation (FM) A technique for altering (modulating) an electrical signal in radio wave form to encode information by changing how often it oscillates.

Front-end (online searching) See gateway.

Front-end processor Computer whose primary purpose usually is to receive and send communication signals to relieve the central computer of some of the communication tasks.

Full duplex See duplex.

Function key Key on a computer keyboard that is designated to carry out a particular operation, e.g., to call up a help screen or quit the program.

Functional dependency Relationship between data elements X and Y in a relational database management system, such that given the value of X, the value of Y can de determined.

Gateway In data communications, a switching function that allows access from one communications system to another and that may facilitate access with enhancements such as protocol conversion; or, in online searching, front-end or intermediary applications software that provides a simple interface between the end user and the information retrieval system during an online search.

Geosynchronous orbit A circular orbit in which a satellite moves around the earth once while the earth rotates once on its axis, thus remaining fixed above a particular point on the equator.

GHz Gigahertz. See hertz.

GID In Germany, the Society for Information and Documentation (Gesellschaft für Information und Dokumentation).

Gigahertz See hertz.

GMD In Germany, the Society for Mathematics and Data Processing (Gesellschaft für Mathematik und Datenverarbeitung).

Graphics The term used for visual images appearing in documents or on a display screen.

Graphics adapter A device that enables a monitor to display graphics as well as text. Types include Hercules Monochrome Graphics Adapter (HMGA), Color Graphics Adapter (CGA), and Enhanced Graphics Adapter(EGA).

Graphics card See graphics adapter.

Green book Standards developed by Philips and Sony for compact disc interactive (CD-I).

Half duplex See duplex.

Handle Codename by which a user of an electronic bulletin board is known to other users.

Hard copy Printed paper output, or output in a nonelectronic form such as microform.

Hard disk An electronic data storage medium using a rigid material (for example, aluminum) on which a coating is applied. Hard disks provide much higher storage capacity than floppy disks.

Hardware Physical equipment comprising a computer and its peripheral devices (keyboard, monitor, printer, disk drives, etc). Also used generically in relation to any type of electrical or electronic equipment (videocassette players, micrographics cameras and readers, etc).

HBO Home Box Office, a cable television channel featuring high-demand entertainment programming.

HDLC See High-level Data Link Control.

Head The part of an audio or video recorder that comes into direct contact with the tape and serves to record, reproduce, or erase electromagnetic pulses on it.

Help screen One of many displays built into computer software, usually accessible through a function key or simple command, that explains an operation or process to users.

Hertz A measure of frequency equal to one cycle per second, named for nineteenth-century German physicist Heinrich Hertz. Often abbreviated to Hz. KHz refers to a thousand cycles (kilohertz), MHz to a million (megahertz), and GHz to a billion (gigahertz).

High-definition television (HDTV) Any of a variety of video formats offering higher resolution than the current NTSC or other foreign broadcast standards. Current formats generally range in resolution from 655 to 2125 scan lines, with an aspect ratio of 5:3 and a bandwidth of 30 to 50 MHz. See also Advanced Compatibility Television, enhanced definition television, Spectrum-Compatibility HDTV.

High-level Data Link Control (HDLC) A bit-level communications protocol that manages the transmission and reception between data terminal equipment of blocks of data placed in frames.

Highlighting Process of emphasizing certain characters on a visual display screen by underscoring, blinking, or increasing intensity.

High Sierra Group An ad hoc standards group, including representatives from the hardware, software, and publishing industries, set up to establish nominal data format and compatibility for CD-ROM.

Hit rate The proportion of items located when conducting an online search, often applied to known-item searching in a bibliographic network.

HMGA Hercules Monochrome Graphics Adapter. See graphics adapter.

Horizontal market Mass market, or market catering to the general public.

Host The principal or controlling computer to which other computers or terminals are connected in a distributed data-processing environment.

HyperCard Software developed by Apple Computer for the Macintosh that allows users to link terms to each other in a personalized network and move directly from one to another as required by clicking a mouse.

Hypermedia Hypertext-type software that links not just terms, but also moving images, still images, sound, etc., particularly in CD-ROM systems.

Hypertext A generic term used to describe the type of computer software similar in function and operation to Apple's HyperCard, as well as the applications developed using such software.

Hz See hertz.

ICCP The Information, Computer and Communications Policy Group of the Organization for Economic Cooperation and Development Science Policy Committee, which later became an OECD Committee (the ICCP Committee) in its own right.

ID Identification code. See password.

Identification code See password.

I-D-S Integrated Data Store, built by Charles Bachman at General Electric in 1964, considered to be the first significant database manager.

IEEE See Institute of Electrical and Electronics Engineers.

IIA In the United States, the Information Industry Association.

ILL Interlibrary loan.

Impedance The resistance to the flow of electrons, and therefore of signals, that exists in metallic circuits.

Import To move text, tables, or images from a scanner or documents developed using other software into the document being worked on. Compare with export.

Inference engine In an expert system, the component responsible for applying the reasoning or logic mechanism to the knowledge base to arrive at an answer.

Information provider An independent contractor or organization, also known as a service provider, that supplies the databases available through videotex systems. See also umbrella information provider.

In-house Produced entirely within a company or organization, using its resources, facilities, and expertise.

INIST In France, the National Institute for Scientific and Technical Information.

Inkjet printer Printer that creates characters and graphics by applying dots of ink by spray nozzle rather than impact and thus operates very quietly.

INSPEC The Information System for Physics, Electronics, Computers and Control in the United Kingdom.

Institute of Electrical and Electronics Engineers (IEEE) An information exchange, publishing, and standards-setting organization, responsible for many of the standards used in local area networks.

Integrated services digital network (ISDN) An emerging standard and system for digitizing all communications traffic, including voice, data, and video.

Integrated software Applications software that combines two or more types of general-purpose software (e.g., word processing, spreadsheet, and database management) into one package with a common command structure.

Interactive A type of computer processing in which users at online terminals can communicate with the host on a real-time basis.

Interactive videodisc (IVD) A videodisc player linked to a microcomputer system such that the microcomputer software permits the indexing and retrieval of the video images as required for the application.

Interface A circuit board that attaches a particular peripheral device to a microcomputer. See also controller.

Interlaced scanning The practice of transmitting the horizontal scan lines that compose a complete television picture in two frames; the first frame consists of the odd-numbered lines, while the second consists of the even-numbered lines.

Interleaving The technique of transmitting signals from two or more devices, via time division multiplexing, over a single path.

Intermediary A person who acts as an agent for a user in carrying out an online search; or applications software that converts online searching into a simple, user-friendly process.

International Organisation for Standardisation (ISO) An international body that has developed standards for pin assignments in data communications plugs, has promulgated Open Systems Interconnection (OSI), and has approved protocols for many of the layers in this model.

IPG The Information Policy Group of the Organization for Economic Cooperation and Development's Science Policy Committee, which was operational between 1965 and 1975.

ISBN International standard book number.

ISDN See integrated services digital network.

ISO See International Organisation for Standardisation.

ISO 9660 The standard entitled "Volume and File Structure of CD-ROM Information Interchange."

ISSN International standard serial number.

IT Information technology.

ITAP In the United Kingdom, the Information Technology Advisory Panel reporting to the Cabinet Office.

ITV British independent television stations.

IVD See interactive videodisc.

Jack A connecting device to which the wires of a circuit may be attached and which is arranged for the insertion of a plug.

Jacket A flat, transparent, plastic carrier with single or multiple film channels made to hold single or multiple microfilm images.

JICST The Japan Information Center for Science and Technology.

Joystick A remote-control device for a computer that looks similar to a gearshift on a car, often used in video and arcade games and in some interactive video applications.

Jukebox A CD player that can hold and access several discs.

K (K byte, KB) Abbreviation for kilobyte, which is 2^{10}, or 1024, bytes. A computer's size often is expressed according to the number of kilobytes of memory it offers, and the number is usually rounded off to the nearest 1000 bytes. See also byte.

Kb See kilobit.

Kbps Kilobits per second. See bits per second.

Key In a relational data model, a group of one or more attributes, or columns, that uniquely identifies a row, or tuple.

Keyboard A device that contains numbers and letters similar to a typewriter keyboard, by which information is input to the computer. In addition, the keyboard utilizes other keys such as reset, control, clear, escape, etc.

Keypad A control device comprising numerals and function keys used to access teletext or videotex.

Keyword In databases, a specific text string that can be retrieved, along with any records or documents in which it is located.

KHz Kilohertz. See hertz.

Kilobit (Kb) One thousand bits. See bit.

Kilobits per second (Kbps) See bits per second.

Kilocharacter Unit of 1000 characters. See character.

Kilocharacter traffic Units of 1000 characters transmitted or received via a telecommunications facility.

Kilohertz (KHz) See hertz.

Knowledge base Component of an expert system that comprises the facts of the subject domain.

LAN See local area network.

Land The reflective area between two adjacent nonreflective pits on a CD-ROM. In CD-ROM coding, a binary 1 represents the transition from pit to land and from land to pit, and two or more 0s represent the distances between transitions.

Laser A device for producing a coherent, monochromatic, high-intensity beam of radiation of a frequency within or near to the range of visible light. Acronym for light amplification by stimulated emission of radiation.

Laser disc See optical disc.

Laser printer Computer peripheral that is capable of printing in a screen-designed font. Laser printer output is closest to typeset in quality.

LaserVision The Philips tradename for its videodisc.

Latent image The invisible image that is produced by the exposure of photo-sensitive film and made visible by the process of development.

LC Library of Congress.

Leased line A dedicated circuit, typically voice-grade telephone, used for private purposes, rather than as part of the public switched network. Often used for low-speed data transmission. See also dedicated line.

Light-emitting diode A semiconductor that produces light when it receives an electric current.

Linear access Available for retrieval serially, that is, a search for specific information or a particular image must proceed in order through all the data recorded until the required location is reached. Contrast with random access.

Linked Systems Project (LSP) A major initiative to link the large library databases in the United States so that data can be shared and the widest access to this data can be achieved.

Local area network (LAN) A communication network that typically uses coaxial cable to connect computers, terminals, printers, facsimile transmission machines, etc., within a limited physical area such as an office building, manufacturing plant, or other work site, in order to share computing resources efficiently among users.

Local loop or local subscriber loop That portion of the public switched (telephone) network that links a telephone or other customer premises equipment with the central office.

Log on In online searching, to initiate a search at a terminal establishing contact with a remote computer. When the activity is completed, a signal is sent to log off.

Logical format Specifies the organization and location of data files on a CD-ROM. The logical format is now standardized by ISO 9660.

Loop In computer programming, a sequence of computer instructions that repeats itself until a predetermined condition is satisfied; or, in data communications, see local loop.

Low-power television (LPTV) Television broadcast by stations limited to 10 watts VHF and 1000 watts UHF, in order to avoid interference with full-power TV stations. Signals can be received within a 10- to 35-mile radius.

LPTV See low-power television.

LSP See Linked Systems Project.

Mac Apple Macintosh Computer.

Macro A set of computer instructions that can be named and treated as a single instruction.

Magazine Frames of teletext information and related menus, covering topics such as news headlines, weather, and sports scores.

Magnetic tape A recording medium consisting of a thin tape coated with a fine magnetic material. Data is recorded in the form of changing magnetic levels on the tape coating.

Mailbox Unique address stored in a central computer for a particular user to which other individuals can send messages via electronic mail or videotex and from which the user retrieves these messages.

Mainframe Largest and fastest class of common commercially available computers. Contrast with minicomputer and microcomputer.

MARC Machine-readable cataloguing. A communication format originally developed by the Library of Congress and now used worldwide for producing and distributing bibliographic records on computer.

Master In micrographics, a document or microform from which duplicates or intermediates can be obtained; or, in CD-ROM, an original recording in a form ready for mass replication.

Mbps Megabits per second. See bits per second.

MDS See multipoint distribution service.

MEDLARS The Medical Literature and Retrieval System, produced by the U.S. National Library of Medicine.

MEDLINE An online service operated by the National Library of Medicine. It offers a number of databases on the medical literature and its specialized areas.

Megabits per second See bits per second.

Megabyte Roughly 1 million bytes, or 1024K bytes. See also byte.

Megahertz See hertz.

Megazine A word coined to describe a CD-ROM that has a variety of source materials combined with bibliographies or indexes, usually related to a particular topic.

Memory The integrated circuits of a computer that store information. See also random access memory and read-only memory.

Menu A list of options displayed on a computer terminal, which prompts the user to select one in order for the software to proceed.

Menu-driven Refers to the technique of using menus for the user to choose options. Contrast with prompt, command.

MHz Megahertz. See hertz.

Microchip See microprocessor.

Microcomputer Smallest and least expensive class of computer, often used in the home as a personal computer. Contrast with mainframe, minicomputer.

Microfiche (fiche) A transparent 4-inch-by-6-inch (105-mm-by-148-mm) sheet of film, with microimages arranged in a grid pattern and an eye-legible heading.

Microfilm Any sheet or strip of transparent plastic base coated with a light-sensitive emulsion used in recording and preserving microimages. See also diazo, silver halide and vesicular film.

Microform A generic term for the various formats used for storing and retrieving microimages.

Micrographics The technology of creating microimages for storage and retrieval in an information system.

Microprocessor (microchip) An integral piece of hardware that houses the logic functions of a computer on one circuit board or in one set of integrated circuits. The microprocessor contains neither the input/output interfaces nor the memory unit.

Micropublishing The issuing of previously unpublished material in multiple-copy microform for distribution and sale; or, the use of desktop publishing software for producing the proofs for and publishing small print runs of books.

Microrepublishing The issuing of previously or simultaneously published hard copy material in multiple-copy microform for distribution and sale.

Microwave A high-frequency, tightly focused, line-of-sight radio transmission capability, operating at frequencies above 1 megahertz.

MIDIST In France, the Interministerial Mission for Scientific and Technical Information.

Minicomputer Medium-size class of computer. Contrast with mainframe, microcomputer.

Minitel The inexpensive, monochrome, stand-alone terminal developed for the French Teletel public videotex service.

Mips Million instructions per second.

Modem (modulator-demodulator) Data communications equipment that typically transmits and receives digital information over telephone lines by converting digital pulses or bits into audible tones for transmission (modulating), and converting audible tones back to digital bits for reception (demodulating).

Modulation (modulate, modulating) The technique of placing information onto a signal by modifying the signal in one of three ways: changing its strength (amplitude modulation), its frequency (frequency modulation), or its phase (phase shift keying).

Modulator-demodulator See modem.

Monitor An electronic device similar to a television that receives and displays a nonbroadcast video signal sent across wires within a closed circuit (from, say, a videotape or disc player), but that cannot intercept a broadcast signal; or, in computing, another name for the visual display terminal.

Mosaic images Groups of block graphic characters that have been combined to form images on a display screen, similar to the way traditional mosaic art images were inlaid using small pieces of glass or tile of different colors to form a picture or design.

Mouse A small hand-held device rolled freestyle on a flat pad that moves a cursor around a computer screen.

MS-DOS See disk operating system.

Multiplexer (mux) A piece of data communications equipment that combines two or more signals so that they can be sent along a single transmission path and reconstructed at the receiver. This is accomplished either by dividing the bandwidth into two or more lower-speed discrete channels (through a frequency division multiplexer, or FDM) or by using time-slicing, or interleaving, techniques (through a time division multiplexer, or TDM, or its derivative, the statistical time division multiplexer, also called STDM or stat mux).

Multipoint distribution service (MDS) A private company that is authorized to receive satellite transmissions of premium cable or other subscription-style TV programming and to rebroadcast that programming for profit via super-high-frequency or microwave signals to homes or businesses with modified receivers.

Mux See multiplexer.

NAPLPS North American Presentation Level Protocol Syntax, the standard for constructing alpha-geometric screen displays in videotex systems.

Narrowcasting Programming aimed at particular or minority audiences.

National Technological University (NTU) Organization that provides a range of satellite-delivered telecourses.

NATIS A UNESCO program concerned with national documentation, library, and archive infrastructures, which grew out of activities dating back to 1966. The NATIS conference was held in 1974, but by 1977 the program was merged with the UNISIST program, resulting in a General Information Program (PGI).

NCLIS U.S. National Commission on Libraries and Information Science.

Nesting In an online search, the use of parentheses in a search statement as a means of indicating the order in which operations should be carried out.

Network System using data communications equipment to connect two or more computers.

NHK See Nippon Hoso Kyokai.

Nippon Hoso Kyokai (NHK) Japan's national broadcasting corporation.

NLM The U.S. National Library of Medicine.

Node In data communications, a station, terminal, or host computer in a communications system, at which a signal may enter or leave the system; or, in an expert system, a point in a semantic network describing a knowledge base.

Noise The interference with transmission caused by external factors such as electromagnetic interference, or by internal factors, such as a poor transmission path or switching.

Nordforsk Scandinavian regional science policy body, established in 1972.

Nordinfo The successor to Nordforsk, established in 1977.

Normalization The process of creating well-formed relations between data elements in a relational database management system.

NTIS In the United States, the National Technical Information Service.

NTSC (National Television Standards Committee) The U.S. color video standard established by the committee of the same name.

NTU See National Technological University.

OCLC Online Computer Library Center, a bibliographic network. Formerly known as the Ohio College Library Center.

OCR See optical character recognition.

OECD Organisation for Economic Cooperation and Development, Paris.

Offline Mode of computer operation in which terminals or other equipment continue to operate while disconnected from a central processor. Contrast with online.

OMB The U.S. Office of Management and Budget.

Online Mode of computer operation in which a computer or terminal operates interactively with a host or in a network rather than in a stand-alone mode.

Online public access catalog (OPAC) An automated library catalog that is available to users via a computer terminal, with a range of search options including author, title, subject, keyword, etc.

Online teleconference Meeting that can be carried out in real time, or non-real time, by participants. Participants are linked by computer terminals so that they can communicate by sending messages to all other participants.

OPAC See online public access catalog.

Open Systems Interconnection (OSI) Framework within which standards for communication between different types of computer systems are being developed.

Operating system (OS) Software that controls the execution of computer programs and that may provide scheduling, debugging diagnostics, input/output control, and other related services.

Optical character recognition (OCR) A method for converting printed characters to machine-readable character codes through an optical sensing device and pattern-recognition software.

Optical disc A disc read from or written to by light, generally a laser. Such a disc may store video, audio, or digital data. Also called laser disc.

Optical fiber See fiber optics.

Optical scanning Use of a device that can view text or graphic images, sense the light emitted (and thus the position of the images), and translate those findings into data comprehensible to a computer graphics system.

ORACLE Teletext system operated by British independent broadcasters. It is an acronym for Optical Reception of Announcements by Coded Line Electronics.

ORBIT The commercial information retrieval service operated by the System Development Corporation.

OS See operating system.

OS/2 IBM operating system that supports networking.

Oscillation A repetitive fluctuation or vibration of an electrical signal.

OSI See Open Systems Interconnection.

Output Data transferred from computer storage to some external document or display, such as a printer or terminal.

Packet A group of characters assembled by a packet assembler-disassembler (PAD) for transmission in a packet-switching network. Typically 128 or more characters in packets, with addressing and continuity controls built in, may flow via two or more channels to arrive at the same destination, where they are disassembled to constitute a whole message.

Packet assembler-disassembler (PAD) A piece of data communications equipment that assembles data coming to it from a terminal or other data terminal equipment into packets and passes them on to the next facility for transmission. Packets arriving at a PAD are disassembled and converted to the original communication or message.

Packet switching A system of data communications developed in the 1960s, that uses multiple data paths with computer-controlled links and switches. Packet switching is the method by which value-added networks such as Telenet and Uninet transmit their traffic.

PAD See packet assembler-disassembler.

Parallel A mode of transmission in which the bits composing a character travel separately with each positional bit assigned to a separate wire. Used widely in very short distances, particularly in sending information to printers. Contrast with serial.

Parallel processing Carrying out computer processing activities by using multiple central processing units simultaneously.

Parity A measure of the number of binary 1s in a digital character. Parity can be used for verification and control purposes.

Parity check A technique for verifying the accuracy of data received in a communications system.

Password A code given whenever a person accesses a computer system, in order to identify that person as a legitimate user. Also known as ID.

Pay per view (PPV) Fee-based cable programming using a sophisticated decoding device such that subscribers pay for each program that they watch.

PBS Public Broadcasting Service, the organization representing U.S. public noncommercial television stations.

PBX See private branch exchange.

PC Personal computer. See microcomputer.

PDI See Picture Description Instructions.

Peripheral An accessory of a computer system, such as a disk drive, printer, or plotter.

Personal Computer (PC) See microcomputer.

PGI An abbreviation (the French initials) of the UNESCO General Information Program formed in 1977 by merging UNISIST and NATIS.

Phase shift keying (PSK) A modulation technique that alters the shape of a signal by introducing a brief reversal, and then a restoration, of the normal shape.

PhotoVideotex The British photographic standard of videotex display.

Picture Description Instructions (PDI) Method used by the Canadian Telidon videotex system for constructing screen images using a range of graphic elements: points, lines, arcs, polygons, and rectangles. Also known as alpha-geometric.

Picture element See pixel.

Pit A microscopic depression in the reflective surface of a CD-ROM. The pattern of pits on the disc represents the data that is stored. See also land.

Pixel (picture element) One of the thousands of dots used to compose a computer display screen, television, or video image.

Planetary camera A type of microfilm camera in which the documents being photographed and the film remain stationary on a plane surface during the exposure. Also known as flatbed camera. Contrast with rotary camera, step-and-repeat camera.

Point-to-multipoint In telecommunications, a data circuit with several ends, which typically are customer sites with data terminal equipment and data communications equipment used to access a computer system at a central site. Contrast with point-to-point.

Point-to-point In telecommunications, a data circuit with one transmitting and one receiving end. Contrast with point-to-multipoint.

Polling A method of controlling transmission on a point-to-multipoint circuit to prevent contention. Each piece of data terminal equipment is assigned an address and is invited by the polling controller to transmit in a predetermined sequence.

Port Electronic circuitry that provides a connection point between the host computer and the input/output devices.

Postings In an online search, an indication of how many documents in a database meet the parameters indicated by the search statement.

PPV See pay per view.

Precision In an online search, the proportion of citations retrieved that are relevant.

Predicate (expert system) See predicate logic.

Predicate logic In an expert system, the representation of knowledge about a subject domain in the form of propositions consisting of objects, persons, and concepts (arguments) about which something is stated (predicate) as the basis for producing inferences.

Premastering A data-formatting process performed on user data before the mastering process in the production of CD-ROMs.

Prestel Britain's national public videotex system developed by British Telecom.

Print file format Information stored electronically in such a way that it appears on screen as it would if it were printed out.

Private branch exchange (PBX) A local switching system for the routing of telephone messages.

Processor A computer, especially one in a network of linked computers.

Production rule In an expert system, a technique for knowledge representation, usually expressed in an IF-THEN form.

Program A series of instructions to a computer that causes the computer to solve a problem or perform a task.

Prompt A message or symbol appearing on a terminal, indicating that the software or operating system is ready to receive an instruction, command, or data.

Proportional spacing Typeface in which narrow letters such as *i* and *j* occupy less space than wide letters such as *m* and *w*.

Protocol A set of standards or rules that governs the procedures for transmitting and receiving data. Parity checking and bit rate are two of the many possible elements of a protocol. See also bit-level protocol and character-level protocol.

Protocol converter A piece of data communications equipment that converts a signal from one protocol, such as ASCII, to another, such as SDLC. Protocol conversion can also take place in software, or as part of the operations of a communications controller or other devices.

PSK See phase shift keying.

PSN See public switched network.

PTT A national postal and telecommunications authority; an acronym from post, telephone and telegram.

Public access channel Channel provided by cable system operators through which community groups, local authorities, and individuals can communicate with cable subscribers.

Public domain software Software that is not copyrighted by the owners, and thus is freely available for use by anyone.

Public menus Introductory screens of a videotex system that guide users through the broad categories of databases available on the system. These menus are constructed by the videotex operator rather than by the information provider.

Public switched network (PSN) The total of all telephone switches and facilities, often referred to as plant, available to a telephone subscriber.

Pulse Brief variation of electric current, especially as a signal.

Query language In database management systems, an alternative to conventional programming languages that enables users to formulate ad hoc information retrieval requests using English-like phrases.

Radio frequency The frequency of the transmitting waves of a given radio message or broadcast; a frequency within the range of radio transmission.

Radio-frequency interference (RFI) The interference in a communications channel caused by the intrusion of unwanted high-frequency signals or noise.

RAM See random access memory.

Random access Retrieval of information directly by reference to its location on disk or other storage device, independent of the order in which it was originally entered. Random access is available on computers, compact disc players, and optical disc systems. Contrast with linear access.

Random access memory (RAM) Integrated circuits acting as internal memory, capable of being read from and written into, used for temporary storage of data or programs during processing. RAM is volatile; it is lost when power is turned off. It may be expanded by adding memory chips or memory boards. Compare with read-only memory.

RBOC Regional Bell Operating Company.

RCA Radio Corporation of America.

Read In computing, to acquire data from one storage device or medium and transfer it to another medium, usually the computer's memory.

Read-only memory (ROM) An integrated circuit on which data or instructions are programmed at the time of manufacture. It cannot be erased or reprogrammed by normal computer operations and is not lost when power is turned off. Contrast with random access memory.

Real time A computer operating mode under which receiving and processing data and returning the results occur so quickly that the system appears to interact instantaneously. The term is also applied to interactive audio and video links, teletext, and videotex.

Recall In an online search, the proportion of citations retrieved from among all those that are relevant.

Record A collection of related fields of data, treated as a unit. An individual's record, for example, would include data in the fields of name, address, and so on. A bibliographic record would contain data in the fields including author, title, publisher, etc.

Record structure In a database management system, the uniform characteristics of all the records in a given file.

Red book Another name for the compact disc digital audio standard.

Reduction ratio The relationship between the dimensions of an original item filmed and the corresponding dimensions of its image in microform.

Reference database Database that contains bibliographic, directory, or other types of citations describing primary information sources. Contrast with source database. See also bibliographic database.

Reflective optical videodisc See videodisc.

Relational database A database whose software allows data fields within records to be connected to records within other files.

Replication In a spreadsheet, the capability of copying a text string or numerical value from one cell to another.

Report An extraction of data from a database or spreadsheet, generated on a regular or irregular basis, listing or summarizing a particular type of activity, eg, payroll or stock control.

Resolution The number of pixels a display screen can accommodate. The more pixels, the higher the resolution and the better the picture quality.

Response frame A videotex message preaddressed to an information provider, which is filled in by the user's selecting from a menu and keying in pertinent information.

Response time The time required between a user's request at a computer terminal and the computer's reply.

RFI See radio-frequency interference.

Ring A local area network topology in which each piece of equipment is connected to two others, this being repeated until a loop is formed. Data are transmitted around the loop, always in the same direction.

RLIN Research Libraries Information Network, a bibliographic network.

Roll microfilm Microfilm wound on a reel or spool.

ROM See read-only memory.

Rotary camera A type of microfilm camera that photographs documents while they are being moved in synchronization with the movement of the film. Contrast with planetary camera and step-and-repeat camera.

Routing The means of directing users from one display screen in a CD-ROM or videotex database to another for more information, without necessarily having to return along the same path by which they originally reached that screen.

Rule (expert system) See production rule.

Satellite A device that has been launched into orbit around the earth or other planets, which contains receiving, recording, or transmitting instruments for purposes of communication or research.

Satellite master antenna television (SMATV) Cable television service with a satellite feed, available within large residential units as a perquisite or for a fee.

Scandiaplan A regional scheme among the major libraries in Scandinavia, initially organized by Nordforsk, to share subject responsibilities among specialized collections and centers of excellence, subsidizing some of them where necessary to maintain high standards.

Scan lines The horizontal lines that compose a television screen image: 525 in the United States, and 625 in Europe.

Scannet The Scandinavian packet-switched network.

Scanning See optical scanning.

Scramble To transmit a signal in a garbled form so that it can be decoded only by a special receiver and not by normal reception equipment.

Scrolling Moving text up and down, or across, on a visual display screen.

SCSI See Small Computer Systems Interface.

SDC System Development Corporation, the operator of the ORBIT information retrieval system.

SDI Selective dissemination of information.

SDLC See Synchronous Data Link Control.

Sector A data block on a storage medium, such as a floppy disk or CD-ROM, usually with a predetermined length.

Semantic network In an expert system, the representation of properties and relationships of objects, situations, and concepts in the knowledge base.

Semiconductor A device that is based on the electronic properties of substances whose electrical conductivity at normal temperatures is intermediate between that of a metal and an insulator, and whose conductivity increases with a rise in temperature over a certain range.

Serial A mode of transmission wherein all signal data bits travel on a single wire, with the bits for each character arriving in sequence. Contrast with parallel.

Server A processor in a local area network that controls the shared use of a resource such as disk storage or a printer.

Service provider See information provider.

Shareware Software that is copyrighted but not copyprotected, which users are encouraged to try, copy, or pass around. Regular users are asked to pay a nominal registration fee to receive documentation and updates.

Shell A commercially available software package designed for the creation of a specific type of expert system.

SIG See special interest group.

Signal Electrical current or light pulse used to convey information.

Silicon chip See chip.

Silver halide film A film used in recording microimages that is sensitized with silver halide. Silver film is considered by many to be the only film suitable for archival permanence. Contrast with diazo and vesicular film.

Simplex The ability of a communications system to transmit information in only one direction. Contrast with duplex.

Sine wave A periodic oscillation that can be represented geometrically by a curve defined by a trigonometric equation involving the sine.

Slot In an expert system, a subdivision of a frame that executes a specific procedure.

Slow-scan video Process by which video images can be conveyed via video cameras, modem links, and voice-grade telephone lines to a receiving location where they are reassembled and displayed on a video monitor.

Small Computer Systems Interface (SCSI) A standard eight-bit parallel interface frequently used to connect computer disk drives to a microcomputer. SCSI, pronounced "scuzzy," is becoming the preferred connection between CD-ROM drives and microcomputers.

Smart terminal A terminal that has the ability to process data and function as a computer as well as the ability to serve as an input/output device for a mainframe computer. Also called intelligent terminal.

SMATV See satellite master antenna television.

SNA See Systems Network Architecture.

Software Computer programs and accompanying documentation. Also used generically in relation to discs, videocassettes, and other materials that are played on electronic equipment.

Solid state Pertaining to electronic devices that are composed of components in the solid state, including transistors, semiconductor diodes, and integrated circuits.

Source database A database that incorporates full textual or statistical information, rather than citations to printed sources of such information. Contrast with reference database.

Special interest group (SIG) Group of subscribers or participants on an electronic bulletin board, videotex, or other computer system who exchange information on their topic of common interest.

Spectrum See electromagnetic spectrum.

Spectrum-Compatibility HDTV High-definition television system developed by Zenith Electronics Corporation that would use the parts of the spectrum that now separate channels to increase the frequency needed for broadcasting HDTV signals.

Spooling The technique used in computer systems, including local area networks, whereby data to be printed is stored temporarily if the printer is busy.

Spreadsheet A computer version of a financial ledger sheet. Labels, values or formulas are entered in cells defined by columns and rows, as the basis for carrying out numerical data analysis.

SQL Structured Query Language. See query language.

Stamper The metal plate that holds the negative image of a glass CD-ROM master. It is used to mold the mass-production replicas.

Stand-alone system An internally compatible computer or other system that can perform its specified functions without being connected to other systems or equipment.

Star A local area network topology in which all equipment is wired to a central computer that establishes, maintains, and breaks connections between the equipment.

Statistical time division multiplexer (STDM or stat mux) See multiplexer.

STDM Statistical time division multiplexer. See multiplexer.

Stemming See truncation.

Step-and-repeat camera A type of microfilm camera that can expose a series of separate images on film in a predetermined format, usually a grid pattern, to produce microfiche. Contrast with planetary camera and rotary camera.

STI Scientific and technical information.

STIM Scientific, technical, and medical information.

String A series of characters, usually treated as text, that have been encoded for computer manipulation and storage.

Strip-up A technique used for the production of microfiche in which short lengths of roll film are attached in rows to a transparent support, which is then used as a master.

STV See subscription television.

Style sheet A feature of word-processing systems that allows users to record combinations of formatting commands under a specific name, which can be called up for use in creating subsequent documents.

Subscription television (STV) Television broadcasting that uses a scrambling signal, to which viewers subscribe in order to obtain the decoding device to unscramble the signal for reception.

Switch Communications equipment that provides access to the public switched (telephone) network, to a local area network, or from one communications line to another. Examples of switches include private branch exchanges (PBXes).

Synchronous A method of data transmission that relies on fixed time periods to mark the transmission of a character or block of characters, an efficient way of controlling the transmission of large volumes of information. Contrast with asynchronous.

Synchronous Data Link Control (SDLC) An IBM bit-level communications protocol.

SYSOP See system operator.

System operator (SYSOP) An individual or group that operates and manages an electronic bulletin board system, including provision and maintenance of host computer equipment, inbound telephone calls, and the information content of the bulletin board.

Systems Network Architecture (SNA) A proprietary networking protocol established by IBM to enable all IBM computing equipment to communicate in a standard way. Other vendors have also developed products based on SNA so that these products can interact with IBM systems.

T-1 A time division multiplexer system that is a standard for the 1.544-Mbps transmission rate now incorporated as part of the integrated services digital network.

TDM Time division multiplexer. See multiplexer.

Telebanking The videotex facility for depositing money and transferring money between accounts electronically. Telebanking requires a gateway between the videotex computer and the bank's computer, so that a user's transactions are registered on the bank's computer.

Teleconference See online teleconference, videoconference.

Telefacsimile (FAX) The transmission and reception of images, and their reconstruction and duplication at the receiving site. Formerly analog, many new FAX machines are digital.

Telefacsimile board A microcomputer peripheral device containing a circuit board, telephone connection, and special printer that enables the computer to be used as a FAX machine.

Telemonitoring The remote surveillance of a home or business by a computer or videotex system to detect fire or robberies or to control lighting, heating, and air-conditioning.

Telenet A commercial data transmission network that offers customers value-added services such as packet switching through the public switched network.

Telesoftware Computer programs and data that are broadcast to television sets equipped with a microprocessor or to personal computers with a teletext decoder for local storage and use.

Teletel The French national public videotex service using the Minitel terminal and the ANTIOPE broadcast standard.

Teletext Noninteractive (one-way) broadcast transmission of text or graphics stored in a computer database for display on a television screen.

Teletype (TTY) A low-speed ASCII-coded communications terminal and the protocol that controls it.

Teletypewriter A type of telegraph machine equipped with a keyboard on which messages are typed, creating electrical impulses that are transmitted through telegraph wires.

Telex (Teletypewriter Exchange) A communications service that uses a teletypewriter connected to the telephone exchange to transmit messages.

Telidon Canadian teletext and videotex system developed by the Canadian Broadcasting Corporation.

Template A partially completed spreadsheet designed for a particular type of application, with labels and formulas already filled in.

Terminal controller A device by which terminals are connected to a computer.

Text-oriented data managers Programs that manage a body of text by providing an automated index to all the substantive words.

Time division multiplexer (TDM) See multiplexer.

Time-sharing The continuous allocation of successive time periods to multiple simultaneous users of a computer, where switching from one user to another occurs at such high speeds that users cannot usually detect any reduction in response time.

Time-shift To record television programs off air on a videocassette recorder to replay at more convenient times.

Token passing A communications technique used in local area networks whereby a node can only transmit when it receives the "token," that is, a message that circulates around the LAN. Only when the transmission is complete is the "token" passed on.

Token-passing ring A type of local area network that depends on each device sharing access to the LAN through use of a "token" or priority-setting process.

Topology The structure of a network. It includes location, arrangement, and relation of communications devices.

Touch screen A visual display screen on which the user chooses among options by touching designated areas on the screen.

Track A linear, spiral, or circular path on which information is recorded. Refers to optical discs as well as magnetic disks.

Transaction log analysis Use of the full records of online searches, particularly on online public access catalogs, to analyze search strategies, successes and failures, and types of problems encountered in searching.

Translator A low-power television broadcasting transmitter that receives on one channel and retransmits on another.

Transponder The receiving and retransmitting mechanism on a communications satellite. Transponders receive the signal, refresh it, and retransmit it to a downlink at a slightly higher frequency than the receiving frequency in order to prevent the incoming signal from being overwhelmed.

Truncation In an online search, the use of a symbol such as ? or # combined with the root of a word to indicate a search for all terms that contain the root plus any other letter(s) as a replacement of the symbol. Also called wildcard searching when the symbols appear internally as well as in a prefix or suffix position.

TTY See Teletype.

Tuple In a relational data model, a row in a relation or table.

Twisted pair The two insulated copper wires, wrapped around each other in a regular pattern, that currently form the basis of most local loops in the public switched (telephone) network.

TWX A communications service, frequently using TTY terminals, owned and operated by Western Union.

Tymnet A commercial data transmission network that offers customers value-added services such as packet switching through the public switched network.

UDC The Universal Decimal Classification scheme, developed and maintained through the activities of the International Federation for Information and Documentation (FID).

UHF See ultra high frequency.

Ultrafiche Microfiche filmed at very high reduction ratios.

Ultra high frequency (UHF) Any frequency between 300 and 3000 megahertz. In the United States, UHF frequencies are used to broadcast television channels 14 to 83.

Umbrella information provider Videotex database provider who sublets pages of a database to other individuals or organizations for a fee.

UNESCO The United Nations Educational, Scientific and Cultural Organization.

UNISIST A UNESCO program that began in about 1969. UNISIST is not strictly an acronym, but was intended to imply a "United Nations International System for Scientific and Technical Information," which was the program's early goal.

Unitized Pertains to microforms that bring together all filmed images pertaining to one item or topic.

Updatable microfiche Microfiche on which new images can be added and outdated ones deleted over time.

Uplink A satellite earth station with the capacity to receive standard terrestrial video and audio transmissions, convert them to a satellite-receivable frequency, and transmit them to a designated satellite.

User friendly Computer system with software simple enough to be accessed by untrained users.

UTLAS The University of Toronto Library Automation System, a bibliographic network.

Value-added network (VAN) A communications carrier, such as Telenet, Tymnet, or Uninet, that adds protocol, packet-switching, or other performance enhancements to its carrying capacity. The Federal Communications Commission refers to value-added networks as enhanced service providers.

VBI See vertical blanking interval.

VCR Videocassette recorder.

VDP Video display processor, used for the compression of data for the production of digital video interactive.

VDT Visual display terminal, or computer monitor.

VDU Visual display unit, or computer monitor.

Vendor A commercial organization that offers telecommunications, online database searching, or other computer-related information services.

Vertical blanking interval (VBI) The unused scan lines in a television picture field that occur when the electron gun that creates the image moves from the bottom of one screen to the top of the next.

Vertical market Market that demands specialized products suited to professional needs. The medical and legal professions are two examples.

Very high frequency (VHF) Any frequency between 30 and 300 megahertz. In the United States, VHF frequencies are used to broadcast television channels 2 to 13.

Very large scale integration (VLSI) A chip that incorporates thousands of integrated circuits.

Vesicular film A film used to record microimages, which contains a light-sensitive component suspended in a plastic layer that creates bubbles when exposed. These create a visible, permanent image when the plastic layer is heated and then cooled. Contrast with diazo and silver halide film.

VHF See very high frequency.

VHS The standard that has emerged as the leader for videocassette recorders.

Viatel The Australian national public videotex system.

Video A system of recording and transmitting primarily visual information by translating moving or still images into electrical signals. These signals can be broadcast via high-frequency carrier waves or sent through cables on a closed circuit.

Videoconference Conference or meeting held with the aid of video and satellite technology. Participants in many locations are able to see and hear conference presenters in real time.

Videodisc A generic term describing an optical disc that stores color video pictures and two-channel sound along a spiral track, usually in analog form. Videodisc uses the same optical readout principle as compact disc, but the discs are larger (12 inches or 30 cm in diameter) and double-sided, and the rotational speed and data transfer rate are higher.

Videotape Magnetized plastic tape upon which a video-frequency signal is recorded; videotape can record both images and sound.

Videotex Interactive (two-way) system for transmitting text or graphics stored in computer databases via voice-grade telephone lines for display on a television screen or personal computer monitor. Videotex, originally known as viewdata, was developed as a simple, low-cost system for mass use.

Viewdata See videotex.

VINITI In the USSR, the All-Union Institute for Scientific and Technical Information.

Virus Program inserted into computer software or operating system designed to destroy data, disrupt processing, and replicate itself in other software.

Visual Display Terminal or Unit (VDT or VDU) A computer monitor.

VLSI See very large scale integration.

Voice mail A technology included among the applications of autiotext, that allows the recording and digital storage on computer of messages received via the public switched network. These messages can be routed, copied, forwarded, replied to, etc. This is in contrast to an answering machine that records messages as analog signals.

VTR Videotape recorder.

Wildcard See truncation.

WLN Western Library Network, an online bibliographic network; formerly known as the Washington Library Network.

Word processing Computer software for inputting, editing, storing, and printing documents.

Worksheet The grid made up of columns and rows that defines a document in spreadsheet applications software.

WORM Write once–read many optical disc, a technology in which the user may write to the disc as well as read from it.

Write-protected A disk that has no notch or has a label covering the notch, so that the contents of the disk cannot be updated or erased.

WYSIWYG An acronym for "What you see is what you get," referring to screen displays that approximate the final layout of a page to be printed.

X.25 protocol The most common packet-switching protocol, developed as a standard by the CCITT.

X.400 CCITT standard for interfaces between electronic mail systems.

Yellow book Another name for the CD-ROM standard.

Index

Glossary terms are not included in the index.

Contributing Authors

Joseph Ford is president of Joseph Ford and Associates, a library automation and data communications consulting firm. Formerly he was the executive director of the CAPCON Library Network, the executive vice president of Biblio-Techniques, and a Library of Congress intern. From 1983 to 1985, he was a member of the OCLC Users' Council and the American National Standards Institute's Joint Telecommunications Standards Coordinating Committee. He is the author of several articles on library automation and data communications.

Kerry Webb is the director of the systems branch at the National Library of Australia, a position which he has held since 1985. He has a B.A. in computer science from the Australian National University and is currently completing his qualifications in library and information management at the University of Canberra. He is convener of the Australian Working Group on Library Systems Interconnection and in 1986 was a UNESCO consultant to Malaysia on the establishment of a national library network. He is presently coauthoring a book on microcomputers for Australian libraries.

Joel M. Lee is the marketing manager for the Auto-Graphics company in Pomona, California. He was previously the senior manager, information technology publishing, with the American Library Association from 1986 to 1988, and ALA's headquarters librarian since 1977. In 1983 he was named System Manager of ALANET, ALA's electronic mail and information service inaugurated in 1984, and he was involved in a variety of electronic publishing projects including the 1988 ALA CD-ROM *Directory of Library and Information Professionals*. He holds an A.B. in English from Oberlin College and took his A.M. at the University of Chicago in the Graduate Library School. His publications include numerous articles on electronic publishing, electronic mail and telecommunications, and the literature of library and information science. He was associate editor of the *ALA World Encyclopedia* *of Library and Information Services* (1st ed., 1980; 2nd ed., 1986), and editor in chief of *Who's Who in Library and Information Services* (1982).

Margaret E. Chisholm is the director of the Graduate School of Library and Information Science at the University of Washington in Seattle. For six years prior to this, she held the appointment of vice president for university relations at the University of Washington. She has also been a professor at the University of Oregon and at the University of New Mexico, and served as dean of the College of Library and Information Services of the University of Maryland for seven years. Her master's degree in librarianship and Ph.D. in administration were completed at the University of Washington. She served as president of the American Library Association in 1987-88. She has served two terms on the national board of the Public Broadcasting System, was a member of the transition committee that established the National Association of Public Television Stations, and is currently a member of the board of trustees of that organization. She is also a member of the KCTS/Channel 9 advisory board of the public television station in Seattle, Washington, and on the advisory council of the National Public Broadcasting Archives.

K. Michael Malone graduated with a master's degree in librarianship from the University of Washington and participated in the 1989-90 Library of Congress intern program in Washington, D.C. He holds a bachelor of arts degree in Russian language and literature from Arizona State University. There he wrote extensively for ASU's paper, the *State Press,* and other local newspapers and magazines. He is a member of the American Library Association and the Alpha Mu Gamma foreign language honorary society.

Nancy D. Lane is the head of the Centre for Library and Information Studies at the University of Canberra, Australia. Previously, she was head of the Department of Library and Information Studies at the Western Australian Institute of Technology (now Curtin University). In 1987-88 she was a visiting scholar at the University of Washington, Seattle, where she presented a number of continuing education courses on CD-ROM. She received her Ph.D. from the University of California, Berkeley, and her master's in information science from UCLA. She has served as president of the South Australian branch of the Australian Library and Information Association, and on the board of the State Library of Western Australia. Her most recent books include *Techniques for Student Research: A Practical Guide* (1989) and *A Guide to Commonwealth Government Information Sources* (1988), and she is on the editorial board of *International Library Review.*

Duncan MacKenzie is the director of special projects, Bell & Howell Australia. He has also served as director of planning and director of sales and marketing. Previously, he was a director of Data Conversion Corporation, which took over Bell & Howell Australia in 1987. He is the South Australian state chairman of the National Information Technology Council of Australia and, for 10 years, he was the federal president of the Micrographics Association of Australia. He was made a fellow of MAA in 1982. For three years, he was a board member of the International Micrographics Congress and received the IMC Award of Excellence in 1981. He is a member of the editorial advisory board of the *International Journal of Micrographics and Optical Technology*. He has written numerous articles on micrographics and information technology.

Andrew Link is product director, document management systems, with Bell & Howell Australia, where he is responsible for the marketing and support of document management systems based on both optical disc and micrographics technology. During the past 5 years with Bell & Howell, he has also worked with computer-assisted retrieval systems. Prior to this, he had 10 years experience in electronics, computers, and related fields, holding positions as a systems engineer and computer service engineer. He holds qualifications in electronics engineering and is a member of the Association for Information and Image Management.

Linda Main is an assistant professor in the Division of Library and Information Science, San Jose State University. Previously she held various research assistant and tutoring positions at the University of Illinois; and at Trinity College and University College in Dublin, Ireland. She holds a Ph.D. in library and information science from the University of Illinois, Urbana-Champaign; an M.A. in political science from the University of Dublin, Trinity College; an M.Lib. from the University of Wales College of Librarianship (Aberystwyth); and a B.A. in history and political science from the University of Dublin, Trinity College. She has published articles in several journals and is a reviewer for *Library Software Review* and *Library and Information Science Annual*. She has given numerous conference papers and workshops throughout the United States.

Terrence A. Brooks is an assistant professor at the Graduate School of Library and Information Science of the University of Washington, Seattle. He has previous teaching experience at the University of Iowa. He received a Ph.D. in information science from the University of Texas at Austin and has an M.B.A. from York University, Ontario. He has published several articles on relational database design and is currently writing a book on the application of artificial intelligence concepts and relational database design for bibliographical data.

Donald E. Riggs is dean of university libraries at the University of Michigan, Ann Arbor. His education includes a B.A from Glenville State College; an M.A. from West Virginia University; an M.L.S. from the University of

Pittsburgh; and an Ed.D. from Virginia Polytechnic Institute and State University. He has given papers on expert systems at state, national, and international conferences and has published several articles on the application of expert systems in libraries. He is coeditor of the book *Expert Systems in Libraries*. In 1987-88, he served as the chair for ALA's Artificial Intelligence and Expert Systems Interest Group.

Raya Fidel is an associate professor at the Graduate School of Library and Information Science, University of Washington, Seattle, where she teaches courses in information science, database design, and indexing and abstracting. A former head librarian for the School of Applied Science and Technology at the Hebrew University of Jerusalem, she obtained a doctorate from the University of Maryland in 1982. Her research focuses on online searching behavior, expert systems, and indexing and abstracting for online systems. Her ongoing research has been supported by grants, including one from the National Science Foundation. She has written articles for a number of journals, and her book *Database Design for Information Retrieval: A Conceptual Approach* was published in 1987.

Peter J. Judge is an information consultant and an honorary research associate of the Centre for Library and Information Studies of the University of Canberra. He has a B.A. and M.A. from Cambridge University. His experience includes 12 years with the Organisation for Economic Cooperation and Development in Paris, where he headed the secretariat of the Science Policy Committee's Information Policy Group, and 14 years with the Commonwealth Scientific and Industrial Research Organization (CSIRO) in Australia, where he was responsible for Central Information, Library and Editorial section. A member of the Australian Library and Information Association, he set up its Information Science Section in 1975, served on the association's council as president of that section, and was convener of its Committee on the Future. He is a fellow of the Institute of Information Scientists, U.K. He has been vice-president of the International Federation for Information and Documentation (FID) and president of its Commission for Asia and the Pacific region. He was the Minister of Science's nominee on the Australian Libraries and Information Council (ALIC) and has been a chairman or member of a dozen Australian government committees in the information field. He has been a consultant for UNESCO, the Australian International Development Assistance Bureau, and other bodies in Australia and overseas, and has published three books and numerous professional papers.